Trish —
I hope you
enjoy my book!

Best,
Kimberly Marlowe Hartnett
2015

Carolina Israelite

Carolina Israelite

How Harry Golden

Made Us Care about Jews, the South,

and Civil Rights

Kimberly Marlowe Hartnett

The University of North Carolina Press CHAPEL HILL

Excerpts from Harry Golden's works reprinted with permission of literary executor Richard Goldhurst. Excerpts from Abraham Joshua Heschel and Susannah Heschel, eds., *Moral Grandeur and Spiritual Audacity: Essays* (New York: Farrar, Straus and Giroux, 1996), vii, and from Charles Peters, *Tilting at Windmills: An Autobiography* (Reading, Mass.: Addison-Wesley, 1988), 49–54, reprinted with permission of the authors. Excerpts from William Targ, *Indecent Pleasures: The Life and Colorful Times of William Targ* (New York: Macmillan, 1975), 277–81, copyright © 1975 by William Targ. Reprinted by permission of Roslyn Targ Literary Agency, Inc.

The paper in this book meets the guidelines for permanence and durability of the Committee on Production Guidelines for Book Longevity of the Council on Library Resources. The University of North Carolina Press has been a member of the Green Press Initiative since 2003.

Cover illustration and frontispiece: Harry Golden, 1957.
Photo by Tom Nebbia; LOOK Magazine Photograph Collection,
Library of Congress, Prints & Photographs Division.

Library of Congress Cataloging-in-Publication Data
Hartnett, Kimberly Marlowe.
Carolina Israelite : how Harry Golden made us care about Jews, the South, and civil rights / Kimberly Marlowe Hartnett. — First edition.
pages cm
Includes bibliographical references and index.
ISBN 978-1-4696-2103-6 (cloth : alk. paper) — ISBN 978-1-4696-2104-3 (ebook)
1. Golden, Harry, 1902–1981. 2. Jewish journalists—United States—Biography.
3. Civil rights workers—United States—Biography. I. Title.
PN4874.G535H37 2015
818.5409—dc23
[B]
2014044785

For Tim, my Beloved

and

Barbara Wessel Hurst,

of Blessed Memory

CONTENTS

A section of illustrations appears on pages 145–56.

Introduction

Harry Golden was a middle-aged, raspy-voiced, cigar-smoking, bourbon-loving Jewish raconteur from New York's Lower East Side when he landed in Charlotte, North Carolina, on the eve of the civil rights movement. He spent the next three decades roasting the painful realities of segregation in the warmth of his wit, first in his improbably titled one-man newspaper, *Carolina Israelite*, and then in more than twenty books, five of which appeared on the *New York Times* bestseller list.

Golden was an irrepressible contrarian, both humanitarian and mountebank, and an old-fashioned newspaperman who blogged before blogs existed. He was beloved for exalting the little guy—factory workers, prostitutes, shopkeepers—and well known for his voluminous correspondence (and in some cases, real friendships) with the likes of Carl Sandburg, Edward R. Murrow, Billy Graham, and Robert and John Kennedy. He hid a shameful past as a Wall Street swindler and federal convict until his bestselling first book, *Only in America*, outed him in 1958 in nearly every major newspaper in the country. In 1963, in *Letter from Birmingham Jail*, the Reverend Martin Luther King Jr. cited Golden as crucial to America's soul, even as the intelligentsia of the era were baffled and loudly annoyed by his wide appeal.[1]

Golden might well have served out his working days as a salesman instead of the celebrity he became. He took up the former as a boy in the early years of the twentieth century, selling afternoon newspapers on the corner of New York City's Delancey and Norfolk Streets. He caught on fast: Shouting out the most lurid headline was sure to sell more copies to the weary sweatshop workers trudging home. A few years later he honed his cold-call salesmanship hawking stocks in 1920s Wall Street bucket shops, long before telemarketing's sanitized scripts, and his success relied on charm, a lot of nerve, and a gift for coming up with quick, entertaining lies.[2]

Those persuasive skills had an alchemic reaction when mixed, at midlife, with Golden's allegiance to the labor movement, his dream of publishing a personal journal, and the need to escape a haunting prison past. He landed in Charlotte, selling ads for the *Charlotte Labor Journal and Dixie Farm News*, and on his own time he pursued mill workers, radical poets, segregationists, and politicians with like aggression. He charmed his way into their sitting rooms and their lives, then pecked away on his manual typewriter set on a card-table desk, turning their stories into *his* stories for the columns of the *Carolina Israelite*. Soon his little paper was a full-time job. He was a writer.

A favorite ploy of Golden's was to add a well-known author, philanthropist, politician, or actor to the circulation list without the celebrity's knowledge, then mention the famous person in print as one of the newspaper's loyal subscribers. An astonishing number of real connections grew out of these manipulated courtships, including one with presidential contender Adlai Stevenson. Soon after the Illinois governor won the 1952 Democratic Party nomination, Golden fired off several witty memos to Stevenson, who in turn invited him to come to Springfield for a campaign speech-writing confab. After a long day of punditry-by-committee with a gang of journalists and political operatives, Golden retired to a guest room in the Governor's mansion.

Some hours later, the intercom next to the bed buzzed, and Stevenson's voice wafted through: "Put on your robe and come to my room. We'll have some champagne and talk," he urged his startled guest. Golden jumped out of bed and pulled on his clothes, tying his necktie as he hurried down the hallway. Stevenson, sitting in an armchair next to piles of newspapers and speech drafts, wore a smoking jacket, cravat, and elegant slippers embroidered with AES across the toes. Taking in Golden's outfit, Stevenson said, "I thought you were in bed." Golden answered, "Give me a drink, Governor, and I'll tell you the whole story. What ghetto boy ever had a bathrobe?"[3]

Perhaps it was that night that Golden first engaged a statesman in an exchange on civil rights. The issue of segregation was already shaping the

Carolina Israelite, and Golden worked it into almost every conversation he had, whether with cabbies, bricklayers, ministers, or college presidents. When *Only in America,* his first collection of essays drawn from the paper, became an overnight blockbuster, Golden was launched. He had, it seemed, found the goods he was meant to sell, and people across the country—Christians, Jews, liberals and conservatives, blacks and whites—were lining up to buy.[4]

I did not meet Harry Golden, who died in 1981, nearly twenty years before I decided to write about him. Yet he was as present in my childhood as an admired out-of-town uncle, his wit and folksy commentary spilling out of the books piled on tables and nightstands. Economic realities and child-raising philosophies in my 1960s New England home meant that I read whatever my mother read, and she read Harry Golden the way her southern grandparents had whiled away the hottest part of a summer day with Scripture, closely, and with the comfortable conviction that real truth sat on the pages.

Montrose Buchanan, my mother, grew up not far from Charlotte, where Golden launched the eccentric *Carolina Israelite.* As a young woman, she worked briefly for him as a secretary in the mid-1940s, and decades later the clever writing she did for various small newspapers was heavily influenced by Golden. She died secure in the knowledge that I was just what she wanted me to be—a newspaper reporter and a book reviewer with at least some of her facility for humorous writing on serious subjects—but not knowing I would someday try to keep her hero alive in a book of my own.

I followed in her footsteps, dropping out of college to write obituaries for a good, independent, small daily newspaper in New Hampshire, the *Concord Monitor.* Many years and newspaper jobs later, I left the newsroom of the *Seattle Times* and went off to be an Ada Comstock Scholar at Smith College in Massachusetts. There I had resources only dreamed of by most writers: world-class libraries, a seat in the lecture halls and offices of some of the country's leading historians, and a scholarship to keep it going for three demanding, invigorating years. Research on Judaism in the American South led me back to Golden. I saw an opportunity for a full-length biography of a remarkable and influential individual and the rich times in which he lived, from Ellis Island to Wall Street, into prison and through the Depression, into the postwar South and on to the most visible years of the civil rights movement, with its frightening, exhilarating changes.[5]

THE BECHARMED EARLY readers who gobbled up Golden's homely little newspaper in the first few years and delighted in his first bestseller would have been decidedly less impressed had they been around to see his unspectacular arrival in Charlotte in 1941. He was a middle-aged Jewish ex-convict leaving wife and children behind in New York City, where they had to scratch out a living. Bespectacled, short of inseam and wide of waist, he came armed with little more than a week's worth of cotton shirts, trousers, a couple of neckties, and an armload of books. Within a few years he was putting out his oddball newspaper and taking on the Ku Klux Klan, just as lunch counters, buses, and schools were turning into southern battlegrounds. As Golden himself might have put it: There's something to upset nearly everyone—what's not to like about *this* story?

Golden spun his experiences and observations into his popular books and scores of magazine and newspaper articles. With the help of his eldest son, editor and writer Richard Goldhurst, he became a household name; his book titles (*Only in America, Enjoy, Enjoy!, You're Entitle', So What Else is New?*) became vernacular expressions. "So, can you beat it?" Golden asked an interviewer in 1961, a few months before his fourth book came out. "Half a million hardcover books for $4 each and 3 million paperbacks for 50 cents—without using any four-letter words or pictures of naked women."[6]

We Americans love our storytellers and splashy showmen; Golden was both. He repackaged the hard past in more appealing wrappings; he brought the powerful and famous down to size and exalted plain people by preserving small but important moments in their lives. He explored some of the biggest themes a writer can put to paper—prejudice, dignity, and the daily struggle of the working person—with slices of real life, humorously rendered.

Golden liked to pause and look at the foibles of daily life, then put it all in perspective for his readers: "America," he declared in 1957, "is on a huge breast binge." Pondering the change from his boyhood, when a flash of exposed leg on a woman boarding the streetcar could make a man's day, to the abundance of cleavage evident in movies and magazines by the late 1950s, Golden theorized that "in times of peace and more placid living, legs are important, but during times of stress and great uncertainty the instinct to seek the safety and comfort of a 'mother' is probably an important factor in this current tremendous interest in the female chest."[7]

Along with such amusing cultural digressions, Golden sounded a warning for America to appreciate and accelerate its social progress. His immigrant childhood and his midlife move to the South convinced him that discrimination was dead weight pulling down the nation and its people. Golden grasped something few white mainstream journalists or historians fully understood at the time: the vital role of African American churches in the movement's progress. He also saw early on that the nonviolent platform of the church leaders would be followed by more militant activists, changing the shape of the movement and America in the process.

Golden was not a conventional newspaper editorialist, and he was most definitely not a model Jewish activist or member of the Jewish intelligentsia of his day, those writers and activists who dismissed the value of his work and looked down on the readers who pushed it onto the bestseller lists. Yet he managed something that most of the editorial pages and intellectuals of his day did not. He held on to his moral outrage over racism, believing that America could and would do better.

Later, critics would complain about his one-note refrain, and they are not wrong. But as historian Stephen J. Whitfield wrote about Golden, "Most writers come to realize that they are blessed with—or imprisoned by—only one subject anyway (with variations), and by making himself into a shrewd observer of the battle for racial justice, this outsider, who had been something of a drifter, found his destiny."[8]

Golden did all this by revealing rankly foolish and hateful manifestations of racism in everyday life, and he did it in his own paper, in hundreds of magazine articles, in radio interviews, in syndicated newspaper columns, and in millions of American living rooms as he traded witty one-liners with the likes of TV hosts Jack Paar and Johnny Carson.

Some of his writing—indeed much of it—seems dated today. Historian Hasia R. Diner rightly faults Golden as having helped invent the myth of the Lower East Side as America's one-and-only genuine Jewish experience. There is not, and never has been, a monolithic "Jewish community." But there are few historical images as stubbornly ubiquitous as that of the brave, ragged Eastern European Jew landing on America's shores at the turn of the twentieth century, with his dashed hopes of gold-paved streets replaced by determination to transplant Jewish culture to the Lower East Side. Golden was not the only popular-culture figure to push this myth, but he understood its sentimental appeal and played to it. The timing of his fame coincided with the flowering of Judaism within mainstream American life, and he proved to be a master at marketing a version of Lower East Side *Yiddishkeit*—cultural Jewishness—in ways that appealed to a very large range of readers. There were, in fact, endless variations on the immigrant experience, including the many paths followed by the millions of Jews who deliberately bypassed the Lower East Side and New York City to settle in other towns and cities throughout America and Canada. Their stories are compelling but were not the ones Golden offered his readers.[9]

He chose to stay with the vantage point of entertaining memoirist, passing on his own recollections in short essays. He evoked the shared struggles and successes in one very concentrated Jewish community and paid less attention to the darkest aspects of poverty, drudgery, sexism, and anti-Semitism that also existed in his world. This was, in part, a commercial decision. Golden was a canny promoter, and success with his first book persuaded him to stick with a winning formula. Later when he wrote about Jews in the South or even in Israel, his style and approach didn't vary much. Golden was fully capable of writing about difficult and unpleasant subjects, and he did so. But much of his audience accepted those subjects from him only after he had won their hearts in the earlier days with more sentimental fare.[10]

Viewing Golden's life today is to pull up a chair and watch the most fascinating and telling events in America's modern history pass by—a bit of a *Forrest Gump* tale. His family steps ashore, a small band of adventurers in the great wave of newcomers who changed and enriched this country. The young Harry Goldhurst (his earlier surname) grabs money with both hands during the frenzied rise of the stock market and ends up behind bars, and we are at the keyhole of one of the millions of businesses and families brought down in the crash of 1929. The news of *Brown v. Board of Education* and its death knell for "separate but equal" finds him celebrating with joyful students on the campus of a southern black college. As John F. Kennedy sets out to be the first Roman Catholic president, Golden and his friend Carl Sandburg talk and sing along the campaign trail. While bus boycotts, sit-ins, and marches become national news, as soldiers guard the entrances of segregating schools, and as blacks register to vote throughout the South, Golden is there to watch and write about it all. He breaks bread with NASA insiders as Apollo 11 heads for the moon. He faces angry college audiences when he refuses to condemn Lyndon Johnson's war in Vietnam.[11]

Golden's work can warn, teach, and invigorate us as we wrestle with our versions of those maladies that sickened his era: financial industry meltdown, the searing arguments over immigration, and the scourge of unemployment, poor schools, and too many Americans with little or no health care. He wrote about all of these things with provocative originality. His life story also traces the evolution of an influential pop-culture figure and reveals how a humorist criticized by intellectuals for sentiment and kitsch was able to change public opinion on the most serious subjects.[12]

The body of Golden's work will be valuable to future historians. The best biographers have that rare ability to continually place the past in context. In their hands, context is not apologetic or pedantic but a lens that magnifies and sharpens. Such historians are deft and tireless in mining the newspapers and books that regular folks were reading, and in doing so, they transport us back to that time. Golden's books and articles were so widely read by mainstream America that revisiting them today is to see quite clearly what many people did *not* know about race issues and religious and class differences. He wrote about African Americans as parents, workers, or students—in short, as people with the same responsibilities, wants, and needs as white people. It is too easy to forget the shameful truth that the concept of blacks as equals—or even as human beings—was a new idea for many of Golden's white readers.[13]

The expression "civil rights movement" is so embedded in our language today that few of us consider its breadth and depth. Countless popular movies, documentaries, novels, histories, and articles have helped preserve the legacies of many of its heroes and enemies. It's no accident that military terms are so often used to describe it: This was a *fight* for rights, a *battle* for change, a *war* against prejudice. There were casualties, martyrs, and prisoners. Women, men, and schoolchildren were clubbed, murdered, knocked flat by fire hoses, and jailed. But it is vital to understand, as historian Jacquelyn Dowd Hall has explained in her scholarship on the "long civil rights movement," that this was more than the tidy historical period bracketed by *Brown v. Board of Education* in 1954 and the Voting Rights Act of 1965. It took place on a bigger stage than the South, and its key players were more complex than that narrower view suggests. Golden's fascination with what might be called the sidebar stories—the details behind the big news of the day, the reactions of regular folks to segregation and protests—enabled him to grasp these points, albeit without anything close to Hall's robust academic exploration.[14]

There were other writers and journalists in the South who bravely stood against Jim Crow and racism, but very rarely were they lone operators without the protection of a large news organization. Many of the intellectuals and academics studying the history and sociology behind bigotry were not as widely known outside their own circles as Golden would be at the height of his popularity. (The problem there, according to Golden, was that scholars live in deathly fear of putting even the smallest bit of *charm* into their writing.)[15]

A gratifying number of white celebrities lent their names to get the cause into the headlines and provided money to feed, transport, and bail out marchers, Freedom Riders, and other protestors. As important as such contributions were, they were often just that—occasions of giving. Golden, from the moment his first book became a bestseller in 1958, used his celebrity to push for civil rights with a single-mindedness that set him apart. He fought in and covered that war, and he did it with a potent mix of bravery, humor, anger, and hope. And finally, there is the incontrovertible fact that Golden was a *character*, an irreverent bookworm, a Shakespeare-quoting, political-handicapping—and extremely funny—character.

Confronted with the question of gradualism—How fast can cultural change really happen?—Golden liked to tell of a sight spotted in a hospital emergency room in Gainesville, Florida, sometime during the 1950s. There on a shelf sat three containers, each holding a thermometer. The first one was labeled "White-Oral"; the second one, "Black-Oral"; and the last one, "Rectal." Golden would take a long pause, shift his cigar to the other side of his mouth, grin, and growl, "Now that is what I call *gradual* integration."[16]

CHAPTER ONE

Putting Down Roots in the
Goldeneh Medina

Leib Goldhirsch, father of the boy who would become Harry Golden, was a predictable man. Whenever he prepared to leave the family's tiny tenement flat on the Lower East Side's Eldridge Street, he would enact the same ritual: put a foot up on the chair by the door, then wait for his wife to rush to his side with a polishing rag. As soon as she bent to her task, the elder Goldhirsch would moan, "*Oy, mein vei'idike rikken!* (Oh, my aching back!)." The joke was always the same—she was polishing, *his* back ached.[1]

Golden found his best story material in his own beginnings. As a writer, he used his origins like sourdough-bread starter, working the mix until it was ready to turn into a fragrant treat, pulling bits off for years, each offering born of the same stuff but made unique by time and temperature, climate and handling. The good storyteller, the true teller of tales, sizes up a listener or a room, even an entire readership at a particular point in time, then delivers what best feeds them. Golden knew that if he shaped a tale to fit his audience, they'd be hooked. He did not consider this method, which sometimes involved generous reworking of the facts, to be on a par with the self-aggrandizing lies of some other self-made men. Those revisionist histories didn't feed others, he felt; they just served the storyteller.

Depending on the setting, Golden declared himself either a native New Yorker (a fiction) or, more often, an immigrant from what was then

Austria-Hungary (true) and born anywhere from 1902 to 1905. (Some of the entries in his FBI files and death certificate agree on a birth year of 1903, but the former lists the day as 6 May; the latter, 28 May.) When he claimed his true immigrant status, he recalled the ship that brought him to New York as the SS *Graf Waldersee*, which was accurate, but he couldn't resist adding a proud claim about the speed record it set on the journey: "It only took eleven days for the *Waldersee* to get to the New World, compared with three months for the *Mayflower*." Actually, the sturdy thirteen-ton ship chugged into New York Harbor on 31 March 1907, a full sixteen days after it left Hamburg. The story usually went that immigration officials at Ellis Island forced the family name change from Goldhirsch to Goldhurst, although this actually happened later, when Harry and his sisters changed their surname as young adults entering the work world. But countless other immigrants lost their names at the hands of government officials, and Golden knew which story played better to his audiences.[2]

But even the most practiced storyteller can't always keep up with the odd truths of real life. Golden made the stories of his various name changes part of his immigrant-story collection, from Goldhirsch to Goldhurst to Golden, and from Herschel to Harry. But he did not write (and may not have known all the details) that his given first name and the names of his mother and two sisters were changed en route or soon after arrival in America. Sometime before the family's answers were recorded on the U.S. Census in 1910, Nechame Goldhirsch became Anna, mother of Chafke, who became Clara; Soni, who became Matilda; and Chaim, who became Hyman and, later, Herschel. "Harry" would come about by the boy's own choice before he graduated from eighth grade.[3]

Family lore holds that two older Goldhirsch sons died of influenza before the family emigrated, and daughter Matilda later listed a mother other than Anna Goldhirsch on official documents, all suggesting an earlier marriage for Leib. These details were largely ignored by Golden in his nostalgic stories; such diversions would have just muddied his simpler view of Jewish immigrant life. "All of us are on a single ball of twine, and every few yards or so we meet," he liked to say, emphasizing one of his favorite themes, the common ground shared by American Jews and other immigrants to their new country.[4]

In 1905, Leib Goldhirsch, then forty-three years old, left the grinding poverty in Mikulintsy, a town in Galicia located in what was then Austria-Hungary and is now Ukraine. He was part of a mass migration of almost 35 million Europeans, 22 million of whom arrived and changed the face of America between 1881 and 1914. Close to 2 million of these newcomers were Jews, many driven away by the threat of what historian Oscar Handlin summed up as "pogroms . . . persecution, compulsory military service, and the confinement . . . to the Pale of Settlement." The Pale comprised several provinces in which Russia had forced Jews to live; *shtetlach* were the small towns within the provinces. The Goldhirsch family did not experience pogroms in Galicia, but Leib, who among other things taught in the *shtetl* school, knew there was little hope for his children to improve their education or achieve satisfactory occupations. As Golden once wrote, "Though there were no bars on the *shtetl*, still it was a cage."[5]

So Leib sailed to North America more than a year before his wife and children, staying first with cousins in Canada, then crossing into the United States at St. Albans, Vermont. With $18 in his pocket—an amount neatly noted on the border-crossing manifest—he headed for New York City. Along with son Jacob, he earned the passage money for the rest of the family. Despite his claim of being a skilled "cloth cutter" on the official forms, Leib probably made money giving Hebrew lessons, while Jacob, then about seventeen and called Jake or Jack in his new country—worked at selling clothing, dishes, and anything else he could buy wholesale, from a wooden pushcart.[6]

In that era, the Lower East Side neighborhood was generally defined as those streets bordered on the north by Fourteenth Street, on the east by the East River, on the south by Fulton and Franklin Streets, and on the west by Pearl Street and Broadway. For the Goldhirsch family, their close-knit community of fellow immigrants from Galicia was *the* Jewish America. Once settled at 171 Eldridge Street, the family got on with life in the *goldeneh medina* (golden land) in their four-room tenement flat, a fifth-floor walkup. Their flat's rooms opened one behind another; the only real windows with anything like a view were the two in the front room, where Matilda practiced the piano and Anna's precious sewing machine and dressmaker's dummy were kept.[7]

A smaller, windowless room held two small beds and a cot for Jake, Harry, and Max, born in 1909. The kitchen, with its uneven wooden table, mismatched chairs and stools, big black stove, sink, and icebox complete with drip pan, was where Leib held court, homework was done, and Clara and Matilda shared a bed in the corner. The room at the back of the flat, with the small window's beam of light almost blocked by the fire escape, was Leib and Anna's room, with a row of wall hooks for clothing, a high bed, and a polished pine dresser. A bathroom down the hall served five families. "Originally the toilets were in the yard in back of the tenement; an urban out-house divided into about four or five separate booths with a latch on the inside of each," Golden recalled. "The board that served as a toilet cover was of a piece, and so when one fellow lifted it up in his booth, it caused quite a disturbance in the other enclosures which led to constant communication among the occupants." Once a month, a crew came to clean. "They were Poles usually and I have never forgotten how those men remained standing in the ditch in their hip boots eating their lunch," he wrote.[8]

Everyone in the crowded household put in long days; everyone but Leib brought in regular money toward the $14-a-month rent and other expenses. The patriarch's days were always busy, but rarely with compensated work. Pushing a cart full of apples or sewing sleeves on shirts was fine for others—women, children, and *landsmen*, fellow immigrants from Galicia who regarded him in awe as he dispensed Talmudic wisdom or read aloud from spirited letters to the editor of *Der Morgen Zhornal* (*Jewish Morning Journal*). Leib's status as a teacher in the old country earned him the honorific "Reb Lebche," and that, along with his own confident bearing, lifted him to a lofty place above his neighbors. The tall silk Prince Albert top hat Leib acquired somewhere in his travels would have looked foolish on most short, middle-aged men, especially one with a round, owlish face and big spectacles; old-fashioned wool trousers; and snugly buttoned, high-collared topcoat, but on Leib it worked. Seeing him striding down Eldridge Street without his elegant hat would have been as unseemly as glimpsing him in a nightshirt, Golden wrote, adding,

> I should start the story of my father by saying that he was a failure.
>
> But his type of failure has not yet been explored in immigrant sociology. We have had stories of the "Horatio Alger" immigrant who went from cloaks operator and peddler to manufacturer and retail merchant. We've also had the story of the immigrant in terms of the class war; the fellow who worked all his life in a sweat-shop and got tuberculosis, or died when he had his head beaten in on the picket line. But we have not yet had the story of the immigrant who failed because he refused to enter the American milieu on its terms—to start earning status on the basis of money.[9]

Leib's aloof attitude toward money extended to all corners of his life. Sometime in the 1920s, a congregation in Montreal invited him to deliver a lecture on Eastern European Jewry. One of his sons chided him: "Papa, you only have one dollar in your billfold. You're going to a strange country, you're going to need more than that." Leib shook his head, answering, "The committee has sent me the ticket. They will meet the train and take me to where I am to speak. They will provide me with dinner and return me to the train." When he came home, Leib had the same dollar in his billfold.[10]

His greatest gift, at least in the eyes of his young son Herschel, was his ability to argue just about anyone into the ground. The Goldhirsch kitchen table was a training ground for the well-honed debate. There Leib and his cronies filled their days, as Golden put it, with "tea and anarchy, anarchy and tea." Leib's dearest friend, whom Golden called "Dudja Silverberg," was another middle-aged man more devoted to spirited conversational dueling than breadwinning, and the only visitor who regularly bested his host. Herschel loved to watch their routine, which rarely varied. "When my father pinned Dudja logically, when he proved Dudja did not know his facts, had not read his Talmud, then Dudja would suddenly lean across the table, pick up a quartered lemon, put it between his teeth, bite hard, suck deeply, quickly sip the hot tea from the water glass, and sigh. '*A glazl varms*, Leib. *A glazl varms* [a glass of warmth].' All the while, while the others watched this acidic test, Dudja's mind was clicking, and invariably he left my father frustrated."[11]

So Leib lectured, gave the occasional Hebrew lesson, and read his newspapers. He often paused to admire and read aloud some bit of nervy prose in the *Jewish Daily Forward* and express his admiration for publisher Abraham Cahan, a crabby Socialist who went on to enliven and preserve Yiddish literature for a half-century. Leib also regularly served as *ba'al tefillah*, a master of prayers, who led the congregation at the small *shul*, or synagogue, around the corner. His religion "tended toward the rational," wrote his son. "He was conversant with Spinoza, Darwin and Kant, yet he never failed to observe every Sabbath."[12]

That Leib indulged his commitment to things both secular and religious so satisfactorily—and was often heard to express gratitude that he could do so without fear of reprisal from government or Gentile neighbors—left a deep impression on his son. When Golden later wrote of America as a land of opportunity, he was not simply cleaving to the rags-to-riches story line but was celebrating the freedom to live as Leib had—observing only those religious practices and customs that suited him, soaking up arguments of every political stripe, and arguing them from various starting points with a joyful contrariness. Leib modeled what historian Jonathan D. Sarna described when characterizing Jewish immigrants of the time as often embodying piety, entrepreneurial hustle, and freethinking—a combination possible in this new world that social/literary critic and historian Irving Howe had touched on when he wrote, "We make distinctions between religious and secular ideologies, and we are right to make them;

but in the heated actuality of east European Jewish life the two had a way of becoming intertwined."[13]

Leib's secular views allowed his son to choose which aspects of an otherwise smothering orthodoxy he would accept. This Golden would do throughout his life, cobbling together bits of Socialism, Judaism, capitalism, Zionism, and—always—commercialism.

Leib was elected, year after year, to the unpaid presidency of the Mikulintsy *Verein*, a society for *landsleit*, those men from his hometown who regarded his opinion as the last word on any of the number of puzzling new challenges they encountered in America. The case of a Romanian rabbi who came to the Lower East Side collecting for Jewish relief in Eastern Europe was one of the dilemmas brought to Leib, and his son wrote about it in the 1960s, four decades after it happened.

> Though [the defendant] was a rabbi, he was also more unfortunately an embezzler. He had defrauded these Lower East Side Jews and they caught him at it. He was tried and convicted. . . . Though a Jewish prosecutor had argued the state's case and a Jewish jury returned the verdict, the judge summoned my father to his chambers, where he confessed to Leib the whole affair was deplorable. He wanted to know what the neighborhood Jews thought was fit punishment. "Send him to Matteawan," said my father. "It is a hospital for the criminally insane. But there he will be able to keep his beard, and there he will still keep the dietary laws because someone can bring food to him. In a few years he can get out, and it won't be such a disgrace." Which is precisely what the judge did."[14]

Leib was licensed to perform civil marriages and did so for immigrant couples married in Jewish religious ceremonies in the old country who needed a legal certificate to establish their marital state in America. The weddings were held in the Goldhirsch flat, often with the couple's many children looking on. By the time he was in grade school, Herschel was handling the paperwork for these unions, while sister Matilda played a wedding march on the secondhand spinet piano wedged in a corner. Leib charged $5 when the couples could afford to pay. Decades later, after he became well known, Golden was regularly contacted by people who remembered standing in the Goldhirsch parlor as Leib made their marriages legal in their new country.[15]

If any of Leib's offspring resented his supreme indifference to earning money, it didn't surface in their correspondence, in the fond stories they traded, or in any of Golden's essays about his father. Leib's children were passionately independent: All were determined to earn their own way, particularly Clara and Matilda, who remained single and worked into old age. Perhaps their early acquaintance with the hustling instincts needed to survive in the workplaces of their youth gave them their nerve; whatever the source, as young adults they shared a willingness to take a flier at a risky scheme. Harry was most decidedly his father's son, drawn always to a lively life of the mind, even as he ventured into his own periodic ill-fated moneymaking ventures.

When Leib Goldhirsch died in 1942 in his early eighties, a judge and grand master of the B'rith Abraham Order read the eulogy that Golden would quote, with uncharacteristic consistency, for the rest of his life: "Reb Lebche, whose body lies before us, could never borrow three hundred dollars on his signature at any time in his life, but he distributed hundreds of thousands of dollars entrusted to him by others for charity; there were factory workers and peddlers who stopped off in Reb Lebche's apartment on their way home and handed him two and three dollars in an envelope without their name or their address but with one message—'Reb Lebche, this is for someone who may need bread tomorrow.' "[16]

Although friends, neighbors, and members of the Mikulintsy *Verein* deferred to Leib's erudition, and his wife and children supported him without complaint, Anna Klein Goldhirsch was the one who actually ran the household. Her days started before the sun rose, when she tiptoed into the kitchen to fire up the stove and begin a cycle of cooking and cleaning that would last until long after the younger children were asleep. While her potato soup and fillings for stuffed cabbage bubbled on the stove, Anna worked her knee-pedal sewing machine in the front room, turning out trousers, shirtwaists, and skirts for her older children and knee pants and jumpers for the younger ones. Wedding gowns and suits were made or altered for her many acquaintances in the neighborhood. She urged food on her children, brushing aside young Herschel's worries that at five feet tall and 145 pounds, he was too fat. Nothing to worry about, she told him. "In America the fat man is always the boss and the skinny man is always the bookkeeper."[17]

Anna was a sturdy woman and a bit over five feet tall. Her face was round, with soft brown eyes and a wide mouth bracketed in smile lines, and her expression was gentle. Her long brown hair, streaked with gray before she turned thirty-five, was pulled back in a bun and often covered with a neat kerchief. Anna never seemed to stop or even lean against the back of her chair. Six days a week she hauled a basket of groceries up five flights of stairs from the pushcarts and markets. Anna spoke little English but had no difficulty making her will known in the busy, small world in which she moved. The neighbors, the kosher butcher, the bread baker, and produce merchants all spoke her language, as did the Singer salesman who stopped by for tea, waiting for Anna to fish coins out of the small pewter dish in which she saved up the payments for her sewing machine. Anna learned to make herself plain to Angelo, the Italian delivery boy she befriended who lugged ice and coal up the stairs and served as the *Shabbos goy*, or non-Jew who lit the stove during the Jewish Sabbath. Then Anna observed Jewish law and avoided all labor from sundown Friday to sundown Saturday. For everyone else, Anna's two all-purpose English vocabulary words worked just fine: "Enjoy!" and "Likewise!"[18]

She prayed out loud as she worked, a friendly running conversation with God, exhorting him to protect her family. She spoke in homely Yiddish vernacular, not the Hebrew her husband chanted for admiring listeners. Anna finished most exchanges with some variation of "*mit gutt helfin!*"—"with God's help!" To son Jake leaving for his job at a pocketbook factory, she said, "Go! Work! With God's help!"; to son Herschel begging pennies for the new cowboy-movie matinee, "With God's help, you'll go to the movies! Repeat after me, with God's help!"[19]

Although she could not read or write, it was Anna, not the learned Leib, who insisted the children attend school as long as possible; Anna who propelled Clara and Matilda through secretarial courses; and Anna who made it possible for her son, by then called Harry, to be the first in the family to graduate from high school. She embodied the Eastern European Jew whom Nathan Glazer and Daniel Moynihan later described as having "a passion for education that was unique in American history." She did not lecture her children on the value of acquiring an education; her means to that end were directly practical. She stitched up neat career-girl suits for her daughters to wear as they learned shorthand and typing, and she carefully tended the finicky gaslights in the flat so her bookworm son had reading light. Then she nagged him if he stayed up too late reading. "I've always had trouble with women and books," Golden liked to say. "All of them have offered the same complaint: 'You're always reading. You always have your nose in a book.' The only woman I ever closed the book for, however, was my mother."[20]

Shabbat and New Suits

The Goldhirsch siblings came and went from the tenement flat constantly, working their various jobs and attending school. The only time they could be counted on to be home together was Friday night. As the sun set, Anna would be lighting the Sabbath candles in the candlesticks she'd carried to America in her small bundle of belongings. The simple Sabbath prayer, uttered by Jewish women the world over brought the busy household to a halt each week: "Blessed are you, Lord God, King of the Universe, who sanctifies us with his commandments, and commands us to light the candles of the Sabbath." Once every seven days, Anna could outshine Leib's ability to parse the Pentateuch, the first five books of the Hebrew Bible. Yet, as devout as she was, the practical-minded Anna did not raise a fuss when her son Jake got a job at a hotel that meant he had to work Friday nights. She packed gefilte fish, chicken soup, and *tzimmes*, a stew of carrots and plums, into two brown enamel pots. After school, Herschel, carrying the pots, boarded the Sixth Avenue streetcar to West Thirty-Eighth Street. He delivered them to a friendly chef at an adjacent restaurant who would keep the food warm on a steam table until Jake took his dinner break.[21]

Although Golden wrote several times about the magic of the Shabbat ritual and the delicious food that accompanied it, he rarely mentioned other Jewish ceremonies in his own life. Raised in what today would be called an Orthodox Jewish home, he became *bar mitzvah* at thirteen, a "son of the commandment" through the ritual Torah reading by a boy entering manhood. Yet in all his references to Jewish life and culture, and to events in his own boyhood, he did not write in detail about this ceremonial passage. True, it was not the large, festive occasion it later became for Jewish families, but it might also have been a deeply held memory he chose *not* to write about—there were a few such things in his life. His eldest son, Richard, remembers: "Most of the time we were growing up, Harry was a Jew when it suited him. He'd eat a ham sandwich and tell entertaining stories about the Jewish immigrant experience. But as he got older, it meant more. . . . His Jewishness meant something different to him. He kept that to himself though. He told the Jewish stories people asked to hear."[22]

Golden didn't eat crab and sometimes let people believe it was out of respect for Jewish dietary law. In fact, his son said, he never got over a boyhood experience of seeing a dead horse crawling with the hungry crustaceans pulled out of the East River. On his album *Harry Golden*, recorded for Vanguard in 1962, Golden did describe parading through the streets from the *shul* to one's home after a bar mitzvah ceremony, and that same year he wrote a thoughtful piece in the *Carolina Israelite* about Jewish identity and conversion to Christianity. Readers had deluged him with angry letters after he printed a story about a young Jewish man who was planning to become a Christian. "I admit I feel a little sad . . . but I feel no anger or resentment [when I hear of someone converting] and that may be due to the fact that I am secure in my own Jewishness. When a convert angers you it means his 'desertion' has weakened your own faith. He has created a new doubt for you."[23]

One of Golden's stories that became a classic, co-opted later by comedians and writers, was in fact about bar mitzvah preparation: "Buying a Suit on the East Side." Golden told it often to audiences and interviewers; it grew longer and the details shifted, but by and large it remained the same story as the version included in *Only in America*, where Golden recounts a carefully choreographed family shopping expedition to get adolescent Hymie a new suit for his big day in the synagogue. "When did you buy a winter suit or a heavy overcoat? In the middle of summer, of course. In July, August was even better. In the summer you could get a bargain," Golden begins.[24]

The story tracks the elaborate feints and dodges acted out by a cast of sharp characters: the "pullers-in," who literally dragged shoppers into the stores along Canal Street and Stanton Street; the beleaguered salesman, a "*mayvinn*" as Golden spelled it, the person in the family who knew all about cloth and workmanship, maybe an uncle who worked as a presser in a garment factory; and of course, young Hymie and his parents. Father barely utters a word, and Mother contributes only well-timed, deep sighs as she sits on a chair by the dressing room. After extensive wrangling between the *mayvinn* and the salesman, a price of $14 is quoted. The family leaves in a huff. "They all follow the mother who is already outside the door talking to the puller-in. The salesman catches up with the party on the sidewalk. The mother is annoyed. She shakes her head and in a low, compassionate tone of voice explains, 'There's nothing further to talk about. If you said maybe ten dollars, we would think you were crazy.' They keep walking." Several hours later, they return for more bargaining, and a deal is cut for $12. Everyone is happy. The family goes home for dinner and then, Golden concludes, "The mother resumes her traditional place within the family circle—'Hymie, did you give your father a big kiss for the suit he bought you today?' "[25]

Another garment-trade technique Golden described with a flourish was the "hard-of-hearing salesman." When a buyer found a suit he liked and asked about the price, the floor salesman would yell to the back something like, "Louis, how much for Number 2734?" A voice would holler back, "Sixty-five dollars." The floor salesman would then turn to the customer and say "thirty-five dollars." At that point, Golden said, "the customer pulled out thirty-five dollars, grabbed the suit without waiting for it to be boxed, and hustled off with his bargain, while Louis and the 'deaf salesman' went out to Davis's Saloon for a cold beer." In these stories, the fall guy was a guy; women were always the smart ones when Golden was telling the story.[26]

Anna Goldhirsch died at age fifty-seven of cancer of the spine, an illness that was spoken about only in whispers and which she kept from her children until the last days. When her son Harry stood next to her hospital bed as she was dying, she could no longer speak but could still turn the cuffs of his shirt back to see if they were clean and nod approvingly that they were. She was not eulogized by a Jewish community leader as her husband would be years later. But in his autobiography, Golden wrote an epitaph as fitting as any: "When she died in 1924, she had never driven in a car, never been to a movie, never, for that matter, seen Grand Central Station. But she had come from one world to another, borne seven children, seen two of them die, and had worked hard every day of her life."[27]

The Poets Were Paid

When Herschel wasn't at home or in school, he could often be found nearby at University Settlement House. Golden praised the settlement houses, those free institutions that gave immigrants safe and clean places to learn about their bewildering new country, borrow books, listen to music and lectures, bathe, and take classes in English. In an essay called "The Poets Were Paid," written early in his career, Golden put into words the view of America he held close all of his life:

> Hundreds of sweatshop employees, men and women who sat at machines for nine and ten hours a day, came home, washed up, had supper . . . went to the settlement house to learn English or listen to a fellow read poetry to them. *Paid* readers of poetry. I saw it. I saw gangsters and bums, but I also saw poets, settlement workers, welfare workers, scribes, teachers, philosophers, all hoping and striving for one goal—to break away—and they did, too. The second generation came along and soon the sons took the old folks away, out to Brooklyn or up to the Bronx, and thus they made room for new immigrants. American gave them all hope and life, and they repaid America.
>
> There has never been a more even trade.[28]

Shelves and shelves of books waiting to be borrowed were what caused Herschel to fall in love the minute he walked into University Settlement's lending library. "A book is the supreme thing of mankind," he said reverently, describing that moment nearly half a century later in a television documentary about his life. He also liked to say that as a youngster he had sighted Eleanor Roosevelt in one of University Settlement's high-ceilinged rooms, teaching a dance class for immigrant girls. The story was rooted in truth: Roosevelt did teach there, but Golden would have been an infant at the time, so his enticing description of her blue dress was a pleasant fiction. When he met Roosevelt in the late 1950s and told her the story, she was either convinced or too polite to question his remarkable memory.[29]

He was not overstating anything, however, when he frequently crowed over the legacy of Eleanor Roosevelt and other young idealists who supported or volunteered in settlement houses like University and Lillian Wald's famous Henry Street Settlement nearby. "And so the secret is out!" he wrote in the *Carolina Israelite*. "Now you, too, know where Franklin D. Roosevelt got the New Deal. Right out of the settlement houses of the teeming slums. Bury the dead, take care of the widows and orphans, teach the young mother how to take care of her baby, and make sure the fellow has a doctor when he gets sick."[30]

For the Goldhirsch children and millions of others, the closest thing to what would now be called a social-services safety net was HIAS—the Hebrew Sheltering and Immigrant Aid Society, the best-known Jewish organization of its kind. Started in 1881, HIAS provided newcomers with guidance on getting through the various inspections and bureaucratic hoops at Ellis Island and on to the American life that lay beyond its gates. By the time the Goldhirsch family arrived, HIAS had merged with another immigrant-aid organization and was a veritable relocation machine, helping with everything from paperwork to clothing and food and sometimes even paying the $25 landing fee for those who arrived without a penny.

HIAS was founded by Russian Jews, but most of the Jewish organizations that the Goldhirsches heard about after their arrival were supported by well-established German-Jewish businessmen and their families, including the American Jewish Committee (AJC), which would figure prominently in Golden's life years later. By the time the waves of Eastern Europeans were arriving at the turn of the twentieth century, the German-Jewish New York burghers were reluctant to be associated with the bearded Jewish men and their wives and children in old-fashioned clothing who fled homelands to escape the pogroms. "Emotions were stirred and conflicts arose," wrote historian Peter I. Rose about the arrival of the Eastern European Jews. "The German Jews, both elite and parvenu, came to be grouped willy nilly with their 'cousins' from Russia, often to their profound dismay."[31]

Golden minimized these divisions, more often focusing on the philanthropic side of the German-Jewish society, not the prejudices some of its members directed toward fellow Jews. "No matter what we said publicly," he once insisted, "every Jew was extremely proud of the German Jews." This was not Golden bending history but a reflection of the awe with which immigrants such as the Goldhirsch family viewed America—with admiration for its democratic system and free enterprise, snooty German Jews and all. They took pride in the likes of Sears, Roebuck & Company magnate Julius Rosenwald, who gave millions of dollars to benefit Jewish children, the YMCA, and African American schools and colleges in the South. Another hero was the influential lawyer Louis Marshall, who fought to protect the rights of a stunning range of people in need, including blacks, Socialists, and would-be homeowners kept out by restrictive covenants, and who would figure prominently in the AJC and the Leo Frank lynching case. Furthermore, as historian Gerald Sorin wrote, however uncomfortable the German Jews were with the idea of uncouth newcomers, they were united in opposing restrictive immigration policies when the Russian pogroms in 1903 and 1906 made emigration a matter of life and death for so many Jews.[32]

Golden's approbation of these Jews increased as the advocacy groups they helped form or supported played prominent roles in the civil rights movement: the Anti-Defamation League (ADL), the AJC, the American Jewish Congress, the National Association for the Advancement of Colored People (NAACP), and the National Urban League. He was not always in sync with these groups; he had ups and down with the leadership of the AJC in particular. But throughout his life, he rarely missed a chance to remind people that Jewish leadership fueled the important groups, and countless middle- and working-class Jews continued to contribute money, serve on boards, work for the agencies, or do all of the above.[33]

Despite his positive public take on the contributions to American life made by German Jews, Golden was not above enjoying a joke at their expense, such as the one in a 1962 letter from his friend Charlotte businessman Hermann E. Cohen, who remembered the various Jewish factions of their youth: "If there is segregation in heaven," wrote Cohen, "it is not by skin pigmentation, but among Hebrews . . . it is those who went there from Poland, Russia, etc. in one Pale, and those from Germany, Holland, etc. in another ghetto."[34]

When a U.S. Census worker visited the Goldhirsch flat in 1910, he probably spoke to Matilda, then 13. The use of "Tillie" for her name on the census form—the only time it appears in her records—betrays a teenager's longing for a more vivacious name. The other siblings were listed as Jacob, 17; Clara, 15; Hyman, 7; and Max, 1. Jake was at least 20 at this point, something Matilda might not have known, or perhaps the family misrepresented his age intentionally for some financial benefit.[35]

Clara was on the tall side for her family, about five feet, four inches, with frizzy brown hair, a wide smile, and a confident walk. While still in her teens, she completed secretarial training and found clerical work in a broker's office. Clara caught on fast; she became Wall Street's first modern-day female stockbroker and built her own brokerage into a buzzing office by the early 1920s. (Victoria Woodhull had already scandalized America by opening her brokerage on the Street back in 1870.) Matilda was smaller than her sister, with a snub nose and smooth brown hair. She was a quick study too and found her niche as a designer, skilled in copying couture and adapting the patterns for use by the knock-off factories that mass-produced garments for a fraction of the chic designers' prices. She waited outside uptown churches on Sundays to see the latest styles, capturing them with a few quick strokes of her pencil in a sketchbook. Max, born in 1909, probably had the luxury of attending school without holding down a part-time job. Anna called her last child "*mein Columbus'l*" (my little Columbus) and, along with his doting siblings, described him proudly as "looking like an Irishman," meaning he did not look "foreign" or Jewish.[36]

Throughout Herschel's childhood and beyond, the consistent family provider was Jake, who worked nearly every day from the moment he arrived in America on his $34 steerage ticket until he became ill in his seventies. Jake was stronger and bigger than his father at a young age, and he quickly moved from his pushcart to better-paying jobs in factories, eventually landing one as a machinist, operating a press that sealed the metal clasps onto cloth and leather handbags. When a press caught the tips of three of his fingers, Jake was rushed to the hospital, where he refused to let doctors sedate him. He would later tell his three daughters he was afraid the doctors would amputate his fingers completely, and that a damaged hand was less likely to deter potential employers than one missing whole fingers.[37]

"I remember a policeman came to the house to tell us 'Jack' had been taken to a hospital," wrote Golden later. "In those days, as now, a policeman came to the house only to bring bad news. He asked neighbors where your family lived and the neighbors knew it was bad news and were hesitant in telling him. They thought, of course, if they didn't tell him where you lived, the bad news would dissipate." Jake's lost wages were not covered, but his hospital stay was paid for by his employer, a gesture the family thereafter cited as proof of the regard in which Jake was held for his work ethic.[38]

Jake's quick grasp of the ways of the business world was probably the only reason the family didn't end up in the streets when a fire broke out in their Eldridge Street tenement, sometime around 1913. "We were bribed with tears and admonoshings [*sic*] not to say a word till the insurance money came, because my kid brother Maxie started the fire looking for something under a couch filled with straw," Golden wrote an acquaintance in 1956. The $86 that the insurance company paid to the family, along with help from relatives, kept the family afloat.[39]

Jake's factory shifts gave way to front-desk work in one of New York's small theatrical hotels. He worked in the hotel business for the rest of his life, eventually buying one, then others, with the help of his wife Lillie's widowed mother. One of Jake's daughters remembered, "My grandmother worked in a factory, she sewed buttons on blouses. Somehow she saved up a couple of thousand dollars and gave it to him." He was not a success in the conventional sense; his hotels were never big moneymakers. More than once he lost one to the bank holding the mortgage, but somehow he always managed to pay his creditors off over time. Jake's siblings respected him in a way they felt toward few others.[40]

For all his big brother's oversight, Herschel had to fend for himself at school and in the neighborhood streets. He survived the usual challenges put to green youngsters who came from homes where English was not spoken, and hazing rituals would provide page after page of fodder for his writings later. In 1965 when a fan sent him a cake of Pears soap, the subject of ubiquitous billboards on the Lower East Side of his childhood, Golden responded with alacrity:

The first English words us immigrants learned in America were:
(1) Fuck
(2) Son-of-bitch
(3) Post-no-bills
(4) Moxie
(5) Good morning—have you used Pears soap?[41]

Herschel was encouraged to stay in school—Jake's labors made that possible—but his part-time jobs started when he was no older than ten. The first was selling newspapers, all with the muscular names of that era: the *New York World*, *Telegram*, *Mail*, *Sun*, and *Globe* and sometimes the *Jewish Daily Forward* and a Chinese weekly that he remembered the newsboys pronouncing as *Mong Gee*. He would buy bundles of papers, fan out copies of each on a busy sidewalk corner near sweatshops, factories, and office buildings, and call out the most promising headlines. A good day was selling 150 papers.[42]

A headline in 1915 marked one of the most influential events of Golden's life: FRANK LYNCHED!

The story, carried by many of the major newspapers of the day—and certainly all the Jewish publications—covered the mob hanging of Leo Frank, a Jewish factory superintendent in Atlanta who had been convicted of the strangulation murder of thirteen-year-old Mary Phagan two years earlier. Twenty-nine-year-old Frank, a college-educated Jew from New York who had married an Atlanta girl, was arrested, tried, and convicted in a trial conducted amidst extreme anti-Semitic threats and intimidation and then sentenced to hang. The governor of Georgia, John M. Slaton, put his own life in danger to commute Frank's death sentence to life imprisonment. A lynch mob dragged Frank from his prison cell in the dead of night, drove him over miles of country roads, and hanged him from an oak tree. The story was a shocker even in the South. Lynching was still a fact of life there, but the majority of victims were African Americans, not well-off white men.

By the time Herschel learned of Frank's murder as he hawked newspapers, he was twelve, a bookish boy well able to understand the stories. That day, he bawled out the gigantic red-inked headline as "FRANK MURDERED!" instead of "FRANK LYNCHED!" knowing that his immigrant customers would not understand this distinctly American word. The grisly nature of the lynching, captured in the lurid prose of the day's journalistic style and repeated in passionate neighborhood discussions, seized the boy's imagination. It grew into a lifelong fascination for Golden, who wrote often about the explosive convergence of prejudice and poverty that ignited in the Frank case. His keen interest would culminate fifty years later in his book *A Little Girl Is Dead*, about the Frank case.[43]

One of the favorite newspaper-selling spots for Herschel was on Allen Street, near Norfolk and Delancey, which for a time was lined with brothels. Not only did the men frequenting the bawdy houses typically buy newspapers on their way home, but the prostitutes regularly paid newsboys to fetch them cigarettes, magazines, and candy, and they were good tippers. His eye for rich storytelling detail began to develop; Herschel noted with interest that the foot of each bed was fitted with a strip of black oilcloth, so the men didn't have to remove their shoes. Golden was neither a prude nor a romantic when it came to sex-for-hire, and he often referred to the women as "whores" rather than "ladies of the evening" or other euphemisms of the day. He had a lifelong affinity for prostitutes and regarded them as admirable pragmatists and excellent sources of reliable civic gossip, although by all accounts he was not a patron. His kind view of professionals simultaneously condemned certain other women. "I [respect] the professional, but have no use for the amateur who has chased the professional out of business; the amateur, the so-called call-girl who does it for money but who poses as a model, an actress, or a housewife. These are the lowest tramps in the world."[44]

Such distractions aside, selling newspapers on the streets of New York was not an easy occupation for those youngsters who, unlike Herschel, lived by their wits on the streets, surviving brutal conditions without protectors. Photographer-turned-muckraker Jacob Riis famously captured the life of these young toughs, who stole or bought newspapers for a penny, then sold them for two cents each while scavenging food and catching sleep in alleys, abandoned buildings, or dooryards—wherever they could hole up for a night or an hour. Herschel came to respect the turf of those newsboys and the lines drawn by ethnic gangs. Finding himself in territory hostile to Jews was a mistake he would not repeat after three Irish boys caught him on their turf and "cockalized" him. "There are hundreds of men in their sixties who know what it is to be cockalized," he wrote. "Indeed cockalization was universal. My father once told me there were specific Polish and Russian words for the process. The enemy kids threw the Jew to the ground, opened his pants, and spat and urinated on his circumcised penis, while they shouted 'Christ killer.'"[45]

By the time he was fourteen and attending East Side Evening High School, Herschel had become Harry, and his world was expanding considerably beyond the Lower East Side. Not that his was a narrow intellectual existence; far from it. Leib and his cronies provided a lively education in Talmudic debate and the roots of Socialism and Marxism, along with their running commentary on the machinations of American politics. Jake, Clara, and Matilda told plenty of dinner-table stories of doings in their various workplaces and regularly talked their bosses into hiring their younger brother for odd jobs, from telegram delivery boy to pretzel vendor at the Polo Grounds. He had an avid curiosity about this wider world, at least the urban part of it. Any rural fantasies disappeared after he spent part of the summer on a small farm in Connecticut the year he turned fifteen, courtesy of a settlement house project for inner-city youth. Driving the horse and buggy into town to get the mail was fun, but when one of the farm's resident spinsters pounced on him in the barn, he was so unnerved that he "squirmed from her caress and ran, red-faced, to the house." A few months later, back in New York, "it dawned upon me what embarrassment she must have suffered. I felt terribly ashamed, but I knew that now boyhood was over."[46]

Single Tax and Shakespeare

Harry next got a taste of labor politics when he lost his first good job, working in Arnold Rosenbloom's hat factory, for talking up a garment-workers' union. "At this moment, which could have been decisive, I was offered a job with the Trade Union of that industry. This would have made me a pioneer in the coming expansion of the labor movement," Golden wrote later to a magazine editor in need of a biographical blurb. "But I became a Single Taxer and joined the Shakespeare Society instead."[47]

Indeed, Harry's next job introduced him to one of the strongest influences of his life, an eccentric, intelligent furrier named Oscar H. Geiger. Harry was hired as a delivery boy, and his new boss took a shine to him when he spied the young man sneaking a volume of Shakespeare into the stockroom to read on the job. Geiger invited him to join the study group of young men that met at his Harlem home, where he introduced his new employee to the radical economic theories of Henry George and the beauty of the Single Tax system. The Round Table Literary Club and its leader immediately expanded Golden's horizons—as a thinker, a Jew, and a man.[48]

Geiger led discussions and prodded the ten young men (including his own son) to read aloud and debate one another as they delved into great literature and political commentary, but his heart was always closer to George's tax platform than anything else. These radical economic ideas excited the group members and many other reform-minded Lower East Siders, who devoured George's 1879 book, *Progress and Poverty*. As a society of poor renters at the mercy of a favor-the-rich tax structure, they found much to like in George's argument that all taxes should be abolished except one on land—a move he insisted would encourage productive use to the benefit of everyone, not just landowners. George also favored rent control, public housing, and a minimum wage. "Naturally," observed Golden, "Henry George was considered a lunatic. So were his disciples, men like Oscar Geiger." Geiger left his career as a hospital administrator and went into retail to be free to devote more time to the Single Tax cause. He also ran, unsuccessfully, for mayor of the city and was always addressed by that title by the Round Table boys. Consequently, the fur business on West Thirty-Seventh Street was not a notable success.[49]

The sort of parlor discussion group led by Geiger was very popular at the time, especially among immigrants fascinated by the American political process, who formed Henry George Clubs and attended forums and rallies of like-minded thinkers. Their keen interests brought them to the attention of Tammany Hall, the political machine that grew from an eighteenth-century alliance between an Irish fraternal organization and the Democratic Party. Many immigrants, including Leib Goldhirsch, viewed Tammany with mingled disgust and admiration, as its efficient, corrupt patronage system reached into every aspect of daily life. Its representatives were present at every funeral and parade, always ready to help out a man in need—in return for his vote, of course.[50]

Later Golden would recall, with great roars of laughter, the election day strategies of Tammany's sachems as they went all out for the vote: Sister Clara was one of the precinct vote "counters" who earned a few extra dollars by smudging every few Republican ballots and rendering them ineligible. (A ring with a piece of charcoal in the place of a diamond did the trick.) Golden wrote often about Tammany's control of elections, always with a touch of hometown pride even as he reported their questionable methods:

> Tammany boss Big Tim Sullivan had about fifty student barbers working for him on every election day. . . . Here's how it worked: Along about August Big Tim sent word around the Bowery flophouses for the bums to let their beards grow. By election day, Big Tim had at his disposal several hundred Bowery bums, each with a full-grown beard. First each bum would vote with a full beard under one name. He would rush to one of the stand-by barbers who immediately clipped off the chin fuzz. So then the bum voted under another name with sideburns . . . then he would rush back to the barber who shaved off the sideburns, and now the bum would vote for the third time with just a mustache; and finally that came off and he would go forth to vote a fourth time—plain-faced, as Tammany called it. For this day's work the bum got one dollar, three meals, a pint of whiskey, and of course, a lesson in civics and good government.[51]

The Round Table also introduced Harry to the likes of Ray Stannard Baker, a crusading journalist who, along with Ida M. Tarbell and Lincoln Steffens, embodied the muckraking school of commentary and news coverage. He was particularly intrigued by the Socialist Baker's work on black Americans, such as *What Is a Lynching? A Study of Mob Justice, South and North*, published in 1905. His first awareness of the history of black

Americans had come when Geiger introduced his young charges to the writings of W. E. B. Du Bois with *The Souls of Black Folk* and the contrasting views of Booker T. Washington's *The Future of the American Negro* and *The Life of Frederick Douglass*.[52]

Workplace reform movements fired up all the Round Table members, but Harry was especially passionate. Worker injuries and deaths were not abstract subjects to him; Jake's maimed hand was a daily reminder of the perils of factory work. After the terrible 1911 fire at the Triangle Shirtwaist Factory killed 146 workers, mostly young immigrant women, some of the Goldhirsches had been among the thousands who followed the funeral cortege to the mass grave in the Arbeter Ring (Workingman's Circle) Cemetery. When the grieving public learned that the dilapidated building had frayed fire hoses and that the shop doors were locked to prevent employee pilferage, their fury forced the city to launch a groundbreaking investigation by a blue-ribbon committee. The factory owners were acquitted of manslaughter charges, but the publicity played a part in the creation of workplace safety regulations and laws and strengthened labor unions, especially those representing garment and other factory workers.[53]

Just as the family memories of the Triangle fire fostered sympathy for the worker in young Harry, the aggressive newspaper coverage of the aftermath planted the idea that timely, bold commentary brought about reforms. More than fifty years later, when Golden looked through newspaper clips from the Triangle fire, he was inspired as he rediscovered the vivid descriptions and human interest vignettes that arrested his family's attention when the headlines were new. "The stories," he insisted, "brought out some of the best reporting in American journalism."[54]

As he became more sophisticated and read more widely, Harry began to feel the pull of two cultures—the secular Americanized intellectuals with whom he was making friends, and the Eastern European Jewish thinkers around his father. He also began to admire some historic figures for their ability to create stimulating and meaningful lives that drew from more than one culture—in Douglass's case, both black and white worlds. Along with this intellectual awakening, when Harry put on a necktie and ventured to Geiger's home sometime around 1917, he had his first brush with assimilated Jews and educated Gentiles his own age. Fifty years later he could call up the thrill he felt that day: "For the first time I was looking at the middle class. We are a middle-class society, and that first vision is almost apocalyptic." With blunt introspection he added, "I know that the middle class inculcates a selfishness and a carelessness in us, a wish that it all be for us and us alone, I know the middle class victimizes the best and encourages the worst, yet to this day I want it."[55]

Embarking on lifelong friendships with these bright, more worldly young men, Harry realized for the first time that it would be possible for him to live somewhere beyond the streets of the Lower East Side—and perhaps even beyond New York. Oscar Geiger lived a life that was light-years from Eldridge Street, in a roomy apartment with stained-glass panels alongside the entry door, polished floors, and comfortable furniture, presided over by an Irish wife, Nina Geiger. Her beauty and the partnership she seemed to share with her husband so impressed Harry that he would later credit her for motivating him to find and marry an Irish Catholic wife of his own.

An Irish Bride

Genevieve Alice Marie "Tiny" Gallagher was Harry's version of Nina Geiger. Smart and capable, with a lively expression, a pleasing figure, and a fast wit, Tiny was a catch. The two met while working in the same office building; Harry, then in his mid-twenties, managed to be waiting for the elevator whenever she went to lunch or out on an errand. Tiny was employed as a secretary and was finishing the course work for a teacher's certificate. Typical for an unmarried woman in her twenties, she lived at home with her family. Later, Golden loved telling the story of an early date when he escorted Tiny home in the wee hours, only to discover she had forgotten her key. Rather than wake everyone up, she decided to get a room at a nearby hotel. When Harry worried aloud that her mother—whom he had yet to meet—would be upset, Tiny assured him it would be fine. "She doesn't know you, but she knows *me*."[56]

The members of the extended Gallagher clan, headed by Tiny's widowed mother, were devout Roman Catholics. They were a large, noisy, musical bunch, and even with their mighty misgivings they still managed to accept this unexpected choice of a Jewish husband. His family was another story. Leib and Matilda were aghast; Jake didn't pick sides. "A Jewish wife can make as much trouble for you as an Irish one," he said with a shrug. Clara, as always, supported her little brother. But in the end, no one from his family went to the wedding. Although he softened somewhat, for years Leib referred to Tiny as "the Shiksa" in front of his grandsons—Richard, Harry Jr. (known as "Buddy" in the family), William (Billy), and Peter. "I cannot re-create the moment in which I decided I wanted to marry Genevieve," Golden wrote in his autobiography. "I loved her until it hurt. I loved the home that sheltered her, I loved her brothers and sisters, I loved her widowed mother, I loved hearing Genevieve play the violin."[57]

Even though they had grown up fearing rival gangs of Irish youth, Golden and his friends admired the Irish for their ability to remain close-knit while so effectively moving into American politics and business. He offered various explanations for this admiration, most amusingly in an essay in his third book, *Enjoy, Enjoy!* Jews, he wrote, perpetually live in fear that one of their own will bring down society's wrath through some bad behavior or even too much visible success, while the Irish stick up for their own regardless of conduct. "This noble trait of the Irish struck me most forcibly when I witnessed the funeral of Bill Fallon, the 'great Mouthpiece,'" wrote Golden. "Bill (a notorious attorney known for defending mobsters) had been convicted of subornation of perjury, bribing a juror, a very serious offense. The Jews and the Italians would have buried such a guy in the middle of the night with the family holding their hats over their faces. But there was Bill, 'God love him,' carried out of the Cathedral after a High Mass, with ten or twelve acolytes walking ahead of the casket, and the Irish lined up and weeping on both sides of the street." With his usual need to end with a catchy kicker, Golden concluded, "This is why forty million Protestants and two million Jews wear green neckties on the Seventeenth of March."[58]

Little Blue Books and the "Material Cause"

At some point during these years, Harry became acquainted with the books and newspapers produced by Kansas publisher Emanuel Haldeman-Julius, a Socialist-Jewish-atheist who first became well known as editor and drama critic for the *New York Call*, a leading Socialist newspaper. Later, Haldeman-Julius held forth in his own newspaper, the *American Freeman*, the content of which veered from politics to stories of the publisher's early love of history and his childhood as a Jewish immigrant from Eastern Europe. Golden initiated what would be a long correspondence with the older man. After he became famous, Golden would declare that "Haldeman-Julius was what Aristotle would have called the material cause for the *Carolina Israelite*."[59]

Haldeman-Julius was a worthy hero to Golden for reasons other than his journalism; he was also a hugely successful pioneer in the mail-order book business and the creator of Little Blue Books. These cheap, pocket-sized paperback editions of the classics sold hundreds of millions of copies, as did works commissioned from contemporary authors who went on to fame and notoriety: Margaret Sanger, H. G. Wells, Will Durant, Theodore Dreiser, Havelock Ellis, and Bertrand Russell, among others. When Haldeman-Julius started his publishing company in 1919, he offered the books for a quarter each, later cutting the price to a dime, or even a nickel if customers ordered in sufficient bulk. One of his many marketing inspirations was to change the name of a slow seller, then list only the book titles in his mail-order catalog. A yawner such as *A Short History of Russia* became the more popular *Rasputin: The Lustful Monk*. Various censorship boards throughout the country banned his catalogs and the advertisements that appeared in pulp magazines through the 1930s. Still, by the time of his death in 1951, Haldeman-Julius had sold an estimated 300 million books, 95 percent of them through the mail.[60]

As the years went on, it was evident that these bookish showmen had much in common, most noticeably their good-sized egos cloaked in humor when they analyzed their place in American publishing. Haldeman-Julius once observed, "At the close of the twentieth century some flea-bitten, sun-bleached, fly-specked, rat-gnawed, dandruff-sprinkled professor of literature is going to write a five-volume history of the books of our century. In it a chapter will be devoted to publishers and editors of books, and in that chapter perhaps a footnote will be given to me."[61]

But Harry Goldhurst was not yet able to see journalism or writing as his métier. The influences of Leib Goldhirsch, Geiger, and Haldeman-Julius, strong as they were, were drowned out by the Siren's call of easy money as the stock market began to boom. Harry got a glimpse of what seemed like a direct road to opportunity and success, and he made a sharp turn away from the life of a bookish, original thinker with a useful grasp of the changing labor market and some precocious insights into the class wars in America. Instead of a traditional and respected position in the Jewish community, a seat in a newsroom, or a place at a podium in a smoke-filled union hall, he took up a desk on Wall Street. That detour would cost him dearly before he was done, robbing years from his life and all but guaranteeing his failure as a husband and a father. It would also imbue him with a fierce empathy for the underdog, for prisoners, and for victims caught in the crosshairs of powerful political wars.

Wall Street Woes

Twenty-six-year-old Harry L. Goldhurst, perspiring and pale, stood in U.S. Court trying to make sense of what he was hearing. Federal Judge Francis J. Coleman had just sentenced him to five years in federal prison, the maximum allowed for the mail fraud Goldhurst committed through his stock-selling operation, Kable & Co. After a moment of stunned silence, reporters raced out to file their stories for the evening editions of the 17 October 1929 newspapers and the pre-dawn runs for the next day. As it turned out, they didn't stop running after this story for quite some time.[62]

It wasn't Goldhurst's get-rich-quick stock cons and blatant playing of clients as suckers that made this courtroom action such big news. The newspaper-selling angle came from one very famous name on Kable & Co.'s client roster: Methodist bishop James Cannon Jr., internationally known crusading prohibitionist, sharp businessman, and a political operator intelligent enough to be much more than the "anachronistic crusader and crackpot" he might have been, as Golden observed in his reminiscences about the bishop.[63]

The power wielded by the cleric in America was enormous. Cannon was "one of the most significant and most ominous figures of his time, a man whose tempestuous career holds lessons for all of us," wrote biographer and newspaper editor Virginius Dabney in 1949. He was also the first of several national celebrities to influence Golden's life from close association, in this case to a ruinous extent.[64]

Cannon, a Virginian, was at the peak of his influence in his sixties. He had entered the ministry at age twenty-four, and he became a bishop in the Methodist Episcopal Church, South, in 1918. Early in his career he rode in the wake of vice crusader Anthony Comstock and also raised stentorian pronouncements against such evils as prize-fighting, football, theatrical performances, and immodestly dressed females on billboards. He possessed the drawing power that only preachers from below the Mason-Dixon line seem to command. He was the driest of "drys," to use the parlance of the day for the antialcohol platform, and he was separated from the "wets" by a wide ocean of whiskey. "I never understood the genesis of his hatred of liquor," wrote Golden; "he was a humorless man; one of his friends once remarked that few had ever seen the bishop laugh and none had ever seen him smile. I suspect that like most humorless men, he had to make his life into a crusade to make sense of it."[65]

Whatever its roots, Cannon's successful battle against the bottle and his private deal-cutting with office-holding southern Democrats made him powerful enough to control outcomes in political races in Virginia and beyond. With this clout came serious enemies in high places. When his foes dug for dirt, they discovered Cannon's penchant for stock speculating. That discovery led to revelations of more weaknesses, exaggerated and real, in the mighty man's character. The controversial bishop would emerge from this first round of stock-scandal muckraking with a long battle ahead and a bespattered reputation. Harry Goldhurst would be behind bars.

The bishop made for excellent copy. If Cannon had not existed, Hollywood would have done well to make him up. The white-haired, stern-faced cleric had the look of the nineteenth century about him, right down to the high-buckled shoes Golden would never fail to mention in later descriptions. He was not a big man, but he exuded the self-confidence that so often envelops self-appointed moral guardians; he was nicknamed the "Dry Messiah" for good reason. A testament to Cannon's impact is the fact that even Golden felt no need to exaggerate in his descriptions of the man: "He firmly believed that when he finally enforced worldwide prohibition, the cupboard doors would open and nothing but good men would come out. Which is to say he was a fanatic, but then, in this century, people have been fanatic about far more destructive reforms than Prohibition."[66]

Yet Cannon was also very much a man of the twentieth century, cleverly manipulating media and using his pulpit to hammer home the evils of liquor. He was well educated, well tailored, well married, and comfortable in high-ceilinged chambers of the nation's Capitol and on small-town stages alike. Starting in 1901 with Virginia's Anti-Saloon League, he loosed his rhetoric on the masses and plotted careful, step-by-step organizing to get counties to go dry, one small town at a time. Cannon became a force in the national movement and used this process over and over, eventually ensuring that in 1920, the Eighteenth Amendment (and its guidebook known as the Volstead Act) would become the law for thirteen years in America. "One day the country woke up, and no one was ever going to have a drink again, a resolve that lasted until noon," wrote Golden.[67]

Along with wiping out cocktail hour, Cannon turned his formidable energy to other matters, including an all-out campaign to make sure Democratic presidential hopeful Alfred E. Smith did not get a chance to hang a crucifix in the White House. Cannon hated absolutely everything about the Catholic Church, which he usually referred to simply as "Rome," giving the word an emphasis generally reserved for obscene nouns. In his political screeds Cannon lumped Tammany Hall and the Church together as if they were one. That Smith, a four-time New York governor, was a wet *and* a Catholic made it possible for Cannon to dispense his venom more efficiently. By 1928 Cannon's anti-Smith efforts paid off. Virginia moved away from its Democratic roots to give its support to the Republican candidate, Herbert Hoover, and the formidable bloc of southern Democrats was cracked.[68]

The bishop was known far beyond the South. He traveled extensively; his ministry took him across the South and Southwest, as well as Mexico, Cuba, Brazil, and Congo. But in his case this globetrotting did not lead to deeper cultural understanding. He reflexively attached moral failings to entire races, countries, and religious denominations, justifying his xenophobia by connecting the objects of his wrath to alcohol. In Cannon's eyes, all of France was an immoral virus that sickened young World War I soldiers sent overseas from rural America. These tainted troops then brought back new attitudes (and diseases) that eroded the morality of American women. Cannon's claims of Gallic abandon quoted in the newspapers probably did more for French tourism than any promotional advertising campaign ever could. Italians, it turned out, were morally lax, too. By World War II, scurrilous leaders used alcohol in the war effort: "No less authority than Mussolini called upon the Italian people to drink more wine because the effect of wine-drinking was to increase the natural activities resulting in the birth of more children for Italy," wrote Cannon in the memoir published after his death.[69]

"The Bishop did not like many people but he did like Jews," Golden wrote. "He always introduced me as the son of a rabbi. . . . The bigotry and prejudice that animated his soul about Catholics never clamored about Jews."[70]

The real story of how this Methodist clergyman changed the shape of America would have been woefully incomplete but for historian Robert H. Hohner and his *Prohibition and Politics: The Life of Bishop James Cannon, Jr.* Hohner's scholarship and thorough portrait of Cannon also reveal the common ground shared by the fallible bishop and the foolish Young Turk Goldhurst on Wall Street. Cannon, like Golden, was the son of a religious man. And he too was a niche journalist who turned a small-time newspaper, the *Virginian*, into an influential voice in the South. Cannon was perennially short of money, and his forays into good works and profit-making businesses often included financial irregularities. Cannon's widely published slurs against whole populations and his denouncing of Franklin D. Roosevelt were in direct opposition to the views for which Golden would become famous, but both men won hearts by standing up for certain underdogs, such as child laborers and textile workers. Further, neither ever lacked opportunities for female companionship, something that completely baffled most other men.[71]

In the most unfortunate of their common experiences, Cannon and Goldhurst suffered at the hands of Senator Carter Glass, who like the bishop was a Virginian, a Democrat, a dry, and Methodist. The son of a

Confederate officer and the owner of the *Lynchburg News*, Glass was a state senator before he went to Washington as a representative in 1903. He was secretary of the treasury for two years and served forty-two years in the U.S. Senate (then a record) until his death in 1946. Glass was also frequently mentioned for higher national posts. He had, as *Time* magazine noted when it put him on the cover in 1924, "a way of getting things done without catering to the donors." Admirers and foes alike acknowledged Glass's work ethic and tenacity; his colleagues considered the Virginian to be a difficult "snapping turtle" of a fellow. "In manner he is quiet and capable. He has a strong chin, graying red hair. In constitution, and hence disposition, he is inclined to be dyspeptic," was how the *Time* writer put it.[72]

Glass hated Cannon with a ferocity that still rolls off his telegrams and letters like steam. He was not Cannon's only enemy in Washington, but he was the most single-minded. In his determination to take down the Dry Messiah, Glass would have unhesitatingly hauled in all twelve of the apostles, never mind one bucket-shop bungler named Goldhurst. The seeds of Glass's hate were planted at least as far back as 1909, when Cannon worked alongside other conservative Virginia politicians who pushed their own dry candidate over Glass in the governor's race. The animosity grew over the years, along with Cannon's power and his dogged town-by-town approach to making liquor illegal. Cannon was willing to take progress in small sips, and when he stumped for a "personal use" provision in a 1916 prohibition law that allowed some liquor and beer to be kept in one's home, Glass sneeringly labeled him "One Quart Cannon."[73]

Glass quietly gathered evidence against the bishop, and by the late 1920s, he had found what he was seeking: The bishop, sermonizing guardian of morals and sworn foe of gambling, was playing the tables in the country's biggest casino—the stock market. It was true that speculating was by now a pastime for countless Americans who had absolutely no idea what they were doing, but the specter of a man of the cloth so bullish that he was getting advances on his salary and cabling his broker on Sundays was a different matter. Glass knew that the American public, not just Methodists, would look askance at Cannon's frenetic trading if the details were laid out before them. And he was just the man to do it.[74]

Cannon, who throughout his life took considerable risks as a businessman, already knew his way around a stock portfolio when he went to the office of Kable & Co. at 32 Broadway in New York City. Cannon's interest in the firm's promises of fat profits had drawn him in by 1927. When a respected banker tried to warn Cannon off these unreliable agents, he ignored the advice. Buying stock through Goldhurst appealed to the bishop; he enjoyed the company of the engaging young man. Cannon dined at the Goldhurst home in Larchmont, and he often stayed at Jake Goldhurst's Cadillac Hotel while in the city. The bishop's willingness to gamble on the market made him more likable, of course. But it was his aura of power that counted most. "I was awed by the Bishop. He had made Prohibition happen," wrote Golden.[75]

The lights went up on this disastrous drama with a scene that had become very common by the end of the 1920s: a bankruptcy filing. After his introduction to the business from sister Clara and a stint working under a brash broker known as Big Bill Ebel (who would also go bust more than once), Goldhurst started Kable & Co. in 1926 touting the "partial-payment" plan for stock purchases. He paid Charles W. Kable, a casual acquaintance, to lend his name to the company in order to avoid confusion with Clara's stock operations. He set up the office with the latest equipment, which at the time meant heavy wooden desks and chairs, clattering manual typewriters, adding machines that looked like one-armed bandits, a Burry stock ticker, several black Bakelite telephones, and of course, a few comfortable armchairs for friendly investors with time to kill.[76]

Kable & Co., like the many other bucket shops of the time, was an operation that briskly reeled in one fish after another, only to eventually leave them flopping and gasping on dry sand. A bucket shop lured clients, put their money in a bucket (that is, the broker's pocket), and did one of two things: waited for the share price to drop before placing an order to buy or waited for it to rise before selling. If an investor handed over funds expecting to buy shares at $100 and the broker waited until the price went to $90 before purchasing the stock, the broker made $10 a share by using the customer's money. Likewise, if the investor ordered the broker to sell at $100 and the broker instead waited for the price to climb to $110, again the shop made $10 a share. This worked perfectly until the broker guessed wrong.

The partial-payment plan allowed customers to "buy now, pay later," with the shop raking its commission off the top and the stock not being put in the investor's name until the full price was paid. Goldhurst, who had sharpened his copywriting skills putting out a market-watch newsletter for Clara, was particularly gifted at composing letters and brochures that promised market expertise and low risk for huge returns.

Goldhurst worked these angles and other scams at Kable & Co. for close to two years, juggling cash and fast-talking investors into buying more stocks rather than withdrawing their "profits." Eventually the pile of unplaced stock orders, an uncooperative market, the empty cash drawer, and suspicious clients came together in one big train wreck.

Hence, the name of Kable & Co. came to lead the small-type "Bankruptcy Proceedings" column on 25 May 1928 in the *New York Times*.[77]

Goldhurst always insisted that his clients were not widows and orphans but seasoned investors, and that appears to be the truth. However, his claim that he never took money from any woman was meant to be gallant and true—and it was neither. But whatever their knowledge level, the clients handed over as much as $444,000 to Kable & Co., which the defendants' books showed as purchasing stocks that came to be worth $2.3 million. Yet only $1,100 remained in the company coffers, and only some of the money could be followed. The bankruptcy process was barely under way before people in high places were paying very close attention to Kable & Co. Quiet questions were asked; stool pigeons surfaced, blabbed, and were rewarded; and finally a very useful tidbit made its way to Glass. The discovery that Bishop Cannon was on the client list of an indicted bucket-shop operator was about as good as good dirt could get.[78]

Hot on the heels of the Kable & Co. bankruptcy filing, Glass saw to it that Cannon's involvement was leaked to several New York City daily newspapers. To the delight of political cartoonists, the "Bucketshop Bishop" had arrived in print. Now Goldhurst realized that the terrified Charles Kable had stopped wringing his hands just long enough to sell Cannon's confidential investment records to the press. The tone of the bankruptcy hearings became ominous. Kable & Co. stayed in the headlines as questions put to Goldhurst and his quaking partner followed every clue that might lead back to Cannon. Did the bishop shill for the firm? Did Goldhurst lure other clients by bragging about his famous customer? Goldhurst was even asked if the size of the handwritten notation "James Cannon Jr." atop a ledger sheet was written intentionally *larger* than the other names.[79]

Right about the time the bankruptcy matter should have been slipping into history, followed by a quick trial on the mail-fraud matter (with, perhaps, a sizeable fine and an order to stay away from Wall Street), things got worse. Goldhurst, it seems, had started another shady stock shop after Kable & Co. failed, this one called Cosmopolitan Fiscal Corp., located at 225 Broadway, just down the street from the first office. The precaution of listing himself only as a manager, when in fact he was an owner, fooled no one. Now he looked like a brash young man thumbing his nose at both his investors *and* the courts. When the operation went bust, Goldhurst scrambled to pay back as many outraged customers as possible, but the damage was done. In August he was indicted a second time for mail fraud, with bail set at $20,000 on top of the $2,000 bond he'd posted for the first round.[80]

Like most juicy political scandals, this one had a lot of smaller, more personal stories hidden behind the headlines. For the Goldhurst and Gallagher families, the cost in money and shame was great. Tiny's family had already made sizeable loans to the couple, as had several friends, while Harry tried to bail out his sinking businesses. This generosity led to the donors being interrogated by the bankruptcy referee about their knowledge and involvement in Goldhurst's business activities.

Clara Goldhurst was among the first called for questioning. She'd made a name for herself eight years earlier as Wall Street's first female "puts and calls" broker, opening her operation with a $5,000 investment from an acquaintance. She had started her kid brother in the business, shared her Broadway office space with him, covered his losses while he learned the ropes, and then bailed him out (figuratively and literally) when his own business failed. She must have been especially dismayed by the prospect of such questioning, having been in the hot seat herself just a year before. In August 1928, Clara had been sued by disgruntled customers tired of waiting for their earnings. Then in 1929, she was enjoined from doing business as a broker. Still one of few women in the business, her case made headlines. The *New York Times* noted her success; she "had the reputation in the financial district of acquiring wealth." The paper generously refrained from questioning her unconvincing defense that the bull market was entirely to blame for her ruination. She was also tactfully described as "an interesting character," when in fact she was mercurial and prone to rambling rants in letters and on the telephone. The family was relieved for any number of reasons that the sibling connection was not covered in more detail in the mainstream press.[81]

Tiny's family, the Gallaghers, also got splashed with more mud when the newspapers reported that the Goldhursts' suburban Larchmont home was put in her name right before Kable & Co. filed for bankruptcy. That revelation was more than just embarrassing; it also made it unlikely anyone would sympathize with Goldhurst's claims on the stand that he'd had to borrow against his family home in a valiant effort to save the failing company. Once the bankruptcy proceedings began winding down, press coverage made it sound as if Goldhurst might soon be out from under the dark cloud. But the bishop, knowing the depth of Glass's animosity, understood that the fight was not finished. "They are trying to get me over your body," he warned Goldhurst.[82]

With the Cannon scandal still roiling, a series of very-well-publicized raids by the U.S. attorney's office in the summer of 1929 whipped up public interest and indignation against "Bucketshops, tipster sheets and other alleged illegal stock enterprises which have prospered under the stimulus of a bull market," as one story labeled the culprits. Among those rounded up in the offices of Cosmopolitan or served with subpoenas were various Goldhurst cronies and Goldhurst's sister Matilda. Now another family member had her name dragged through the dirt. The walls were closing in, and Goldhurst panicked. He borrowed more money from his brother Jake and used it to bribe an old girlfriend who worked as a lawyer in the U.S. attorney's office, handing over thousands in cash and a diamond bracelet. The folder of material she gave him outlining the prosecution's case was very useful—or it would have been had Goldhurst not been caught with it a short time later.[83]

Thus this routine case of one con artist fleecing investors had become a sensational mission. By the time it was over, it had become an assortment of clumsy bribery, outright theft, unethical legal maneuvers, conflicts of interest, and frantic attempts to cover the innumerable tracks left by those involved. It would be years before the pieces of this story came together, and some secrets of subterfuge died with the actors. Goldhurst, desperately hoping for leniency from the court, surprised the prosecution by pleading guilty at the last minute. Cannon had no comment. He had sailed away to check on his Methodist flock in Brazil.[84]

Behind Bars

In the fall of October 1929, Goldhurst began his prison stay in the Atlanta Federal Penitentiary. Tiny, who had just returned to work seven weeks after giving birth to their third son, William, moved in with her mother in Jersey City. Wall Street continued to fall apart. Carter Glass kept on plotting and planting stories designed to bring his ordained enemy to his knees. Rumors resurfaced that rationed food was hoarded during World War I at a school under the bishop's direction. And even the bishop's allies were driven away by reports that Cannon had had an affair with his secretary after his wife's death in 1928. That he and companion Helen McCallum were married in 1930 didn't prevent the press from delving into their earlier relationship with innovative energy that today's tabloids would admire. "The Bishop managed all at once to get himself in trouble with money, food, and women—which was more trouble than any that ever afflicted alcoholics I have known," observed Golden.[85]

The imprisoned bucket-shop operator, meanwhile, might have been working some angles as well. White-collar criminals were being moved from Atlanta to military camps, presumably to free up space for hard-core criminals. In the early 1930s, Department of Justice prison officials stumbled on a ring of inmates operating a sort of prison-cell upgrade service, somehow influencing the selection of prisoners slated for transfer to Fort Meade, Maryland, and elsewhere. The press got hold of the story in the summer of 1931 and noted that Goldhurst was among the Atlanta prisoners transferred around the same time. Due to either a reporter's hunch or sloppy editing, the article implied that Goldhurst was among those who paid or bartered their way into a move to Fort Meade. Oddly, this development—be it unfortunate coincidence or the latest example of terrible judgment on Goldhurst's part—did not last long as a news story. His parole hearing on 31 May 1931 focused on the Kable & Co. mess and his resulting remorse and financial ruin. When asked by parole board member Irvin B. Tucker about the losses to clients, Goldhurst made his no-widows-and-orphans excuse, waffling slightly on the female-client point. "I very seldom took an account from a woman," he said. Tucker's next question was rhetorical and sarcastic: "They are bad squealers?"[86]

Despite his understandable nervousness, a glimmer of the quotable one-liners that would later define Harry Golden comes through in the hearing transcript. Asked "How much do you have laid aside to enjoy when you get out?" he intoned, "All I have in this world are my eyeglasses and my fountain pen." Before being ushered out, Goldhurst voiced one more plea: "I feel positively that I will die a first offender. . . . I think probably by that time I will have accomplished enough even to wipe that out. . . . I will do probation for 40 years." The board listened to Tucker's analysis: "The applicant is a Jewish person. He has a good record of accomplishment behind him, has undoubtedly had fine opportunities and good associations in the past. His background is entirely favorable to parole consideration." He continued on to acknowledge the seriousness of the crime, adding that an adequate sentence would be served if parole was granted for 15 October, five months away. The others agreed.[87]

But as the scrutiny of bucket shops continued and Glass worked his back channels to keep the Cannon case alive, the three parole board members went back into a huddle. The blow fell on 10 December 1931 and made headlines the next day: "Cannon's Broker Loses His Parole." Goldhurst would serve his entire sentence with the customary time off for good behavior.[88]

The passage in Goldhurst's autobiography concerning the day that he was told of the parole revocation is probably the most unvarnished and accurate recollection of all: "There are disappointments in this world so devastating we do not know how we can possibly survive them. Perhaps we survive them as I survived this disappointment, because we have no choice. A man cannot go to pieces in jail, nor can his fellow convicts shoulder any of his troubles. I knew that night I would have to serve the whole of my sentence, one of the few federal offenders who had to do so. I knew I would have to serve three years and eight months and twenty-two days, which is exactly what I served."[89]

Cannon soldiered on, suing politicians, publishers, and just about anyone else who leveled public criticism at him. By one account, he had traded nearly $500,000 worth of securities though Goldhurst's shop, but at the end of his life he lived modestly in Richmond. While both his influence and wallet were by then very thin, Cannon's hatred of Demon Rum remained fierce. He was in Chicago for a 1944 meeting of the Anti-Saloon League when he died at age seventy-nine.[90]

Carter Glass died in 1946 at age eighty-eight. He was lauded as a fiscal-policy pioneer for shepherding the Glass-Steagall Act and other laws intended to regulate banking and securities and insure consumer deposits. "In the field of banking and finance no member of either house had studied more deeply than he, or brought a more superior equipment to the work of molding our fiscal policy," wrote President Harry Truman to Glass's widow, Mary Scott Meade Glass. He also assured her that Glass was glorified to the end as "Unreconstructed Rebel," a nickname bestowed by President Franklin Roosevelt.[91]

Glass's obituary did not revisit an extraordinarily disingenuous statement he had made nine years earlier during an interview on his seventy-ninth birthday: "Looking back on his long career . . . Mr. Glass reflected that he had 'never any desire to do anything but publish my newspaper' and added that he 'never much cared for public life.' "[92]

Back to the Real World

When Goldhurst got out of prison in 1933, he left in a blue suit and shined black shoes, with $10 in his pocket and a story that creatively recast his trouble with the law. The Kable & Co. saga, in his telling, became a sad commentary on the economic times; his business had failed *after* news broke that Bishop Cannon played the market. The ensuing scandal caused a run on accounts by Kable customers, which caught the firm without adequate funds to cover all the demands. For the most part Goldhurst kept his prison past a secret, but when he did have to sum it up, this fiction worked nicely. It appeared in his FBI records more than thirty-five years later, unchallenged by the field agent who recorded it.[93]

"It is a great temptation to rationalize a prison record, to excuse or senti-mentalize the experience," Golden told journalist Joseph Wershba in a 1961 interview. "And in its way, this is a good sign. It proves a man is ashamed of having been in prison, [and that] you are hopeless and must forever con-sider yourself alienated from society."[94]

Goldhurst faced the challenges awaiting any man in his circumstances. Money was tight during the years he was away, but Tiny was resourceful, a hard worker who somehow kept a grip on her sense of humor. "I would be a frugal woman if I had anything to be frugal with," she told her sons. She had taken charge, helped by the moral and financial support of her extended family. Now her husband reappeared, a stranger to his sons, and assumed his place as the head of the household. More accurately, he traded a small cell for a titular role at home. They rented a house in Red Bank, New Jersey. Tiny continued to work as an office manager, and Harry commuted into the city to work a "temporary" job as a desk clerk at Jake's Hotel Markwell at 220 West Forth-Ninth and Broadway. That temporary job lasted until 1940.[95]

There are certain things virtually guaranteed to create marital friction when the partners are not on the same wavelength; money, parenting, and alcohol are among them. The Goldhursts wrestled with all three, and their differing values on these points were exaggerated by the time apart. Had things gone differently, parenting disagreements might have been over allowance, how to mete out punishment for boyish infractions, and the like. For Harry and Tiny, parenting now broke down along religious lines. The boys were caught in the confusing tensions of an interfaith marriage in the 1930s. They had a Jewish name but were being raised as Catholics. Later, they figured out that when asked "What kind of name is Goldhurst?" the best answer was "a surname." They weren't part of a Jewish household and knew nothing of Judaism's rituals. Gentiles didn't accept them, except for Tiny's relatives who feared for the boys' immortal souls. "The indif-ference we received from one side, and the strain of perfect behavior in the presence of the other, made my brothers and me viciously anti-family on every conceivable level," wrote Richard Goldhurst in 1953. "One of my brothers later told me, in jest supposedly, that the reason he married his wife was because she was one girl with whom he could keep a distance of 500 miles between themselves and all relatives."[96]

Harry had agreed at the time of their marriage that any children would be raised in the Catholic Church, which, as he later argued, was exactly what any man would do in order to get the woman he loved. "Tiny knew what Jews were, as I knew what Irishmen were. It didn't make much difference in 1926. But now there was a difference, and that difference was Adolph

Hitler," he wrote. When the likes of the hugely popular and anti-Semitic Father Coughlin filled radio airways with suggestions that the Third Reich's plans for Jews were "understandable defense mechanisms" and encouraged boycotts of Jewish businesses, there was no ignoring the changed atmosphere, especially in New York. Talking about the problem failed to bring the couple to an understanding, so Harry pulled down a crucifix and picture of Jesus off a wall in their home and threw them into the trash.[97]

Money was tight, and in a more profound and frightening way than Goldhurst had experienced before. The last time he'd been a working man, cash had flowed (albeit that cash rightfully belonged to clients). Before that, he'd been a poor boy among other poor people. Now he discovered that there was no humiliation quite like being broke and having to keep up suburban appearances. The middle-class life he'd dreamed about was swallowed up by prison time and, more ominously, the Depression: "There were mornings at the Red Bank Railroad Station when I did not have the $14.70 to buy the monthly commutation ticket," Golden wrote. "When the conductor stopped by my seat, I told him nonchalantly that I had left my ticket at home. I paid him the single dollar for the ride. . . . I was not the only man in those days without the $14.70 who needed the good graces of a conductor to preserve his dignity. The conductors pocketed the $1, and the trip back and forth for the next twenty-five days cost $50, instead of $14.70. The most embarrassing aspect of the Depression was handing over that $1 with the aplomb of a man who has a million in the bank."[98]

Finally, there was alcohol. When Jake couldn't make payroll on time or the money didn't stretch far enough, the Goldhursts borrowed from friends and relatives, paying them back with postdated checks, if at all. Now that prohibition was over, Harry could more easily invest in his favorite coping mechanism. "There might be no milk in the refrigerator, but there's a bottle of whiskey in the house," was Tiny's accurate observation. Goldhurst never hid his drinking, which in many circles today would be cause for a full-on intervention. Most often he wrote with humor about his affinity for the bottle. The most honest examination came in the essay "How about Whiskey?" included in his 1962 book *You're Entitle'*. Along with its surprisingly serious view, it refers to his prison years, an uncommon aside:

> For years there has been a debate between prohibitionists and sociologists. The one has said, "He's poor because he drinks," and the other replied, "He drinks because he's poor." . . . We are certain of this: He's slowly destroying himself because he drinks. . . . I have less excuse to drink than anyone else. Why? Because I once saw a brilliant man bang

his head against the wall of a cell and laugh uproariously every time his head crashed against the solid concrete. . . . We whiskey drinkers rationalize the process in a million different ways. "It's a food." "It's stimulating." "It brings out the best in me." But mostly "I can take it or leave it alone." This last statement is never made unless you are holding a drink in your hand.[99]

Tiny, in her usual fair-minded way, told son Richard years later that she'd seen Harry drunk just once, and it was during this demoralizing time: "She told me he was walking home [from the train] and he'd dropped his newspaper. It was on the ground and he wouldn't bend over to pick it up. He just kept kicking it. He kicked it all the way home."[100]

Later, by the time his life was circumscribed by putting out the *Carolina Israelite*, Golden had the bourbon routine down pat: A little branch water and "a healthy dollup in the morning, a drink or two before lunch, two in the afternoon, one before dinner, but never anything after sundown," Golden wrote. It wasn't unusual for him to go through the better part of three fifths of liquor in a week. "You didn't serve him cocktails, he poured his own glass," Richard Goldhurst remembered. "Sometimes late in the day Harry would look in the icebox for a piece of cheese and leave his drink in there by mistake. You'd hear him say, 'Where's my damn drink?'" Over the years, Goldhurst added, his father tried many times to persuade advertising agencies to place lucrative liquor ads in the *Carolina Israelite*. During these telephone conversations, the ad men always ultimately rebuffed Golden with the claim that many of his readers were the wrong demographic because "Jews don't drink." Once, upon hearing the familiar argument, Golden paused, sipped his bourbon, and said: "Yeahhhhhh . . . Christians drink . . . but we Jews are catching up."[101]

"Take Five Dollars Off . . ."

These tough years produced some of Golden's most enjoyable stories, as he drew on his days and nights at the slightly seedy Hotel Markwell. "Give him credit," Goldhurst wrote later; "Harry was far from humbled." He had a particular soft spot for the actresses who lived in the residential hotel or just stayed for the run of a touring show. They were all, by necessity, a streetwise lot:

Bessie Dwyer was an actress in her early thirties with red hair and a voluptuous figure. She was unfailingly polite, industrious and kind. . . .

The day clerk, Ross Peyton, was fascinated with her good looks and personality. One morning, when Bessie came downstairs to pay her bill, he leaned over the counter, put his hand down her dress, and squeezed her breast. Bessie didn't start; she made no movement; she just tolerated Peyton's affections. Two or three times his hand bounced her breast. Then he withdrew his hand with a smile that looked like a cracked plate. He presented the weekly accounting. Bessie said, "Take five dollars off that bill." When Peyton asked why, she responded, "For the free feel. Why do you suppose you're going to take five dollars off?" Peyton hurried through the subtraction, the smile long vanished. His amorous adventures with Miss Dwyer came to an abrupt end.[102]

The ten-story, 120 room Markwell hosted other colorful clientele, including a handsome "beard" hired to tag along to nightclubs with an adulterous couple, and "cardsharks" as Golden termed the smooth gamblers who made their livings sailing aboard luxury liners back and forth across the Atlantic, getting paid in traveler's checks by their marks. There were cheaper hotels, but the Markwell's more casual etiquette allowed a guest to walk through the carpeted lobby carrying a laundry bag or come home with a sandwich and a bottle without ordering room service or tipping a bellboy. The front door hinted at an earlier stab at elegance: "Markwell Hotel" in gold script and a crest sporting the motto "Bonus-Melior-Optimus,"—"Good, Better, Best."[103]

Managing a Broadway hotel involved bookkeeping and other paperwork. It also meant heading off certain problem guests, especially rent-by-the-hour prostitutes, who could get the place shut down by vice cops. A manager needed to keep a sharp eye out for opium addicts, who would do anything for money, skipping out on a bill being the least troubling. Just as important for a successful deskman were maintaining utmost discretion and a polite poker face. Goldhurst polished all these skills.

Despite its value as a source of entertaining stories, hotel work just did not pay well enough. Richard Goldhurst later wrote about the entire family climbing down a fire escape to skip out on the rent, then speeding away in the car that his father had prudently kept hidden from the "repossession thieves." Harry Goldhurst kept his ears open for promising business deals, continuing to evidence the unquenchable optimism that resides in the DNA of a true salesman.[104]

He was delighted to have the chance to invest a couple hundred dollars in a new theatrical troupe preparing to mount productions of some wily-villain-and-helpless-female melodramas such as *Nellie the Beautiful*

Cloak Model and other gems. Whatever the plays lacked would be more than offset by the imaginative casting: a midget in every part. The opening of *No Mother to Guide Her* was, as he later recalled, "the shortest run in the history of Broadway—a one-night run of two-and-a-half acts of a three-act play." The performance went off the rails as soon as the shaky pianist in the orchestra pit began playing one-handed in order to hoist her whiskey glass and the diminutive cast members erupted in a full-volume disagreement on stage. Goldhurst resigned himself to the loss of his money, figuring to leave the whole mess behind him. The actors, however, had other ideas. They wanted their full rehearsal pay. "The next two weeks were rough ones for me," he wrote. "Wherever I went, I saw midgets. They called me on the telephone and every morning a midget was waiting for me in the lobby." A delegation even paid a visit to Tiny, to whom her husband simply said, "I am not even going to try to explain this." Eventually accord was reached, and all parted on civil terms.[105]

Another man might have taken the midget revolt as a clear sign that successful investing in untried schemes was not likely to happen—unless, of course, that man knew about the New York World's Fair coming in 1939 and clearly a gold mine. While he pondered various ways to get a piece of this tourism pie, Goldhurst was moonlighting as a newspaper-advertising salesman. Sales could be done over the telephone, and much of his pitching passed through the Markwell switchboard. He worked for various publishers, selling ads and writing ad copy for "puffs"—special sections full of what was later called "advertorial" material—for the *New York Daily Mirror* and the *New York Post*, among others. The added income became more important when Tiny took a break from work in 1938 after the birth of their fourth son, Peter. The baby suffered seizures and other health problems from birth, and soon Peter's severe developmental disabilities became clear. He lived eighteen years and died in a state home for the disabled.[106]

Along with access to the switchboard, the Markwell job came with a satisfyingly thick pile of New York's daily newspapers, seven days a week. Harry Goldhurst read them all, front to back; the staid *New York Times* and the tabloids with their pinup photos and shocking crime news got equal attention. One story he followed closely was that of the 1931 arrest and subsequent trials of nine young black men charged with raping two white women in Scottsboro, Alabama. All the "Scottsboro Boys" were tried and convicted quickly; eight were sentenced to death, and the trial of the youngest, age thirteen, ended in a hung jury arguing over death or life imprisonment. The Scottsboro defendants were not executed but were tried and retried, jailed, paroled, and deprived of anything like a normal life. Three of the men received posthumous pardons in 2013.[107]

The case hit a tender nerve for Goldhurst. He first read about it while sitting in prison, where life sentences and death row were real things. The attention given to the Scottsboro story reminded him of the Triangle Shirtwaist Company catastrophe back in 1911, although the events were two decades and many miles apart. Once again he felt that reporters, editors, and photographers were the people bringing about real change; without them the advocates and lawmakers would not rise to the occasion—or at least not until much later. This was not a "civil rights" story to him then; that term wasn't even in common use yet. It wasn't a black story or a southern story either. It was a story about journalism, the good journalism that made people rally for the underdog.

A World's Fair That Wasn't

As the promoters of the World's Fair geared up their publicity machines, they promised Americans a dazzling look at the triumphs that lay ahead in industry, science, arts, and commerce. Naturally, Goldhurst loved the idea. He hatched a proposal to sell advertising space in a special magazine sure to be snapped up by the hordes descending on the city. Everyone he told about the idea could see the genius in selling ads wrapped around event programs. (Alternative weeklies and blogs would prove it to be so decades later.) And no one doubted that hotels could rake in good money for the duration. "Along about 1938 all of us hotel managers . . . raised the rent of all the permanent guests in the hope that they would move," Golden wrote. "They obliged us." The showgirls and actors left the rooms renting for $8, $10, and $12 a week. The hotel keepers thought they would get this rate once a night instead of once a week. "But after the World's Fair had been going about three months, they even promised to help move these actors and showgirls by taxicab if they'd only come back and take their eight dollar room again," wrote Golden.[108]

On the Road

Goldhurst's small role in the newspaper business was both a balm to his ego and a straw to be grasped as his home life grew more tense. He became a traveling ad salesman for the "puff" papers, journeying farther south and staying longer with each trip. Now Harry L. Goldhurst became Harry Golden. (The middle initial L, for Louis, would still come and go for a few years.) Harry simply started using the new name. It's hard to imagine today, tethered as we are to official records and unyielding databases beyond our control, but in 1940 a clever person could still rename himself armed with little more than a pen, a bottle of black India ink, and the presence of mind to keep his story straight.

The name change has been explained various ways by relatives and in writings about Golden: The switch provided a fresh start after prison. It was a means of dodging creditors. He wanted to avoid recognition and embarrassment to Bishop Cannon while working in Virginia. Whatever the first motivation, it was also a change to something that sounded catchier and more writerly to him. Reporters of the day, even those with nothing to hide, often changed surnames. (Frequently to less ethnic, more WASPy bylines.) By the time Golden was living the life he'd made for himself in Charlotte, the new name was firmly attached to the man.

Besides being a demarcation in Golden's personal history, this name change reflects the continued confused family-name dynamics of the clan. Tiny and Richard kept "Goldhurst" as their surname; two of the sons became "Golden." "Billy and Buddy had no choice," said their older brother, Richard. "Harry changed their names when they lived with him for a bit [in the late 1940s] and went to school in the South." Continuing the family tradition of mixing things up, Billy went back to "Goldhurst" as an adult. Harry Jr. found that using "Golden" was more attractive as a byline when he became a newsman himself. Many years later, Richard asked his mother why she didn't change her name. Tiny responded without missing a beat. "I went through the war with this one," she said firmly.[109]

CHAPTER TWO

Heading South

"After the World's Fair flopped in '40, Harry traveled around, working and kiting checks," Richard Goldhurst remembered. "He wound up in Charlotte in '41 on one of his peregrinations around the South." Charlotte is not the first place one would imagine a Socialist-leaning New York Jew with a felonious past would choose to launch his personal journal. But in the early 1940s Golden began to trade on connections he had made during his stints with the New York papers and went to work for the *Norfolk (Va.) Times-Advocate* to sell ads and continue to write content for "puffs." It was tough going; his goal of sending Tiny $35 a month was more often than not unmet. But Golden liked the sound of the paper's slogan: "Independently devoted to the labor movement—without a radical policy."[1]

Among his various side jobs, Golden wrote material for a United Mine Workers annual report and spent some days in the company of labor giant John L. Lewis. Both lovers of Shakespeare, they quoted passages to each other in genial competition. Long after, when summing up the role of unions, especially in the mines and mills of the South, Golden would respectfully quote Lewis as saying, " 'The life of a miner used to be ten years in the pits. Now it's twenty-seven years. That is what I gave my men—seventeen years of life.' " Over the next eight months, Golden connected with other compatriots in the southern labor press in and around

Charlotte, and when a job offer came from the tiny *Charlotte Labor Journal and Dixie Farm News*, he jumped. Tiny said she thought working for a labor journal in wartime was about as innovative as importing rickshaws to solve New York's traffic congestion.[2]

Two aspects of life in Charlotte intrigued Golden from the minute he arrived in the early 1940s: hookers and segregation. "All the whores frequented the post office," he wrote. "On a weekday evening, dozens of salesmen repaired to the Charlotte post office to send in their reports to home offices in Cincinnati or New York or Chicago. The minute a man dropped that brown envelope in the brass out-of-town slot, the women watching knew he wasn't a cop and that he was probably lonely." He added, "The cheap night rates for [telephone] long distance did more to subdue prostitution than all the vice crusades ever mounted."[3]

Perhaps Golden did not intend to settle in as completely as he ultimately did, but Charlotte had some other pluses: It was far enough from New York to allow him to hide his shameful prison time, yet it was "a charming city; big enough to support a symphony orchestra and small enough to have an almost provincial friendliness," as he put it in a barely fictionalized rendering of the city for a later piece in *Commentary*. It had the largest newspaper presence in the Carolinas—the *Charlotte Observer* in the morning, the *Charlotte News* in the afternoon, and one of the oldest black-owned newspapers in the South, the *Charlotte Post*. The reporters, editors, and freelancers at the papers, and their other writerly friends, were a talented bunch, and several would become his good friends.[4]

Within a few years of arriving, and throughout the rest of his life, Golden credited himself with anticipating the great changes that loomed for the South and claimed he had deliberately moved there to start a newspaper dealing with race issues. "The last homogenous area of the country was about to transform itself and not transform itself gradually but suddenly and painfully," he wrote, describing the South he first encountered. "It wasn't that it was easier to start a newspaper in Charlotte than it was in New York—it is hard to start a newspaper anywhere—it was that the big story was in the South." Golden said he "guessed correctly that the daily papers would miss the event completely, leave it alone, because to report this story meant describing the lot of the Negro." The truth was that he possessed the ideal combination of nerve and curiosity about his fellow human beings, along with an accident of timing that positioned him in a front-row seat for the revolution. The powerlessness of prison and desperation of the Depression reinforced Golden's empathy for the downtrodden and forged something stronger. He was gearing up for a fight, even before he quite realized it himself.[5]

He was fascinated and baffled by the two-color society. "As I, a stranger to Charlotte, an immigrant in America, walked down the street, Negroes, whose [ancestors] had been in this country for two and sometimes three hundred years, stepped off the sidewalk and tipped their hat," he wrote later. "When I went into a drugstore, I never saw a Negro. . . . Almost half of Charlotte's population, the colored half, was invisible." When African American writer James Baldwin, much more traveled and worldly than Golden, journeyed South for the first time in 1957, he wrote a friend after two days in Charlotte that he would not have made the trip had he known the unique, painful sense of isolation and fear that awaited him.[6]

Even to an outsider used to a world where black and white didn't mix much, the southern conventions of separate water fountains, restrooms, and schools felt surreal. The fact that the "Colored Only" versions of these basic things not only existed but were always inferior to those used by whites was just the first hint of how ingrained racial segregation was here. There is a reason that a decrepit water fountain labeled "Colored" is such an enduring symbol in photographs depicting the segregated South. As a metaphor, it would be hard to beat: the most basic of human needs—water—dispensed grudgingly from aging fixtures in the hottest states.

Legalized discrimination and the accompanying racism were not confined to the South. Across America, blacks were at best second-class citizens. As pointed out by Swedish scholar Gunnar Myrdal in his landmark 1944 book *An American Dilemma: The Negro Problem and Modern Democracy*, there was a solid history of racial discrimination and rationalization in the North and elsewhere. But the fact that 90 percent of the country's 8.8 million African Americans lived in southern states in the early years of the twentieth century and had relatively recently been legally considered property, much like livestock, furniture, or farm equipment, made for very different regional stages on which the fight for integration and civil rights would play out.[7]

As Golden would discover, the business of making and selling yarn and cloth had a great deal to do with this new world he encountered in North Carolina, along with its racial makeup. "In nearly every region of the state, particularly the piedmont, textile production has shaped every facet of life—business, politics, architecture, social relations, culture," wrote historian Brent D. Glass in his cogent book on the industry. North Carolina was not of the plantation born. It was built on the backs of yeomen, farmers who by the 1840s were starting to venture off their small acreage to do "public work"—meaning labor in textile mills in hopes of more secure, if very low, wages and housing.[8]

Changes in farming after the Civil War expanded this workforce of poor white women, children, and men willing to work long days for little money. What had been a family enterprise moved into sharecropping, in which a tenant farmer worked the land and was forced to remain in near-constant debt to the landowner. Laws that favored the moneylenders by putting liens on crops and regulating open-grazing lands kept the small farmers at subsistence level, or worse. Those who moved from farms settled in mill and market towns that sprouted along the expanding railroad lines. Then, backed by northern investors who saw the rich possibilities, the Cotton Mill Campaign of the 1880s took off with evangelical fervor. "Next to God what this town needs is a cotton mill," went one slogan. Men with and without actual church pulpits took to sermonizing about the righteousness and Christian nature of new mills. (Indeed, the railroad barons who were out ahead of these changes *were* almost godlike, reaching down to change even the time of day to suit their needs when they created the country's time zones.) The various evangelists succeeded. In the last decade of the nineteenth century, looms in the South increased tenfold to 110,000, and half of those were within 100 miles of Charlotte. But the ultimate cost to southerners would be enormous. Locally run, the mills were making money for distant stockholders. In the early-twentieth-century Cotton Belt, as historian David R. Goldfield put it, "the profits went North, and the human and environmental refuse stayed behind."[9]

This was all part of the call for a "New South," what Glass characterized as the "steady drumbeat of support for industry, laissez-faire capitalism, public education, and diversified agriculture" sounded by persuasive voices such as those of Henry W. Grady of the *Atlanta Constitution*; engineer, entrepreneur, and journalist Daniel A. Tompkins; Francis W. Dawson of the *Charleston (S.C.) News and Courier*; and Henry Watterson of the *Louisville Courier-Journal*.[10]

In North Carolina, the New South took the form of villages, mill towns, and small cities, including Charlotte. Urbanization started slowly and would accelerate after World War II. As historian Milton Ready observed in *The Tar Heel State*, Grady and his ilk framed a new role for the state and the region, but "not surprisingly, their dream failed to transform North Carolina or the South into an industrialized, urbanized region smacking of Yankee values and ambitions."[11]

In fact, the rise of the cotton mill culture was at first seen by many southerners as a means to "finally conquer the frontier left us by the Yankee," as W. J. Cash wrote in his classic *The Mind of the South*. Cash, who grew up in a mill town in South Carolina and worked for newspapers in Charlotte and elsewhere, wrote that the mill and factory were "sanctuary for the falling common whites" that created further, deeper separation between races by putting "thousands of them in an employment, which, by common agreement, shall be closed to the Negro."[12]

The deeply entrenched anxiety about black men having proximity to white women was a useful excuse for not hiring blacks to work in the mills. It wasn't until the 1960s that African Americans made real inroads into that workforce. Golden, like Cash, believed that many poor white southerners who supported Jim Crow did so because "the Negro stands between them and social oblivion," as Golden put it. "They are aware of their inadequacies in education and earning power. . . . If the poor whites lose the segregated Negro, where would they now find self esteem?"[13]

The work in mills was dirty, dangerous, lung-clogging labor that shortened the lives of most who did it. The chance to look down on someone, anyone, as inferior to yourself had to be tempting if you moved from childhood to old age in the shadow of clattering mill machinery. By the turn of the century almost all workers lived in company-owned housing and went to stores, doctors, schools, and even churches supported by their employers. This was no utopian or Socialist community; workers paid dearly for everything they got. In a sense, mill towns were an updated version of sharecropping, where the laborer almost always stayed trapped, owing his or her soul to the company.[14]

Some of Golden's neighbors during his first years in Charlotte were descendants of the first farm-to-mill workers. For a time he rented cheap rooms in one of the many mill settlements that ringed Charlotte, ramshackle houses that the mill owners began to sell to workers during the 1930s, which the new occupants proudly and poignantly called "duplexes." One morning as he readied himself for work, humming along with one of his cherished classical records, a noise outside sent him out to the porch to investigate:

> She was the grandmother who had done her hitch in the mill and was now taking care of home and grandchildren while her daughter and son-in-law were on the "day-shift" looms. She quickly explained: "When you start to play that music I always pull my chair outside your door, but the chair broke a leg, and I am mighty sorry." She confessed that she had been listening for nearly a year while I was playing my recordings of *Traviata*, and *Otello*, and a Lotte Lehmann album of Brahms lieder. I said to the woman: "I'll leave you my key and when I go to the office you just come on in here and play all this music you want." She thanked me: "You reckon

my son-in-law can show me how to work the machine?" By this time all I could do was turn my face away from her and say: "I reckon."[15]

Bigotry Begets Myth

In these prewar years, there were rural communities where poor blacks and whites lived without serious friction, but the poorest white man—who might be disparaged as a hillbilly, a "lint head" (mill worker), or worse—was typically deemed superior to a poor black man. Even if a political candidate had presented the plight of blacks as a worthy campaign platform, there was no substantial black voting bloc to push that leader into office.[16]

Black Americans could no longer be the property of whites, but the cumulative effects of being denied civil rights for so long magnified and solidified conventional racism and fortified the myths used to subjugate them. This mindset declared African Americans as less intelligent than whites, morally loose or oversexed, and—a particularly heinous fantasy—generally satisfied with their lot. These prejudices didn't end with the character of blacks; they included prejudices about vocational aptitude as well. In *American Dilemma*, Myrdal tracked the evolution of black labor in the South: African Americans were generally allowed only the jobs whites deplored; were discouraged if not prevented from developing more advanced skills (as painters, builders, construction workers, drivers, craftsmen, and so on); and then were declared uniformly to lack the mechanical abilities needed to move beyond menial jobs.[17]

The Race Beat, by journalists Gene Roberts and Hank Klibanoff, starts its riveting exploration with these dismal Myrdal findings. As the authors explain, "As bad as the economic conditions were, Myrdal found that the treatment of Negroes in the courts was worse. . . . [Myrdal] found no weakening in the resolve of southern whites to deprive Negroes of equal educational opportunities."[18]

This generalizing has real risks, of course. Not all southern whites, even those with little education, who were poor and without prospects, were racists. Nor were all blacks living lives of poverty, suffering, and fear. Cities, including Charlotte, had a black middle class. Golden, unlike some of his Yankee friends, understood from the first that southern states were not a monolithic racist region. Alabama was different from South Carolina; Georgia, from Mississippi. It has been rightly said that North Carolina, in many ways, was considerably more progressive than most of its neighbors. By the first years of the twentieth century, it was the leading tobacco-manufacturing state, thanks to James B. Duke, whose American Tobacco Company had a monopoly until a 1911 court order forced the company to be split up. He also pushed North Carolina into the hydroelectric power and railroad businesses. One result was Charlotte growing fast enough to become the state's largest city by the early years of the twentieth century; it was a center for financial, legal, and land-development operations almost four decades before Golden arrived.[19]

When Golden met his new neighbors, they were all undeniably part of a caste system like none he had seen—more rigid than any enclave of Boston Brahmins or the original Dutch families of New York and more entrenched than the Gentile-Jewish divide of his childhood. He saw the tangible economic damage from this history. The large white underclass was uneducated and poor. Emancipated blacks had gained earning and purchasing power just seventy-five years before his arrival. As historian Goldfield put it, wages had stayed low for so many workers of both races for so long that buying power was stalled and a shadow society of "nonconsumers" was created. This meant production and service industries stayed small; government was provincial. Those at the top of this chain also suffered from the lack of good schools and health care, to say nothing of missing out on cultural and recreational benefits that increase with healthier economies.[20]

The bold Depression programs of the New Deal had improved the quality of life for the poor before Golden's arrival, but that potential, too, was limited by the same attitudes and history that spawned the caste system. A mix of antifederal feeling, antipathy for the practice of paying relief to the poor, and the complications of segregation meant that North Carolina had what historian Ready calls "paradoxical" results from Roosevelt's programs. North Carolina's Senator Josiah Bailey, who voted against the Federal Emergency Relief Act and the National Recovery Administration in 1933, publicly worried about the burden on his poor state to meet the act's one-third matching funds requirement, and privately he predicted that once poor people were on the federal dole, they would never get off.

When the act passed, $40 million was distributed over three years in the state for public projects and relief, including direct aid to blacks from the federal government for the first time since Reconstruction—another thorn in the side of southern politicians. The state's contribution of $700,000, far below the required match, and its stalling on complying with various other conditions denied North Carolinians the full benefit of the programs. Yet the public works funding built an impressive number of schools, airports, hospitals, stadiums, sewer lines, roads, and homes. The New Deal pushed North Carolina into the modern era, with higher wages and stronger industry, and, Ready writes, the state, "for the first time abandoned its centuries-old tradition of disregarding the welfare of its citizens."[21]

Following the Money, to Charlotte

Even with the limits of the state's legacy, Golden grasped that Charlotte had real promise. This sprawling, 173-year-old city in Mecklenburg County was a pleasantly feisty place, differentiated from its sister cities by progressive and aggressive development. Had he chosen another southern city for his home, Golden would have been unlikely to succeed as he did. Charlotte had the right combination of commerce and tolerance to allow him to flourish. It was also, like Atlanta, a city "too busy to hate," with considerably less tension over the race question than those urban areas deeper into the South, such as Selma and Birmingham, which would not have tolerated such a rabble-rouser. Charlotte would eventually be the rare place where leaders quietly enabled desegregation in public places. Atlanta's more expansive commerce might have squashed the small, shaky newspaper business before Golden hit his stride.[22]

By the time World War II production boosted urban economies, city leaders in Charlotte were already savvy enough to see the valuable synergy of growing on all fronts—schools, housing, transportation infrastructure, factories, and businesses. Golden enjoyed poking fun at chamber-of-commerce types and their eagerness to market their hometowns, but—a master salesman at heart—he never lost his appreciation for the power of good public relations. Back in 1939–40, business leaders had launched a highly publicized effort to help census takers account for every citizen, in hopes of being recognized as the first metropolis in the Carolinas with 100,000 residents. Boosterish supporters, including the *Charlotte News* and the *Charlotte Observer*, were eager to include the 30,000-plus black residents living within the city limits, a part of the population roundly ignored by the newspapers most of the time. This advocacy paid off when the city topped the goal by a few hundred, and both papers announced Charlotte's first-place finish on 9 June 1940. Seven years later the Charlotte Planning Commission enacted a zoning plan that changed the loose residential patterns of the city, effectively confining blacks to an area of lower property values in the northwest section of the city. By then Golden was used to the ironies of a segregated society.[23]

Golden settled in with apparent ease. After checking into the Willard Hotel the first night, he went for a stroll, keeping his usual deliberate pace—suitable for a man just over five feet, six inches, and weighing 190 pounds. "All of Charlotte that I needed was contained in a few blocks. Looking over a Southern town is a strange sensation for any New Yorker," he recalled. He found Charlotte's skyline shockingly low, its pace sleepy, and its women prettier—"if not as stylish as the girls in the big cities." Within a short walk the newcomer found the Little Pep Delmonico and the Oriental restaurants, the New York Café, and the S&W Cafeteria. There was also a poolroom, several Bible stores and—oh, happy day!—a newsstand with out-of-town daily newspapers. Belk's, Ivey's, and Efird's were the big department stores. Some years later, when a Belk matriarch donated a chapel to Charlotte's Queens College, she asked her lawyer to prepare remarks for the ceremony. The lawyer tapped his writer buddy Harry for help. "Thus it was that an unwitting Mrs. Belk used my words in addressing herself to 1,000 virgins who listened to her dedicate a chapel to Jesus Christ," Golden wrote.[24]

The post office on the corner of West Trade and Mint Streets, a grand limestone structure expanded in 1934 to become the largest federal building in the Carolinas, was the center of his new universe. Golden's chosen sport was letter-writing, and he played it with a fervor usually seen only in obsessed golfers. He mourned the gradual decline of mail deliveries over the years, from twice a day to once. The closing of a post office occasioned indignant commentary; the death of postmarks from towns with names such as Adamant and New Russia was tragic.[25]

Along with its intended purpose, as well as the opportunity to watch the working ladies preparing to pounce on traveling salesmen, the post office served as the starting point for any adventure. Golden had a terrible sense of direction, but he navigated without a map, relying on the one landmark he could trust. "As long as I have lived in Charlotte I have always gone to the post office first to start on any journey," he wrote. "If it's a dinner invitation, I go to the post office and then proceed to my friend's home. . . . If I have a speaking engagement in Utica, I go to the post office and then to the airport." (Later, Golden's companion Anita Stewart Brown would usually drive when the two went anywhere, relieving him of the need to use his post-office directional system.) The post office also provided another service to someone willing, as he was, to poke around in its lobby trash cans to see what people were reading and discarding. In 1955 he reported in the "first Post Office trash-can survey ever made" that he had uncovered an abundance of copies of the status-conferring *Wall Street Journal*, still folded in their mailing wrappers. No religious publications were tossed, he noted, and of course, "you won't find a *Carolina Israelite*, either."[26]

Charlotte Labor Journal

When Golden wasn't living in the drab mill-village "duplex," he lived in various cheap rooms in the city and tiny bachelor apartments designed for men who didn't cook at home. For the next few years, when he was flush he rented small quarters in more presentable buildings, such as the brick Blandwood apartments on South Tryon Street. This was one aspect of his life in the South he did not lighten in the telling. "When I first came to Charlotte, I was the only poor Jew in town. I lived in drab bungalows whose siding often sprang for want of nails and there were occasions when I couldn't meet the rent for my room in a semi-transient hotel whose curtains were stiff with a decade's dirt."[27]

City directories first listed H. L. Golden in 1943 as "advertising manager" of the *Charlotte Labor Journal and Dixie Farm News*, although his actual duties ran more along the lines of watching the office when publisher William Witter was sleeping off a drunk. Here was a perfect subject for Golden. Witter was a flawed hero, a bigot who stood up, when he was able, for the noble cause of the worker. "William Witter had been a newspaperman for 40 years," wrote Golden in his autobiography. "Had he been able to overcome alcohol he would have been governor."[28]

That overstatement was grounded in some truth of actual political genius. Even thoroughly pickled, Witter was able to predict any race "within 1,000 votes," Golden recalled. A lot of people told stories about Witter, but Golden could always enthrall listeners with his versions. Witter's wife, Lula, was "a big buxom woman who hated liquor with a passion Bishop Cannon might envy," Golden would begin. "One night walking home, Witter stopped under the railroad viaduct . . . for one last snort before he came under the ever-watchful eyes of Lula. As he savored the white lightning . . . one of the water pipes overhead sprung a leak, and drops cascaded on Witter's suit. He said to himself, 'Raining. Can't go home in this.' He finished the bottle and fell asleep under the viaduct." Thereafter one of Golden's regular duties was to leave a bottle of alcohol-rich Virginia Dare vanilla extract in Witter's mailbox on Saturday nights, a hedge against the long, dry Sunday at home with Lula.[29]

Witter was the first of several friends Golden made in the South who violently disagreed with his views on racial equality. "What made me despair about the segregation I saw was not only the cruelty it inflicted on

Negroes but the total self-corruption it inflicted on white men," he wrote. "William Witter had given his life to the labor movement. He championed workingmen when bricks and bats broke up picket lines. Yet when I told him how unjust and iniquitous segregation was, he looked up at me and said coldly, 'Don't pull that stuff around here, son.' "[30]

Golden's ability to tolerate this, to give the benefit of the doubt to a bright and interesting person, believing logic and decency would eventually prevail over old hatreds, was key to his success as a speaker and writer on civil rights. He did not polarize or preach, and he managed to tease humor out of some blatantly offensive moments. His appreciation for Witter's dogged championing of the working stiff existed in its own compartment, alongside but not overlapping with his dismay at the man's segregationist stance. The liberal southern friends Golden would make in the coming years—including those who won Pulitzers for writing about race issues—admired him for this. He made it look easy.

It was while working for Witter that Golden wrote his first editorials in the short-essay style that became his signature. Most of his copy was unsigned and hewed to the labor agenda. On the occasions when Witter was away, such as his "four month rest at the Union Printers Home in Colorado Springs" in 1942, Golden branched out with a front-page piece headlined "What Are the World's Greatest Books?" He trotted out that subject twice that year, in fact, and dozens of times more in his books and the *Carolina Israelite*. The list changed a bit over time, but *Hamlet* always made the cut.[31]

When Witter died, Golden fondly recalled the publisher's habitual ostentatious crossing of the street outside the *Charlotte Observer*, the result of a long-ago dust-up that barred the labor leader from the premises. At union gatherings, Witter was always introduced as "Old Man Witter who brought bread to the strikers at Shelby!" wrote Golden. This invariably led to a call for Witter to pull up a trouser leg and show all where he'd taken a bullet during one of the clashes started with the historic Loray Cotton Mill strike in Gastonia, North Carolina, back in 1929. "On one of these occasions, Mrs. Witter snorted to me, 'Bullet wound, my foot! He got that when he broke his leg running out of an old-timey whorehouse.' " At the end of the telling or writing of this story, Golden liked to add a heartfelt epitaph for his old boss: "Charlotte was better for his presence. So was the South. So was I."[32]

Movers, Shakers, and a Lifelong Friend

Golden became acquainted with leaders of Charlotte's Jewish community soon after he arrived in the city. Later, after he had achieved some fame as an author, stories circulated that this Jewish professional or that leading citizen had invited and then sponsored Golden's move to the South, but that was not the case. He had arrived under his own steam. His first encounters with Jewish leaders were with Arthur Goodman, a prominent attorney and, later, a state legislator, and Hermann E. Cohen, a hosiery jobber—a middleman who put buyers and manufacturers together in deals that suited both. At age eighty-seven, Cohen dictated his reminiscences about the early years of his acquaintance with Golden, recorded as part of research by Morris Speizman for his 1978 book, *The Jews of Charlotte, North Carolina*. A leader of various civic and Jewish community efforts, Speizman founded and ran a successful business dealing in textile machinery. He and Golden had a prickly relationship, yet Speizman's writings preserved evocative stories about Golden as well as other important aspects of Charlotte's history.[33]

The Cohen transcript is one of the earliest plausible recollections available of Golden's first years in Charlotte. Cohen himself was a witty and prolific letter-writer, "a wonderful reprobate," in the words of his nephew, and he and Golden were natural allies. They shared a similar appreciation for the universal ridiculousness of their fellow man and were not above a juvenile joke or two between them. ("Roses are red, violets are blueish, if it weren't for Jesus, we'd all be Jewish," went one piece of doggerel exchanged.) Cohen's early company was called Priestly Knit Goods, a nod to his surname, which designated him a member of the *Kohanim*, a priestly caste considered in Jewish tradition to be descendants of Aaron, the brother of Moses.[34]

As Cohen recalled in his 1976 dictation, the men crossed paths for the first time a few months after Golden's arrival. Cohen wanted to advertise his company more cheaply than the rates the dailies were charging, so he climbed the dirty stairs to the offices of the *Charlotte Labor Journal*. "The Journal was on College Street, upstairs, in an old rickety building, because it was not in a prosperous condition," began Cohen. There he encountered "a short, dark complexioned fellow who wore (I believe) a piece of rope around his waist for a belt"—none other than Harry Golden. Witter was ill-disposed as usual, and Cohen must have hesitated briefly at the prospect of placing an ad with this stranger. More than three decades later, Cohen could clearly recall Golden's quick and confident response: "I can do anything around the paper. . . . I can put it to bed. I can set the type, I can do anything—just tell me what you want." The two introduced themselves, and Cohen, with welcome directness, asked the newcomer if he was Jewish. Golden answered affirmatively. Did he know anyone in town?

Just Witter and my bootlegger, replied Golden. Next Cohen noticed several quotations from great thinkers pinned on the wall near Golden's desk and began talking about the works from which they were drawn. The two avid readers took each other's measure and liked what they found. So began their long, sometimes bumpy friendship.[35]

By then Golden had already met Goodman, whom he read about in newspaper stories before moving to the city. Years later Golden told Cohen, "I wrote to Arthur Goodman [because] I felt that it would be chutzpah NOT to write to a leading Jew in the city," when planning to move there and publish "an Anglo-Jewish paper." Golden had also wangled an introduction to I. D. Blumenthal, the successful business leader who owned the Radiator Specialty Company and later became the philanthropist whose family name remains well known in Charlotte today. When Golden printed a small trial run of the *Carolina Israelite* in 1942, it was made possible because Goodman and Cohen had reached for their wallets. When Golden commenced uninterrupted publishing in 1944, their support and Blumenthal's money and interest in interfaith issues were key factors. Publisher Witter, for his part, heralded the first issue of Golden's paper by wishing it a "successful voyage on the sea of journalism," in the pages of the *Charlotte Labor Journal*.[36]

Along with his labor-press work, Golden did some ad-selling stints in 1942 and 1943 for the *Hendersonville (N.C.) Times-News* and the *Charlotte Observer*, where he also wrote copy for special sections. Burke Davis, a writer for the *Charlotte News* and, later, a hugely prolific author, was the first close Gentile friend Golden made in town, and he helped with introductions to other newspaper folks. The two men were so close that when Davis's daughter Angela was born in 1942, Golden got to carry her from the hospital to the Davis home on Lombardy Circle. Soon Golden was a regular at the newsman poker game with Davis and others, including reporter Pete McKnight of the *News*; Harry Ashmore, editorial writer at the *News*; and writer Legette Blythe, also a novelist, who then covered city hall for the *Observer*. "I discovered in due course that he was a bad poker player and a great talking man," Ashmore wrote later. Golden had yet to start the *Carolina Israelite*, and Ashmore added, "I remember feeling the . . . vagrant sense of regret that the great tales and profound wisdom which interfered with the game would be dissipated with the blue smoke that hung over the table."[37]

Golden liked Ashmore right away, recognizing his intelligence and wit and the steel in the younger man's spine. Ashmore had grown up in Greenville, South Carolina, where poverty among blacks was a given, and his overseas service during World War II sent him home certain that the old way of doing things was going to change. In 1946, Ashmore arrived at the *Charlotte News* and was hailed by Golden as the *Carolina Israelite*'s "Man of the Month," in some musty-sounding rhetoric: "Those people who are ever on the alert to take advantage of an opening to spread dissension and hatred and further try to set one group of people against another, will find a vigorous and a very worthy opponent in Mr. Ashmore." Golden rightly observed that the unrest in the South made Ashmore a better writer. He was among those southerners "whose imagination and moral sense has been stirred by the struggle integration has engendered in the South," as Golden later wrote. Ashmore went on to win a Pulitzer Prize in 1958 for his editorials on the desegregation of schools in Little Rock, Arkansas. The two men remained friends throughout Golden's life, and their affection for each other was well known. They were often mentioned together by their peers when the subject turned to bold commentary. "Editorial pages of American newspapers are a disgrace," declared James Reston in 1959, who was then bureau chief for the *New York Times* in Washington, D.C. "The only two editorial voices that rise above the din of those singing commercials are Harry Ashmore and Harry Golden."[38]

The first official issue of Golden's paper, published in February 1944, bristled with large, bold headlines and was jammed with entreaties to readers to share the paper with friends. It included a reprint of a famous letter from George Washington to a Jewish congregation in Savannah and a column called "The Fighting Jew" featuring news and photographs of Jewish soldiers and sailors. Well-known members of Jewish congregations or social groups were quoted in the various features. The introduction to "The Fighting Jew" was written by Rabbi William Silverman of Temple Emanuel in Gastonia, North Carolina. "The conception of the passive Jew is an example of fallacious thinking," Silverman lectured his readers, "and indicates an ignorance of Jewish history and Jewish spirit."[39]

The front-page banner was crowded with the name of the paper in Middle Eastern–influenced calligraphy and its uppercase motto, "TO BREAK DOWN THE WALLS OF MISUNDERSTANDING—AND TO BUILD BRIDGES OF GOOD WILL," as well as an American flag, a menorah, the commandment tablets, and biblical excerpts marked "Jewish" and "Christian" notable for their similarity.

When the war ended, along with mourning the deaths of so many and cheering the defeat of Hitler, Golden made a pointed attack on German civilians. Viewed in the context of national euphoria, Golden's tough-talking headlines and reckless subtext probably did not raise many eyebrows, although there was a jarring contrast with the ecumenical-humanitarian graphics at the top of the page. "GERMANY LOSES ANOTHER WORLD WAR," thundered the front-page headline on the April 1945 issue, with "Hitler Joins Wilhelm and Others in Failure" as the underline. "The 'master race' idea now revealed as a 'front' for German passion to wear medals, strut, let others work for them, and a mad desire to bring Parisian perfume to their women without paying for it."[40]

It is a kind understatement to say that Golden had not yet found his writer's voice. But he wasn't worried. The writing would get better. The important thing was that somehow he had put together a newspaper, had some copies printed and distributed, and was on his way to do it all over again in a month or so. The look and content of the paper improved with each issue; the adherence to a publishing schedule did not. Throughout the 1940s he skipped and combined issues. Subscribers who had paid $2 for a year of the *Carolina Israelite* were kind enough (or inattentive enough) to overlook the uneven production. In a burst of ingenuity Golden simply renumbered the issues a couple of times to skip over the empty months.

By 1946 he had the use of a small office at 324½ Tryon Street, which he proudly listed in the city directory as the office of Southland Publishing Company, publisher of the *Carolina Israelite*. That summer he told his 3,481 "subscribers" (those who elected to get the paper and those who had it thrust upon them via second-class mail) that he was making the paper into a magazine. The closest he got was a magazine-style front page with teaser headlines promoting content inside. That didn't last long, simply because no newspaperman can go too long without a real A-1 for a story and headline the likes of "Rabbi Fineberg Lectures on Crucifixion," which must have caused a few double takes around town.[41]

Even the *Carolina Israelite*'s rough early pages looked promising enough that friends and backers encouraged him to keep it up. It helped that Goodman and Cohen were listed as the editorial board and Rabbi Philip Frankel, the first leader of Temple Beth El, the new Reform congregation in town, as contributing editor. Blumenthal and others made loans to Golden several times during the 1940s—the amounts and terms were disputed between them for years, in one case leading to arbitration in 1948. What lenders characterized as generous support and lenient repayment terms, Golden later described as powerful community leaders taking advantage of a good idea and a small-time *arriviste* who needed their stamp of approval in order to succeed in Charlotte. "I was alone, starting a little paper," Golden angrily reminded Cohen in 1959, in answer to the latter's reminder of some $2,013 he'd given Golden in the early days without repayment.[42]

The records of the business arrangements from this time are sufficiently contradictory that they cannot be fairly reconstructed today without the key players around to speak for themselves. What is clear is that Goodman helped Golden with the legalities of setting up Southland in 1943 to publish an "Anglo-Jewish" newspaper and contributed operating funds, as did Cohen. Blumenthal funneled seed money to the paper, hired Golden to handle advertising for his own company during the lean early years, and paid for the printing of a book on the history of Jews in America in 1950. Along with providing start-up funds, Cohen wrote more than a dozen checks for $50 to $450 between 1943 and 1945 when Golden was broke and was in danger of defaulting on his life insurance premiums. He may well have given Golden more money, but these early checks rankled sufficiently for him to mention them later. At least once when federal and state income taxes came due on Golden's business earnings, he used Blumenthal's money, then put the touch on another acquaintance to pay off the shortfall.[43]

Golden's benefactors knew he was broke, but they were not aware of the lengths he'd already gone to in order to stay afloat since moving to the South. In December 1943 Golden was caught kiting checks out of state and attempting to scam businesses, most notably the Tutwiler Hotel in Birmingham, Alabama. He wrote the hotel in advance posing as a spokesman for the "Advertising Trade Service Inc. of New York City," asking that the trade group's soon-to-arrive representative be "extended all courtesies." The hotel might have written off the lodging and meals, but when their visitor bounced personal checks as well, the police were called. Off Golden went to U.S. District Court, where he received a suspended sentence, five years' probation, and orders to check in with the Charlotte Police Department when he got back home. Local officials apparently did not make the connection between the case of Bishop Cannon's broker and the small-time crook running up a tab in a Birmingham hotel—a remarkable circumstance given that the Birmingham arrest record was under "Goldhurst" instead of his new surname. Then the FBI showed up on Tiny's doorstep in New York. With her young sons watching, she stood up to the agents who questioned her. She told them she had no idea where Harry Golden could be found. When one of the agents tried to strong-arm her, saying, "Tell us or you're going to headquarters," Tiny retorted, "Drive me." The agents tried various other threats to no avail. "Tiny hated snitches," said her son Richard Goldhurst.[44]

The Internal Revenue Service (IRS) was more determined than the FBI and more alert than the police and the court system. Charlotte agents started dogging Golden within a year of his arrival and kept it up until royalties from his first book flowed in and he finally caught up with his taxes in 1959. That was not the result of improved money handing on his part; it was made possible by his hiring of an endlessly patient attorney who made sure income was tracked and reported. It also helped that an exasperated IRS agent finally gave Golden a pile of stamped, self-addressed envelopes for weekly payments.[45]

Ruth Allman, a secretary to Golden during the war years, wrote him when his autobiography was published in 1969, recalling the tough early days. "I remember the time you came in the office trembling and perspiration streaming, and told me you had just called the man in the Internal Revenue office a son-of-a-bitch." At her urging Golden went back and apologized. The agent and his fellow agents remained watchful, and Golden took great pleasure in writing the government a fat check to finally pay off his debt when *Only in America* hit the bestseller list in 1958. Along the way, with his usual knack for getting just about anyone to like him, Golden became quite friendly with the tax men. A 1960 affidavit contains his sworn statement that there was nothing untoward about their long chats or his gift of a $1.60 bottle of Mogen David kosher wine for one IRS agent's father. As to rumors that Golden served liquor to the agent, he was able to "state categorically that I have no recollection" and add with obvious relish that he happened to know that the agent in question did not drink anyway.[46]

Through all of this Golden's relationship with I. D. Blumenthal might have been closer, despite the differences in their station, had Golden not so grossly mishandled his boss's money. This was an alliance of two colorful operators, far apart on social and income levels, who both loved a good moneymaking idea. Blumenthal made a fortune when he recognized the value of a radiator-sealing chemical mix invented by Charlotte tinsmith G. G. Ray in 1924. He bought the company and within a decade expanded it to include a rubber plant in Los Angeles. Blumenthal multiplied his success many times over, manufacturing parts for B-24 and B-25 bombers during World War II. He was deeply committed to interfaith activities on the community level, and his enthusiasm was behind Golden's decision to launch the newspaper with that theme.[47]

Golden was always looking for a big ticket to success—a miraculous asthma medication seemed promising for a brief time, and a plan to cash in on restorative spring water actually did get out of the gate. He registered the trade name of "Midas Mineral Water" and touted it as pure, healthy, and rejuvenating in ads and with photographs of an attractive young secretary alongside a Midas office water-cooler. But Midas Mineral Water came on the scene decades before bottled water became an ever-present American accessory. The venture was a bust. "The only fly in the water, so to speak, was that the famous mineral spring was really a faucet in a deserted shack of a bankrupted ginger ale company and the demographic fact that Southerners don't drink water, they drink Coke," said Richard Goldhurst. "After a summer, Harry and the spring went broke. At the time he just sighed in regret and said, 'Oh, what Coke can do to the teeth and a good idea.'"[48]

On paper, the *Carolina Israelite* brought in impressive revenue, around $12,000 to $15,000 a year in the late 1940s, according to income-tax worksheets done by an accountant. Some of that money could have mistakenly come from the gross totals of advertising billings Golden handled for Blumenthal, rather than his own commissions. But even at half that amount, and factoring in the high costs of printing and mailing the paper, the numbers were hefty. Golden never drew a large salary, but his habit of spending first and worrying about paying the piper later quickly became his modus operandi in Charlotte. His bookkeeping was a disaster. Bills run up on Blumenthal's tab went unpaid. When the *Carolina Israelite* needed typing paper or Golden's electric bill was due, he paid with whatever checkbook he laid his hands on first. Blumenthal demanded an accounting, and the two ended up in arbitration in December 1948 before a panel of three local businessmen, one of whom was Arthur Goodman. The proceedings concluded with Golden signing two notes: the first to the Radiator Specialty Company for $6832.03, "as a result of their several business transactions, payable at 3 percent interest and a minimum monthly payment of $50 . . . if I. D. Blumenthal so desires said note." The second was for $800 payable to Blumenthal personally for an advance he'd made to cover costs of printing a Jewish history book. The arbitrators "recommended" that Golden assign future royalties to Blumenthal from the as-yet-unpublished book. The signed agreement would not have withstood legal challenge, but that was not the point. Golden's inept or dishonest handling of advertisers' money he'd collected as Blumenthal's agent was not going to go unnoticed, nor were any murky tax questions going to be left open. There the matter stayed for some years, with neither note repaid by Golden and no real effort made by Blumenthal to collect.[49]

Golden was largely circumspect about the whole disagreement, but his grudge against what he considered small-minded bean-counting surfaced with regularity. One of his often-quoted short pieces reflected this prejudice neatly: "They never met a payroll: 1. Copernicus 2. Galileo 3. Newton 4. Einstein." He was sometimes more pointed, as in a letter to acquaintance

Lewis Bernstein, a Charlotte jeweler and friend. Bernstein had asked Golden what subscribers got out of the *Carolina Israelite*. Golden fired back, in obvious reference to Blumenthal, "I know a millionaire in the city who has made a million dollars on a product where the catalog page explaining the uses of the product costs more to produce than the product itself. . . . I dare say that never in a million years would anyone say to the manufacturer, 'what do they get out of it?' "[50]

Twenty years after the arbitration, Blumenthal wrote to Golden about the unpaid notes, suggesting he make good on the debt in the form of a contribution to the Blumenthal Jewish Home for the Aged in Clemmons, North Carolina. "I really should have kept up with you about this, but for a long time I did not press you because I felt you just did not have the money to pay it," wrote Blumenthal in 1960. "Then after your books became so successful, I thought all the time you would come to me yourself and pay off this old balance." Golden responded, "Thank you for a warm-hearted letter. I think the fact that you did not press me . . . was due to your innate decency about pressing me for a debt I did not owe." Their relationship remained predictably cool.[51]

By the end of the 1940s, Golden was clear on one thing: He was incapable of working with partners. He'd made the mistake twice in his life, first on Wall Street, and now, after tussling with his Charlotte investors, he resolved to avoid partnerships—and employers—as much as possible. Not since boyhood had he held a job for any length of time that put him under a boss's close scrutiny. "I have NEVER kept a check stub in my life . . . and I must NEVER be beholden to anyone," he wrote Cohen in 1959. And for Golden, in some instances that would mean simply *deciding* not to be obligated, whatever his benefactor might expect.[52]

Making Friends and Influencing People

Golden had a couple of close Jewish friends in Charlotte. One was Rabbi Frankel, who led the small congregation of Temple Beth El founded in 1943. "Phil and Harry's conversations would jump from Goethe to Goodman and from Blum to Blumenthal," recalled friend Walter Klein, a fellow writer Golden met during the war years. Golden drafted the first temple constitution and taught Sunday school. (One imagines him with an unlit cigar clamped in his mouth while he spun his version of Hebraic history.) Later Golden left the congregation, irritated that he was being dogged for dues and feeling underappreciated for the fundraising speeches he gave for the temple. But, Klein added, he continued to accept speaking invitations from time to time, "usually preceded by a taste of bourbon from his flask as he got out of his car."[53]

Along with his poker circle of ink-stained staffers of the two dailies, Golden made friends with typesetters and pressmen, loading-dock workers and delivery truck drivers, and ad salesmen, engravers, and photographers. Among them were Klein, then in charge of *Morris Code*, the military newspaper for personnel at the busy Morris Field airbase and, later, the owner of a successful Charlotte advertising agency; Henry Stalls, who printed the *Carolina Israelite* and was a force in local trade unions; and Golden's gregarious ad salesman, Ken Robertson. As was so often the case in his life, Golden was accepted by local newspapermen in spite of not being a peer in the usual sense. He was not, and never would be, a conventional daily journalist. But those men and the occasional woman whose days were timed by copy deadlines and press runs knew a brother when they met one. For the first time since the Round Table in Oscar Geiger's home, Harry had a circle of real friends.[54]

Golden and some of these buddies took to meeting regularly for refreshments at a local printing shop. He particularly liked the large bay window that opened up on Fourth Street, where he could entreat his fellow worshippers (usually Stalls and Robertson) to join him in "bellowing hymns out the open window, bourbon bottle in hand," said Klein. Golden took great pride in his repertoire of window-rattling Christian standards, some learned around the piano while courting Tiny in her mother's living room, others acquired in less domestic settings. More than once during a gathering in a southern church Golden startled his hosts by joining enthusiastically in the singing of "The Old Rugged Cross" or "Higher Ground." One of his more memorable impromptu concerts occurred after he became well known around town, when he happened upon a Salvation Army band grinding out "What a Friend We Have in Jesus" on a downtown street corner. He promptly joined in, then captured the scene for his readers:

> I had no sooner started than the conductor was in front of me, waving his baton to lead me onward. He was trying to edge me into the solo spot in the front of the band. I had two alternatives. I could run away, but I am no coward; or I could sing along with him, which I did. First thing you know I was right there in deep center field among the folks with the trumpets and the drum and the cymbals, and they all seemed to perk up and take on a new exhilaration. . . . I had to sing several verses before I found the opportunity to make a graceful exit. Nor was this the end of it. . . . More people saw me singing with the Salvation Army (or

so they said) than read my paper. The rumor went that I had joined, repented, that now I was a Salvationist, and it spread from Richmond, Virginia, to Augusta, Georgia.[55]

Golden (and many of his friends) always insisted that Charlotte's Jewish society shunned him because of his outspoken support of labor unions and civil rights. Some did, but long before that happened, his gospel performances surely sent more than one of Charlotte's Jewish matrons in search of a fainting couch.

Outside his small circle, Golden was a foreign creature to just about everyone around him, Jew or Gentile, who was unused to his most unsouthern demeanor. He cared little for convention, whether in dress, diet, or social small talk. Golden's account at Mellon's, a Charlotte clothier, reveals the simplicity of his wardrobe in those days. One big purchase in the late 1940s was a shirt and two changes of underwear, totaling $7.26. "When I wore tan and brown summer shoes in December, Gentiles thought me eccentric. They were right." He maintained this rumpled, careless look until his fortunes changed.[56]

Young Jack Claiborne, who went on to work for the *Charlotte Observer* for forty-one years, started his own lifelong love affair with newspapers while collecting for his older brother's paper route. There he met Golden and was immediately impressed that this Yankee, while not gracious in the usual sense, treated him as an adult. "He did not talk down to a little boy," Claiborne recalled. "When you went to collect, if he was eating, he'd offer you whatever he was having—something like oysters and bourbon." Golden was always worrying a stub of a cigar, remembered Claiborne. "He waddled. He was always kind of out of breath, as if he'd just run up the stairs. He always—*always*—had opinions, and he told a lot of little jokes. What I really remember is that whenever he'd finish a sentence, offering up some observation or another, he'd lean back and say, 'Yeahhhh' in this satisfied-sounding gravelly New York drawl."[57]

Courting the Big Shots

Golden didn't let his frayed trouser hems or negligible social standing deter him from pressing the famous into service. Celebrity power, he thought, was the surest way to promote the *Carolina Israelite*. Few things guaranteed participation of luminaries like the public bestowing of honors and awards on them. With urging from Blumenthal, Golden joined in organizing an event that honored North Carolina governor J. Melville

Broughton. The front page of the February 1944 *Carolina Israelite* featured a reproduction of a letter from Broughton expressing his pleasure that the issue of the paper was "devoted to the theme and purpose of 'Brotherhood month.'" Golden must have supplied some of the text; the length and floridity of the sentences match his style at the time: "It seems likely that the enlightened consciences of all who are resisting the cruel aggression of the Axis forces and of all who are now sympathetic with that resistance will unitedly create a sentiment and power throughout the world that will make a recurrence of these conditions forever impossible."[58]

Golden proved extremely skillful at bringing together all the pieces for this event, sending flattering invitations to bigwigs, then rounding up local businesses for support. He was also adept at sliding the whole operation into his corner. Brotherhood Week—a respected event created by the National Conference of Christians and Jews (NCCJ), which had been holding it for more than a decade—soon became the "*Carolina Israelite*'s annual Gold Medal Award" determined by reader ballot and given to that "Carolinian who has made an outstanding contribution to interfaith amity and human rights." The formality of ballot counting was questionable, given that the men most admired by Golden were invariably the winners. The award program eventually ran into "jurisdictional and financial problems," as Speizman put it in his book on Charlotte's Jewish history—another way to say the business crowd distanced itself after the award became an obvious promotional tool for the *Carolina Israelite*, with Golden leaving bills unpaid for NCCJ supporters and others to sort out.[59]

After Broughton, the 1945 recipient was Josephus Daniels, editor and publisher of the state's leading Democratic newspaper, the *Raleigh News and Observer*. Daniels had served as secretary of the navy during Woodrow Wilson's administration and as ambassador to Mexico under Franklin Roosevelt. Golden ensured that the event would be a hit by boldly inviting financier Bernard Baruch to speak at the banquet honoring Daniels. Baruch and Daniels crossed paths when the latter was serving as an economic advisor to Presidents Wilson and Roosevelt. "Harry suspected, reasonably enough, that Baruch was an egomaniac and probably couldn't resist coming to Charlotte," wrote Charles Peters, publisher of *Washington Magazine*, who became friends with Richard Goldhurst in postwar New York City. "The great man came to Charlotte and the locals were impressed. They might not have heard of Harry Golden, but they had certainly heard of Bernard Baruch."[60]

In 1946 Golden reported that a majority of *Carolina Israelite* readers chose Charlotte native Frank Porter Graham, then president of the

University of North Carolina and an appointee to the President's Commission on Civil Rights under Harry Truman. Graham had been a respected member of the NCCJ long before Golden stole the Brotherhood award idea, so his election as an award winner only helped the *Carolina Israelite* effort. The two men had met soon after Golden came to Charlotte, and Graham earned his lifelong gratitude by stepping forward to lend Golden and his newspaper enough respectability to survive. "In the beginning, I had trouble," Golden wrote. "[In 1943 and 1944] some of the Jews in North Carolina organized a 'Golden Go Home' committee. They used to complain, 'What kind of Jewish newspaper is this, that talks about the Scottsboro boys in Alabama, that urges the textile workers to join the union?' " Or as he more bluntly put it in a question-and-answer interview with the *New York Times* in 1960, "The Jews . . . were scared to death I was going to kill them with the Negro problem." Graham, he said, sent a letter inviting him to meet. "And he didn't say, like most Southerners, 'Come to see me some time.' He gave me a date, a place, and an hour. It was a Saturday afternoon and I went. And there in his home he had [novelists] Jimmy Street, Noel Houston, and three or four professors, and I was photographed with them. When the Jews of Charlotte saw a picture of me with all those Gentiles, they figured I was kosher, and I was on my way."[61]

His admiration was well directed and widely shared. Graham, a history professor who took over leadership of the university in 1930, was a unique mix: kind mentor, sophisticated politician, and Roosevelt-administration insider. He was a southern gentleman able to achieve unusual freedom for his faculty and students through extraordinary diplomatic skills. He dealt with issues connected to segregation as he had dealt with Golden's troubles, by quietly lending his presence, not by pointed speeches or stands. Graham had detractors on both sides—hard-line segregationists and civil rights activists—but he remained at the helm of the university for two decades, building it into a leading institution and nurturing talent among faculty and students. His calm tenacity was legendary. During his wartime work as a negotiator for the National Labor Relations Board, Graham went head-to-head with John L. Lewis, the powerful labor leader who had traded poetry lines with Golden. Lewis later complained, "Who locked me in with that sweet little S.O.B.?"[62]

Graham became even more of a hero to Golden when he faced down the House Un-American Activities Committee (HUAC) and triumphed over accusations that he was a Communist. HUAC's supposed concern was his participation some years earlier with the Southern Conference for Human Welfare. This group of southern educators came together in the 1930s to push an agenda of improved education, employment, and health care regardless of race, color, or creed. The alleged tie to the Communist Party was based on unconvincing observations of conference speeches and discussions and the damning fact that the group's activities were reported in the *Daily Worker*. Graham was named to fill one of North Carolina's seats in the U.S. Senate in 1949. He then ran for the office the next year but lost after one of the dirtiest fights in regional political history. The *New York Times* called Graham "one of the most outspoken liberals [North Carolina] has ever produced." He went on in 1951 to serve in the United Nations as a mediator, retiring in 1967 at age eighty-one.[63]

The 1947 medal winner was Herschel V. Johnson, another Charlotte native, former U.S. ambassador to Sweden, then acting ambassador to the United Nations, and a significant voice for adoption of the UN's Partition Plan for Palestine in 1947. The medal went to Judge John J. Parker of the U.S. Court of Appeals for the Fourth Circuit in 1948 and to Governor W. Kerr Scott in 1949. Parker, then serving in the middle of a long career on the bench of the Fourth Circuit and as an alternate judge for the Nuremberg tribunal, later sponsored Golden's entry into the venerable Philosophy Club of Charlotte, a group of influential men who met monthly to present papers on issues of the day. The Republican Parker lost his chance at a Supreme Court appointment in 1930 in part because of an unpopular ruling he had made in a labor case, and in part due to vigorous opposition by the NAACP over a past statement supporting a lily-white political process. Golden remained indignant enough on his friend's behalf that he was virtually incapable of mentioning Parker's name without taking his listener through what he considered the faulty logic used by both sets of the judge's opponents. To take this Republican southerner's side over organized labor *and* the NAACP was proof of Golden's regard for the man, as well as of his refusal to stay neatly inside any party lines. "Nothing in this world would make me happier than the opportunity to vote for Judge Parker for President of the United States, before I die," Golden gushed.[64]

As for Scott, he too was Golden's kind of candidate. He upset the usual way of doing political business in North Carolina by winning in 1948 when the party machine intended to seat someone from the other side of the state. Promoting his progressive "Go Forward" platform, Scott fought for utilities and new roads in rural areas and better treatment for blacks, and he continued to do so after his election in 1954 to the U.S. Senate. He appointed the first African American to the state's board of education, yet he did not favor desegregation, arguing that blacks themselves did not want it. He too was a showman with a gift for turning a memorable phrase.

Born on a dairy farm, Scott often said that other farmers, whom he called "branch-head boys," got him in office and kept him there. He deliberately downplayed his prosperity with his folksy one-liners. When he dressed up, he donned what he called his "two-cow suit," explaining that he had to sell two cows to buy it.[65]

The gold medals and declarations of brotherhood were blatantly promotional for the *Carolina Israelite*, but they were also personally significant for Golden. While he had admired and learned much from his father, Leib Goldhirsch's age and the respectful distance kept between parent and child at the time circumscribed their relationship. The role of an assimilated child in an immigrant family is complex, requiring the offspring to live in two worlds, balancing roles as dutiful child, translator, and ambassador. Perhaps as a result Golden courted mentors throughout his life, first older and accomplished men (Graham and Parker fell into this group) and later those of any age who represented principles he admired. By midlife his most valued friendships were with men who could be both illuminating teachers and appreciative audience. He found an extraordinary group of them.

The few women to whom he was close were self-sufficient, intelligent, and of course, good listeners. (He always said that Tiny was the wittiest woman he'd ever met.) In his writings Golden portrayed women at large as an exasperating or mysterious bunch and often affected a clumsy chauvinism for comic purposes. In reality he harbored many a sexist attitude while successfully disarming any number of women. A sharp-eyed observer could guess who among Charlotte women were his paramours; they were the ones sporting very large bruises on a lower shin, the result of an unexpected edge on the metal bed frame in Golden's boudoir. Characterization of Golden as a womanizer cropped up often in interviews with those who knew him, and many of the observations had the distinct tang of sour grapes. Men acquainted with Golden rarely understood what, exactly, an attractive woman saw in the overweight Yankee, short as he was in both stature and funds.[66]

"He had a way of being very charming when he wanted to be," remembered Ruth Ben-Joseph, a Charlotte businesswoman who, with husband Marc Ben-Joseph, was friends with Golden beginning in the 1950s. "He had a way of acting as if you were the only one, the smartest one, in the room." He tended to stand very close and gesture in ways that brought him even more into his listener's space; another friend likened this to Lyndon Johnson's legendary intrusive body language. "Most women didn't know how to get out of it," said Ruth Ben-Joseph. "They'd always be a little shaken up and very flattered later."[67]

Broadcast journalist Charles Kuralt, whose career began to blossom in 1950, became a storyteller after Golden's own heart. Years later Kuralt made fun of his own regrets at middle age by recalling, "Harry Golden, the old editor and author who lived in my hometown, told me when I was a young newspaper reporter, 'When you get to my age, sonny, all you ever think about are the women you could have gone to bed with and didn't.'" Kuralt added ruefully, "I laughed then."[68]

A Book Misses the Mark

Almost anyone who did business in Charlotte and knew Golden eventually got talked into advertising in the *Carolina Israelite*. The wise ones avoided the "discount plan" available for purchasing multiple ads in advance. They instead paid for one at a time and learned to ask in *which* month their ad would appear. Golden referred to variously named entities as parent company of the paper, but often he did not set them up legally. In 1946, the existing Southland Publishing was dissolved and was later reborn with Golden as the sole owner and publisher of the newspaper. A new entity was formed in 1949 as a book-publishing arm, the Henry Lewis Martin Company, a compilation of the officers' names—printer Henry Stalls, Harry Lewis Golden, and Martin Rywell. Within a year Golden and Rywell cowrote and published *Jews in American History*. Although Golden promoted the book enthusiastically on the front page of the *Carolina Israelite* and later offered subscribers the book at a bargain rate, it did not sell well, nor was it a critical success. Golden's friend Rabbi Philip Frankel reviewed it for the *Charlotte News* and loyally called it "an encyclopedia that reads like a novel." The kindest scholarly review claimed "as history it lacks all interpretation, critical evaluation, and synthesis. Essentially it is a directory of names, with bits of history thrown in and often very casually, at that."[69]

Unfortunately, the scholarly reviewer was spot on. *Jews in American History* is, in a word, terrible. Its only redeeming feature was the single-page introduction written by Graham, which carefully avoided promising the reader any real edification. Five years later Golden put out a seventy-two-page pamphlet called *Jewish Roots in the Carolinas: A Pattern of American Philo-Semitism*, an inevitable improvement on the earlier book. Still, the pamphlet contained entertaining, scattershot narrative that gave respected historical works and his own fan letters equal weight as historical sources. In the endnotes for *Jewish Roots*, Golden listed the book he and Rywell had co-authored, one of the rare times he mentioned it in print. A perusal of *Jews in American History* reveals one good explanation for Blumenthal's failure to put much energy into dogging Golden for reimbursement of the printing costs. He probably hoped the publication would fade from memory.[70]

Carl Sandburg

Golden's native ability to bounce back from failure coupled with his hunger to be a real writer allowed him to remain undaunted by the failure of his book. He had ego and imagination, and he had a respected writer who believed in him: Carl Sandburg. Golden was in awe of the renowned poet and author of the monumental work on Abraham Lincoln. The two-volume set *Abraham Lincoln: The Prairie Years*, published in 1926, had been followed by the four-volume *Abraham Lincoln: The War Years*, winner of the 1940 Pulitzer Prize. (Sandburg toiled to condense the six into a single book, published in 1954.) The Pulitzer was his second; he had shared the prize in 1919 for his poetry collection, *Cornhuskers*. Sandburg's observations of Chicago ("Hog butcher to the world . . . City of the big shoulders") would lodge in the brains of countless twentieth-century schoolchildren unknowingly memorizing the work of a stalwart Socialist. The grandchildren of the early poetry readers would co-opt another Sandburg line in the Vietnam era: "Sometime they'll give a war and nobody will come."[71]

When the two men met in 1948, Sandburg was long established; his first poetry had been published forty-four years earlier. Golden was just becoming known as the colorful editor of the *Carolina Israelite*. Don Shoemaker, editor of the *Asheville Citizen-Times*, introduced the two after a public appearance by Sandburg, who had moved to a farm in Flat Rock, North Carolina, a few years earlier. Golden was flattered when Sandburg realized, "You're the fellow with the newspaper," as they shook hands. A correspondence grew up between the two, and when Golden asked for an appointment in 1956, Sandburg replied quickly. Golden quoted the invitation this way: "Dear Brudder Golden: All signs say I'll be here April 3 and if you're here we won't expect to save the country but we can have fellowship." Golden endeared himself to both Sandburg and his wife, Paula, when he arrived at their home, Connemara Farms; he took in the vast acreage and said, "Well, I wonder what old Victor Berger would have said if he had seen this place." The joking mention of one of the founders of the Socialist Party in America, a friend of both Sandburgs, delighted them.[72]

Golden planned this first visit with care. He did not want to act like the reporters who came to the office of the *Carolina Israelite*, "standing first on one foot and then on the other," asking inane questions. "Nor did I carry a book for him to autograph, or a camera to snap his picture, or a manuscript for him to read in his 'spare time.' All I brought was a bottle of whiskey." He wasn't sure Sandburg was a drinking man, but that did not deter him. "I figured that even if he doesn't drink he probably would not think it in bad taste if I drank a few toasts to him—right on the spot." One of Sandburg's daughters kept the clear North Carolina branch water coming.[73]

Golden wrote about that first meeting in the next issue of the *Carolina Israelite*, with Sandburg's permission. They bemoaned misunderstood Socialism. They remembered heroes: birth control pioneer Margaret Sanger, Emanuel Haldeman-Julius and his Little Blue Books, and lawyer Clarence Darrow. Sandburg read aloud one of his poems, "Home Fires," about Rivington Street on the Lower East Side in the 1920s, with its title drawn from the last line: "Here the stranger wonders how so many people remember where they keep home fires."[74]

After that, the two men met often at Sandburg's book-filled home overlooking the sprawling acres of pasture and woodlands. Lilian "Paula" Steichen Sandburg (sister of photographer Edward Steichen), an intelligent, well-educated woman of multifarious talents who kept the household on an even keel, always welcomed Golden warmly. "Harry loved Paula Sandburg," said Richard Goldhurst. "You know why? Well, she was very smart. . . . But when they'd be working, she'd tiptoe in the room with hot chocolate and put it down and tiptoe out and never say a word."[75]

The two men make a memorable tableau: One is a short, stout, middle-aged fellow leaning forward and gesturing with a cigar in one hand and a coffee cup or bourbon glass in the other. Across from him in a rocking chair sits a tall, thin, white-haired man with every one of his seventy-plus years writ on his craggy face, wearing a green printer's eyeshade against the still-strong afternoon sun. The older man listens intently. A typical conversation is going on: They are putting together a list of the five biggest phonies in America. They settle on the following:

Norman Vincent Peale
Bernard Baruch
Francis Cardinal Spellman
General Douglas MacArthur
Cecil B. DeMille.

They ruminate about Peale, the minister who made "positive thinking" into an industry; Baruch, the close friend of presidents; Archbishop Spellman, the equivalent of Roman Catholic royalty; then the war hero;

and finally the moviemaker. Now they are finished and can get up, stiff-backed from sitting so long, and head off for a couple hours of sleep before daybreak.[76]

For Golden this was heaven on earth. In Sandburg he found a man whose writings, public recognition, and even his marriage were his own ideals. Sandburg didn't bring about Golden's love of long and genial debate—those affections were born in childhood at Leib's kitchen table—but coming together on the Connemara porch was as sacred and fulfilling to Golden as any religious ritual could be to the most orthodox worshipper. For the older man, the new friendship was welcome. Sandburg, as happens with many popular American poets, went in and out of fashion. His writing career was so long that he experienced this wax and wane more than once in his own lifetime. He had not been happy with the reception of his 1948 novel, *Remembrance Rock*, which critics variously called "an epic and a testament" or "huge, muddled, overdone," as Sandburg wryly noted to historian Allan Nevins, a reviewer who wrote warmly of the novel. A third Pulitzer, awarded in 1950 for his *Complete Poems*, was all the more sweet given those recent mixed reviews. Golden came along at a time when Sandburg could most value the friendship he offered. As the years went on they would have another common experience: Both were revered by a large lay readership and punished by intellectual critics.[77]

"It was a very important relationship to both of them," said Richard Goldhurst. "Sandburg had reached the age you get to when many friends are gone. . . . Then along came Harry with this little newspaper, came to him at Flat Rock, and they just got along. He was a fan and they read and knew a lot of the same people." (Paula Sandburg shared her husband's respect and affection for Golden. Years later, after Sandburg had died, she asked Golden to serve as a literary executor if something happened to her.) The two men visited often, usually alone or often with Ralph McGill. They also spent time with newsman Edward R. Murrow and Adlai Stevenson, and later Sandburg and Golden would campaign together for John F. Kennedy.[78]

Golden's writing abilities grew within this friendship; his style owns something to Sandburg's loving treatment of society's invisible workers and wanderers. The men shared a certain ability to use wicked humor as indictment, as in Sandburg's line, "Tell me why a hearse horse snickers when he hauls a lawyer's bones?" Sandburg's early poems touching on race were psalms to Golden. "I walk away asking where I came from," wrote the poet at the end of his "Singing Nigger," which appeared in 1918 in *Cornhuskers*. Some of Sandburg's writing about African Americans is dated and reads as patronizing today, another commonality he shared with Golden. But at the time of its creation, Sandburg's poetry about blacks, workers, war, and progress was radical in subject and original in construction. To read his collected poems today is to enter an America captured with unique acuity.[79]

Golden regarded friendship with Sandburg as a unique pastime: "It is so complete that at every stage of the relationship you feel yourself helpless because he gives so much more than he receives. . . . If you are his friend, it means that everybody associated with you, your family, your publisher, your editors, your friends, associates and even your employees, none of whom he knows or has ever seen, are his friends too, taken in one fell swoop."[80]

In 1963, when a big party was held to celebrate Sandburg's eighty-fifth birthday and the publication of his thirty-fifth book, the tall, white-haired man looked out at the crowd full of famous people from the literary world, political circles, academia, and Hollywood, taking it all in with obvious pleasure. He remarked on only one: "I see Harry Golden, eminent citizen of North Carolina. He has a face that says who he is."[81]

CHAPTER THREE

A New Life and a New Cause in Dixie

As the war years gave way to the promise of the 1950s, Golden was a fixture in Charlotte, waddling from the post office to the newsstand six days a week and driving a rattling car to outlying mills and businesses to sell ads. He was on his own now with the *Carolina Israelite*; the patron entanglements were over. When he wasn't peddling ads or writing, he served as a resident expert on matters Jewish, foreign, or anything seen as plain unsouthern. The Baptists, Episcopalians, and Presbyterians counted on Golden to provide the Jewish view on everything from Noah's ark to Israel bonds.

True, it was sometimes irritating to give his all to a speech in front of an appreciative church audience only to be asked afterward if he knew "Mr. Cohen, who lived next door to us in New Orleans." "It never ceases to amaze me how so many Gentiles believe that all the Jews meet in some cellar once a week," he wrote in 1953. But Golden was more often amused by such incidents, which were rooted in efforts to be hospitable and correct. "These Southerners are deeply concerned over the possibility of an 'oversight' occurring when there are Jewish guests at their annual banquets. If pork is on the menu, they automatically serve you chicken, without comment or inquiry," he wrote. The fact that the chicken was usually fried in butter or lard was beside the point.[1]

In the early days on the Christian-listener circuit, Golden quickly learned what played well. One bit that he repeated often had been introduced on a pleasantly warm weeknight in the late 1940s. Golden dropped his chewed, unlit cigar in the pocket of his rumpled suit jacket and ambled up to the front of the audience at Covenant Presbyterian Church in Charlotte. Surely the first transplanted Lower East Side Jew to stand there, Golden looked around the full room and pushed his black-rimmed glasses up on his nose. "Folks, I have a secret to tell you," he rasped. "If Jesus put Charlotte on his itinerary for the Second Coming, I would be his contact man. This is not blasphemy. In the first place, I'm a cousin. In the second place, he would need an interpreter, for he probably doesn't speak this 'you-all' business." Golden paused, pointing a pudgy finger at the well-dressed crowd. "In the third place, he would want a trained reporter. He would want to know, *what in hell are Presbyterians?*'" The audience loved him.[2]

Eccentricities of religious communities, especially those common to both Jew and Christian, delighted Golden. His style of ecumenical comedy, in which endearing foibles made Baptists and Methodists, Jews and Catholics seem to have much in common would play well as an era of brotherhood-as-national-religion unfolded after the war and flowed into the next two decades. In the postwar years, growing families and resurgence in construction meant bigger congregations and fancier houses of worship, which in turn led many a proud clergyman to take the visiting Golden on a tour of bright new facilities: "Today when the rabbi or the Protestant clergyman shows you through his newly constructed edifice he shows you the kitchen first. . . . Five hundred years hence, people will dig up the churches and the temples . . . and they will conclude that this American decade was the most pious era in world history. But the steam tables, bakeries, and barbecue pits will puzzle them. This may send them off on a brand-new line of research—to find out the nature of the sacrifices we performed."[3]

Golden's success was enmeshed with these postwar shifts in American Judaism, changes in both its practice and how Jews were viewed by others. Historian Stephen J. Whitfield, in his extensive writing about Jews and American culture, focused on the national mood that provided such fertile ground for Golden's popularity to take root. In 1954, as American Jews celebrated 300 years in the New World, they "injected their own upbeat mood into the triumphalist spirit of a moment in which national power and prosperity were at their peak," he wrote. Harvard professor Oscar Handlin published his book *Adventures in Freedom* that year to mark the tercentenary and observed that by the early 1950s American Jews "wondered whether something valuable was not lost in the accommodation" to this new life in America. Not that American Jews pined for those earlier times, exactly. Positive daydreams of that Jewish past, as Handlin phrased it, were satisfying enough. As the children and grandchildren of immigrants moved more fully into mainstream culture, the experiences of their elders began to take on the patina of a romantic past. "Now that few remnants of the immigrant culture remained," Handlin wrote, "the idealized image of the ghetto was strangely fascinating, in its implacable resistance to change, in its stubborn devotion to learning." Enter Harry Golden with his well-timed idealized tales of the old country and the Lower East Side.[4]

With migration from urban neighborhoods to the suburbs came recognition of Judaism as one of the "Big Three," a development chronicled in historian Will Herberg's influential book *Protestant-Catholic-Jew*, published in 1955. Open anti-Semitism was now becoming less acceptable, and while experiences of Holocaust victims and survivors were more visibly threaded into the narrative of the war, there was an ecumenical consensus to focus on America's prosperity and the opportunities at hand. The increased acceptance of Jews by the majority culture meshed with what historian Jonathan D. Sarna called the "cult of synthesis"— the determination by American Jews, from their earliest days in this country, to "interweave their 'Judaism' with their 'Americanism' in an attempt to fashion for themselves some unified, 'synthetic' whole." All of these changes played into the expanding cultural pluralism, in which "brotherhood became a civil religion," as historian Leonard Rogoff neatly put it.[5]

Meanwhile, the *Carolina Israelite*, urged by its early backers to court a mixed audience of Jewish and Christian readers who favored this evolving Brotherhood-with-a–capital-B, was now becoming more of a personal journal with wide-ranging subject matter. Letters praising the newspaper were peppered throughout, as were mentions of the literary and political big hitters who received it. By the time the February 1951 issue came out, the paper had a mix and voice Golden liked. The front-page topics included his plans to bring a professional production of Shakespeare's *King Lear* to Charlotte, titles of the books he was reviewing for other publications, and original pieces, including "The First Time I Heard of Anti-Semitism"; "Swampum, Swampum, Get the Wampum— Tammany!"; and "The Seven Men Who Took The World Apart." (This list covered a wide time frame, from Copernicus to Einstein.) Golden ran a wire-service news release on prisoners deported from Hungary to the Soviet Union as slave laborers. He pointed out that there was an eclipse in 1178 B.C. and explained that it moved Homer to write, "The sun that day perished out of the heaven." He shrugged off the celebrity of Frank Sinatra. He reminded readers to send in $2 for their subscriptions. In July he extolled his progress in a note, "I Am Hitting My Stride," and in the November 1951 issue he ran an item headlined, "I'll Write the Entire Paper from Now On," adding, "Slowly but surely I am coming around to the idea to write everything in my paper myself, except for the 'letters to the editor.'" He was confident enough of his newspaper's staying power that he now paid extra for the slightly larger boldface business listing in the city directory.

Golden's Lower East Side tales appeared on many of the paper's pages, while news of synagogue dedications and interfaith events dwindled and eventually disappeared. In their place were biographical and historical tidbits such as "How Dr. Samuel Johnson Prepared Oysters." Observations of the South and its racial issues steadily increased. By 1952 the circulation was still modest, under 5,000. He expanded his ploy of adding "subscribers" by sending free copies using mailing lists purchased from far-flung Jewish groups. Golden's circulation arithmetic was predictably loose, and he reported the numbers with a wink. "I'll bet there must be at least 25,000 readers of the *Carolina Israelite*, on a basis of at least 5 for every subscription," he theorized. "I get a letter from a fellow in Portland, Oregon, who received [the paper] from a friend in Los Angeles . . . sent by his sister-in-law in Washington, D.C., whose husband brought it home from the office—a traveling salesman from Atlanta having left it with him. . . . Now all you folks sit down and send me $2 and get you a nice fresh one." This boastful ratio actually became accurate in the coming years when his books of collected *Carolina Israelite* essays hit the bestseller lists; at its peak the number of subscribers would top 55,000.[6]

The paper was not graphically inviting, and its look would never change much. Photos and illustrations were almost nonexistent; even the ads were usually plain "tombstone" blocks, like those in a high school yearbook. The average issue was eight pages, filled with as many as 20,000 words. Golden's "editorials" (the term he preferred to "essays") were set in 8-point Century, 24½ picas wide, with 10-point bold heads, all caps. No sections or departments existed in this paper. "The only arrangement I adhere to, is to have a long piece followed by two or three short ones," Golden explained.[7]

The *Carolina Israelite* made close to $22,000 in 1953, but as was the case in earlier years, relatively little ended up in Golden's pocket after the overhead was covered and his rob-Peter-to-pay-Paul method of bookkeeping was carried out. Now, at least, checks to the staff usually did not bounce. The business end of the operation was a patchwork held together by secretaries and other helpers who came and went until the spring of 1955, when a good Presbyterian named Maureen Titlow arrived and stayed. Each helper quickly learned the boss's priorities. Secretary Mamie Hill helped hold down the fort in the 1950s, too, and once watched with disapproval as a "shabby, down-at-the-heels character wandered in off the street" and was hired to sell ads. "For three weeks, this man pretended to be working out promotional schemes while in actuality he merely got in my way," she remembered. The man sneaked sips from Golden's bourbon, a habit of which the boss was aware and was willing to tolerate—up to a point. Mr. Golden knew what a bit of good liquor can do for a fellow down on his luck, as his secretary put it. But when the poacher *watered down* the bourbon, all bets were off. "Mr. Golden returned from his lunch and as usual reached for his bourbon.... Then a look of pure disgust crossed his face.... 'Some son-of-a-bitch put water in my liquor,' he said. The fellow was out on his ear in short order."[8]

The fact that the paper survived at all was cause for admiration among other writers and editors. At the 1952 meeting of the National Conference of Editorial Writers, novelist James Street interrupted proceedings to call for his friend Golden to be introduced: "I want to meet the fellow who makes a living out of a Jewish newspaper in North Carolina." Golden had provided an official blurb for the conference program, describing his paper this way: "It's run by a happy and contented Jew in one of the most thoroughly gentile regions on earth."[9]

Golden the writer now began to operate on two levels: as a transplant intrigued by southerners, both Gentiles and Jews, and as an observer of the national scene and the changing attitudes about race issues. Opportunities to publish his essays started to come from *Congress Bi-Weekly*, the house organ of the American Jewish Congress, and *Commentary*, the editorially independent magazine published by the AJC. Other respected national publications would follow suit.

Profiles by journalist friends appeared with increasing frequency and lessening objectivity. Often the reporters wrote their paeans for publications other than their own; the thinking must have been that this preserved objectivity. The Raleigh bureau chief for the *Charlotte Observer* wrote in the *Nation* that Golden was a "highly literate, astonishingly well-read editor who lets his thoughts free-wheel through his column." Being recognized in the *Nation* pleased Golden, who would write for it himself in the coming years.[10]

Well-Timed Arrival

Golden's arrival in Charlotte had paralleled an important event in the country's civil rights timeline, and he was strongly influenced by it. In 1941, the NAACP sued and won the right for black men to apply for spaces in the Army Air Forces. The same year, A. Philip Randolph, founder of the Brotherhood of Sleeping Car Porters and an influential African American activist, issued a blunt challenge to President Franklin Roosevelt: Open up defense jobs to blacks or deal with the headache of a massive march on Washington, D.C. The resulting Executive Order 8802 signed that year made it illegal for defense industries and federal agencies to discriminate against workers based on race. Randolph used the tactic for many years. "Randolph . . . for thirty years frightened Presidents of the United States out of their wits with his sepulchral announcement of an impending protest March on Washington. . . . President Eisenhower ducked out of Washington every time he heard that Randolph had arrived at Washington's Union Station," wrote Golden later.[11]

Working alongside Randolph to push for the executive order was the intrepid Walter White, executive director of the NAACP who had used his light skin as a disguise to investigate violence against southern blacks. White anticipated that wartime military service offered a rare opportunity to break down discrimination, but he feared that even heroism and sacrifices by black troops would not be enough to change official policies. He fearlessly pushed for a "double victory"—abroad and at home—against Jim Crow. As historian Morton Sosna pointed out, this worried even some of the most liberal whites, who feared the reaction if black leaders appeared to be using the war to bring their grievances into a more public debate.[12]

Golden didn't share their fears; he focused on the gains, such as the growth of the NAACP, which began to attract a mass following. By 1946, membership ranks had swelled to close to 600,000 people. Another organization making changes in response to wartime shifts was the Fellowship of Reconciliation, an international interfaith pacifist organization that had been around since World War I. In 1941 that organization created the Congress of Racial Equality (CORE), headed by Bayard Rustin, an African American jailed in the early 1940s for being a conscientious objector and who would become one of the key figures working with the Reverend Martin Luther King Jr.[13]

Golden joined both the Fellowship of Reconciliation and CORE as a dues-paying member, convinced the organizations would bring about real change. His relationships with both would be long; he spoke often at fundraisers for CORE and the NAACP in the coming years, waiving his fee after fame raised his marketability. More than two decades later a group of CORE members slept on his floor as Freedom Riders traveling south to protest segregated interstate transportation. When the fellowship came under fire from the John Birch Society for being "un-American," he defended the group in poetic language: "The truth is that the Fellowship of Reconciliation does lie outside the mainstream of American life and culture, but it feeds into our society from fresh springs, enlarging, cleansing, bringing new ideas of a better life. It is good to know someone is lobbying for peace."[14]

He cheered the breaking of the color barrier by baseball great Jackie Robinson in 1947, as he had the election of Harlem politician Adam Clayton Powell Jr. in 1941 as the first black on the New York City Council and then, in 1944, the state's first black member of the U.S. House of Representatives. Golden didn't much like Powell, criticizing him for his elastic ethics, even though the politician was not so different from the Tammany Hall types he treated with more humor in his writing. "Every minority group has had its share of Adam Clayton Powells," he allowed. Golden did credit the congressman's various doomed antisegregation proposals. "They proved an irritant and a goad. They served their purpose for Negroes and for Powell too."[15]

Golden was among the early readers impressed by Myrdal's massive and damning *American Dilemma*. But, already feeling protective of those southerners who abhorred racism, Golden made the point that Myrdal "was only one among a vast number of people who deplored segregation." There were novelists, housewives, taxi drivers, and editors—and many southerners—who also opposed it and did not need a Swedish sociologist, no matter how brilliant, to prove what they already knew, he said. Giving credit where credit was due was a trait that helped build the tolerance— and admiration—that Golden got in the South, especially among those touchy about Yankee criticism.[16]

Golden was alert to changes in the magazine publishing world regarding the subject of race. Others came to know *Jet* when the magazine ran a shocking photograph of the corpse of Emmett Till, a fourteen-year-old boy murdered in Mississippi in 1955, whose story made international news. Golden was a rare white person who had been reading *Jet* for four years by then. He was also a regular reader of the *Crisis*, the house organ of the NAACP, which published him beginning in the late 1950s. He saw that *Ebony*, the first glossy magazine aimed at a national black readership, was a hit from its launch in 1945.[17]

Black Press

Another phenomenon with which Golden became better acquainted was the long reach of black-owned newspapers. These weeklies and monthlies had existed since the late nineteenth century and boldly "ridiculed white hypocrisy, spoke out bitterly against racial injustice, [and] reinterpreted the mainstream press," as well as covering social and local news, as the book *The Race Beat* put it. The writers and publishers within the black press had surprising latitude in times when saying aloud the things printed in their columns could have meant harassment, an end to livelihood, or even injury and death. This freedom to publish was not owing to the desire of the American public for a color-blind free press; papers like the *Baltimore Afro-American*, the *Atlanta Daily World*, the *Chicago Defender*, and the *Pittsburgh Courier* were left alone simply because they were distributed quietly and white people rarely read them. Race was ignored by mainstream newspapers for the most part until the early 1950s. By then, circulation of most black weeklies was dropping.[18]

Golden was well acquainted with the *Charlotte Post*, written by and for African Americans since 1878. He visited the *Post* while making his ad-sales rounds for Witter's paper and his own. Golden's speeches and writings were quoted in black publications often, beginning in the 1950s with the *Chicago Defender*, and his syndicated column ran weekly in that paper (by then the *Chicago Daily Defender*) in the 1960s. He drew ideas from these papers, as he did from his regular reading of New York's dailies; of *Life*, *Time*, *Saturday Evening Post*, and *Commentary*; and of various Socialist publications, including the *Forward* and the advertising-free newspaper *PM*.[19]

Yet Golden gave the black publications little public attention. This was, in part, because he was embracing the image increasingly assigned to his paper by white liberals, especially in the Northeast, who saw him as a front-row observer of southern race matters. As with the popular musicians of the day—Jerry Lee Lewis and Elvis Presley, to name just two—white America tended not to notice the chroniclers of an issue or creators of a genre until one of their own took it up and repackaged it. Golden encouraged the view of himself as a lone voice in the South able to amuse and then motivate white America by revealing the idiocy of racism.

Coverage of the news in mainstream media was as segregated as any southern church, and he *did* express anger about this circumstance. It bothered him on two levels: It was discriminatory, and it deprived readers of important viewpoints. He knew that Jonathan Daniels, editor of the *Raleigh News and Observer,* while on leave to serve as President Roosevelt's special assistant, had struggled to make even the smallest change in this area. Daniels managed to get the first black reporter, Harry McAlpin of the *Atlanta Daily World,* into White House press conferences in 1944. Otherwise, white journalists stood by while black reporters and photographers were kept out of the House and Senate press galleries until 1947. African American reporters stood in line with the tourists, hoping to get a seat in order to cover important votes and debates.[20]

Upstart that Golden was, he still automatically had more rights than did the black journalists, many of whom had more education and experience than he did. Golden didn't harbor the deep guilt that many of his middle-class liberal compatriots felt about his white advantage, but he never fully lost his astonishment at seeing it play out.

Truman and Civil Rights

Golden admired President Harry Truman for putting the groundwork in place to support the civil rights movement. But even before those accomplishments, Golden was attracted to the very thing that repelled Truman's detractors: the great contrast between the straight-shooting Missourian and Franklin Roosevelt, the "aristocrat who wore a Navy cape, was a senior warden of the Hyde Park Episcopal Church and a descendant of Mayflower stock," as Golden described him. Truman, on the other hand, once won a farmer's vote by telling a mule's age after examining its teeth, or so the legend went. Golden did not revere Franklin Roosevelt as so many did. (There was, however, no hedging in his fierce, lifelong love for Eleanor Roosevelt, "the greatest woman in the world.") Yet he admired and believed in the accomplishments of the Roosevelt administration and tirelessly mocked those who did not. Those detractors were, to Golden, on a par with a Charlotte taxi driver he met during the Roosevelt years whose story he retold countless times. The driver was fuming when he picked Golden up; it seems the previous passenger was a black preacher who had paid the fare with a $5 bill. "Now when did you see a nigger with a five-dollar bill before Roosevelt?" the driver demanded.[21]

Nothing was more appealing to Golden than an unassuming person who turned out to have courage and depth. At first he felt a bit sorry for Truman. Here was a regular fellow who "wore a colored sport shirt and interrupted the pinochle game to ask 'Do you boys think I did the right thing today?' " Underestimating Truman was a common mistake, and one Golden soon corrected. Truman was the last president from the simpler, low-tech America, but as biographer David G. McCullough has said, Truman was not a simple man. Nor did he lead the country in simple times.[22]

Golden was not around to read the transcript of Truman's personal diary discovered in 2003. In the long-hidden, blue-covered datebook, Truman wrote this on 21 July 1947: "Had ten minutes conversation with Henry Morgenthau about Jewish ship in Palestine [sic]. . . . The Jews have no sense of proportion nor do they have any judgment on world affairs. . . . The Jews, I find are very, very selfish." He continued on in that vein. Golden may have been big-hearted enough to attribute those thoughts to a man exhausted by proximity to so many forms of human barbarism and loss.[23]

Instead, Golden was won over when Truman spoke to an NAACP convention in 1947, a first for a president. Truman's creation of the President's Commission on Civil Rights in 1947 proved he was "president of both whites and negroes" in a way his predecessors were not, said Golden. Even the commission's name meant progress; now the term "civil rights" began to enter general use.[24]

With the release of the commission's report, *To Secure These Rights*, in 1947, and the next year's order desegregating the military, Golden started to believe that black Americans could get an equal shake in those areas controlled by the federal government. It was a biracial commission with both Jews and Gentiles and heavy-hitters from business and academia. Golden's friend Frank P. Graham, then president of the University of North Carolina, was an appointee. The report's recommendations were ambitious, promoting improved access to employment, voting rights, medical care, housing, and other areas of need for African Americans. The breadth of the report surprised even Truman. More than a million copies of the report were distributed, and several black newspapers serialized it. Political leaders who played big roles in the civil rights battles ahead were spurred by the report, and policy made years later—including affirmative action—could be traced to the panel's work.[25]

To Secure These Rights opens with as fine a summary of oxymoronic American prejudices as ever came out of a government typewriter:

The cultural diversity of the United States has flavored the whole political, economic, and social development of the nation. Our science, our industry, our art, our music, our philosophy have been formed and enriched by peoples from throughout the world. Our diversity, however, has had one disadvantage. The fact that the forebears of some of us arrived in America later than those of others, the fact that some of us have lived in separate groups, and the fact that some of us have different customs and religious beliefs, or different skin colors, have too often been seized upon as justification for discrimination.[26]

This sober government report also distinguished itself by quoting a statement made by a president of baseball's National League. Ford Frick (later appointed baseball commissioner) had that year faced down threats of a strike when African American Jackie Robinson joined the Brooklyn Dodgers: "If you do this you will be suspended from the [National Baseball] league. You will find that the friends you think you have in the press box will not support you, that you will be outcasts. I do not care if half the League strikes. Those who do it will encounter quick retribution. All will be suspended and I don't care if it wrecks the National League for 5 years. This is the United States of America and one citizen has as much right to play as another."[27]

To Secure These Rights set up Truman's most important domestic accomplishment: desegregation of the U.S. military. When Randolph delivered his ultimatum to Roosevelt about opening war-industry jobs to blacks, he had also demanded desegregation of the armed forces, but without success. Now the Commission on Civil Rights put the issue in front of the world, showing dispassionate evidence that mixed-race military units could serve the country well. And the military, unlike general society, did not take steps back after initiating change. Golden's friend Harry Ashmore quoted a wry colonel of his acquaintance: "The Army is slow to change, but it changes. I would never have believed I'd live long enough to see the cavalry give up its horses. Letting Negroes come in through the front door is nothing compared to dismounting George Patton."[28]

Whatever troops felt about military desegregation, the order from on high infuriated those southerners back home who saw it as blatant interference in states' rights. Residents in communities with military bases nearby were especially angry. One was Montgomery, Alabama, where Maxwell and Gunter air force bases poured millions of dollars into the local economy. The order "reminded everyone that the source of Montgomery's new identity was the Yankee government itself, which was imposing a regimen of full-fledged race-mixing at the two huge air bases," wrote historian Taylor Branch. "The city was helpless to stop it, but its council could and did make sure that such practices did not spread into the city."[29]

Branch's observation hits the heart of the civil rights fight. The South had a very long history of being force-fed by outsiders. Belief that a state had the right, if not the duty, to rule itself was not a political position in Dixie; it was something bred to the bone. The content of federal edicts—whether from the high court, Congress, or the president—became less important. It was the source of the orders that rankled.

Lynching

Nowhere was the southern politicians' resistance to federal muscle more unyielding than on the subject of lynching, which so fascinated Golden. He began to delve into its provenance and grew steadily more articulate, framing it first as a historical phenomenon of a lawless frontier, then as more complex eruptions among poor whites, directed almost exclusively at blacks. It was sympathy for the underdog taken to an unusual extreme; the study of hate crimes was not the visible field it is today. Golden felt that if he came to understand all the components enabling mob murder, he would grasp something that eluded him about the roots of race hatred.

Mobs killed at least 4,700 people, 3,400 of them black, from 1882 to 1944. (These are recorded killings. Actual totals were higher, perhaps dramatically so.) Lynchings were on the decline by the 1940s, but some of the most widely publicized and influential cases came in that decade. As Truman's Commission on Civil Rights put it, "It is still possible for a mob to abduct and murder a person in some sections of the country with almost certain assurance of escaping punishment for the crime. The decade from 1936 through 1946 saw at least 43 lynchings. No person received the death penalty, and the majority of the guilty persons were not even prosecuted."[30]

Men and women of all races and ages were killed or maimed with some fanfare in America as far back as Revolutionary days, when tar and feathers were favored means to get a message across to Loyalists. But lynching was most often a southern crime, and its victims were most often black men. "Lynching" is used as a synonym for hanging, but the methods of murder were more numerous and cruel. Dragging, beating, mutilating, shooting, and burning were common, carried out in ways that kept the victim alive as long as possible and watched by boisterous crowds, including young children. H. L. Mencken famously referred to lynching as a form of southern entertainment that took the place of merry-go-rounds and theater.[31]

Golden wrote, "There were always lynchings along the American frontier. The frontier was raw and dangerous, the people populating it violent and quick. But the number of frontiersmen summarily hanged was not in itself a sign of national weakness any more than the number of frontiersmen who succumbed to dysentery was. What does reveal a temperamental American weakness is the melancholy fact that when the frontier closed, lynching had an independent career."[32]

From its 1909 founding, the NAACP was a force against lynching, and this determination to stop mob murders played a large part in Golden's affinity for the organization. Golden avidly read the expert work on the subject by Arthur Raper and Walter White. (Golden was also a rare writer who credited "I. B. Wells" for dramatically raising awareness of lynching, but he did not realize the activist writer, Ida B. Wells, was female.) "The grotesqueries of lynching are a direct result of the American belief that law and politics are synonymous," Golden wrote. "Despite all our piety, we are a violent country, ruthlessly brutal and ruthlessly materialistic; and we learn our lessons all too slowly. As a nation we may venerate many things, but law is not one of them."[33]

Repeated efforts were made to legislate change by making lynching a felony under federal law, but the powerful bloc of southern Democrats was so adept at preserving states' rights—and so skilled at filibustering—that these efforts were doomed. Pushing and nagging by Golden's heroine Eleanor Roosevelt could not convince President Roosevelt to publicly support antilynching legislation. (Even Sara Delano Roosevelt, Eleanor's oppositional mother-in-law, agreed with her for once.) But the president knew his other reforms would get no support from southern Democrats if he waded into the lynching debate. He would not take that risk. Truman didn't have the eyes and ears of a constantly traveling First Lady and had much to learn about black America, especially the dangers faced by blacks in the South. His understanding improved fast when he met with White and members of the National Emergency Committee against Violence in the summer of 1946. They described recent episodes of southern violence, including an African American war veteran who had both eyes gouged out by a white sheriff. A shocked Truman exclaimed, "My God, I had no idea things were as terrible as that. We've got to do something."[34]

Golden, unlike Truman, was familiar with this aspect of these hate crimes. "While studying the history of lynching, I was amazed at the incidence of lynchers burning and hanging Negroes after World War I, the sole reason being that the Negro was wearing an army uniform," he wrote. The uniform, Golden said, symbolized both a temporary equality and protection of the federal government, and "the symbolism was a portent which enraged the lynchers."[35]

Adlai Stevenson

Golden would become even more appreciative of Truman when Dwight D. Eisenhower took office in 1953. Ike, the war hero president, just plain irritated him. After Truman's salty bluntness, Eisenhower was utterly bland, Golden thought, a man who was distant and unresponsive on any issue beyond development of interstate highways. He did his best to avoid any discussion that touched on the words "civil rights," and Golden said often that he could never forgive the president for grabbing a microphone and yelling, "I always stand up when they play Dixie," as a high school band struck up the tune at an "I Like Ike" rally in Columbia, South Carolina. (The actual remark by Eisenhower was worded a bit differently but was just as offensive.)[36]

"What General Eisenhower thinks about William Shakespeare we do not know," Golden wrote after Eisenhower left the White House. "But what Shakespeare thought about General Eisenhower is as clear as anything can be. He drew the former President full length in the character of Polonius in Hamlet. . . . He is the mediator, the smoother-out, the man who meets every crisis with an old-fashioned homily, 'Give every man thy ear, but few thy voice' . . . and 'to thine own self be true.' "[37]

But Golden's biggest gripe—if he had been honest about it—was that Eisenhower beat Adlai Stevenson twice. Golden deeply admired Stevenson, as did Carl Sandburg, and this was an important common bond. When Sandburg said, "I am one of the host that love Adlai with a respect bordering on reverence," he captured the fierce dedication that the Illinois Democrat inspired in Golden and others. Eleanor Roosevelt was a close friend and protector of Stevenson. Golden treasured a two-sentence note typed by the former First Lady: "Thank you for your letter and your loyalty to Gov. Stevenson. I am enjoying your latest book." And when Eleanor Roosevelt died, Stevenson delivered a eulogy after Golden's own heart: "It was said of her contemptuously at times that she was a do-gooder, a charge leveled with similar derision against another public figure 1,962 years ago."[38]

Newton Minow, Stevenson's law partner and, later, chairman of the Federal Communications Commission, was an amused reader of the *Carolina Israelite*, and many years later he said he was likely the one who introduced Stevenson to Golden's work. Golden had also happily sent Stevenson copies of the paper, proclaimed him a subscriber, and wrote an appealing, intelligent fan letter or two. Stevenson was charmed. "Every now and then I look through the *Carolina Israelite* and invariably end up in a gala of mirth or with a knitted brow—or both!" wrote Stevenson to Golden in 1955.[39]

When Stevenson rode a presidential campaign train through North Carolina in 1952, he wisely invited Golden, who knew his way around his adopted state but was yet to become famous. (It was then that Golden made the visit to Stevenson's Libertyville, Illinois, home that inspired his "What ghetto boy ever had a bathrobe?" line.) That visit involved the sort of group writing that Stevenson enjoyed, especially when he could then dismember and rewrite the work himself. "No one, as far as I was ever able to learn, wrote speeches 'for' Adlai Stevenson," said Golden. "You submitted titles for speeches, sometimes the speech itself, and if you were lucky and very good, sometimes you occasionally heard a word or maybe even a sentence—but only occasionally."[40]

Golden was well suited to do the work of a political speechwriter. He had a trove of historical references filed away in his memory, and he wrote very fast. He admired the man who took the high road but rarely judged the one who took an expedient shortcut to elected office. A political hack writer could easily find work, and ghost writers, he said, were always needed. "Approximately 90 percent of political candidates are lawyers, and that fact alone makes ghost writers necessary," he declared. "By education, training, and practice, lawyers are concerned entirely with what has already happened." He sometimes wrote remarks for candidates on both sides of a local or state election and loved to tell the story of a congressional candidate who hired him to write a campaign brochure in the 1940s. The politician was so pleased with the result that he ordered, "Golden, get me twenty thousand of this here paper. Get me ten thousand with the union label and ten thousand without."[41]

Golden did not figure large in Stevenson's busy private life; their connection has rarely been acknowledged by historians. Yet Golden's presence was felt. Golden's papers include more than seventy personal notes and letters of the even larger number that passed between them, the last coming just days before Stevenson died in 1965. Stevenson was among the savvy public figures who recognized the value of Golden's cogent summaries of the day's issues. Golden was called into Stevenson's orbit again during the 1956 and 1960 presidential races; he supported John F. Kennedy in the latter race only after Stevenson lost the Democratic nomination. "I had with Stevenson something of the influence George Burns has with Jack Benny," wrote Golden. "Burns has but to say 'Hello, Jack' for Benny to double up in laughter." His oldest, corniest joke, Golden said, would cause Stevenson to "push away from the table to give himself lots of room to laugh." Anyone who has spent a grinding week or two on a campaign trail or been served by the sycophants who populate political entourages can understand how welcome a companion like Golden could be. "Yes, there was a huge gulf," said Minow, when asked about the unlikely pairing. They were not what he would call close, he said, "but both men loved good stories . . . and they both had wit and charm."[42]

In fact, Stevenson, as scrutinized in biographer John Bartlow Martin's two volumes, does not seem like such a stretch as a friend for Golden. He was the kind of old-fashioned moneyed liberal that Golden admired in spite of himself. That and the WASPy Stevenson's curiosity about an immigrant's past helped forge this liaison. Both men were prolific correspondents who worked out some of their most arresting ideas in letters. They both hankered after the newspaper business. (Stevenson's family had a share of the *Daily Pentagraph* in Illinois, and he had covered the famous so-called Monkey Trial of John Scopes.) Both men felt the tug-of-war between their fame and doing "the right thing." Martin quotes a letter written early in Stevenson's career in which he laments, "I know perfectly well that if I am to make a 'success' of myself, sooner or later I must 'sell out.' " Golden was in the room during some of Stevenson's most trying moments: lost elections, concession speeches, and the difficult news that president-elect Kennedy would not be naming him secretary of state. Golden was among the supporters who encouraged Stevenson to take the post of ambassador to the United Nations when Kennedy offered it in 1961.[43]

Biographer Martin describes his subject's casual anti-Semitism, but by the time he and Golden met, Stevenson had evolved to his trademark above-the-fray liberalism, presumably shedding some earlier prejudices. It is possible that Golden had a role in pushing Stevenson away from old influences about race and religion. Back in the early 1950s, admirers, including sympathetic newspaper columnists, had already begun to couple the word "integrity" with Stevenson's name. This became less than a compliment over time and more a coded way of saying "not tough enough." Stevenson broke the stereotype of his state's corrupt politician; he "reminded us that the machine is not supreme," as Golden put it. He stood up for free speech amidst the rising anti-Red tide, and despite his mixed record on race issues, he used the considerable power of the governorship to push back racism in Illinois. Richard Goodwin, who served Presidents Kennedy and Johnson as a writer and special assistant, eulogized

Stevenson as a man who "told an entire generation there was room for intelligence and idealism in public life."[44]

Finding a Voice, and New Courage

As he was tapped to help Stevenson, Golden was showing two talents that served him well: disarming the reader with humor and frankness, and boiling down complex social issues. Today, someone with Golden's skill would be a popular cable-channel pundit and prolific blogger. Then he was a lone operator who had experienced the addictive gratification that comes with taking on the bad guys and being recognized for it.

In the November 1951 *Carolina Israelite* he used a fraud case against a small-time Klan member to call out the citizenry against white supremacists, who in their "thoroughly evil" way represented much more than their malevolent cross-burnings and lynchings. In the piece headlined "Ku Klux Klan Head Convicted," he asked, "The negroes can stand it, the Jews can stand it, the Catholic[s] can stand it, but can North Carolina, South Carolina and Georgia stand it?" "Basically the Ku Klux fellows are really saying this: 'Look, your courts are no good; your judges are no good; your peace officers are no good; your state, county, and city officials are no good. . . . We have decided that you are all unfit, and that we, with masks on, shall take over the job.'" It was an effective approach. Four years later, twenty-six-year-old Martin Luther King Jr. galvanized listeners with a similar theme: "If we are wrong, the Constitution of the United States is wrong. If we are wrong, God Almighty is wrong. If we are wrong, Jesus of Nazareth was merely a utopian dreamer that never came down to earth. If we are wrong, justice is a lie."[45]

The few other white newspaper editors who took similar critical stands against the Klan were also taking risks, but they had the protection that came from being part of larger, more established institutions. The supremacists threatened all such commentators, but Golden was answering his own telephone and opening his own mail. He collected a cache of kiss-offs he used in response to phone threats. Asked why he was "stirring up the nigras," as callers often asked, Golden might answer, "Well, I'm half Negro myself." Or when greeted by a stream of threats and obscenities, he would interrupt and say, "Oh, you have the wrong number. This is the office of . . . ," then adding the name of the current Chamber of Commerce "Man of the Year." Inevitably the caller hung up and immediately dialed again, at which point he answered, "Hello, this is [Man of the Year], may I help you?" The bewildered ranter generally gave up at that point. Friend Walter Klein was visiting once when a hateful call came in. The man was so loud that Klein could hear him call Golden a "goddamn nigger-loving Jew bastard" from across the room. Golden calmly rejoined, "I want to thank you. Duke University pays me fifty dollars for every threat recording I send them and yours was just right." The caller banged the telephone receiver down in a fury. On another occasion, Golden and his son Richard were sitting in their car waiting for a stoplight to change when an aggrieved local walked up and leaned close to Golden's window. "Harry Golden, you git outta that car and Ah'm gonna kill you," he threatened. Golden threw out a comeback line borrowed from his Mississippi editor friend, P. D. East: "That's not incentive enough." Then he drove off.[46]

Obvious racist thugs were not the only villains. Golden was among the early, consistently tough critics of Senator Joseph McCarthy, the infamous Red-baiting liar who turned a lackluster political career into history. The first widespread newspaper coverage of McCarthy came after 9 February 1950, when he made a speech at a dinner of a Women's Republican Club in Wheeling, West Virginia, claiming to have a list of known Communists in the State Department. As media historian Edwin R. Bayley discovered when he analyzed press coverage of McCarthy, the editorial stands taken by many daily newspapers were quite fluid. Golden was no doubt pleased that while the *Charlotte Observer* started out saying McCarthy's charges were "too specific to be ignored," the paper also called for more facts; within days the editorialists declared, "McCarthy has failed to make good his charge" about card-carrying Communists.[47]

Golden recognized the con artist in the Wisconsin senator early on. He saw McCarthy as a transparent tyrant. "There's very little in politics that Tammany Hall didn't invent," wrote Golden. "Senator McCarthy is using one of its oldest tricks. The trick is to make an accusation, trail off in the explanation by talking about something else, and just let that business of 'where there's smoke there's fire,' do its worst." Golden despised the effect McCarthy had on the Letters to the Editor pages of newspapers and magazines, a sacred territory. "I know of at least a half-dozen North Carolina New Dealers who, for years, were regular contributors to open forums," wrote Golden. "They have as much use for Stalin and communism as they had for Hitler and Nazism, but they no longer write 'letters to the editor.' They quit. They know that in times of hysteria, the slightest raising of an eyebrow [brings] all sorts of complications."[48]

Marriage at a Distance

With the differences with Blumenthal behind him, and the *Carolina Israelite*'s growing readership, Golden worried less about offending Jews in Charlotte, shrugging off his outsider status. That was just as well, because gossip about his business dealings and his absentee wife—who was a Gentile at that—put him out of the running for genuine, widespread acceptance.

In city directories and other records, Golden took pains to list himself as married, even though Tiny never made her home in Charlotte. There had been talk about the entire family moving to the South once Golden was established; but that didn't happen, and he explained his marital separation in various ways depending on who was asking. He might say that one of them needed to live in New York in order for youngest son Peter to remain in the care of a state institution. Or Tiny's Catholicism might be regretfully cited to an overeager female companion who was hoping a divorce was in the offing. Such a woman, no doubt imagining her rival as a devout churchgoing wife, could not know of Tiny's irreverent penchant for beginning grace at a meal by intoning "Our Father, who art in Charlotte," with a prayerful upward gaze. None of this cramped Golden's social pleasures. "Harry still managed to go through every widow in Charlotte," said Richard Goldhurst.[49]

The question of a divorce was never really on the table, for reasons known only to the husband and wife. "There have been some good and enriching years for which I am grateful to you," Tiny wrote her husband in 1959 when the couple decided to draw up legal separation papers. "To our friends who have so often deplored the tragedy of this union we can simply say: 'It never quite jelled.'" After Golden died, his attorney showed his eldest son a large file drawer stuffed with copies of separation agreements waved off by one or the other of the couple. They never stopped writing new ones and ignoring old ones, said Goldhurst, who added drily, "It would take me a week to describe that marriage."[50]

In 1944 Golden was flush enough that sons Billy and Buddy (Harry Jr.) could go south to live with him. Buddy graduated from Charlotte's Central High School and attended Belmont Abbey, then a junior college established by Benedictine monks. Later he fast-talked his way onto the state news desk at the *Charlotte Observer*, evidencing a talent for clever headlines written on deadline. He was the desk man who handled the story of a tobacco farmer who went on a bender, passed out, got robbed, and contritely told police it was God punishing him for his sinful behavior. His headline, "Farmer's Roll Is Called Up Yonder," won him a place in copyeditors' hearts for a long time to come.[51]

Richard served as a U.S. Army paratrooper in the 11th Airborne Division. While stationed at Fort Bragg, he twice wangled weekend passes home, explaining that his father's "work for the war effort" could use his help. Once in Charlotte, he passed the time playing pool with Buddy and ate meals with the others. It was the closest the Goldhurst males ever got to a domestic existence. "Three times a day, Harry led the three of us to the Little Pep Delmonico or to the S&W Cafeteria or to the Oriental for either breakfast, lunch or dinner," Goldhurst said.[52]

Back in New York, Tiny made the most of the empty bedrooms in the crumbling apartment four flights up at 200 W. Ninety-Second Street. The housing market was tight, and she had no trouble finding two boarders. She slept on the couch, draped her nightgown over a built-in desk in the living room, and stored her underwear in the desk drawers. One boarder who arrived in 1946 was the Charlestonian Charles Peters, a military veteran and aspiring writer attending Columbia who would found the engaging *Washington Monthly* in 1969. He rented the room for two years and ate dinner at Tiny's table for five more years after that. Meals, usually spaghetti and cheesecake, were marginal. The real draw was the hostess.

"She was about five feet tall and must have weighed around 160 pounds," wrote Peters in his memoir *Tilting at Windmills*. "Her hair was steely gray, she had the shoulders of a linebacker, and her jaw made Dick Tracy's look weak." Most nights Tiny came home exhausted from work, but after a restorative cigarette she'd perk up and start dinner—and stories. "She would assume you knew all the characters. When she mentioned Sam, she did not bother to explain who he was. It usually took half the story to figure it out, and sometimes it took several stories over several months before you had him clearly in your mind. But you were never to interrupt with a question like 'Who's Sam?' " A frequent character in Tiny's stories was Clara, Harry's sister, whose calls, letters, complaints, and battles with creditors were unrelenting. Tiny described her sister-in-law in various unflattering ways. As Richard Goldhurst quoted one of her jibes, Clara's job on Wall Street was a profession "that did not survive the Depression but far outlived her virginity." But Tiny was always there, calmly talking Clara in off the ledge of the moment. Her expertise at this was much admired by Golden's brother Jake and, later, Jake's daughters, who came to understand the challenge themselves. "However [Harry] may have wronged Tiny, he continued to occupy the center stage of her stories. I understood why when I met him in 1947," wrote Peters. "Expecting to dislike him because he had run out on his family, I was totally charmed." Within a few hours the two men were singing all the old hymns Peters remembered from his Charleston Sunday school days.[53]

The "Disturber" Holds Forth

His marital situation aside, by the 1950s Golden's growing reputation as a chronicler of the Jewish South was a thorn in the sides of those prominent Charlotte Jews who worried that he might be regarded as their representative. Golden dismissed these Jews as those who lived "in deadly fear of a disturber." The shift in views about America's "Big Three" religions and its effect of relaxing worries about anti-Semitic backlash was still in the wings, especially in the South.[54]

It was one thing for him to spout off in his raffish little newspaper but another thing entirely when his byline started showing up in national publications. One piece published in 1950 looked at a peculiar regional evangelism. A sort of Jews for Jesus crowd, these "Hebrew-Christian preachers" took up the ministry of bringing the message of Christ to Jews, who would presumably then see the light and convert. Golden wrote,

> The vast majority of our Christian neighbors, friends, and associates simply remain amazingly naive. A Gentile friend or neighbor meets you on the street during one of the revivals and, in an obvious attempt to be pleasant, says, "Great work that [evangelist Hyman] Appelman is doing, isn't it?" Occasionally, a Christian clergyman will invite the local rabbi to hear a "great Jewish preacher" during one of these revivals. And this is not for any lack of respect for the rabbi and his congregation: it is just that to many Christian Southerners a Jew is a Jew the way a Frenchman is a Frenchman. More than one Jew in the South has at one time or another been asked in all sincerity: "Are you a Baptist Jew or a Methodist Jew?"[55]

This sort of observation of Christian cluelessness embarrassed many in Charlotte's middle-class Jewish circles who wanted to stay comfortably assimilated into the larger Gentile community and who felt they needed to carefully avoid public acknowledgment of religious affiliation. Golden found various amusing ways to make the point. "On many a Monday morning, as a Jewish merchant opens his store, he may not know it but the group of women passing by on the street are on their way to the Baptist church to pray for his salvation," he wrote.[56]

"In the forties and fifties, most Jews [here] tried to keep a very low profile; they wanted to go along and get along," recalled Mark Bernstein, a Charlotte attorney and friend of Golden's. "So now people were asking, 'What is Harry Golden writing, *now*?' A lot of them were amused, but the community was split about him." Historian Leonard Rogoff, when writing about Golden, quoted Jews with stronger feelings, including "a Charlotte rabbi who bemoaned, 'We wish he'd go away and leave us alone.'" Golden appeared to many of his Jewish neighbors as one who "wore his Jewishness too loudly, and his public advocacy of unpopular causes jeopardized their status as solid, middle-class Americans," observed Rogoff.[57]

When *Commentary* ran Golden's 1951 essay "A Son of the South and Some Daughters," worries about his unseemly views and irreverent humor escalated. Now Golden pronounced that Jews, Gentiles, ministers, and rabbis alike could all claim narrow-minded conflict-avoiders within their ranks. The debacle behind this article took place in 1948 and grew out of a proposal to place a historical marker on the spot where Confederate cabinet member Judah Benjamin, a Jew, had been given sanctuary in the home of merchant Abram Weil in 1865. As Golden related it, the local chapter of the United Daughters of the Confederacy came up with the proposal, and he got their letter over the transom at two synagogues in town, which in turn happily put up the money. A date was set for the marker's dedication. Then one of the Daughters received an irate letter from her son in New York, which Golden quoted this way: "My pleasure in scanning the pages of my home-town [Charlotte] newspaper was interrupted this morning when I saw and read the enclosed article relative to a memorial to Judah P. Benjamin. This leaves no doubt in my mind that the United Daughters of the Confederacy have been completely 'taken in' by the editor of this 'Jewish [*sic*] Carolina Israelite' and, unless they withdraw their support of this project, will be made an unwitting tool in another scheme which is nothing else but propaganda for the Jewish race."[58]

The good local Daughters went into a tizzy, the leading Jews blanched, and the big event never came off. The marker was later quietly dedicated with a few hardy souls looking on, including the stubborn Daughter who had researched Benjamin in the first place, Golden, and the admirable Presbyterian minister who "delivered a prayer for brotherhood just as the memorial to old Judah was being firmly set into the concrete of a Charlotte sidewalk."[59]

In 1953, *Commentary* ran Golden's "A Pulpit in the South." Set in "Elizabeth, North Carolina," the short and one-sided story about the woes of a young Reform rabbi and his timid congregants was not even thinly disguised in its indictment of Golden's real-life community. Golden, as Bernstein and several others remembered, was not above using the race issue to create heroes and villains without much in the way of nuance. If a congregation fired a rabbi and the rabbi had integrationist views, then ipso facto, it was the race issue that caused the parting. And Golden was most definitely willing to include himself on the side of the righteous, as he did in this *Commentary* piece: "The few Jewish 'non-conformists' in the South such as the union organizer, the public welfare worker, or the member of the Urban League, were sources of great anxiety to the Jewish community at large, who feared the 'Gentile reaction,'" wrote Golden. "Yet somehow these very same Jewish odd-fish seem to have more contacts and friends within the white Protestant society than do the main body of Jews, for all their desperate effort to reflect the habits and the prejudices of the majority."[60]

After that piece ran, a letter to *Commentary* from Charlotte businessman and Jewish leader Morris Speizman reflected some of the worries and mixed feelings toward Golden. "Mr. Golden, instead of giving us a piece of literature, has written what citizens of the various communities here in the Southeast feel is an accusation of 'Babbittry.' Actually, we are not quite as bad as he pictures us." This was not the last time Speizman would write a letter with some variation of "Harry Golden does not speak for me."[61]

Speizman's was not a lone voice. Virtually everyone, Jews and Gentiles alike, who was interviewed about this period in his life in Charlotte recalled the days when members of the Jewish community expressed such worries. This was not an unreasonable concern, since so many of Golden's readers were introduced to Jews and blacks for the first time through his writings and would be likely to take his word as at least somewhat representative. Golden made sweeping statements about Jews constantly, usually in the time-honored tradition of a comedian who indicts entire groups by gender, race, or nationality in order to entertain his readers and listeners. Most of the time he wielded his broad brush to entertain, playing up stereotypes on all sides of an issue with a wink to readers. In a *Carolina Israelite* piece headlined "What I've Done for the Jews of the South," Golden called himself a "normalizing factor" in that he disproved the claim that "the Jews have all the money." In a later piece, "It's Wonderful to Be a Gentile," he declared, "Perhaps the great advantage to being a Gentile is that you don't have to tip much." When his subjects grew more serious, as with the *Commentary* pieces touching on anti-Semitism and Jewish assimilation, his words were sharper. And however embarrassing, combative, or off-putting his stance was to some, Golden was hitting on some tender truths. By the time these race questions were called, the Jews in

Charlotte—and elsewhere throughout the South—had a long history of working very hard in order to fit in with the majority.[62]

Jews in the South

"In the South the Jews faced a special breed of American," wrote Eli N. Evans in *The Provincials*, his rich memoir of growing up in a southern Jewish family. "Who can even imagine the strange and twisted soul of the Civil War Southerner . . . the man at war with the values of the nation and yet its most ardent defender . . . rhapsodic in defense of his institutions . . . intolerant of dissent . . . the believer in caste." The view of the southern Jew was also complicated. He was "everywhere the eternal alien; and in the South, where any difference had always stood out with great vividness, he was especially so," as W. J. Cash wrote. To racists, the Jew was tolerable (just) because he was white. Writer Thomas Dixon (his work *The Clansman* led to the 1915 film *Birth of a Nation*) told an audience in 1903 that Jews, at least, could be assimilated in America without damage, but "you can't swallow one nigger without changing your complexion."[63]

Golden knew little about the history of Jews in the South; he learned it as he became part of it. When he arrived, some 750 Jews lived in Charlotte, and most he met in his early days were not native to the city or the South. But the longer-established families he met over time in the South proudly traced their southern roots. These Jews had been working to assimilate for generations. Their ancestors were barely on the fringes of white southern society in the pre–Civil War slave trade. The trafficking in human beings was controlled by white Protestants who sold, for the most part, to their own, not to the Jewish merchant or tradesman who had little use for slave labor. Yet even in these roles Jews attracted prejudice. "A swarm of Jews, within the last ten years, has settled in nearly every Southern town," sniffed the influential critic (and designer of New York City's Central Park) Frederick Law Olmsted in 1861. "Many of them men of no character, opening cheap clothing and trinket shops . . . and engaging in unlawful trade with the simple Negroes which is found very profitable."[64]

Olmsted's words were hateful, but he was correct in one sense. There was one group of Jews who made a real mark in the antebellum South: the immigrant peddlers who walked the countryside carrying huge folding packs filled with all manner of goods such as needles and thread, petticoats, cooking pots, small toys, patent medicines, clothing, and other items for sale to rural customers. Many of these peddlers opened small stores, and a few of these grew into major department stores, including Rich's and Neiman-Marcus in the South.[65]

Golden would write his 1963 book, *Forgotten Pioneer*, to celebrate this neglected part of American history, one that even Jews tended to ignore. "Maybe because so many of the peddlers in the last hundred years have been Jews is the reason no one pays much attention to their role," he wrote. "The Jewish novelists, writers and historians who wrote about America were understandably anxious to identify with the majority." Our society, he added, "generally frowns on the commercial man and he has rarely appeared as a hero in American literature." Despite this short shrift from descendants and historians, the Jewish peddler was a valued person in rural life. Besides bringing much-needed goods and a break for those exhausted from plowing or laboriously wresting turpentine from pine trees, the visiting peddler was often respected by these God-fearing southerners for what they believed was his direct connection to the Old Testament stories they revered. Historian Rogoff calls this "southern philosemitism, that romantic religiosity that viewed Jews not as Christkillers but as People of the Book, of the Savior's very flesh and blood."[66]

By choosing one of the only niches available to him, the peddler latched onto the coping mechanisms that would well serve Jews in the South right up to Golden's day: toil at selling goods or providing services that do not threaten a Gentile workforce and transact business with blacks in ways acceptable to the white majority. "They had to acquire knowledge of local social and political relationships, to figure out who were the most likely customers and where they lived, what topics to avoid, and what aspirations to play upon," wrote historian Hasia R. Diner.[67]

Diner, Golden, Evans, and others have written about Jewish purveyors as the first to allow black customers to try on clothing before purchasing it; whites refused to buy clothes that a black person had "used" in any way. A crucial part of a Jewish merchant's survival and success was the element of trust placed in him by his white customers on this point. These patrons had to see him as being discreet and staying within certain bounds as he brokered various transactions, sometimes with individuals living far outside polite society.

In much of the South, Jews who sold to African Americans were also the first to extend credit and write insurance policies for them. In his rebuttal to the prejudice that Jewish merchants are usurious by nature, Golden argued that in the twentieth-century South they gave black men their first boost in status since Reconstruction. He did not paint this as heroism, however. "What the Jewish merchant did was completely devoid of politics, idealism, paternalism, and charity," he wrote. "He was interested only in making a profit and expanding his own business, and those motives are the very foundation upon which rests the self-esteem imported to the Negro."[68]

A Jewish southerner could be a racist, but he was not part of the poor-white vigilante crowd. As a merchant, he might well be the white person most familiar to a black customer. This didn't mean that Jews and blacks socialized. "Jews understood that such a blatant transgression of the color line would lead to serious retribution by the white community," wrote historian Clive Webb. This was a fine balance, and the small-town Jewish businessman and his family had been maintaining it for generations.[69]

Old Fears Made New

Around the time Golden arrived, the rate of anti-Semitic incidents was lower in the South than in other parts of the country, and most of the Jews he met seemed to him to be southern first, Jewish second—the opposite of his own family and boyhood friends, whom he described as Jews or Catholics from this or that neighborhood. But southern Jews were not complacent. Golden discovered quickly that old scars remained, especially those from the Leo Frank lynching in 1915 and the Scottsboro Boys case in 1931. Decades later, these events were still discussed in hushed and sometimes fearful tones.

Both cases proved that a backlash against well-off, assimilated Jewish citizens could be easily provoked. The nine defendants convicted in the trumped-up Scottsboro rape case had been represented by Samuel Lebowitz, a Jewish lawyer from New York, and much of the funding and support for the trials came from the American Communist Party. Jewish groups were also very visibly involved in protesting, covering the news story, and fundraising for the defense. This proximity of Communists and Jews had made for another occasion when anti-Semites painted all Jews with a red brush. This worsened in the years after World War II; rising panic about Communism allowed white supremacists to cast integrationists as agitators working against the racial status quo, surely an un-American activity if there ever was one. As Melissa Faye Greene put it, "If anti-Communism and segregationist extremism can be seen as two mighty rivers that met and flooded the South, then the Jew can be seen as the hapless fisherman on the far bank who has gotten tangled in his line and pulled into the torrent."[70]

One opinion poll in the late 1950s showed that southern Jews were actually more enthusiastic about desegregation than were white Gentiles, but as historian Clive Webb pointed out, the poll also found that most southern Gentiles did not know that. No wonder any mention of moving the color line even an inch was enough to make many a southern Jewish heart sink. When Golden got wind that Speizman and fellow Jewish leader Alfred Smith had approached the American Jewish Congress in 1952 expressing deep concerns that the organization's support of school desegregation could result in an anti-Semitic backlash in the South, Golden inserted himself into the matter. Apparently the Charlotte contingent had suggested to the American Jewish Congress that local dues might not be forthcoming if the national organization failed to tone down its support. Golden grandly offered to help make up the difference. The totals were not large, but his gesture was just the sort that ensured he would remain an outsider in his home community. The Charlotte Jewish leaders later also appealed to the ADL on the same point, and Speizman was commendably honest when he wrote, "Subsequent events proved that the ADL was correct in its judgment that actively supporting the desegregation cause would not result in Jewish blood being spilled throughout the South."[71]

Golden didn't detail the matter of the dues threat in his public writing, but he got at the same issue nonetheless. He described a "proprietary class" of southern Jews in unflattering terms in "Jew and Gentile in the New South: Segregation at Sundown," written for *Commentary* in 1955. His blunt description of the small group of liberals, Jews and Gentiles, who banded together in southern cities was not inaccurate but was bound to engender resentment. He managed to worry those Jews who avoided getting involved in civil rights matters, and he probably insulted some who *were* involved and who felt that he downplayed their efforts. He wrote,

> In all of the larger Southern cities, there are always a few Jews, calling themselves liberals, for whom the "racial problem" is a major concern. Together with like-minded Gentiles—Protestant clergymen, Unitarians, Quakers, labor-organizers, writers, artists, scientists (many of whom also occupy a marginal social position)—and even some members of the Jewish proprietary class, they have welded themselves into a small but cohesive, active minority. Often the membership in this group cuts across racial lines, and in some cities represents the only direct line of communication between the white and Negro races. . . . Such a liberal group may just "talk," or it may expand into an Urban League or some other well-defined educational or political organization interested in

desegregation. . . . But the Southern Jewish proprietary class is inclined to be nervous about too liberal a concern with the Negro problem on the part of fellow Jews—they call it "rocking the boat."[72]

The next year Golden contributed a piece to a group of articles on race issues in *Midstream*, a Jewish quarterly put out by the Theodor Herzl Foundation in New York. "Unease in Dixie: Caught in the Middle" considers the place of the Jew in the "troubled South." Golden again generalized about the southern Jew, depicting him as one who did not dwell overmuch on being "for" or "against" segregation: "Instead, he sees the problem as merely one of certain fixed 'jeopardies,' any one of which is serious enough to threaten his security." Golden used the example of a textile mill going out of business. "It would mean economic disaster for the entire South, but to the Jew it would mean much more. It would involve his constant fear that those who may deem themselves responsible for such a tragedy would automatically seek to shift the responsibility to the Jew."[73]

Any unhappy local Jews who saw the magazine could at first console themselves that at least the periodical was not widely available. Golden took care of that by getting permission to reprint the article, slapping on a cover with his name and *Carolina Israelite* in large type, then distributing it far and wide beyond his now approximately 10,000-name mailing list. He drew on it for an essay in his paper, and it migrated to his first book, *Only in America*, thereby guaranteeing that his subversive view was not going to be tamped down by unhappy Jews.[74]

Golden's highly readable opinion pieces did what such writing usually does: The problem—too few influential southern Jews standing up against segregation—was made to sound simpler than it actually was, especially to readers unfamiliar with the segregated South. The benign climate he felt on arrival in the early 1940s changed in the next decade. One estimate cited by Webb found that anti-Semitic material being circulated in the South increased 400 percent in the second half of the 1950s, and while Golden did not have the benefit of knowing about these results then or Webb's analysis of their effect, he certainly knew that these were more tenuous times for Jews in the South. He knew, too, that at the time he was writing these editorials criticizing the lack of Jewish leadership, brave exceptions existed.[75]

In 1954, for example, the board of directors of Rabbi Jacob M. "Jack" Rothschild's Hebrew Benevolent Congregation Temple in Atlanta (the city's Reform congregation) was horrified by Rothschild's idea of forming an in-house discussion group on racial issues. The proposal was soundly rejected, despite Atlanta's comparatively liberal atmosphere. The first Jewish chaplain to see combat in World War II, Rothschild did not shrink from any challenge. He came to be known as one of the leading clerics in the movement, a career path full of risks and trials for him, his family, and his congregation, including a dramatic 1958 bombing of the Temple.[76]

There was also Rabbi Charles Mantinband, who served three southern communities from 1946 to 1962 and made a commitment at the start of his rabbinate that he would not let race, segregation, or bigotry temper his friendships, his behavior, or what he said. Mantinband was threatened throughout his tenure in Hattiesburg, Mississippi, from 1951 to 1962. Not only were the Gentiles up in arms about Mantinband's open socializing with blacks in his home—the former mayor who was heading up the White Citizens Council was especially peeved—but members of his temple board of directors were appalled and frightened. When the board argued that the rabbi's house was an extension of temple property and therefore subject to their restrictions, Mantinband refused to conform to the segregationist status quo: "Yes, it is your house," he told the board members. "But it is my home."[77]

Close to home, the North Carolina Association of Rabbis had issued a strong statement in 1955 supporting *Brown v. Board of Education* and desegregation of schools. As Rogoff noted, the timing was significant and bold, coming just weeks after Governor Luther Hodges asked both races to continue segregation voluntarily. A year later the rabbis again called for "a swift end to segregation." Rogoff noted, "They had Christian cover. Baptist, Episcopal, Quaker, and Unitarian groups had acted, and Roman Catholics integrated their schools. In 1955 the North Carolina Council of Churches resolved 'in the spirit of Christ to realize an integrated school system.' "[78]

Golden did know these heroes—his correspondence with Mantinband was particularly charming—and he wrote about them occasionally. He also described some of the very real threats to the Jewish community, such as the discovery of a pile of unexploded dynamite meant to destroy Charlotte's Temple Beth-El in 1957, the first in a series of attempted temple bombings in the South. But he did so more often in his small newspaper, not in his pieces for national publications. He chose, instead, to highlight the case of Rabbi Seymour Atlas of Montgomery, whom he believed was discharged by his congregation because of his outspoken support of civil rights for blacks. Golden could have a tin ear when it came to disagreements within the Jewish community, which he usually held up for scrutiny only to make unflattering or funny points.[79]

He did not, for example, give as much attention as he could have to the handling of the attempted bombing in Charlotte, which created real anguish among Jews in the city and elsewhere. The board of directors of Temple Beth-El kept quiet about the attempt for eleven days, during which time five Ku Klux Klansmen were arrested in connection with a plan to dynamite a nearby school. Rabbi E. A. Levi of Charlotte's Temple Israel angrily insisted that the silence by Beth-El's leadership gave the Klan thugs assurance they could bomb with impunity. When Golden revisited the subject of synagogue bombings the next year in the *Carolina Israelite*, he did not dwell on the seriousness of these threats, instead arguing that it wasn't Jewish support of desegregation that caused them in the first place, but anti-Semitism. Jews, he sighed, could never win in this equation: "If all the Jews in the South joined the Ku Klux Klan, the anti-Semites would say, 'Aha, the Jews are smart. They have joined [the Klan] in order to mongrelize the south.' "[80]

Golden's insistence on sticking with the controversial subject of segregation and drawing attention to those who did or didn't stand up against it (without much in the way of nuance) cost him more than social marginalization. Starting in 1955 and '56, white supremacists had hit on the idea of writing Golden's advertisers and threatening to boycott them, or worse, if they stayed in the paper. The national advertisers, such as Katz's Deli, couldn't have cared less. But these threats caused many local advertisers and businesspeople, both Jews and Gentiles, to shy away.[81]

Golden turned to outsiders for help and was kept afloat by loyal supporters, including Irving Engel, president of the AJC, and philanthropist Kivie Kaplan, the tireless chairman of the NAACP's Life Membership Committee who would go on to lead the organization as president. Golden borrowed at least $20,000, much of it from constituents of these two leaders, and wrote in his autobiography that it was all paid back "with interest" when his first book came out, which was not true. He made contributions to the AJC and other groups in cash and by waiving speaking fees, but at least some of the money he received came from individuals, not their organizations, and was often treated by Golden as gifts, not loans.[82]

The interactions with Engel and Kaplan, which continued for much of Golden's life, were emblematic of his remarkable good fortune in keeping friends who had every right to resent his unreliability on matters of money. He particularly valued his friendship with Kaplan, whom he loved and admired for his generosity to workers while he was a Boston factory owner, and for his later determination to build the NAACP into the force for equality it became. The support of these friends kept him going, and advertisers returned as the paper and Golden's fame grew.

Jews and Blacks: The Bigger Picture

While Golden did his best to make a name for himself as a "disturber" down home, American Jews were becoming increasingly identified with the cause of civil rights in the 1950s. Historians and journalists often refer to the "Black-Jewish alliance" at the heart of the civil rights movement, a complex partnership that over time has become discussed in ways too tidily condensed to be accurate. It was never a firm cleaving together of two minority groups joining forces to slay Jim Crow. A better description might be "Black-Jewish joint venture," with its implied meaning of allies brought together for mutual benefit and common good but still remaining in their separate camps.

By the 1950s, circumstances for most Jews across America were better than those of blacks, by whatever measure one might choose—economic status, education level, or employment opportunities. By the same token, there were shared issues, both secular and spiritual. Both groups were minorities in a country espousing democracy that was undercut by racial apartheid and anti-Semitism. After World War II, segregation and racism did not end for African Americans who had fought for their country, and even Hitler's genocide had not routed American anti-Semitism.

In some quarters, the shared theology of the Hebrew Bible and the Christian Old Testament could reach across color and denominational lines. More obvious elements of this connection would surface later, when the Reverend Martin Luther King Jr. moved to the national and international stages and used scriptural references, often the prophetic narratives, in nearly every speech. Taylor Branch, writing about King's close relationship with brilliant theologian Rabbi Abraham Joshua Heschel in the 1960s, noted the power of this shared embrace of the Hebrew prophets. "The distinctly molded personality of the Negro preacher . . . was a cousin to the blazing psychic originals such as Jeremiah and Daniel—marked by passion, vivid images of slavery and deliverance, and arresting combinations of the earthly and sublime," wrote Branch. To both the preacher and the rabbi, "the prophetic tradition came naturally as a grounding language."[83]

It must be remembered that the common bond of slavery was more spiritual than literal. "If Jews were once slaves . . . that was in the remote past," wrote historian Milton R. Konvitz. The American blacks and Jews from Europe and Russia who grew up hearing accounts of oppression had very different pasts. Jews were by then an urban population, forced by their isolation to develop professional crafts and the kind of supportive community that American slaves were forbidden, he explained. What American blacks and Jews did share was, however, very powerful: some common enemies and a sense of unease that even when stability and safety were achieved, they could disappear in an instant.[84]

By the 1950s, several Jewish organizations that already had long histories of battling discrimination were known for more than their stands against anti-Semitism. German American Jews had formed B'nai B'rith ("children of the covenant") as a safety net for poor Jews in 1843, providing burial expenses and other emergency help for setbacks that could cripple families living in poverty. Its ADL was born in 1913 in response to the ugly climate of anti-Semitism in the country and soon took on discriminatory entities across the board, including the segregated schools that would be challenged in *Brown*. The AJC, its founders galvanized by pogroms in Russia, was founded in 1906 to protect religious and civil rights of Jews. Under the leadership of a small group of urban, reform-minded, and well-to-do German American Jews—"Jewish patricians," as historian Jonathan D. Sarna called them—the AJC raised its voice against Nazism and prejudice based on so-called racial science, which would later be a key issue in gaining rights for black Americans. The American Jewish Congress was organized in 1918 and represented the political views of Eastern European Jews in a way the earlier organizations had not.[85]

As historian Stuart Svonkin discussed in his work on the Jewish intergroup movement, after World War II these organizations energetically took up the position that anti-Semitism and other prejudices were interconnected. The AJC and the ADL generally attracted moderate Jews who had "made it," Svonkin wrote. The more Zionist American Jewish Congress "tended to attract more self-consciously progressive Jews who were dedicated to achieving social change through collective action and political protest." Small wonder that Golden corresponded with leaders of all the groups; over the course of his life he was, by his own admission, drawn to those who had "made it" and was obviously in the camp of those who marched. Yet part of Golden's self-promoted image was always that of an outsider who stood at arm's length from the national Jewish organizations. That was true, to a point. He chafed at staying with *any* institutional agenda, but when it served his purposes, he happily shared the dais and headlines with leaders of any or all of the Jewish organizations. He had easier relationships with the National Urban League, founded in 1908 by a merger of several black-interest groups, and the NAACP, founded in 1909 as part of the "new abolition movement," with Jews providing important financial and leadership support. Of all the organizations, the NAACP was the one he most consistently supported and with which he had the least friction.[86]

The motivations of these Jewish organizations that joined the civil rights movement have been subject to endless reexamination. From the earliest days of the movement, Jews were credited (or berated, depending on the observer) for fighting alongside blacks. One common explanation for the Jewish participation is that their own experience of discrimination made racism against blacks anathema. Some argue that the Jews of the Lower East Side who joined Socialist and pro-labor groups functioned as the farm teams for the later civil rights movement, or that the American Left, including Jews, was a disorganized group seeking a cause to rally around in the postwar years. Still other historians perceive the Jews joining the civil rights effort largely out of a desire to "curry favor" within liberal WASP culture. And not to be overlooked is the paranoia of anti-Semitic rants that claim that Jews were behind integration as an extension of their eternal conspiracy to seize money and power.[87]

For many Jews, it was a matter of decency and a commitment to observing *mizvot*—the commandments—such as the one forbidding Jews from standing by while another is in danger. By the 1960s, however, many of the Jewish young people involved in civil rights protests had grown up with the movement roiling around them. For them, the fight was often not connected to religious beliefs or practices; it was a demand for equality and a rejection of the stain of segregation they had inherited. They were marching "under the banner of Dr. King's Southern *Christian* Leadership Conference and were trained by the National Council of Churches," wrote Konvitz. "Their contribution to civil rights came as an expression of Christian or American idealism, not as an expression of American Judaism."[88]

As for Golden, he continually returned to an emphasis on the courage and strength that came from an ethical brotherhood, just the sort of "rational religion" Leib Goldhirsch would have recognized. "When you are worried about others, you are fearless," Golden said. "When you fight for *others*, you build an impregnable wall of security around *yourself*."[89]

CHAPTER FOUR

Brown, Flames, and Fame

It was a gently warm spring day, just after lunch. Golden finished the short piece he was writing for the June 1954 issue of the *Carolina Israelite* and heaved himself out of his squeaky desk chair. He headed out the door for the short stroll down West Trade Street to see Ken Whitsett, a Charlotte native and talented commercial artist. The men had met years earlier when Golden handled Blumenthal's advertising, and they knew many of the same newspaper types around town. Whitsett had been a cartoonist for the *Charlotte Observer* and had founded an engraving company in the early 1930s. He was articulate and could be charming. He was also a diehard segregationist. "The mention of the word 'Negroes' drove Ken haywire," wrote Golden. "Ken Whitsett had no animosity toward Jews, toward Seventh-Day Adventists, or toward subversives, for that matter. But the image of the Negro transformed him." While others puzzled over this odd friendship, wondering how it was possible that the outspoken integrationist and the man who led the segregationist group called the Patriots of North Carolina got along, the two simply ignored their biggest difference. As Golden put it, "Prudently I left the subject of race alone in his company."[1]

On this day, 17 May 1954, the subject could not be ignored.

Earlier that morning the Supreme Court had released its unanimous ruling against the long-standing "separate but equal" principle challenged in *Brown v. Board of Education of Topeka, Kansas*. Chief Justice Earl Warren told the country that separating black students from others just because of race "generates a feeling of inferiority as to their status in the community that may affect their hearts and minds in a way unlikely ever to be undone." Golden had not heard the news, but Whitsett had. "Ken rose from his chair, advanced toward me and shouted, 'You did it! You did it! You came down from the North and put the niggers up to it.' He slapped me. Only then did I realize what had happened."[2]

The shock that accompanied the slap didn't last long. Golden rushed from Whitsett's office to the Alexander Funeral Home, one of the city's oldest black-owned businesses, run by brothers Fred and Kelly Alexander. When Golden arrived, his friend Kelly was jubilant. "This is the beginning of a new life for us," he said. The two went together to see John Perry, the president of Johnson C. Smith University, where the campus echoed with singing and clapping of euphoric African American teachers and students. As the Reverend Martin Luther King Jr. would put it, the news of *Brown* felt like "joyous daybreak to end the long night of human captivity."[3]

Remarkably, while Golden and Whitsett were thereafter much more careful in their choice of conversational subjects, they remained cordial. Two years later they sat together waiting to testify before the governor's Advisory Education Committee on the Pearsall Plan, a so-called moderate solution to school desegregation that would make black students' transfer requests almost impossible, provide tuition grants to white students who wanted to leave desegregated public schools, and give communities the right to close schools as a way to avoid integrated classrooms. The plan would keep nearly every black student right where she or he was—in inferior, underfunded schools. Yet the "moderate" tag was not wrong. The tiny bit of integration allowed by the plan was considerably more than some other southern states were prepared to accept. Later, outside the statehouse, a reporter sniffed out the possibility of a good story and asked Whitsett to explain the odd alliance. "Harry Golden and I have nothing in common but our friendship," said Whitsett, ending the discussion.[4]

Brown v. Board of Education

The Supreme Court ruling that so enraged Whitsett is always called a landmark decision and a crucial turning point in the civil rights movement. It is both. It is also an often-misunderstood event. *Brown* was not nine powerful jurists announcing that racism was bad. It was not strictly a product of the 1950s. It was not a surprise. It was not clear in its edict. Depending on who described it, *Brown* fell somewhere between a Second Emancipation and a plot hatched by a tyrannical federal government—supported by Yankees, Communists, Jews, and other anti-American factions—forcing its will on southern states. Mississippi senator James O. Eastland is often quoted as calling it a "momentous crime."[5]

The high court had announced a year earlier that it would consider *Brown* and had been heading in this direction for some time. Years of painstaking work and strategizing by activists and lawyers for the NAACP's Legal Defense and Educational Fund, led by Thurgood Marshall, laid the groundwork for *Brown*. Marshall, who later became the first black Supreme Court justice, was a providential fighter for this battle. As a schoolboy he had been ordered to memorize a part of the Constitution each time he misbehaved, which was apparently often. He knew it well.[6]

Brown was a class-action lawsuit that combined five individual cases representing 200 plaintiffs in four states and the District of Columbia. *Brown* did not call just for change in classroom demographics or school-house conditions. It was a complete upheaval, more jarring than same-sex marriage or gays in the military would be in the next century. The numbers were dramatic, affecting nearly 39 percent of the 28.8 million students in America's public schools. In 1951, this meant 11.5 million children of both races in 11,173 public school districts. Those districts were in seventeen southern and border states that required segregation. Four other states left segregation up to local communities, and the custom of segregated schools was deeply entrenched in the District of Columbia.[7]

Much of the NAACP's case for *Brown* hinged on testimony by social psychologist Kenneth Clark. The AJC hired Clark, an African American, to study the effects of segregation on black children. He and wife Mamie Clark performed testing, measuring the responses of the children to both white and black dolls. In this most frequently cited of the tests, the children more often found the white dolls more attractive, and the Clarks used these and other findings to conclude that the black children were made to feel inferior by segregation. Lawyers and researchers of both races questioned the findings then, and in the 1960s black activists in particular would raise louder objections. "Why should we assume, some asked, that black people who admire white dolls . . . necessarily have low self-esteem or succumb to self-hate? . . . Studies such as Clark's, these critics declared, aimed to demonstrate the nasty consequences of white racism in American society but had the unintended effect of demeaning black people," wrote historian James T. Patterson.[8]

For all its historical heft, the opinion in *Brown* is an unvarnished bit of writing, especially the two most familiar sentences of the document read aloud by Chief Justice Earl Warren: "We conclude that, in the field of public education, the doctrine of 'separate but equal' has no place. Separate educational facilities are inherently unequal." As activist Constance Baker Motley wrote later, "The Court's decision . . . [was] sweeping, unusually straightforward, simply written. . . . [It] gained the status of a Magna Carta in the black community."[9]

Brown was a crucial event in Golden's life, in ways both predictable and not. High-profile Jewish organizations, such as the ADL and the AJC, were strong supporters of the challenge to segregated schools, and he reveled in the Jewish association with the case. More significantly, *Brown* alerted Golden to nuances of segregation and costs of racism he had not fully considered.[10]

Before the decision, Golden wrote about segregation as something atmospheric; one could not avoid breathing its fumes. Through the early 1950s, his point of view was that of a sympathetic white transplant. He chronicled things he saw in a typical day, such as restricted stores and restaurants, and the ridiculous musical chairs played on buses and trains. He observed the housing of poor blacks through his car window. He squirmed from the awkwardness of not being able to meet a black friend anywhere public for a cup of coffee. His acquaintance with black classrooms was on college campuses, not inside bleak local grade schools. He was well aware that the separate schools were unequal schools, but the Supreme Court's ruling triggered his first productive questioning of what that inequity meant to the South, to the rest of the country, and to future generations. He would now come to understand something that historian Glenda Elizabeth Gilmore summed up years later when she observed that "through *Brown*, the weight of Jim Crow's destruction fell on the backs of schoolchildren."[11]

Golden still thought a bit like the Wall Street operator he once was, figuring the winners, the losers, and the odds separating them. The more he pondered the separate schools, the more convinced he became that segregationists had made the South into the sucker in this deal. "The Southerner prides himself as a fiscal conservative," he once observed. "He is the original 'balance the budget' fellow in our society. . . . Yet he has spent fortunes maintaining two school systems, each of them inadequate. He established colleges for Negroes to maintain a segregated society." The deal was not good for blacks and not good for the South. "After he spent all that money, he would offer the Negro the chance to become either a preacher or a teacher in the Negro ghetto," Golden wrote. And if the Negro didn't want to preach or teach, he left. The result was a debilitating drain of money, brains, and progress from the South. Life outside the South, away from family, meant facing more subtle discrimination. It might not be pleasant, but the odds of finding work and safety were much better.[12]

At the time Golden pointed to this black exodus from the South, he had no idea of the size of the migration. Few people did, not even those African Americans who were involved. When Nicholas Lemann published *The Promised Land* in 1991, he put the startling numbers in context. It was, he wrote, one of the largest and most rapid mass internal movements of people in history. Between 1910 and 1970, more than 6 million black Americans left the South; 5 million moved after 1940 when cotton picking became mechanized. "In sheer numbers," Lemann wrote, "It outranks the migration of any other ethnic group—Italians or Irish or Poles—to this country." This historical migration, wrote Isabel Wilkerson in her epic 2010 book *The Warmth of Other Suns*, "would transform urban America. . . . It would force the South to search its soul and finally to lay aside a feudal caste system."[13]

Monday Finally Comes

Brown was changing the work and responsibilities of thoughtful news writers all over the country. It put special pressure on the mainstream press in the South to cover this issue fairly and thoroughly. Even more difficult was the question of how to do so without losing advertising or putting staff in danger. A year before *Brown*, Ralph McGill published his editorial in the *Atlanta Constitution* headlined, "One Day It Will Be Monday." He urged readers to face the reality that the court was going to hand down a ruling outlawing the dual school system of the South and that no amount of pretending otherwise could prevent it. "So, somebody, especially those who have a duty so to do, ought to be talking about it calmly, and informatively," he wrote. What today reads like a stating-the-obvious, buck-passing editorial was combustible material in 1953. It brought a barrage of hate mail and threats to the paper and to McGill.[14]

All southern newspapermen, including Golden's poker buddies at the *Charlotte News* and the *Charlotte Observer*, needed access to reliable reporting and the safety in numbers that came with a cooperative news effort. Those big-city newspapers outside the South with resources to cover the story did not yet grasp the importance of what was unfolding, nor were those papers widely circulated among southerners. Wire services could not cover the sprawling issue on their own. Even the most responsible southern newspapers were essentially operating in a war zone when reporting on this topic. Harry Ashmore took on the problem in 1954 by launching the Southern Education Reporting Service. Ashmore's book of research on the southern school system, *The Negro and the Schools*, came out the same year; his work on both efforts was funded by the Ford Foundation.[15]

To put out the reporting service's monthly *Southern School News*, Ashmore brought in nineteen top newspaper reporters and editors and adapted the wire-service model to the needs of the segregated South. His smartest move was to convince Tom Waring of the *Charleston News and Courier*, a member of a respected Charleston family and opponent of desegregation, to serve as vice chairman of the board. Virginius Dabney of the *Richmond Times-Dispatch* served as chairman. Ashmore's task was a daunting one that could have ended his promising career—or put him in the losing position of pleasing no one on any side of the issue. Golden was sympathetic when Ashmore described his role as "running for sonofabitch without opposition."[16]

Charlotte News editor Pete McKnight was tapped to lead the effort—another wise choice. His first move was to "throw out all adjectives and adverbs" and keep the focus on the facts of race news. The *Southern School News* was a fresh, bold idea, and for the next decade it delivered the support and reliable information its creators had in mind. Yet no black reporters were hired. The board did include blacks, but the press release announcing the new service intentionally omitted the race of any board members.[17]

A memorable voice raised in opposition to *Brown* was that of James Jackson Kilpatrick, editor of the *Richmond News-Leader* and another of Golden's unlikely friends. Kilpatrick was one of a very small number of anti-integration editorialists who wrote well and constructed arguments with rhetoric beyond the usual white-supremacist sputum. He was, Golden said, a man he had always wished was on the same side. Kilpatrick's brand of segregation reflected the city in which he lived and wrote. Richmond, like Charlotte, escaped much of the racial turmoil of other southern cities, and in similar ways. "By supporting the local African American elite, Richmond's white elite made concessions without undermining the forces that maintained strong patterns of segregation and privilege," wrote historian Daniel Horowitz.[18]

Kilpatrick's first reaction was that the South had no choice but to accept *Brown*, however misguided it was. The key, he believed, was for the Supreme Court to come back with a plan allowing states and municipalities the widest possible discretion in carrying it out. Kilpatrick became a hero among opponents of segregation when he dredged up the idea of "interposition," a hoary concept that allowed states to refuse to follow federal mandates under certain circumstances. Empowering states to face down the feds sounded good to segregationists, but the idea had no legal legs in mid-twentieth-century America.[19]

By the late 1950s he and Golden were corresponding regularly: friends in private and opponents on newsprint. They delighted their fellow newsmen by going head-to-head at a state editorial writers' conference, each arguing his take on integration. "Your bout with Kilpatrick . . . some said it was the greatest search for absolute truth since the Council of Nicea. They may be right," wrote *Charlotte News* editor Cecil Prince in a letter to Golden. Like Whitsett, Kilpatrick made no bones about his seemingly contradictory admiration of Golden. He once sent his $2 subscription fee for the *Carolina Israelite* with a note saying, "Here's my $2. Half of what you write is good, the other half drives me crazy." Golden kept the letter on the wall near his desk.[20]

While the newspaper folks hustled around, trying to figure ways to deal with the story, much of the rest of the South was quiet. "I thought this silence was because the South was stunned," wrote Golden in his autobiography. "But I was wrong. The South was mustering its forces. . . . The leaders of the South created a vacuum, and into the vacuum came the white supremacists, the racists, the White Citizens Councils, the Ku Kluxers, a sad price to pay for maintaining the Southern way of life."[21]

Golden did not yet acknowledge the extent to which leadership embraced white supremacy; that observation would come from him in the 1960s. Scholarship advanced by historian Clive Webb half a century later argued that highly visible members of these racist groups were the "perfect foil for a segregationist leadership seeking public respectability." By comparison to the extremists, those in power seemed moderate, even as they blocked integration of any kind and protected systemic racism. In the time of *Brown*, Golden painted marauding sheet-wearers as greater and more effective villains than those leaders actually in power. He was correct in one important sense: Sensational images of such extremists (usually in full Klan regalia) became ubiquitous symbols of southern bigotry.[22]

More Law, but No More Leadership

After *Brown* came the so-called *Brown II* in 1955. This was the Supreme Court's attempt to help states figure out how to desegregate schools "with all deliberate speed." Now Golden took to reminding his readers—especially those in the North—that changing bad law was gratifying and necessary, but it was up to state-level leaders to make it work. Southerners were looking to their governors and legislatures for guidance, "but it did not materialize for even a single moment," Golden said. When *Brown II* came down, there was another chance for leadership, and this time the failure was even worse, he thought. Most southern governors responded by saying they would find a way out of the ruling. A disgusted Golden wrote,

> At the moment the situation stands something like this:
> 1. The Supreme Court decision will stand.
> 2. The Governors of the South say No.
> 3. The public school system must be preserved at all costs.
> How these three points will eventually dissolve themselves into each other is not quite clear, but it will take far more wisdom than the Governors have shown to date.[23]

Golden's criticism did not end with recalcitrant governors. He felt that the effect of *Brown* was lessened in part due to flabby discussion by liberals who wanted to sweep all manner of social ills into the same pile. In an argument not unlike one voiced by some of his racist opponents, Golden condemned the use of the buzzwords "social equality," which he described as a construct "about as real as the ghost I saw at a spiritual séance some years ago." He argued that no race or nationality has real equality within its ranks. *Brown*, he wrote, was about racism and equal *opportunities*; it was not going to erase societal divisions built on class divisions or plain old snobbery. The present-day racial equivalents of "lace-curtain Irish" looking down at the "shanty Irish" would continue, and lumping such tribal barriers in with the huge disparity in public education was distracting and damaging to the civil rights cause, he declared.[24]

Golden's writing and speeches on the immorality of Jim Crow and its dispiriting hold on daily life now provided the first look at this injustice for many in his white American audience. He began to gain a larger following and became a stronger advocate for African Americans. He was focusing on practical, achievable, and therefore incremental progress. Golden would soon be regarded as a level-headed commentator by a growing group of magazine editors and politically active liberals, as well as an entertaining pundit to mainstream audiences who saw him on shows hosted by Dave Garroway, Steve Allen, and, later, Jack Paar and Johnny Carson. Yet within a decade this shift would bring him scorn from Jewish intellectuals in particular, who decried him as too facile, and then dismissal by more militant blacks tired of tolerating the pace set by whites and moderate blacks in the movement.

Friends of the Mind

The news fraternity and political backrooms provided Golden with camaraderie, status, and material. The forming of the Charlotte-Mecklenburg Council on Human Relations in 1955 cemented some of his important relationships, including one with the group's founder, respected physician Raymond Wheeler, a steady voice against racism in the community. Golden also became closer to the Alexander brothers. Fred Alexander went on to be the first black elected to the Charlotte City Council in 1965, and in 1974 he became the first black member of the North Carolina senate since Reconstruction. For forty years, Kelly Alexander was a force in the local and state NAACP, and in 1983 he was elected head of the national chapter.[25]

Golden's finer sensibilities were served by the Philosophy Club of Charlotte. Formed in 1912, with Frank P. Graham among the founders, the Philosophy Club was made up of "presidents of the universities, the leading clergymen of the city, and those of us who do not wince when called intellectuals," said Golden. Every month a different member took the floor and, uninterrupted, presented a paper on a subject ranging from constitutional law to religion and evolution. Once the presentation was finished, discussion and debate could commence. Golden was brought into the fold in 1954. The rumor was that Judge John J. Parker told his fellow club members, "We need another member. We need a Jew. I propose Harry Golden."[26]

Golden spoke on Jewish topics more than once. A paper presented in the winter of 1955 carried the lofty title of "Judaism and Its Influence on the Evolution of the Human Race." In a letter that became a draft of the paper, Golden wrote, "Anti-Semitism, is an instinctive aggression against the confines of Christian ethics—actually it is an assault upon Christianity." Ensuring animated discussion, he added, "I do not believe Christianity would survive ten years after the elimination of the Jew. Because the Jew represents the basic tie with civilization."[27]

In 1957 and again in 1964, the club asked Golden to present on the race question. He was very cautious the first time, stating that the only sensible course was for the South to follow the law of the land in regard to segregated schools. (It was three years after *Brown*.) The listeners were polite but did not engage in discussion. When he spoke on the subject to the club in 1964, he was blunt and forceful about the "evil" of segregation and its cost to the South. "The reaction was one I will never forget. Each man rose and thanked me for my views."[28]

Golden had friends outside his writerly circle, too; the closest were Dave and Bea Wallas; for a time Marion Cannon, connected to the Cannon textile fortune; and Anita Stewart Brown, his companion in Charlotte from the late 1950s until his death. Among the first "Lady Agents" to work for Eastern Air Lines during World War II, Brown married and was widowed, then returned to the airline to work for another thirty years. She took Golden's frequent calls as he planned trips to speeches around the country. "We became telephone pals," she remembered. "He started calling me just to talk, especially when I was working from three to midnight." She took to reading the *Carolina Israelite*—"I kept it on my lap at work." After two years of phone chats, they met in person on 15 July 1958; Brown quoted the date without hesitation during an interview more than forty years later. When she showed up at his book-signing at Ivey's Department Store and introduced herself, "He looked at me like I was from Mars," laughed Brown. "Then he realized who I was and said, with a big smile, 'Oh, for God's sake!'" The two became a couple, with Brown accompanying him to speeches and meetings around the South. She quickly discovered that it was much better all around if she handled both navigation and driving. When a bomb threat was made during one of Golden's speeches at Belmont Abbey, Golden and Brown stayed put while others made for the exits. It wasn't bravery on her part, she insisted. Golden wasn't leaving, and "I just thought 'if something happens to him, it will just have to happen to me too.'"[29]

At first glance they were an odd couple. Brown, in her fifties when they met, was Old South Presbyterian, a direct descendant of early settlers of the county, and a former sorority girl and graduate of Charlotte's Queens College. She had the bearing and manners of her generation and background. She also knew how to have fun. She had an appreciation for Golden's earthy jokes, and when interviewed at age eighty-five, she still made herself laugh when recalling his better lines. "He wrote for the people, regular people, like Shakespeare did," she said. Brown shared Golden's views on segregation but let him do the talking about that, and pretty much any other subject. She and Tiny knew about each other. "There were *differences*," was the extent of Brown's dignified summation of the separated couple. Tiny's observations of Golden's Charlotte companion can only be imagined.[30]

Soon after they began spending time together, Brown invited Golden to her family home for dinner. "I told them not to make a commotion," she said. "But when he got there—late, he'd gotten lost—Mother flew out ahead of me to meet him. She was so excited she called him 'Mr. Goldman.'" Golden was unperturbed by the mistake and pleased to be so warmly welcomed. Brown remembered every detail of the evening. "Mother looked so pretty that night," she recalled in her gentle drawl. "She had this lovely dress with thin straps." He charmed the family with stories all through dinner. "He could, and did, talk to anybody," she said. "He softened people up."[31]

Dave Wallas, "a liberal's liberal," as his son put it, was a self-educated Jewish Brooklynite who moved with his wife, Beatrice, to Charlotte in the 1930s. After his father's death interrupted his education and sent him into the work world as a young adult, Wallas became a voracious reader both at home and while on the road as a traveling salesman. Wallas and Golden would talk into the night, covering ancient history and the latest desegregation rulings—with many stops in between. Bea Wallas, a graduate of Hunter College, was the glue for the family and their lively social life, raising three children while taking on a dizzying number of civic events and issues. She encouraged Golden to use their home as his own, and he took her up on this generosity often.[32]

Dave Wallas spent Monday through Friday most weeks on the road selling for White Swan Uniforms, later taking up other women's clothing lines. He wrote Golden, scrawling his observations and thoughts in looping cursive on letterhead from White Swan and various motels. In one salty letter, Wallas bemoaned the dullness of the town where he was staying and joked to his friend that having ruled out going to a movie or other racier activities, he might as well read some Jung.[33]

Wink Locklair

If there is one experience in Golden's life that demonstrates his extraordinary talent for friendship, it was his relationship with Wriston "Wink" Locklair, a talented writer in his twenties who covered the arts for the *Charlotte Observer*. Golden shared Locklair's love of opera and literature, and they both followed the theater world and cultural life of New York City. Locklair, who had studied boxing as well as piano and dance, could appreciate another fellow with eclectic interests.[34]

Golden and others in their circle were shocked when Locklair was arrested in a police "sting" raid in 1955 as an alleged member of a "homosexual circle." Locklair was immediately fired from the newspaper before any facts were known and was sentenced to five years in prison. Questionable police work leading to Locklair's arrest certainly could have been challenged. But the horror of a public scandal dragging on for his family was great enough that Locklair chose to quietly go from the local holding cell to the state penitentiary in Raleigh within the month. Golden wrote Locklair immediately: "I extend the hand of friendship to you—now and always." He was frank with his friend: "I was terribly shocked first at the news that you were involved in it, and then even more shocked at the severity of the sentence." When Golden asked the presiding judge in the case what he was thinking in sending a young man accused of being homosexual to prison for five years, he encountered unexpected venom: "You Jews did it. You Jews prescribed stoning. All I did was cut down the severity. I gave him a break," the judge snapped at his questioner.[35]

While in prison Locklair read constantly and wrote short stories. One of the three letters he was allowed to send each week often went to Golden. The humiliation of prison has embittered and ruined men tougher than Locklair. It surely took its toll on him. But reserves of humor and his talent as a writer helped sustain him. Locklair was eligible for parole within the first year, and his record as a prisoner ensured his release—if he had a job waiting. The one person who stepped forward was Golden, who created a position at the *Carolina Israelite* for a writer/collections agent. The necessary work could be done, he wrote the parole board, from Locklair's home "under the eyes of his loved ones." After serving nine months, Locklair came home. "You are doing the Christian thing," Locklair's mother told Golden. "The humor did not escape me, neither did the sincerity nor the compliment involved," Golden wrote to a friend.[36]

Locklair's highly disciplined approach to work served him well. His time at the *Carolina Israelite* was short lived, though productive. A neatly typed tally sheet dated 14 April 1956 showed debts collected from nine businesses, yielding a $97 paycheck. He moved to New York City (living just a few doors away from Golden's childhood tenement), took up the first of his writing jobs, and quickly wrote to Golden: "I feel like I've known Delancey Street all my life! The freedom, the peace of mind, the relief, the feeling of doing a creative job again—all this is wonderful." Locklair never stopped writing about the arts and continued to do so with spirit and skill for various respected publications. He kept it up even when his career path took him to a prestigious post as assistant to the president and director of public relations at the Juilliard School, where by all accounts he was indispensable, until his death from a heart attack at age fifty-nine in 1984.[37]

Golden was not afraid to risk public disapproval or exposure of his own prison past by hiring Locklair. He wrote to Charlotte police chief Frank Littlejohn about offering Locklair a job and made a veiled reference to "my experience in this wide world" that had acquainted him with the deep prejudices toward criminals charged with sexual offenses. "I have seen the time when hatchet murderers and bank robbers receive candy, flowers and marriage proposals while in Sing Sing, but let a fellow rub up against a girl in the subway and the mob is ready to kill him." Littlejohn, knowing Golden's felonious secret, would have understood the reference to his "experience."[38]

For all his support of Locklair and his family, Golden did not tell any of them about his own time in prison. When that story broke, Locklair's mother and sister were among the first to call Golden. Wink could not get through—the telephone lines were jammed—but he wrote, "While I never did get in my call, you *did* know how I felt. I thought about the episode for days, and reflected on the countless times the fear of exposure must have gone through your mind."[39]

Golden sometimes referred to homosexuals in disparaging ways, but homosexuality was just another human condition in his mind, not an illness or moral flaw. When a middle-aged lesbian overdosed on heroin years before at the Hotel Markwell, Golden thought fast and told the investigating reporter from the *New York Daily News* that the "former Miss Wyoming" was found dead in her room. "I picked Wyoming because it was a small state far away and they probably wouldn't bother to check."[40]

Observing Locklair's precarious place in society moved Golden to see homophobia as racism in a different guise. He couldn't knowledgeably refute the wrongheaded belief that homosexuality was a psychological disorder and sometimes "curable," but he didn't accept it either. He wrote about the then-taboo subject by referencing literature, plays, or movies and briskly dismissed the homophobia of the times. The 1956 release of the film version of *Tea and Sympathy* was one such occasion. The story line, drawn from the play of the same title by Robert Anderson, involves a sensitive prep-school student tormented by his classmates as "Sister Boy" and driven to attempt suicide. The tea and lifesaving sympathy—and love—come from the unhappy wife of his housemaster. Golden observed that while it had taken "courage and wisdom" to perform the play on Broadway in 1953, the most serious issue was removed from the movie. "The problem is NOT the boy who is unjustly, or should I say, erroneously, labeled a homosexual. . . . The problem is the boy who IS a homosexual, and what to do about him, and for his continued creativity; and what to do about our attitudes, laws, remedies." Golden felt that because the film focused on the unfairness of unjust labeling, it also implied that when true, the labeled person *deserved* his distress. In an even more unusual discussion for the time, Golden went on to bluntly liken homophobia to the shibboleths about masturbation and sex that were accepted as truth during his boyhood on the Lower East Side.[41]

Rosa Parks and the Boycott

There was another arrest that drew Golden's ire, and this one reverberated far beyond the South: that of Rosa Parks for her refusal to go to the back of the bus. Her story is one of an inspiring victory, and the basic facts are well known: In 1954, a tired seamstress refused to leave a "white" seat on a bus in Montgomery, Alabama, and was promptly arrested. Blacks in the city boycotted the segregated transit service, and their nonviolent protest was so effective that it inspired a generation of activists.

The story is sometimes framed as a spontaneous action, but it was not. While Parks did decide on the spot to refuse the driver's order to move, the case resulting from her action was a deliberate result of careful planning and action by a serious activist. "Journalists and some historians have taken too literally her ironic remark that she refused to move because she was tired," a *New York Times* editorial noted in 1994. "She was weary, but not politically naïve about segregation and the need to confront it. . . . Long before she got on that bus, Rosa Parks had been touched with the spirit of rebellion through her contacts with the National Association for the Advancement of Colored People and the Brotherhood of Sleeping Car Porters." The editorial noted that Parks knew E. D. Nixon, the brotherhood's local representative, and Montgomery attorney Clifford Durr and his wife, Virginia Foster Durr.[42]

The Durrs were a force to be reckoned with, a white couple of standing who worked for the civil rights cause. They posed enough of a threat that the powerful U.S. senator James Eastland from Mississippi accused them of ties to the Communist Party and hauled them in for a hearing. The fact that Justice Hugo Black was married to Virginia Durr's sister ensured that their appearance made headlines. Virginia Durr made a point of calmly pulling out a compact and powdering her nose while being accused. In a review of a biography of Virginia, writer Rosellen Brown observed, "While the majority of Alabamians considered Virginia and Clifford Durr traitors, not heroes, they represented to many of us the best of the white South, its native strength: they were sensible, outspoken, committed and only accidentally heroic."[43]

Interestingly, Durr, "relegated to near pariah status since her open support of the bus boycott," as historian Raymond Arsenault put it, had little use for Golden. In a letter to a friend, Durr called Golden "a phony, a sincere phony" who "says everything is rosy and segregation can be destroyed by tricks."[44]

Even the attempt by the *New York Times* in 1994 to portray Parks with more accuracy grossly understates her activism. She was not "touched by the spirit of rebellion" but was a seasoned soldier in the fight for civil rights. As Jeanne Theoharis's revealing biography, *The Rebellious Life of Mrs. Rosa Parks*, makes clear, Parks and her husband, Raymond, were effective, brave radicals before and after her famous bus ride. The action by Parks was exactly the sort of test case the NAACP wanted to fight. When Nixon and Clifford Durr bailed Parks out of jail, they asked a tough question. Would she go to court and fight the charge? Parks said yes. Within a day, the news spread through the black community. Parks went to court and was convicted.[45]

The Montgomery Improvement Association, a group of African American clergy and activists led by the Reverend Ralph Abernathy, met the night of 4 December 1954 to plan a boycott of the public bus service in order to draw attention to the case and make what today seem like very minor demands—decent treatment aboard buses and hiring of black drivers. An intelligent, well-spoken leader was needed to take a central role, someone young and without the battle scars and baggage of his elders. The young preacher who was asked to take on the leadership of the group and to address that night's meeting was the Reverend Martin Luther King Jr. The room erupted in shouts as King's poetic words captured the century of righteous anger that had led his listeners to their seats: "There comes a time when people get tired of being pushed out of the glittering sunlight of life's July and left standing amid the piercing chill of an alpine November. There comes a time." It is astonishing to realize that King, then just twenty-six, was delivering remarks he wrote hurriedly only a short time before.[46]

The next day, 5 December, the buses were empty of the usual 30,000 black riders. The scenario was the same the next day, and the next. The boycott lasted 381 days. As Taylor Branch wrote, "Only the rarest and oddest of people saw historical possibilities in the bus boycott." Of course Golden would pull for the bus boycott; it was a homegrown effort that had no earthly reason to succeed. The action appealed to him with its strategy of turning commonplace activity into a powerful object lesson. He had the heart of a union man, and this was a strike. And it was a strike that defeated the bosses. His own protest against transit segregation was brief. "One night I resolved to sit in the colored section," he recalled. "The bus driver saw me in his mirror and yelled, 'Hey, mister, there's a seat up here.' I said, 'I'm sitting here.' When I didn't move, he started to revile me and kept up a blue streak until I got off. . . . I doubt now that I proved anything except my ability to desecrate a hallowed custom." In the end, the question forced by Parks and her refusal to give up her seat on a bus went all the way to the Supreme Court. In 1956, the Court ruled that the segregation on Montgomery's buses was illegal.[47]

Highlander Folk School

Golden and Parks shared a common experience; both were veterans of the Highlander Folk School in Monteagle, Tennessee, a remarkable place for many reasons, beginning with the number of civil rights activists it attracted and created. Parks attended a workshop there six months before her historic refusal on the Montgomery city bus. Golden visited there for the first time in the summer of 1958, just before his first book, *Only in America*, came out.[48]

Highlander was cofounded in 1932 by Myles Horton, who grew up in the poor South and spent his life beating back poverty by training teachers, organizers, and leaders who could bring about change in their own communities. It was inspired by folk schools in Denmark that brought adults together for learning and community; it came into being when a retired teacher and activist named Lillian Johnson donated her farm on the Cumberland Plateau in southeastern Tennessee.[49]

At first Highlander focused on training union organizers, but it had expanded into civil rights issues by 1953. It pioneered "Citizen Education Programs" led by Septima Poinsette Clark. This African American educator perfected methods of rapid literacy training during her forty years of activism, which began in a makeshift classroom for poor black children in Charleston, South Carolina. Clark later recalled a day in Camden, Alabama, where she stood near a line of black citizens waiting to register to vote. When a white official started to make an X for one man's name, the would-be voter said, "You don't have to make an X for me, because I can write my own name." The astonished official, Clark remembered, said, "My God, them niggers done learned to write their names."[50]

When her 1962 autobiography, *Echo in My Soul*, written with Legette Blythe, was about to go to press, Clark asked Golden to write a foreword, which he promptly did. He recalled her arrest at Highlander in 1959, when "it took twenty sheriffs and a half a dozen district attorneys and even more judges as well as two governors to keep Septima Clark from teaching the next day." He was exaggerating the number of law enforcement figures, but not Clark's bravery. A scholar later characterized Golden's contribution as "reminiscent of the practice of having white abolitionists authenticate nineteenth-century slave narratives." (As Golden might put it: "*Gurnisht helfen . . .* Nothing helps.") Clark knew what she was doing; the endorsement of a bestselling author was a wise marketing move.[51]

Highlander was also one of the places at which the civil rights movement's soundtrack came together. Zilphia Horton, wife of Myles Horton, understood the powerfully moving character of Appalachian folk music. Woody Guthrie and Pete Seeger had visited in 1940, and Seeger was quickly hooked, returning many times. Accounts describing the genesis of "We Shall Overcome" as the movement's anthem credit Zilphia and folksinger Guy Carawan with passing the song to Seeger, who performed it at Highlander during a visit from the Reverend Martin Luther King Jr.[52]

When Golden wrote in the *Carolina Israelite* of his intention to speak at Highlander in the summer of 1958 on the same bill as Eleanor Roosevelt, a horrified James Kilpatrick fired off a letter from his desk at the *Richmond News-Leader* begging his friend to get out of the engagement any way he could: "Get sick, Harry. I urge you. Get sick!" Highlander, wrote Kilpatrick, was "set up by Communists, financed by Communists, and as recently as last year, one of its 'integration workshops' was attended by a number of known and avowed Communists." Roosevelt's support was not enough to remove the pink stain of the school. "She is immune in a way, I assure you, that you are not," Kilpatrick wrote. So Golden worked the phones and fired off telegrams asking wise friends for advice, including insiders at the Anti-Defamation League. He was assured it was safe to go if he made clear in any remarks that he was not a Communist. Even if other advisors had been as negative as Kilpatrick, Golden would have been sorely tempted by Roosevelt's presence. He wrote back to his friend and thanked him, assuring Kilpatrick that he would be sure to "deliver a blistering attack on communism" while there. While in the company of Roosevelt, Golden was delighted to hear her say that Horton was actually taking a chance inviting *her* to Highlander, given her controversial support of equal rights for all races. (Golden may have wanted a chance to redeem himself with the former First Lady following an encounter a couple of years earlier when she spoke at a "Bonds for Israel" meeting. Chatting after the event, Golden joked that she must be rushing back to New York to "prepare for Passover." Roosevelt frostily replied that she was "rushing back to New York to prepare for my Christian Easter." Typically Golden wrote about his gaffe in the *Carolina Israelite* under the headline, "I Shall Never Do This Again.")[53]

Golden timed his own arrival on 17 June 1958 for just a few hours before the former First Lady's flight was due into Chattanooga. He took Horton's suggestion that he meet for a chat with journalist John N. Popham, whom Golden knew casually. In his years as a *New York Times* reporter "Johnny" Popham's coverage of southern leaders' efforts to shut Highlander down had been accurate—and therefore invaluable in fundraising. The thick-accented Popham, a Virginia native and an extraordinarily colorful character, was the first reporter—and for some time the only one—to cover the South full time for a mainstream northern newspaper. Enormous changes were afoot, but Popham believed the influential leaders in the South would face the fact that desegregation was inevitable. His premature confidence and closeness to players on both sides of the fight led some media historians to see Popham as being too soft on the South. But they under-value both the unprecedented access gained by his personal style and the solid foundation his reporting provided as the movement took off and the nation's newspapers scrambled to cover it.[54]

It all happened just the way Golden hoped: He climbed into the car with Roosevelt, and the two talked nonstop during the slow, fifty-mile ride from the airport to Highlander. It was a cherished experience in Golden's life, and he wrote often about his conversation with Roosevelt, polishing the story over time. But a hurriedly typed note (quoted here with the errors of the original) that he dashed off for himself to preserve the feelings of the day was the most genuine:

> As I sat with Mrs. Roosevelt during this fifty mile drive I thought about this amazing woman. Some months ago she had been to Moscow and interviewed Khrushchev, she had entertained and honored by kings and queens, and honored by the leaders of the world, and there she was, well-past middle-age traveling a hot and dusty Tennessee road to make a speech and sit on a pine bench and eat off a paper plate and make a speech to a handful of Negro and white students and a handful of hard-working and much-harassed teachers and social workers.[55]

Golden talked for an hour and a half to the Highlander group, and he was entertaining and impassioned. But the speech was significant for reasons other than his delivery and the widespread attention it got him when quoted in Highlander's annual report. Highlander gave Golden a stamp of authenticity as an activist. (It worked in reverse in Parks's case; she lent Highlander greater legitimacy after she became an icon of the movement.) He was now a respected spokesman, teacher, and something of a seer. That day he warmed up the audience with a few jokes at the expense of the segregationist crowd. After the laughs tapered off, he delivered a serious message that contained a theme he returned to often until the end of his life, that of health care inequities between blacks and whites: "What do they mean when they talk about racial segregation? Do you think they mean a Negro child going or not going to a white school? Nonsense. Nonsense. . . . It means, my friends, *death*. . . . Nine Negro women die in childbirth in the South to every one white woman who dies in childbirth. That is what segregation means. . . . It means death." Citing the greater frequency of tuberculosis cases among blacks, Golden continued: "That is what racial segregation is. Don't let them kid you about the social classes. The Negro is not intruding when he moves into a better neighborhood. He is escaping; he is escaping from death."[56]

Visitors came from around the world to observe and learn at Highlander, including government officials sent by the State Department. Southern leaders were not impressed by that distinction, and the state of Tennessee spent years trying to shut the place down, leaning heavily on claims that it was a Communist front. Bogus charges of illegal alcohol sales were ultimately used to make the case. When Grundy County sheriff Elson Clay barred the doors in 1959, Horton famously declared, "You can padlock a building, but you can't padlock an idea." The state succeeded in revoking Highlander's charter and seizing the property in 1960, but the operation moved to Knoxville and kept going.[57]

Black Health Care

Golden's 1958 Highlander speech on black health tied the issue to him more publicly, but he had been arguing for years that decent medical care was a civil right. Since *Brown*, however, he was more often quoted on the inevitability and wisdom of school desegregation. He was firmly insistent that medical care *and* schools must be unassailable priorities in order for the South to move forward. It was a view both moral and practical. Denying health care to some Americans was an abomination. Opening taxpayer-supported schools to all citizens was a manifestation of discrimination that *could* be fixed.

This belief was even more firmly fixed in his mind after one particular event. "A week or so ago I visited the home of Dorothy Counts, the 15-year-old Negro girl of Charlotte, North Carolina, who had been forced to leave the all-white school to which she had been assigned; due to an ordeal of uninterrupted harassment and violence," he wrote in the *Nation* in 1958. The student's father, the Reverend Herman L. Counts, a member of the faculty of Johnson C. Smith University, showed Golden the list of influential Charlotte residents who had called to express support and concern. If these people had spoken up, Golden wrote, "they might very well have settled the matter for at least one of the most progressive cities of the South." Golden never forgot the feeling of looking from the list back to Counts's face.[58]

Golden was impressed by the answer he got when he asked Thurgood Marshall, at the time head of the NAACP Legal Defense Fund, why the integration of public schools was chosen as the main issue to take on segregation in court, instead of health care. "Marshall . . . agreed that forceful action in the courts and in public protest would have resulted in wide gains in health facilities for Negroes . . . but he said the idea of a second-class citizenship would have remained. 'We are a school-oriented society. If we desegregate schools of America, the whole pattern of racial desegregation will inevitably collapse.'"[59]

Before Highlander, Golden raised the subject of health care more often in speeches rather than in his newspaper, usually pointing out the greater likelihood of tuberculosis and the higher rate of black women dying in childbirth. When he did begin to press the issue in print, he compared statistics from New York City to North Carolina's, flatly blaming the southern state's separate-and-unequal medical facilities as the cause for its statistically higher mortality rate for black births. In fact, black infants died at higher rates than whites across America, but holding up his adopted state's medical statistics next to those of the Yankee metropolis in a 1953 article was a far more effective indictment than a wordy moral argument that race (and racism) should not determine the survival rate of a child. After Highlander, Golden pursued the issue often in print: "In facilities, training, and supervision, Negro hospitals are far below the quality and adequacy of white hospitals," he wrote in the *Carolina Israelite*. He zeroed in on a detail that went largely ignored even in liberal circles: "Why doesn't the Negro help himself? First of all, [as a Negro doctor] he is banned from 99 percent of the white medical associations, nor is he permitted in any of the training sessions of specialties."[60]

Now Golden was hitting close to home. In his time, the few black physicians in the area could admit patients only to Good Samaritan Hospital in Charlotte. Good Sam opened in 1891 as the country's first hospital exclusively for black patients, and until Golden spoke out, it was routinely held up as an example of the city's egalitarian character—even by some who regarded themselves as pro-integration. He shamed those doctors: "The Hippocratic Oath doesn't mention black or white," he reminded them in 1962.[61]

In 1960 as national broadcast and print media discovered the lunch-counter sit-ins protesting segregated restaurants, Golden urged students (such as those in the just-formed Student Non-Violent Coordinating Committee, or SNCC) to do the same at hospitals. He didn't need to name names. "Even the most progressive of Southern communities have had case histories where an emergency case involving a Negro was turned away at the [white] hospital entrance because of segregation laws. . . . I have no fear of libeling anyone when I say the 'separate but equal' doctrine is a laughing matter when applied to Negro hospitals." A few picket lines made up of pregnant black women "many of them in their ninth month," would make the point, he said.[62]

Black publications, including the *Chicago Daily Defender*, cited Golden as an authority on these health disparities. Being black in a segregated state meant that "you die in greater numbers, at a younger age, and you die more frequently from diseases like tuberculosis. . . . Syphilis and diabetes, the other partners of poverty, will also kill you in greater numbers than they kill anyone else."[63]

One part of the health care divide that particularly bothered Golden was the involuntary sterilization of poor women. The eugenics movement had lost much of its appeal after the Third Reich took it up, but well after World War II its view of help-the-fittest-survive continued in some quarters. Until an exemplary series titled "Against Their Will" was published by the *Winston-Salem Journal* in 2002, few people knew about North Carolina's participation in this practice. The capsule summary used to promote the series was dramatic on its own: "North Carolina's eugenics law, passed in 1929 and rewritten in 1933, allowed sterilizations for three reasons—epilepsy, sickness and feeblemindedness. But the board almost routinely violated the spirit, if not the letter, of the law by passing judgment on many other things, from promiscuity to homosexuality."[64]

Golden assumed that black women were always more likely to be sterilized, which was true during most of the years he wrote about the subject. (According to the *Winston-Salem Journal* project, the effort was racially balanced in the early days, but by the late 1960s more than 60 percent of the women subjected to sterilization were black.) Many states had similar practices; the thinking was that the identified diseases and conditions were hereditary and needed to be rooted out of the gene pool. North Carolina carried out sterilizations much longer than most states, with the backing of influential and wealthy business leaders. By 1974 the state had ordered some 7,600 procedures. The majority were women, and a third of them were minors, many of whom had suffered incest or rape.[65]

Golden was unaware of the number of people affected in North Carolina. In 1962 he wrote, "No matter what the state—Louisiana, Virginia, Oregon, the legislators invariably recommend sterilization of the wicked woman, said wicked woman being of dark visage." He raised a question unusual for its feminist tone: Why aren't men sterilized? The procedure was simpler and more effective, since a man could father many children in the time it took a woman to have just one. It was a rhetorical question. Male legislators, he concluded sarcastically, get a kick out of the idea of sterilization operations for women, but when it came to themselves, "any kick is a rather uncomfortable one."[66]

Little Rock

Along with health care, the topic that most animated Golden and the others at Highlander that summer was the school year that had just ended at Central High School in Little Rock, Arkansas. Nine African American students had made history by enrolling in the all-white school for the 1957–58 school year.[67]

Some of the photographs that have come to be most associated with the civil rights movement were taken of the menacing crowds bearing down on these students on 4 September 1957. This was public in a different way from other racial violence; it was such an ordinary setting with such extraordinary actions. Governor Orval Faubus had ordered the Arkansas National Guard to be on duty, not to protect the new students, but to keep them from entering the school. A crowd of close to 1,000 angry whites surrounded the black students. The scene had all the ingredients of a lynching. The photographs of Elizabeth Eckford, dressed in a starched shirtwaist dress, hair carefully styled, sunglasses on, clutching her books to her chest, and encircled by a white mob, remain terrifying all these years later. A step or two in back of her was a young white woman, her face contorted with rage. No parents could read or watch coverage and fail to imagine the terror of sending their own child into this danger.[68]

Now furious antisegregationists were real to the rest of America. News coverage pushed a reluctant President Eisenhower to send 1,200 troops from the U.S. Army's 101st Airborne Division from Fort Campbell, Kentucky, and federalize the Arkansas National Guard. Soldiers were assigned to shadow the black students, but angry white classmates still managed to harass the newcomers.[69]

Jews in Little Rock were doing their best to keep their heads down during this unrest. Historian Clive Webb describes an incident in which the head of the Arkansas Council on Human Relations attempted to bolster support for the rights of the black students by sharing a copy of one of Golden's magazine articles criticizing southern Jews who were too fearful to stand up for desegregation. The result was a hysterical rejection of the content. It didn't take particularly tough talk to raise alarm in any community, Jewish or Gentile. Editorializing by Golden's friend Harry Ashmore against Faubus for defying the federal law caused subscribers and advertisers to leave the *Arkansas Gazette* in droves. (Golden lost subscribers in Little Rock, too, but he was already used to such departures and, of course, his tiny operation had much less at risk.) Ashmore's rhetoric does not sound radical or liberal now; it was then: "It is quite true that most of us would have preferred to continue segregation in the public schools. But it is equally true that we cannot do so lawfully." It was another fifteen years before Little Rock's schools were integrated.[70]

World Comes Calling

As the first year of Little Rock's desegregation came to an end, Ben Zevin was feeling understandably smug. Zevin, president of World Publishing, was a devoted reader of the *Carolina Israelite*, and he was about to release Harry Golden's first book. He wasn't expecting a huge response, but he knew the timing was good for Golden's mix of humor and commentary on race issues.

Zevin was an immigrant from Ukraine and, like Golden, had done time in the advertising business. He joined his father-in-law's sturdy Cleveland publishing company in 1935 and energetically expanded World by mass-producing inexpensive reprints in paperback under its Tower and Forum imprints. For a time World's presses in Ohio churned out more bibles and dictionaries than anyone else in the country, including its top-selling *Webster's New World Dictionary of the American Language*. The trade-book division operated out of a busy New York City office. Zevin became president of the company in 1945, and a column in *Time* magazine, headlined "Upstart Printer," described him in its condescending, jaunty style: "The Atlas who hopes to push World to a top place in the reprint business is small, owlish, President Benjamin D. Zevin, 44. A New Yorker and ex-advertising man, Ben Zevin got into the book business by marriage, into mass distribution of reprints by pondering on old jokes."[71]

Zevin understood that the seemingly opposite moods of the time boded well for sales of Golden's nostalgic material. Both the reader who was pleased by postwar prosperity and the one anxious over Cold War threats could find entertainment. Golden could speak the language America was primed to hear. Zevin admired Golden's ability to be outspoken and humorous about something as harsh as racism and saw that *Brown*, the murder of Emmett Till, and the accomplishments of Rosa Parks and the transit boycott had steadily increased interest in the civil rights movement. Best of all, Golden's rising profile and his circulation numbers looked promising to the practical Zevin. With a mailing list of close to 12,000, the *Carolina Israelite* was not a fluke. Subscribers included politicians, clergy, writers, civil rights activists, and as many as 4,500 Jews, all scattered over forty-five states, Canada, Israel, England, and a few other far-flung points. Zevin figured this crowd was made up of good book-buyers. Golden's speeches had long been covered by local newspapers; now national columns mentioned him and his growing influence. In April 1957, *Time* magazine quoted Golden's crack that he was the proud member of three minority groups: Jews, radicals, and Yankees.[72]

The magazine's piece "The Press: Golden Rule" also reported, "At a press conference with North Carolina's Governor Luther Hodges, Golden quipped: 'How does it feel to be governor of a state where one-third of the population is embittered?' Chuckling, Hodges turned to other newsmen and said: 'Gentlemen, I think Harry Golden is one of the most valuable citizens of this state.' Golden maintains that his barbs are not treated seriously because he is Jewish. 'Most Southerners,' he explains, 'think of Jews as surrogate Negroes. Everyone knows where I stand, but they laugh with me and at me.'"[73]

Golden was known, but he was not yet a big star. He was marketable and not yet expensive—an appealing writer for World Publishing.

This partnership almost did not happen. Another publisher contacted Golden a year before Zevin and proposed a book of *Carolina Israelite* reprints, using only the pieces on Jewish life in America. Anything to do with race or politics wouldn't make the cut. "I went back to Charlotte and thought about it. . . . I decided they were dopes," wrote Golden. "So you see, a publisher no sooner discovered me than unfortunately I discovered integrity." Then along came Zevin, who wrote to tell Golden how much he liked a *Carolina Israelite* piece on Senator McCarthy. Here was a publisher who understood, Golden thought. In June 1957, the men met and Zevin laid out his idea for a book of reprinted pieces. He flattered Golden by sending a letter the next day, saying how much he'd enjoyed their conversation and sending copies of two new books put out by World. Golden promptly signed a contract to write *Only in America*.[74]

The rest of 1957 and the first month of the new year were a blur for Golden, who kept up a brisk speaking schedule while putting out the paper and working with World staff on the book project. Golden happily talked content with editor Bill Targ and marketing ideas with Eleanor Kask Friede, both highly respected in the book world.[75]

Responding to Zevin's suggestion for a book, Golden had mailed off a large cardboard box reeking of cigar smoke and stuffed with hundreds of faded clippings and tear sheets from the *Carolina Israelite*, in no particular order. An amused Targ, well acquainted with the idiosyncrasies of writers, politely suggested that he take a stab at selecting his own favorites. With help from his son Harry Jr., by now a reporter for the *Detroit Free Press*, Golden eventually settled on 184 essays. It was scheduled for a modest initial printing of 5,000 copies with an advance of $3,000 against future sales for the author. Although that healthy sum showed confidence on the publisher's part, Golden assumed the first run would not sell out, so he cut a deal with World, agreeing to buy unsold books back at a reduced rate, with the idea of sending them to new subscribers of the *Carolina Israelite* as a premium.[76]

Meeting up with Targ was a lucky accident for Golden, and the two would work together on seventeen books, first at World, then at G. P. Putnam's Sons, where Targ moved later in his long career. They had much in common, particularly their gifts for holding forth on just about any subject, at length and with excellent comic timing. Four years younger than his author, Targ was also Jewish and early on had shed his parents' Russian surname for a shorter version. He was well read and very much at home in the book business, having owned a rare-book shop in Chicago while in his twenties. By the time he met Golden in middle age, Targ had been at World's New York office for more than a dozen years. He had a reputation for navigating writerly temperament and talent of all sorts, from Dorothy Parker to Mario Puzo. He failed to get the aging Parker to write a book for World but charmed her nonetheless, and he made publishing history at Putnam in 1968 when he bought *The Godfather* sight-unseen from Puzo for $5,000. Targ's writers responded well to his low-key confidence; he was sure of his own editorial strengths yet also possessed a self-deprecating, earthy sense of humor.[77]

It was Targ who suggested "Why I Never Bawl Out a Waitress," a classic Golden rumination, as the opening essay for *Only in America*. It was a wise choice that launched the eclectic collection from a strong start. The piece begins, "I have a rule against registering complaints in a restaurant; because I know that there are at least four billion suns in the Milky Way—which is only one galaxy." Golden waxes on for a few hundred words about the inconsequential nature of our lone planet and the infinite nature of outer space before ending with this kicker: "When you think of all of this, it's silly to worry whether the waitress brought you string beans instead of limas."[78]

The book also brought another name change for its author; this one would be Golden's last. He had traveled from Chaim to Hyman to Herschel to Harry Lewis to Harry L. to plain old Harry, and from Goldhirsch (with a very brief try-on of Goldenhurst in grade school) to Goldhurst to Golden Sr., to Golden. "In accordance with your wishes we are going to omit your middle initial and simply print your name as Harry Golden on the jacket, title page, etc.," wrote Targ.[79]

Carl Sandburg wrote to Golden and pronounced *Only in America* to be "a honey of a book" and promptly agreed to write a foreword. "Carl says the 'foreword' to my book will be short but 'the words will be good,'" Golden wrote Targ at the end of December 1957. "He also told me to 'tell the World Publishing Company that this is the first Foreword I have written without pay.'" Sandburg was true to his word. The biographer and poet who wrote thousands of pages to preserve the life of Abraham Lincoln summed up his friend perfectly in twenty-seven good words within the passage, "Whatever is human interests Harry Golden. Honest men, crooks, knuckleheads, particularly anybody out of the ordinary if even a half-wit, any of them is in his line."[80]

Readers of the *Carolina Israelite* were apprised of the book's progress; in fact, Golden touted it even before a title was chosen. "Quite frankly I do not know what they will call it, or the date of publication, but you should begin to think in terms of reserving your copy at your local book store. Just tell them: 'Harry Golden's book, published by World Publishing Company,'—they'll know." World gave Golden permission to hold an early book signing at Ivey's Department Store in Charlotte. In later years most daily newspapers would adopt policies that book reviewers be at least outwardly without personal conflicts of interest, but that was not the case then. Golden announced in the May–June 1958 issue that among the early reviewers would be friends Gerald W. Johnson for the *New York Herald Tribune*, Ashmore for the *Nation*, Kays Gary of the *Charlotte Observer*, and Julian Scheer of the *Charlotte News*.[81]

The Evil Eye

Golden signed off on the galleys for his book, then he relaxed in that luxurious way that a writer can—for a very brief period—when it is too late to change anything but he has not yet panicked about what was left out. His relief was not only short; it was interrupted by a catastrophe.

On 17 February 1957, Golden became reacquainted with the Evil Eye his mother had warned him about long ago. While on his way to a week of speeches in the Northeast, Golden was tracked down in the Newark railroad station by the Charlotte Police Department. There was a fire, they said; come home. A snowstorm was backing things up, so Golden stood up in a crowded train car all the way to Washington. Three Marines riding the train took Golden to the airport, where they caught a flight to Charlotte. Then one of the young men risked being late reporting to his barracks to give Golden a ride to what had been 1229 Elizabeth Avenue. The wreckage was still smoldering.[82]

Police chief Frank Littlejohn (described in the *Charlotte News* fire story as "a long-time friend of editor Golden") at first treated the fire as arson. By the end of the day, it was determined that the heating system was to blame. The unusually cold night pushed the furnace and chimney past capacity, and once started, the fire roared up inside the unlined chimney flue and then the walls of the wood-frame house. Golden and advertising manager Ken Robertson had left around 7:00 the night before. The fire got a crackling start before any of the neighbors noticed it and called in the alarm in the early morning. High heat and structural collapse—the second floor caved in completely—meant loss of most of Golden's belongings, including close to 2,000 books and drawers of correspondence dating back to his arrival in Charlotte. Firefighters first thought Golden was in the house, but when Robertson came dashing into the yard, they got the only good news of the night: The house was empty. The firefighters grabbed the panicked Robertson before he could run inside to get the subscription list. Now there was nothing to be done but stand clear and watch the fire burn down.[83]

Golden, stunned, stood on the street and repeated the same thought: "I'm destroyed. All my years of work are lost." At first he worried most about the readers: "I don't even have a duplicate list of subscribers. It's just carelessness on my part but I don't even have that." But within a few hours, the depth of the loss became clear. Hundreds of letters and files were gone. Golden's letters and the carbons of responses that survive in some of his correspondents' archives show how much was lost that night. Even Golden could not exaggerate this tragedy.

He wrote *World* publisher Zevin and managing editor Jerome Fried on 18 February: "Only about a year ago I promised the University of North Carolina my correspondence, which weighed about two tons. . . . I'm terribly sorry that I didn't send it to them while I was alive—or my building was standing." He did note the one considerable bit of good news: "Thank God the manuscript was sent back to you last week."[84]

The *Charlotte News* and the *Charlotte Observer* published editorials exhorting Golden to take heart. The *Charlotte News* editorialists asked, "How does a paper stay in business when it has lost the names of its subscribers—particularly when those subscribers are scattered through this country and much of the world? We wouldn't know, nor would we expect any of newspaperdom's tycoons to have an answer. But then neither they nor we could understand how an immigrant from New York's East Side could succeed in establishing Charlotte, North Carolina, a provocative journal of personal opinion that does gentle battle with some of the area's prevailing attitude."[85]

Word of the fire brought practical help from every corner of Charlotte, then from farther afield. Jewish business leader Morris Speizman disapproved of Golden making a spectacle of himself, but he was one of the first to step up, offering warehouse space for storing books and other belongings that could be dried out and saved. Walter Klein stood ready to give Golden everything from a desk to a place to live. "If you had been the innkeeper in Bethlehem, He wouldn't have been born in a manger," a grateful Golden wrote Klein. Such offers were not without a price to the giver. Golden stored piles of pro-integration materials in a room at Klein's ad agency. When one potential client happened to spy the stuff, he "curdled and left without a word," Klein recalled.[86]

Sandburg, whose house was stuffed with teetering piles of books and drawers of letters, understood more than most what Golden had lost. P. D. East of *The Petal Paper* took a break from writing satiric ad copy for his own little Mississippi antisegregationist paper (promoting cross-burning kits, kerosene included) and sent Golden the most heartfelt offer: "Realizing that to weep would be of no value, I wish to ask you a question which I hope you will take in the spirit in which it's asked: What can I do for you? Do you need money? I haven't much, but you can have all I have and all I can raise. . . . Damnit, Harry, I'm not being nice; I mean it."[87]

Frank Graham passed the news to Adlai Stevenson, who wrote in sympathy. "I am sure you are rising reborn from the ashes."[88]

A worried James Kilpatrick heard of the fire much after the fact, after "damn near everyone in the country," and wrote to Golden on *Richmond News-Leader* letterhead, offering books from his own library to replace those lost in the fire. Kilpatrick injected some humor that warmed Golden's heart as much as the offer. The segregationist editor said he hoped that the books might persuade Golden to come over to his side of the fence, but failing that, he knew they would serve a crucial need: "Nobody like you or me can live without books . . . whether or not we ever read them."[89]

Another arch-segregationist friend couldn't resist a similar sentiment. Ken Whitsett wrote, "Harry, get started again. I hope you will get started now on the right track, but do get started, and good luck, always."[90]

As for the subscriber list, Golden hadn't reckoned with the determination of Chief Littlejohn, who was indeed a friend, just as the *Charlotte News* had claimed. Two years earlier Littlejohn had written Golden an articulate letter referencing the evolution of attitudes he had seen in his own lifetime: "I think that you are doing a good job in helping erase old animosities and prejudices which we, in the South, inherited from Civil War days." Golden now returned the compliment, and then some. "Now this Chief was worrying himself sick about my mailing list—of all things," Golden wrote in a piece picked up by wire services a week after the fire. "I had a list of duplicates (the originals were on the floor that was the first to cave into the furnace room on top of that unlined, blazing flue); but these duplicates were terribly charred, and the six or seven hundred sheets were water soaked and frozen. On top of that they were on gummed labels. It looked hopeless. The Chief took those four sets of burned sheets, solid as boards, and turned them over to his laboratory. They worked on them for two days with chemicals . . . and the lists were saved."[91]

When a couple of TV reporters (they didn't yet travel in large packs) showed up to cover this story with its appealing visual elements, Golden became the showman: "I said that this was especially wonderful, because as a result of this 'police-work' no one will get into trouble, no one will be 'sought,' no one will be arrested; the Police did all of this so that a Baptist clergyman in Decatur, Georgia; and a Rabbi in Boston, Massachusetts; and a school teacher in Portland, Oregon, will continue to get a little personal journal published down here in Charlotte, North Carolina." Mindful of his soon-to-appear book, Golden added jubilantly, "This could happen (long pause) *only in America*!" Some of the countless newspapers and magazines that picked up the story put the last three words all in uppercase letters, just the way he hoped they would.[92]

After Golden gave the police his glowing, public thanks, a Mrs. Anna Steele of the Chantilly Baptist Church called Golden and clarified things a bit: "I want you to know that Jesus saved you and your list of subscribers because last night our prayer circle prayed for you." Golden promptly sent this nugget to a friend at *Time* and worked it into his next several speeches.[93]

With coverage in just about every major newspaper and news magazine, the *Congressional Record*, late-night TV, and the church circuit, the response was astounding. Contributions came from actors, housewives, hotel clerks, Republicans, Democrats, Socialists, whites, blacks, racists, and pacifists. New subscriptions poured in. Current subscribers re-upped and bought gift subscriptions. Golden moved into a house at 1312 Elizabeth Avenue and was up and running quickly. He turned that into a story as well:

I had what my mother used to call "insurinks." When I went into business with two typewriters and six hundred subscribers I had a $3,000 policy on the business, and I had the same policy with six typewriters and 15,000 subscribers. At that I thank Mr. Nathan Sutker, my insurinks agent of Charlotte, who literally shamed me into a policy. What kind of fire? Who has a fire? But I grudgingly went along, half the time behind in the premiums, which Mr. Sutker paid for me, but thank God for it—a man can move around a bit, take another building, replace the necessary office equipment, and with my list at least 94 percent intact, I am ready to go.[94]

The wire services stayed with the story long enough to announce when the first post-fire issue of the *Carolina Israelite* was in the mail. It was late, as predicted.

A Sleeper

Five months after the fire, *Only in America* was in print. Golden sent copies to a few close writer-friends before the official release date in July 1958. Reactions were gratifying and thoughtful, often expressing the admirer's own inability to write satisfactorily about the race question. Hal Tribble, associate editor of the *Charlotte Observer*, told Golden, "I'm certain you love the South as much as I do, but you can view it with detachment—and I, merely with grief."[95]

Zevin called the early reviews "phenomenal" but warned Golden that it would take a bit of time for that praise to translate into booksellers' orders. "They will follow," he assured Golden in a letter on 16 July. For once, Zevin was off the mark in his sales prediction.[96]

NBC's Dave Garroway gave Golden a valuable boost on the *Today* show. Garroway's large viewership, along with the host's sincere curiosity and charming style, was a gold mine. Garroway introduced the beaming author by reading aloud from the foreword written by Sandburg, then asking about the *Carolina Israelite* and the "distinguished citizens" among its subscribers.[97]

On the official publication day, Golden went to Targ's office at 119 West Fifty-Seventh Street. There he heard that the U.S. Army had placed an order for 902 copies for post libraries, unknowingly purchasing a book by a man who had once been imprisoned at Fort Meade. Early reviews and sales figures started arriving. Things looked good. *Very* good.

But even Targ was unprepared for what happened at their celebratory lunch. As Targ recalled in his autobiography, the two men had barely hoisted their drinks to toast each other when Victor, the maitre d' of the Plaza Hotel's Oak Room, appeared at their table. Would the gentlemen mind if Mr. Richard Rodgers came over to say a few words? Golden's mouth dropped open; even Targ was surprised. *The* Richard Rodgers? Broadway icon and hit-maker behind *Oklahoma, South Pacific*, and *The King and I*? Targ assured Victor the gentlemen would be delighted to welcome Mr. Rodgers to their table. Writing about the incident in his entertaining autobiography, Targ recalled, "Rodgers proceeded to compliment Golden for the 'marvelous book.' . . . He kept on, exclaiming over the merits of Golden's book. . . . Golden stared at me and I returned his look, wondering if this was really happening."[98]

After Rodgers returned to his own table, Targ and Golden finished their drinks and lunch, then hurried over to Scribner's Bookstore on Fifth Avenue. Targ's recollection continued: "We . . . were greeted by Igor Kropotkin, the store's manager. He said they had sold out their entire stock of fifty copies and needed more books at once. He didn't know what it was all about and assumed there was a mammoth publicity and advertising campaign at work. Of course there was no such thing. The demand for the book was pure 'word of mouth'—the only true method yet known for selling books."[99]

With almost no advertising and only a handful of advance copies sent to reviewers, *Only in America* was a runaway bestseller. As if the calls pouring in from wholesalers and bookstores weren't proof enough, Targ and others in the World offices noticed that everyone riding the train or subway had his or her nose in *Only in America*. U.S. military base libraries around the world clamored for it. Jewish readers couldn't get enough of it—"It was *the* book in Miami Beach," Targ's sources told him—but sales crossed all demographics of religion, age, sex, and income levels.[100]

Targ never claimed credit for the hit, even when writing years later: "I still can't understand what happened and why the book was such a success. Of course we all know that genuine humor is a rare commodity and when it is good, when it is right and well timed, it is pure gold. And that, I suspect, is what we had."[101]

World's printers raced to get another 25,000 new copies out to the booksellers. The presses kept rolling until after *Only in America* sold 250,000 copies—a trade-edition record at the time. Book-of-the-Month Club, *Reader's Digest*, and newspaper syndicates dialed up Targ immediately. "We quickly reached the top of the [*New York Times*] bestseller list," wrote Targ in a guest column in the *Carolina Israelite*. "And life was beautiful."[102]

Golden, as almost all writers do, insisted publicly that he had never imagined that the book would sell so well. But in truth he had long believed that the stories of an immigrant childhood on the Lower East Side could be a hit, given the chance. The book was genuinely funny; it exalted the little guy and the working stiff. It captured a certain Jewish experience in America—the version that most people wanted to remember, as it turned out. And, as Golden often said, it was essentially a personal journal, a one-man newspaper in book form that could be read as a narrative thread or dipped into at random. The same things that made the *Carolina Israelite* appealing to such a diverse readership made *Only in America* into a *New York Times* bestseller for sixty-six weeks.[103]

The success made Golden a star, and he had the temperament to savor the moment. "Luckily it came at the age of 56 instead of at 26," Golden wrote in the *Carolina Israelite* the month his book came out. "If it happens at 26 you better be prepared for an entire lifetime of tension, frustration, and even a bit of anger. No matter how good you are, it is never again the same." As it was, the changes brought by fame were delightful. After decades of courting famous and influential people in admiring letters, Golden was now on the receiving end.[104]

As Golden had promised *Carolina Israelite* readers, reviews appeared in major newspapers and magazines, including those written by Ashmore and several other friends. "The book has many distinctions, not the least of which is the unique and remarkably sympathetic view of the white South in its desegregation travail as seen through the eyes of one who himself has felt the edge of prejudice," Ashmore wrote in the *Nation*. Gerald Johnson told readers of the *New York Herald Tribune* that "standing on a bushel of eels would be a relatively simple feat by comparison with reviewing this book.... The only possible approach is to review Harry Golden, for the book is Golden and Golden is the book." The *Christian Science Monitor* praised the book's humor and confidence. *Kirkus* compared Golden to Mark Twain; the *Library Journal* likened him to Will Rogers. "Seldom has that rich if grotesque and difficult life [the history of the Jewish American immigrant] been described with more humor and less of either condescension or sentimentality," said *Saturday Review*. "If there is such a thing as a cracker-barrel philosopher left in our century, Mr. Golden has earned the title," declared the *New York Times*. Golden, never one to let a good, folksy image go to waste, immediately began claiming that he kept an *actual* cracker barrel next to his desk, a repository for his typed news copy. A mischievous friend sent Golden just such a barrel so that hungry photographers could snap pictures of him using it.[105]

(clockwise from top left)

Anna Klein Goldhirsch, Harry's mother, ca 1910. Anna spoke Yiddish, relying when necessary on her two all-purpose English words: "Enjoy!" and "Likewise!" Harry Golden Papers, J. Murrey Atkins Library Special Collections, University of North Carolina at Charlotte.

Leib Goldhirsch, Harry's father, ca 1926. Leib's greatest gift, at least in the eyes of his young son Harry, was his ability to argue just about anyone into the ground. Harry Golden Papers, J. Murrey Atkins Library Special Collections, University of North Carolina at Charlotte.

Jake Goldhirsch, Harry's brother, ca 1959. Jake sold from a pushcart while still a teenager, then worked in a factory, scraping together enough money to buy the Hotel Markwell on West Forty-Ninth Street in New York City. Manning the front desk provided Harry with some of his best stories. Leveton Family Collection.

(left) Harry with his sister Clara Goldhurst, 1922. One of the first women to operate her own brokerage on Wall Street, Clara gave Harry his start, hiring him to write upbeat market reports. Harry Golden Papers, J. Murrey Atkins Library Special Collections, University of North Carolina at Charlotte.

(right) Matilda Goldhurst, Harry's sister, 1922. A skilled seamstress while still in her teens, Matilda would wait outside churches attended by society women and, as they exited, quickly capture the lines of their couture outfits in her sketchbook. Harry Golden Papers, J. Murrey Atkins Library Special Collections, University of North Carolina at Charlotte.

Max Goldhirsch, Harry's brother, and Max's wife, Ann Goldhirsch, ca 1930s. Max was the only sibling born in America; Anna Goldhirsch often referred to him as "my little Columbus." Harry Golden Papers, J. Murrey Atkins Library Special Collections, University of North Carolina at Charlotte.

Round Table Literary Club - 1921
Standing: Lowenberg, Golden, Norwalk, Duff, Gomperts, Davidson, Edelman.
Seated: DeLeeuw, Barrett, O.H. Geiger, G. R. Geiger, Bergerman

(above) Oscar Geiger's Roundtable Literary Club. Harry (*back row, second from left*) was still Goldhirsch, not yet Golden, when this was taken in 1921. The typed roster was added many years later. Harry Golden Papers, J. Murrey Atkins Library Special Collections, University of North Carolina at Charlotte.

(left) Genevieve Alice Marie "Tiny" Gallagher around the time she married Harry Goldhurst in 1927. Her eldest son once declared, "It would take me a week to describe that marriage." Harry Golden Papers, J. Murrey Atkins Library Special Collections, University of North Carolina at Charlotte.

(left) Harry Goldhurst and his son Richard in 1928. Harry Golden Papers, J. Murrey Atkins Library Special Collections, University of North Carolina at Charlotte.

(below) Three of Harry's four sons: Harry Jr., Richard, and William Goldhurst, in 1932. His fourth son, Peter, was developmentally disabled and died at age eighteen. Harry Golden Papers, J. Murrey Atkins Library Special Collections, University of North Carolina at Charlotte.

Harry Golden at his desk, December 1957. Photo by Tom Nebbia; LOOK Magazine Photograph Collection, Library of Congress, Prints & Photographs Division.

(opposite) Golden with *Carolina Israelite* circulation lists after the 1957 fire destroyed his home and office on Elizabeth Avenue in Charlotte, North Carolina. The water-soaked lists were painstakingly restored in a police laboratory. Harry Golden Papers, J. Murrey Atkins Library Special Collections, University of North Carolina at Charlotte.

Golden, Eleanor Roosevelt, and Carl Sandburg shortly after publication of Golden's 1961 book, *Carl Sandburg*. Harry Golden Papers, J. Murrey Atkins Library Special Collections, University of North Carolina at Charlotte.

(opposite, above and below)
Carl Sandburg and Golden in 1958. "If you are his friend, it means that everybody associated with you . . . are his friends too," Golden said. Harry Golden Papers, J. Murrey Atkins Library Special Collections, University of North Carolina at Charlotte.

Golden and entertainer Sammy Davis Jr. backstage at an NAACP fundraiser in 1960. Harry Golden Papers, J. Murrey Atkins Library Special Collections, University of North Carolina at Charlotte.

Golden with President Lyndon B. Johnson at a White House reception in 1964.
"A war President is a role which appeals to him hardly at all," Golden said of Johnson
during the Vietnam War. Harry Golden Papers, J. Murrey Atkins Library Special
Collections, University of North Carolina at Charlotte.

(opposite, above and below)
Golden at the White House reception in 1963 marking the 100th anniversary of the
Emancipation Proclamation. Harry Golden Papers, J. Murrey Atkins Library Special
Collections, University of North Carolina at Charlotte.

Golden on the campaign trail for Robert F. Kennedy's successful 1964 run for the U.S. Senate.
The inscription reads, "For Harry, And afterwards I put on my coat, did what you told me and
won the election. My thanks—Bob Kennedy." Harry Golden Papers, J. Murrey Atkins Library
Special Collections, University of North Carolina at Charlotte.

The Carolina Israelite

VOL. 19, No. 4   Charlotte, North Carolina, July-August, 1961   PRICE $3.00 PER YEAR

Book Review

JUST A DIRTY BOOK?

Tropic of Cancer by Henry Miller. Grove Press. $7.50

My sainted Irish grandmother, the mother of seven, once remarked to me, "You younger people take sex so seriously you are all liable to start writing books about it." Vide Mr. Miller, Grandma.

While Tropic of Cancer may not have distressed her, I suspect my grandmother would have put it down not so much because Mr. Miller does take sex seriously but because (1) he is unoriginal, and (2) he is dirty.

Tropic of Cancer is a personal journal. The arrangement of its chapters, however, its conversational, slangy diction, its personae, the author's foreshortenings and ellipses combine to give the book the social texture we conveniently call fiction. Tropic of Cancer is a novel, but not quite a novel, for it lacks motivated narrative. Its presentation is unique, but Mr. Miller is derivative.

Enthusiasts have said Tropic of Cancer descends from Walt Whitman. Since Henry Miller does not possess a sense of personal purpose, let alone a sense of national purpose, let alone even a political awareness, I think we can safely dispense with this insight and say no, Henry Miller has not cribbed from Walt Whitman. George Orwell, in essay Inside the Whale rather thought Henry Miller sounded like Louis Ferdinand Celine. He rather does, at that, One suspects Miller took much of his inspiration from Celine. Critics have argued that everything regarding the 20th Century that filled Celine with terror made Henry Miller happy, but this is a quantitative rather than qualitative difference. Celine resented more terrors.

Both Celine and Miller were trying to manipulate surrealist materials. Where Celine succeeded in making Europe into a bad dream, Miller failed by assembling his materials too realistically. The result is a mindlessness. The hero of Tropic of Cancer never gets a job, it is gotten for him. He doesn't get in bad with the boss, but a mysterious and inarticulated caprice gets him fired. Even when the hero picks up a girl, it is somehow as though the girl had been procured. Listening to Mr. Miller inveigh against America and the corruption it provides is to realize America to Henry Miller is not an idea, a milieu, or even a geographic unit; it is simply a word.

This mindlessness produces a world of depressing sameness. Though the hero is in bed with someone most of the time, one gets the impression he really isn't having much fun; he is not after joy, but experience. But it is precisely when he reports on sex that Miller is misleading. His women for instance never talk in bed (although one married lady does urge, "Fire! vite!"). Now everyone knows women talk in bed all the time. If an eminent divine like John Donne could write "For God's sake, hold your tongue and let me love," Mr. Miller could be an honest. The great crime the male perpetrated both against himself and the female was not in giving women the vote but in teaching them how to talk. That Mr. Miller never finds female

Continued on Page 2

The Bomb Shelter

The bomb shelter has moved up front to page one of the second section (local news) of our daily newspapers. It is an important local matter. Companies are advertising prefabricated bomb shelter. Trade Fairs are demonstrating samples. A family is photographed in their bomb shelter showing stacks of canned foods on shelves above a chemical toilet.

There is one big flaw in the whole bomb shelter program, which no one has explored.

How can two or three people have a bomb shelter in a neighborhood while the others in the same neighborhood have no bomb shelter? How could it be possible to live with your private bomb-shelter — psychologically, spiritually—and (eventually) physically?

I can see where government, State and local, can establish bomb shelters and say; "The people on this side of the street or in this area go to Bomb Shelter A, and the people over here to go to Bomb Shelter B," etc.

But the fellow with a private bomb-shelter will have to worry about more than mere radioactive fall-out from the skies. He will also have to arm himself, his wife, and his children against his neighbors, to fight them off as they seek a drop of uncontaminated water to drink and a few cans of uncontaminated food to eat. He will have to kill a few of his friends and neighbors to protect his family.

Is it possible for all the 190 million individuals of the great American civilization to wrap themselves in cotton? Ah, how we need a bit of wisdom today!

The Golden Bomb Shelter Plan And A Great Religious Revival

To make certain that everybody, rich and poor alike, is assured of the protection of a bomb shelter, I believe that the responsibility should be turned over to the churches, cathedrals, temples, and synagogues. They should build shelters in every neighborhood and community for use of their parishioners. I have been assured that an adequate shelter can be built in the basement of every religious edifice in our country.

If, God willing, there is never any need for the shelters, it would be all to the good. There are over seventy million Christians and two million Jews who are unaffiliated. They do not belong to a religious institution of any kind. The bomb shelter will bring them in; every last one of them; and think what this would also do for the attendance on Friday nights and on Sunday mornings. Everybody would go to church or temple. They would have a stake in the shelter because the church would mean survival here as well as salvation hereafter. And you would soon have capacity attendance at all religious services. And if, God forbid, there was an emergency, we would be able to use the same posters we have used for years; "Go to the church of your choice—as quickly as possible."

Only In Formosa

While I was judging the Miss Universe contest in Miami Beach, I met Mr. Sidney H. Chang, the American correspondent for the Central Daily News of Taipeh, Taiwan, Republic of China, who was there to write about "Miss Republic of China". Mr. Chang informed me that in the high schools of Formosa they use my book Only in America, in the English classes.

What Else Does A Man Want?

What else does a man want out of life, than to have Carl Sandburg, America's great poet, and the author of the Abraham Lincoln six-volume classic, to say; "Harry, your book about me — is good."

A New Golden Plan To End Racial Segregation

The population of Jackson, Mississippi is 144,422.

A southern city of 144,422 belongs in a special class. Based on population, banks determine the rating of the city bonds, and their prestige among investors. Chamber of Commerce people also use the population figure as an inducement to attract new industry and more distributorships to the city.

What's the population of Jackson, Mississippi? 144,422? But what about the 51,556 of that total who are Negroes? These Negroes are discriminated against in education, political activity, health facilities, employment, and entertainment facilities. They are segregated. But they are not segregated in the population figure.

Jackson is not the only city thus involved; all of the other cities who boast of increased population are guilty of using figures to prove something which is not wholly true. Cities may well be bursting at their seams, but they still want it both ways. They want to include the Negroes as part of their population but exclude their Negroes as people. Therefore the new Golden Plan to end racial segregation; the next time a Southern city applies for a bond issue and boasts of its tremendously-increased population, let the NAACP file a demurrer with the Chase-Manhattan Bank and say, No — the city does not have 144,442 population. It segregates 51,556 of its population and it should also segregate the population in its bond application. This would end segregation in a hurry.

Long Live Latin-America

Jews have at no time been more than ten per cent of the Semitic peoples. These ancient, contentious, gifted ornery Semitic tribes have vexed every generation since they first inaugurated civilization and fought with one another over every imaginable detail of law, commerce, letters, and religion. They are a tough resilient people and their worst enemy can't say that they aren't eloquent, not to say noisy.

The restored Christians of Spain sent their Semitic Spaniards to the New World keeping all the blue-eyed Spaniards at home. And if Spain had memories of the seven hundred years in which the Semitic Moors ruled Spain she little thought that the era would be wistfully remembered as the classical age of Spain's greatest glory.

Now the descendents of these banished Spaniards are below the Rio Grande, in Mexico, Central and South America and in the Caribbean, and they are full of contention richly gifted, as noisy as ever, brilliant, touchy about points of honor, with never a dull moment for themselves or other human beings on this earth.

Diana And John Were Married August 5

Diana Surrah and John Vargo were married on August 5 at 10 o'clock at St. Gertrude's Roman Catholic Church, McIntyre, Pennsylvania.

They sent me an invitation and a letter telling me of their romance.

I had delivered a lecture at Indiana State College, Indiana, Pennsylvania.

After the speech they, among others, came up to me to shake hands. It just so happened that John and Diana remained alone with me for a few minutes and they laughed at the coincidence that they were both subscribers to The Carolina Israelite. John asked Diana whether he could take her home. They talked about me for a little while, and during the next few months they talked a lot not about me.

And so two paid subscriptions have now become one, and may God bless them.

(In reply to my letter Diana says she and John do not mind me telling of their wedding).

The Pope Will Save Us Liberals

The ugly John Birch Society has sent a message to all its adherents through its leader Robert Welch that the time has come to start listing names, names of people who do not subscribe to the ideas of the Birchers. Mr. Welch calls anyone inimical to his society a "Comsymp." He urges his members to make these lists of "traitors" who support foreign aid, the graduated income tax, the United Nations, integration of the schools, and the Supreme Court.

Mr. Welch is playing in good fortune. The day following his order the biggest Comsymp of all, Pope John XXIII, issued his Mater et Magisteri encyclical calling for the greater socialization of the world's riches for the common good of the world society. Not only is Pope John a liberal in the Pius XI tradition, but a "foreigner" as well. He is made to order for the John Birchers.

CHAPTER FIVE

Scandal and Resurrection

Just about two months after the joyful publication-day lunch at the Plaza, Golden's editor got another big surprise, this one as painful as the first one had been delightful. William Targ sat at his desk reading a letter over and over, stunned by its contents: Harry Golden, the anonymous letter-writer said, was a crook and a felon who had changed his name and lied to hide his prison time.

Targ tried to shrug it off; he got a lot of mail, and some was bound to come from crackpots. His name and title at World Publishing were easy to find, and he had been mentioned often of late as the editor responsible for this surprise bestseller. But some small voice in Targ's head told him the letter was the real deal. Postmarked from New York City, the typed, single-spaced, one-page letter was enough to alarm any editor. It said, in part,

> If you don't already know it, you should be made aware of the fact that "Harry Golden" is an ex-convict, who served a prison sentence of five years in Atlanta Penitentiary back in the thirties. . . . He was convicted . . . of operating a bucket shop which fleeced many hundreds of people of huge sums of money. This crook was the most notorious stock racketeer of his day. . . . Goldhurst is an ego-maniac, who, you may be sure, takes great delight in the fact that he has been able to hoodwink you and the

public, just as he did so many innocent victims twenty years or so ago. He is a colossal fraud; the list of names of subscribers for his Carolina Israelite, which he gives you, is a list of those persons he has selected as window dressing, and to whom he sends copies free.[1]

The letter was signed FRIEND and was dated 13 September 1958. Targ was not the only person to receive it. Within minutes an editor from the *New York Herald Tribune* called, quoted the letter, and asked what was up. Targ persuaded the editor to hold off on publishing anything until Ben Zevin and Golden could be consulted. Golden flew in for a meeting, and publicist Eleanor Kask Friede met his flight at LaGuardia. As they sped toward World's offices in a cab, she explained the situation to a horrified Golden. Zevin, Targ, and Judith Crist, the *New York Herald Tribune* reporter covering the story, were waiting at the office, Friede told him. She asked him about the prison story. Golden told her yes, he had been convicted and sent to prison. The cab ride was much too short for his taste. As he sat in the World office and answered Crist's questions, Golden drained several paper cups of water, but his throat stayed dry. "It is hard now to re-create this moment, but the thought I remember flashing through me was that this was exactly how Pandora felt when she opened the box," he wrote in his autobiography.[2]

Crist's lead on the 19 September front-page story was a good one. It began, "Twenty-five years of suspense, of 'constant fear of success,' ended yesterday for Harry L. Golden, author of the nation's top non-fiction bestseller, 'Only in America.' They ended with Mr. Golden's disclosure that twenty-five years ago he served a Federal prison term for using the mails to defraud." The sender of the damning letter must have been apoplectic over the positive descriptions of Golden that followed in Crist's story. He was "one of North Carolina's most influential citizens" and a writer "who has brought the homilies and simplicities of his Lower East Side origins to bear on the complexities and prejudices of Dixie." His adopted hometown of Charlotte and the rest of the country "returned his affection." The story did not mention the anonymous letter, so Golden's confession was initially cast as his own brave decision and a way to "lay the ghost of the past once and for all, curbing possible rumors and poison-pen innuendo."[3]

Others viewed the letter as part of a larger conspiracy. Columnist Walter Winchell, by then on the downhill side of his popularity though still well read, gave it a couple of ominous-sounding lines in the *New York Mirror*, saying "several hateful and envious people" had tipped the newspapers about Golden's prison secret. Julian Scheer, Golden's friend at the *Charlotte*

News, reported that the letters were sent to a much wider circle than the New York newspaper press. Editors at national magazines, including *Life*, *Coronet*, and the *Saturday Evening Post*, received copies too.[4]

Golden got the last word in Crist's piece: "I don't want to be a martyr. I pleaded guilty to something that was wrong. I'd like to be judged on my work and my conduct since." His ability to spin bad news served him especially well this day: "I can only rely again on the inherent sense of fair play that I've encountered before among my countrymen. It may not have been a coincidence that I called my best-seller, 'Only in America.'"

Now Golden and his publisher braced for the fallout. Tiny assured him they could ride it out. Clara stayed at his side, and Jake followed his brother's instructions to scout out small motels for sale in Florida should his writing career be over. For Jake's wife, Lillian, who was very fond of her brother-in-law, the dismay was almost as strong as the first time around. Back then, "she was devastated when she heard," said her daughter Norma Leveton. "She just didn't understand. Of course, in our household, a bill came in Monday, it was paid Monday." The family almost never discussed it around the younger generation, she recalled, "until [Edward R.] Murrow interviewed him [in 1959], and the subject came up." His revelations exposed Golden's secret to the whole family.[5]

Television and speaking engagements were canceled for the rest of September; Golden apologized profusely to newsman Howard K. Smith at CBS for pulling out of a moderated panel on integration, saying he did not want to hurt the important discussion on civil rights. Golden did, however, keep on his calendar more than fifty appearances scheduled for the last three months of the year, saying he would understand if any of the groups wanted to back out. Few did. While detractors surfaced immediately, their number was very small. Both Golden and World received hate mail, and a few editorials excoriating Golden appeared in small southern newspapers. One such editorialist called him a "money-crazed Israelite" whose book was a bestseller because it was "selling so good in Harlem" and was reviewed only "by Jews and Negroes." Golden seized on this last accusation, which he later used to tease his WASP friends who had praised his book in reviews.[6]

The *Charleston News and Courier*, not a fan of Golden or his views on integration, flatly accused him of setting up "one of the most bizarre publicity stunts in book-publishing history." There were others who found the timing a bit too convenient. One southern newspaper declared, "Yep, the devil who tempted the late Methodist Bishop James Cannon Jr. to gamble . . . has turned his talents from crime to writing. . . . It seems, once again, that this conniving Jewish swindler makes easy prey out of gullible gospel guys."[7]

This time, however, Golden was not running a scam. He knew the prison story would surface someday but figured he could control the timing—not a completely fatuous view, given that he had been arrested again in the 1940s and achieved considerable fame as a writer and speaker without detection. Once the story broke, however, he recovered quickly and began capitalizing on it. In this sense, the Charleston editorialist was not off base. The paper made a fair point in another editorial: "We wonder how well *The Herald Tribune* would have received the news that a prominent Southern segregationist had a criminal past."[8]

Golden always said he told just three people about his prison time when he moved to Charlotte: Raleigh publisher Josephus Daniels, Charlotte police chief Frank Littlejohn, and friend Hermann Cohen. But it seems unlikely Golden did not tell writer Burke Davis, and Sandburg obviously knew, despite Golden's claims to the contrary. Sandburg's comment to reporters was "The story only ties me closer to him," a neat way to avoid the question of when he first knew Golden was an ex-felon.[9]

Golden had once come perilously close to the subject in a 1953 piece he wrote for his paper. "The Wall Street Story" tells a tale of stock speculators in the 1920s, several of whom "belonged to a famous church on Fifth Avenue; where the pastor was the famous Rev. Dr. H., as saintly a clergyman as ever lived." The elderly churchman pays a visit to a congregant who is "one of Wall Street's biggest men." In the end, the clever broker dupes the clueless pastor into helping manipulate the price of a railroad stock. Golden's recklessness in writing this is unfathomable; perhaps some low moments in the stock market that autumn of 1953 hit a nerve. Fortunately, readers apparently regarded it as just another amusing yarn.[10]

Daniels, one of many influential Methodists who had been infuriated by the "Bucketshop Bishop," was convulsed with laughter when Golden hesitantly told him the story in his office at the Raleigh paper sometime after his move to Charlotte. Daniels laughed so hard that secretaries in the outer office checked to see if everything was all right. "You were Bishop Cannon's broker?" Daniels kept repeating between roars of laughter.[11]

Realizing that some of his friends in the press would feel both personally wounded and professionally annoyed about being scooped, Golden sent out several apologetic notes immediately after his interview with Crist, hoping his friends could save face by writing something for their papers on the same day. "I knew that the time would come when I would have to tell this story," he wrote Pete McKnight at the *Charlotte Observer*.

"But I had hoped that it would happen so that I could prepare my friends and associates. . . . I wanted my own people to hear it from me first."[12]

But now, finally, the Evil Eye had seen enough of Golden. Once again his fortunes had gone from poor to rich, then tumbled again. Once again he survived. And this time his fortunes soared even higher: Harry Golden, swindler and jailbird, was a *hero*. The accolades came quick and thick. "The skeleton in Harry Golden's closet had no peace today," wrote Scheer in the *Charlotte News*. Reaction to the news came from all parts of the country. "It was all one-sided—favorable."[13]

Adlai Stevenson compared Golden to O. Henry, another hard-drinking writer and a gifted chronicler of regular folks with a prison past. Stevenson said he expected the experience had given Golden a bigger heart, deeper understanding, and a longer view of life. Garroway invited Golden back to the *Today* show. Jack Paar's people called, cementing a long relationship between the *Tonight Show* and Golden. Several newspapers offered big payments for a first-person prison story, something Golden never took them up on. His autobiography gives some detail, but even that says relatively little about the actual prison experience. Several tough reporters who called Golden looking for a more critical angle came away charmed. More than one finished up an interview and promptly subscribed to the *Carolina Israelite*. As Scheer and several others made sure to note, once again Golden was running late with the current issue.[14]

McCandlish Phillips in the *New York Times* wrote a sympathetic account calling Golden "a reader's delight" with gifts of "sagacity and reflection." The next day the paper was more effusive in a follow-up story: "The two telephones in the old frame house of Harry Golden, a cigar-chewing, cracker-barrel philosopher out of New York's Lower East Side, seldom stopped ringing today. There were calls from laborers, bus drivers, priests, rabbis and clerks. And there were seventy-five telegrams." A week after the scandal broke, yet another *New York Times* writer, one who covered the publishing industry, observed, "It appears that book buyers also agreed that yesterday should belong to yesterday." There were 95,000 copies of *Only in America* in print, half of which were ordered right after the prison story made the papers. The columnist ended the item succinctly: "Incident closed, with dignity."[15]

Highlander's Myles Horton wrote to Golden, "Only in America could one have a successful fire and a successful expose in a single year. While I love you for what you are and have little interest in your past, this particular event in your past does explain one mystery which has been bothering me. The suspicions I had from reading the *Carolina Israelite*, heightened by reading your book: how the hell, I kept asking myself, could you have found time to read so much?"[16]

Writer Fannie Hurst teased her friend with a telegram asking only, "So, what else is new?" Golden enjoyed the line so much that he resurrected it for the title of a book of collected essays published six years later. When reporters called Hurst for comment, she said, "I couldn't care less." Supportive calls and letters came from Christian clergy, several convicts and ex-felons, Socialists, millionaires, politicians from both sides of the aisle, and as Golden bragged—likely exaggerating just to needle local Jews who snubbed him—"practically the whole Rabbinate of America."[17]

Golden got the last, catchiest word: "The real moral of my story," he wrote, "is the press taketh away, but the press also giveth back."[18]

Solvent at Last

The success of *Only in America* gave Golden financial stability for the first time in his life. The *Carolina Israelite* was no longer a week-to-week operation that depended on Golden's skill at talking creditors and lenders into going against their better judgment. In 1956, Golden made the last such shaky request of his bank, walking away with $2,000 from American Trust Company and agreeing to steep weekly payments. His credit record at this bank was wobbly at best; the money squabbles with Blumenthal at the end of the 1940s had ended with Golden signing notes on the letterhead of this very bank. For several years before the publication of the book, Golden drew money out of his policy at Jefferson Standard Life Insurance Co., paying down the loans just enough to borrow again. The payday loan storefronts of today didn't exist in the 1950s, but Golden created his own high-interest, small-yield system in which it was impossible to get ahead.[19]

In August, Golden received a second advance against royalties. This one was for $5,000, and by all indications it was the largest *legitimate* lump sum to come his way in decades. He promptly bought Tiny air conditioners for her apartment, sent checks to his sons, and treated himself to a lifetime NAACP membership, an investment made by few people and almost no whites at the time. (He was particularly proud of that investment, given his deep admiration for Kivie Kaplan, the NAACP executive who was responsible for making the "life membership" program a resounding success, growing from around 200 to more than 55,000 in 1972. The admiration was mutual—Kaplan made a gift of *Only in America* to the Reverend Martin Luther King.) By 1960, Golden's books would earn more than $120,000 in royalties, a staggering sum. After paying long-overdue taxes and new taxes, buying the house he had been renting, and sending checks to his long-suffering family, Golden was comfortable, not rich. (And, in fact, some debts to friends and Jewish organizations from the early 1950s *still* went unpaid.) As Richard Goldhurst said, "*Only in America* should have made Harry rich as Croesus," but that would never happen.[20]

Perhaps most valuable was the firm guidance from Zevin introducing Golden to an attorney with enough fortitude to keep the books balanced and the bills in order. "Mr. [Maurice] Greenbaum is a man of great talent and skill and an authority on tax matters relating to creative artists and, particularly, professional writers," wrote Zevin. For once, Golden took sound financial advice and signed on with Greenbaum.[21]

Subsequent royalty checks were divided among the business account of the *Carolina Israelite*, Golden, Tiny, and their sons. And with each new book Golden readjusted percentages of the royalties and fees paid to his sons according to who helped write or edit books and articles. The fame and money brought by *Only in America* meant no more name changes, no need to kite checks, and no sneaking past the landlord. Even the IRS was getting paid. With that maddening language used about popular-culture hits, Golden was now described as an "overnight" success, despite the years of work and some lucky timing. *Only in America* came just as the civil rights movement hit a crucial place. Building on the drama of the Montgomery bus boycott and the shocking footage of black teenagers braving mobs to go to Little Rock High School, the cause now had America's attention.

Golden's new freedom was not most people's notion of Easy Street. It meant traveling the country almost half of the month, making speeches and living out of a suitcase. But, for Golden, going from Charlotte to Cleveland to Los Angeles to Phoenix wasn't difficult, now that he had a decent suitcase and a few dollars in his pocket, and when a packed house greeted him at every destination. He'd come a long way since his trip to Denver a few years earlier. "It was a great event for me; a high honor to have been brought 3,000 miles to appear before these people," he wrote in 1955 after making a speech to a Jewish organization there. "It was the first time in my life I had been out west or further than Chicago." He was pleased and surprised to look out at a room of "handsomely dressed people" who had paid $100 a couple to hear him. "I hadn't seen that many Jews in twenty years," he quipped. Requests for appearances came in every week. Golden hired a speakers agency to handle the details and discovered an unexpected benefit: An agent is a convenient scapegoat if one wants to avoid speaking to the Elks Club lodge of the brother-in-law of a former class-mate in Albany or dodge a dinner date with some lonely female reader convinced that he was her soul mate.[22]

In 1958, reflecting back on his schedule for the previous year, he dictated a list of the audiences he had faced:

> Two societies of lawyers and judges, National Council of Jewish Women, American Jewish Congress, American Jewish Committee, Anti-Defamation League, a Negro college, a Presbyterian seminary, a conference of Southern editors, ten or twelve synagogues, Temples and other Jewish fellowships, an inter-racial high school in the South, the Zionists, an Anti-Zionist group, the Hadassies [he meant members of Hadassah, the women's Zionist group], Rotary, B'nai B'rith, Kiwanis, Lions, O, a Roman Catholic Students' League and the International Ladies' Garment Workers' Union.[23]

The list was accurate as far as it went, but there was more. He also appeared on TV variety shows and panels about civil rights. A few days' "rest" near home was still packed: a women's club luncheon, three more synagogues, and another Rotary chapter. He was a moneymaker too: On a double bill with Sammy Davis Jr. at an NAACP dinner in Detroit in 1960, he raised $50,000. (Golden gave his $500 speaking fee to the group's southern voter-registration project. He had been donating fees with regularity at this point. Davis donated his too.) They were both hits: Golden knew how to work this kind of room like a master, and Davis delighted them with his high-energy singing, joking, and praising those who were fighting the good fight by supporting the NAACP. He took the time beforehand to share a cigar break with Golden. The latter took no little pride in a letter written by a prominent white supremacist who declared Golden the most evil Jew in America . . . except for Sammy Davis Jr. After the NAACP dinner in Detroit, Golden was a moneymaker, even without star power sharing the stage. He now was in the unusual position of reporting on civil rights news while making it himself.[24]

Occasionally a physical ailment—a questionable result in a prostate exam or heart palpitations—would compel his doctor to issue stern orders about rest and better diet. When given such a warning in 1959, Golden canceled a few speeches, but within a month or so he resumed his schedule. Why, asked his friends, do you make all these speeches? Is it the money? Golden answered in an essay: "I do not need the money. . . . I did not need the money, in fact, when I *needed* it. I make speeches today because of the Evil Eye. The alternative to traveling around the country would be to sit at home. . . . Instead of catching me basking, the Evil Eye sees me huffing and puffing through the airport, 70 pounds overweight . . . and thinks, 'Why bother with him? I've got a lot of happy people to bother with.' "[25]

Golden went from speech to speech simply because he loved the audiences and the chance to sell regular, non-activist folks on the need to think and care about racial issues. He was good at imparting information without making listeners feel self-conscious about their lack of knowledge or boring the ones who were more informed about the issues. He had a knack for testing the atmosphere of a room and knew just how far to turn up the heat on racial topics. Early on, before Golden wrote his first book, even an FBI informer watching him speak in Arden, Delaware, had to grudgingly give him this due: "His delivery was what might be described as smooth, and he was rather witty." He usually spoke without a word-for-word written speech, but his easy delivery belied a deliberate routine. When speaking to Jewish audiences, he warmed them up with nostalgic tales of growing up on the Lower East Side. "My whole purpose is to suggest that they unclutch their fingers and relax about the whole business of Jewishness," he explained. If a Christian audience laughed a little too long, he took a break from jokes and gave them the dismal statistics for infant mortality among blacks, asking, "How does that sound to a Christian?" Those people interviewed who recalled hearing a speech by Golden almost always commented on his skill for asking a tough question without sounding confrontational. Making listeners squirm was not his goal—at least not those who came to sit in a room and listen to him. He saved the shaming for the politicians, corrupt sheriffs, hypocritical clergy, Ku Kluxers, and those Jews and Christians he thought were apathetic, pompous, or both.[26]

Golden Plans

Golden got his biggest laughs from his "Golden Plans"; he'd delighted viewers by describing one on Garroway's show. Now that he was in demand by other television shows, radio programs, newspapers, magazines, and a dizzying number of audiences, he perfected this *shtick*. The Golden Plans, which were sometimes likened to Jonathan Swift's eighteenth-century essay, *A Modest Proposal*, that satirically urged poor Irish to eat their young, took on a life of their own. Golden's Plans lacked the bitter dark tone of Swift's work, but the outrageousness of both made for handy comparison. Beginning in the mid-1950s, these tongue-in-cheek routines were delivered with gusto in speeches and sprinkled throughout the pages of his newspaper. The Vertical Negro Plan was the first and most enduring. Golden put out this idea as the North Carolina legislature was about to meet in special session to consider constitutional amendments that would do away with compulsory education (so whites did not have to sit in a classroom with blacks), allow districts to close schools rather than accept black students, and provide education grants to whites electing to send their children to private schools. Golden assured readers of the May–June 1956 *Carolina Israelite* that he had a solution. "A careful study of my plan, I believe, will show that it will save millions of dollars in tax funds and eliminate forever the danger to our public education system."[27]

The Vertical Negro Plan played off the ludicrous practice that allowed blacks and whites to stand in the same lines at the grocery store, post office, and bank. It allowed both races to walk the same streets and enter the same stores. "It is only when the Negro 'sets' that the fur begins to fly," wrote Golden. All the legislators needed to do, he declared, was order public schools to remove all chairs, leaving only desks in the classrooms. "Since no one in the South pays the slightest attention to the VERTICAL NEGRO, this will completely solve our problem. And it is not such a terrible inconvenience for young people to stand up during their class-room studies. In fact this may be a blessing in disguise. They are not learning to read sitting down anyway; maybe 'standing up' will help." This, he added, would also save millions in costs for remedial English classes.[28]

Golden got the glory for this bit of satire, but it was actually already in practice at a Charlotte eatery called Tanner's, a place so small that there was no room for seats. Another practitioner of the Vertical Negro Plan before Golden gave it a name was Durham merchant E. J. "Mutt" Evans (father of writer Eli Evans), who served as his city's first Jewish mayor, from 1951 to 1963. As Golden no doubt knew, the popular Evans took the counter stools out of his department store's snack bar, and both black and white customers ate standing up without a fuss.[29]

Also in 1956, Golden came up with his Golden Plan to Eliminate Anti-Semitism, which recommended that every Jewish-affiliated group in the country sign a statement saying, "At the very first sign of any overt anti-Semitism in the United States, we shall recommend to our membership that all Jews in America become Christians, en masse, overnight." He predicted that most middle-class and upper middle-class Jews would want to join the Episcopal and Presbyterian churches, and that the prospect of 5 million Jews descending on these Protestant strongholds would do the trick. "The Episcopalians and the Presbyterians would organize a strong Anti-Defamation League. They would go from door to door whacking anti-Semites on the head: 'Shh, you don't know what you are saying.'

And so within a few years this form of insanity will have completely disappeared from our national life." The idea for this plan, Golden said, came to him when a Protestant minister of his acquaintance teasingly suggested he convert. He responded to his clerical friend that churches only liked to get *one* Jew, and then only once in awhile. The minister conceded the point.[30]

For Christians worried that church-pew integration could be the next site of Supreme Court interference, Golden offered his White Citizens Plan. If white Gentiles simply converted to Judaism, they could escape the integration of their churches with the additional benefit of using the nice clubs, hotels, and other services created by Jews who were barred from Christian enclaves. Then there was the Bomb Shelter Plan that would put shelters in all houses of worship, forcing a panicked ecumenism. Other Golden Plans advocated a lending system allowing blacks to borrow white babies and pose as babysitters to attend performances without seating for blacks; suggested pogo sticks instead of squad cars so that mixed-race police teams could work together; urged turbans for blacks, to capitalize on the southern willingness to respect exotic foreign visitors and boost the textile industry at the same time; and suggested "Out of Order" signs on "White Only" water fountains and restrooms as a way to quietly force an end to the two-color system.[31]

Golden spun off a few other plans that he didn't publicize but included in letters to friends, such as his thought that if oil could be discovered under land occupied by black sharecroppers in a southern state, it would surely force a racist governor or member of Congress to "file his claim and try to prove that he is 1/64th Negro." This would settle the race question for the entire South, Golden declared.[32]

As the civil rights movement unfolded and violence became more common, Golden's plans became correspondingly bleaker in their humor. In 1964 he announced the Golden Insurance Plan. Workers, black and white, who were traveling south to register black voters could buy life insurance policies on themselves from white-owned companies. The prospect of paying so many claims would motivate the company owners to reason with their white-supremacist neighbors and talk them out of bombings and other attacks, he said.[33]

"Send the Bedspread to the Laundry!"

The reversals of fortune didn't change Golden's day-to-day life much. His office and home looked the same, although now the level of tidiness mattered a bit more. When Edward R. Murrow's production team called to say they wanted to film Golden at work for the popular *Person to Person* show on CBS, he hung up the phone and bellowed to his secretary: "Send the bedspread to the laundry!" He then resumed typing. Golden still liked moderately priced cigars for the ten or so he smoked each day, and while higher-grade bourbon was fine, he was not terribly fussy. (Secretary Mamie Hill, a teetotaler, left his employ assuming "all liquor is called 'Early Times.'") He did replace a few of his oldest, scratchiest opera record albums, Mozart's *Don Giovanni* and the classic canon of Puccini and Donizetti. Now he could keep his eye out for a collector's copy of "the greatest recording ever made," the one performed by Enrico Caruso and Antonio Scotti of Verdi's *La forza del destino*.[34]

There were noticeable improvements to his wardrobe, which had never recovered after his ousting from Wall Street. Sixty years after Golden's arrival in Charlotte, acquaintances still remembered his meager wardrobe during the early days. When the *Carolina Israelite* took off, he started sending *all* his shirts to the laundry, not just the special-occasion ones. And now he traded in his rumpled look for good, tailored suits and polished shoes, custom-made for his short, wide feet. "After *Only in America*, he was positively dapper," said Richard Goldhurst. "He bought suits at Saks Fifth Avenue and he'd tell the salesman that he wanted a suit or a raincoat just like so-and-so had . . . someone he'd met recently: a Broadway producer, say, and that's just what he'd get." At home Golden wore a starched shirt, usually white, often with a red vest and "a pair of pants to whatever natty suit he put his hands on first in the closet," said Goldhurst, "and, no necktie." For formal occasions he brought out an elegant dinner jacket. Women, especially, thought he looked smart. "My wife Doris always said he looked sexy when he dressed up," Goldhurst remembered. One day as the two men rode together in a cab during a visit to New York City, Goldhurst solemnly warned his father of a sartorial shift. "I told him, 'They say fashion dictates no more cuffs.' After a moment's thought, Harry replied: 'Fine. As long as *they* leave me alone.'"[35]

Pushing the Prose

Many a book editor has sweated getting a bestselling author to buckle down and write the next book, but Golden's editor and publisher had the opposite problem. *Only in America* was barely off the presses at World, and Golden was enthusiastically promoting the idea of a second book, this time with son Harry playing a larger role in copyediting the work. Harry Jr. had been struggling with alcohol and stress, and his worried father wanted to nudge him toward work that he did well and that would provide satisfaction without pressure. "It is all right for you to send material to Harry, Jr. for copy-editing," Zevin wrote to Golden. "However, if your next book comes out in less than 2½ to 3 years, it will prove a grievous error. I hope that you will be guided by my judgment and experience in these matters. Let's concentrate on this one."[36]

Richard Goldhurst became more involved with his father's work now too, and his would be an ongoing role, unlike his brothers, who edited or handled research for their father much less often and in smaller amounts. Goldhurst had contributed regular book reviews to the *Carolina Israelite* since 1953, and after *Only in America* established his father's fame, he began to edit copy from his Westport, Connecticut, home and eventually came to spend considerable time in Charlotte. The two men developed a staccato style in their notes to each other, an efficient practice that would serve them well later when Golden traveled overseas and needed to cable anecdotes and quotes home for use in magazine pieces as well as in his own paper.[37]

Golden didn't listen to Zevin or Targ or the critics who reviewed his later books when they urged him to slow down. He paid little heed to Targ's suggestions to take more care with his writing. The editor tried various ploys, such as forwarding letters from respected writers who took issue with this or that in Golden's book. "I send you herewith a letter from a friend of mine," Targ wrote Golden on 31 July 1958. "He is preparing a 10-volume definitive bibliography of American Literature at Harvard University at present." The friend, Jacob Blanck, liked the book and was slightly apologetic for what he called his "bug hunting." He went on to fill six pages with questions and corrections of *Only in America*. The letter made its point, but alas, it came in the mail along with piles of others praising the book—a book that, after all, was still being reprinted to meet demand.[38]

Golden parried by alerting various journalists and critics that he had a plan to write a book a year—"not two books a year, nor one book every two years, but one a year," *New York Times* columnist Lewis Nichols dutifully reported, just a month after Targ's attempt at coercing Golden into more careful construction of his work. Golden also happily collected letters he could use to fend off his editor's suggestions. One came from a Mrs. Jack Levensky—Braille Chairman of the Tifereth Israel Synagogue Braille Group in Des Moines, Iowa. "I think it might be of interest to you to know that today I completed transcribing into Braille your book, *Only in America*," she wrote. "I am looking forward with much interest to the book you are soon to publish. I hope that this new book, too, can be made available to the blind." Well, there you go, Golden said. If even *blind* readers wanted another book, why on earth would you wait?[39]

He wasn't joking. While the literary quality of his books clearly suffered from the speed with which he churned them out, a student of marketing would do well to analyze Golden's instincts on when to push ahead. Even his failures—a World's Fair tourist guide and Midas Mineral Water—were good ideas, just ahead of their time. When his first book was a hit, Golden knew he was part of something bigger that had started earlier in the decade; aspects of Jewish life were increasingly being embraced by the larger culture. "The Rise of the Goldbergs" started as a radio show in the 1920s, then morphed into the hugely popular new genre, the TV sit-com, in 1949. Its star, Gertrude Berg, won an Emmy in 1950, and the show ran until 1956. Bess Myerson, the country's first Jewish Miss America in 1945, was now a TV regular.[40]

Popular Jewish performers were becoming big stars: Jack Benny and George Burns made the move from radio to TV; Milton ("Uncle Miltie") Berle was a superstar; Sid Caesar and his "Your Show of Shows" was a hit. Books by Jewish writers as varied as Herman Wouk, Leon Uris, Bernard Malamud, Saul Bellow, and Philip Roth were transforming American popular culture. Yiddish words, from "bagel" to "kibitz," were becoming so embedded in the American lexicon that Leo Rosten's weighty volume, *The Joys of Yiddish*, would be an instant (and long-standing) hit when it came out a decade later.

Yet Golden was not much driven by the financial aspect. He was making up for lost years. He had dreamed of being a writer for much of his life, and now, in his late fifties, he was not going to waste time. His second book was titled *For 2 Cents Plain*, mimicking the thrifty order given for a large glass of seltzer at stands in New York during his youth. (Flavored syrups cost another penny.) He pushed World to get it out in the summer of 1959 and was rewarded when his first and second book were on the *New York Times* bestseller list at the same time. "Here is a piece of publishing audacity," one reviewer declared. Golden's two books had made him a bestselling author, and he been "Ed Murrowed, Jack Paared, Dave Garrowayed, Arthur Godfreyed and sought as a speaker in all parts of the country." For once, Golden's braggadocio was not misplaced; after seeing Golden's touring schedule and observing his self-promotion, a *New York Times* book-industry columnist conceded that it probably *was* possible that he signed close to 50,000 copies of his first two books, given that some 420,000 copies were in print by 1959. "At airports, in cabs, on foot, he constantly must reach for his pen," wrote Lewis Nichols.[41]

Golden knew that the popular writer's shelf life could be short. As Norman Mailer once described a time when his own popularity temporarily plummeted, "America is a fast country." And Golden had another reason for his rapid-fire production, a strategy familiar to anyone who has ever tried to quit smoking or start dieting: Spread the word, create a crowd of witnesses, and therefore shame yourself into doing the hard thing. "The announcement of a new book, even before the next has come out, is a kind of discipline I seem to need," he told his *Carolina Israelite* readers. "Once I announce it I MUST do it because that temptation to sit back, listen to Mozart, read Emerson, Shakespeare, Sandburg and Steinbeck, and bask, is too great and I know that I should keep a-going."[42]

When *Only in America* came out as a paperback in the summer of 1959, Golden announced the good news in his newspaper. "Paperbacks are the nicest thing that has happened to American literature since Thomas Wolfe," he declared.[43]

A Bestseller Goes to Broadway. Briefly.

Only in America was out less than a month when Golden got a letter from the playwrights who wrote the scripts for *Inherit the Wind* and *Auntie Mame*. It seemed that Jerome Lawrence and Robert E. Lee wanted to make *Only in America* into a Broadway play. Before Golden knew it, Herman Shumlin, a respected producer and director, was on board, and a young actor named Nehemiah Persoff was cast to play Golden. (Big star Paul Muni dropped out for health reasons.) The play was in good company, advertised alongside the big hit *Gypsy* with Ethel Merman, *The Sound of Music*, *The Threepenny Opera*, Tennessee Williams's *Orpheus Descending*, and that enduring show *The Music Man* (the *Cats* of its day). *Only in America* opened in the Cort Theatre on West Forth-Eighth Street on 19 November 1959.[44]

After the opening-night show, the playwrights, Golden, Tiny, and a small group of New York friends gathered and awaited the critics' verdicts. Between them they had connections in every newsroom and so were clustered around the telephone, listening to reviews read sotto voce before the papers hit the streets. The first one set in type was by Walter Kerr, the excellent reviewer then with the *Herald Tribune*. Kerr declared, "Mr. Golden is both the subject and victim of the play." Brooks Atkinson's review in the *New York Times* was thoughtful and complimentary of Golden and the premise but tough on the end result. The resolution of the dramatic tension—when the Golden character triumphs over his prison scandal—was basically a bomb. "Like other aspects of the dramatization, the conclusion seems a little uncomfortable and contrived," Atkinson wrote, adding that "the play not only adds nothing to what we all know about him from the book: it also takes away some of his quality as a writer, a serious student of American affairs and as a man. The tricks of the theatre tend to belittle him." Another reviewer wrote, "Golden is better silent." Yet another began, "God speed, for trying, but . . . ." And so on. "Reviews like this end all pretense at parties," Golden wrote in the *Carolina Israelite* a few days later. "People put on their hats and coats, quietly say goodnight, and go home." Within a few days, some other writers and critics tried to temper the negative reviews. "The daily press treated [the play] rather harshly," wrote Harold Clurman in the *Nation*. "That seems to me unfair. The play is, no doubt, sentimental, indeed corny, but since when have we sworn off sentiment or corn in our theatre?"[45]

Once a man has flopped with a play cast entirely with vaudevillian midgets, as Golden had back in his earlier New York days, not much will surprise him in the theater. So he told the tale of his sudden death on Broadway far and wide, insisting that he felt no bitterness about the experience. Typically, the loss of $2,000 he and Tiny had invested did not bother him at all. (A couple of Charlotte friends who had invested might have been more disgruntled, although Hermann Cohen was a good sport.) Golden gallantly said that the play just had too much of him and not enough of Charlotte and the times. In his autobiography, he wrote that in hindsight it seemed clear that a sensible person would not buy a ticket to a Broadway show "when for $2 at a Hadassah meeting they can hear the real Harry Golden with luncheon thrown in."[46]

Publicity, even about a bad play, along with big sales of Golden's bestsellers brought more subscribers to the *Carolina Israelite*: 52,900 in 1960, and the numbers would climb to a peak of 55,000 the next year. Golden now also got more requests to review or write blurbs for new books— Jewish nostalgia, race and civil rights, humor, and fiction. By the time his third book, *Enjoy, Enjoy!* came out in 1960, requests were coming in a steady stream. As any rising writer finds, this initially flattering inclusion soon becomes a time-eating, often thankless, and usually unpaid labor.[47]

Dolores Ziff, publicity manager for J. B. Lippincott Co., wrote Golden in February 1960 and asked if he would consider reading a galley of a southern novel by an unknown young, first-time novelist and supplying a quote. The book was *To Kill a Mockingbird*, by Harper Lee. "You, of course, realize how difficult it can be to establish a young novelist, so I need hardly add that any comment you may have on the book could be enormously helpful to the furthering of Miss Lee's writing career," wrote Ziff. Golden complied, and perhaps he helped boost sales. In any event, in August 1960, Lee's classic story of Scout, Jem, and Atticus Finch was on the *New York Times* bestseller list along with Golden's *Enjoy, Enjoy!*[48]

Once it became clear that Golden could open doors at a wide range of publications, he was often tapped for help. He became a master of writing a charming "recommendation" in difficult cases. When a casual acquaintance used him as reference for a writing job at *Playboy*, Golden wrote back, " I think B__ is right in suggesting that I write to you because the odds now would be five hundred to one instead of a thousand to one, I hope. [She] is not only well-educated and highly articulate but there are flashes now and then of an original mind."[49]

Writers who had not the slightest need of Golden's support pursued him as well. One in this eclectic fan club was Henry Miller, whose novel *Tropic of Cancer* was the subject of a landmark censorship fight about to go to the Supreme Court. Miller wrote in 1963 that he was pleased to hear from a mutual friend that Golden liked his writing. "I got the notion you didn't like my work," Miller wrote. "A surprise and a great pleasure, let me assure you." In closing, Miller wrote, "But be free not to like my work when it hits you the wrong way." Golden's succinct reply went back by return mail: "Dear Mr. Miller: Thanks for the note. Stay well. You are *not* what's wrong with the country." The high court ruled in Miller's favor the next year.[50]

Golden and John Steinbeck, winner of the Pulitzer Prize and the Nobel Prize for literature, shared jokes and fears in their small stack of missives. A postcard sent by Steinbeck in 1963 about one soon-to-be candidate for president said only, "Barry Goldwater promises to lead us out of Egypt, and I believe he could do it too. Trouble is, we ain't in Egypt." (Golden co-opted that joke in the *Carolina Israelite* the next year.) In another letter, written in his beautiful cursive, Steinbeck wrote movingly about the growing anger and threats of widespread violence in the civil rights movement: "The unbelievable patience and forbearance of the Negro [has] so far been unique in revolutionary history. I am saddened but not surprised to see the edges of patience giving way to rage." After the author died in 1968, his widow, Elaine Scott Steinbeck, wrote Golden, "He felt a bond with you. . . . He was splendid to the very end—and you will rejoice with me I know that his clear, sparkling mind never faltered until he went to sleep. . . . Thank you for being his friend."[51]

But segregation even tainted meetings with well-known black writers. In 1961 Golden wrote to a friend about babbling away on the telephone to visiting writer James Baldwin, realizing that there was no nice place he could take him for a drink. "I felt like such a damn fool," Golden said. In the coming years Golden would take strong offense at some of Baldwin's remarks, but the awkwardness of that day on the telephone was what he remembered most clearly whenever Baldwin's name came up.[52]

Black Churches

As the civil rights movement assumed a shape clearly visible all over America, one of Golden's greatest strengths came to the fore: an unusual gift for seeing and appreciating what others drew from their religious beliefs. This talent seemed ingrained, not sustained by any ritual practices of his own. Golden spent much more time at the front of houses of worship as a guest speaker than he ever did as a congregant. Many things fed this vital part of his nature. He never lost his respect for his mother's piety, even as he gently poked fun at it. ("You'll go to the movies—with God's help!") He reflected many times on the status afforded his father as a cantor and Talmudic authority, and on his own long journey from childhood influences: "My first impressions of Christianity came in the home, of course. My parents . . . had come from the villages of Eastern Europe where Christians were feared with legitimate reason. . . . However Christianity itself, as a philosophy, did not impress me until I began to watch the Negroes of the South fight for their right to enter society as first-class citizens. . . . When I studied this phenomenon, I came to the conclusion that they are using a mighty weapon—their Christian faith."[53]

And he did, after all, have a wife raised in the Roman Catholic Church as well as many friends—and a couple of cellmates—who were Christians. Notwithstanding his anger over his sons being raised in the church and a thorough knowledge of Christians persecuting Jews and nonbelievers throughout history, he was respectful of the institutions—or at least the *idea* of the institutions. Black adults in the South were empowered by their churches, and Golden was both deeply touched and angered by the heartbreaking contrast between daily life and church roles: "[The church] provides the Negro with the only opportunity for both self-esteem and self-expression, which are denied him in open society. The Negro is a truck driver, his wife is a domestic, but over the week-end they are deacons, stewards, elders, communal leaders, Sunday School teachers, and choir directors. It is of particular importance for the children to see their parents, dressed in Sunday clothes, participating in the education, religious, and social activities of the community."[54]

This perceptive curiosity made Golden cognizant of the deep roots of southern black churches. While he did not have a spiritual attachment to the Hebrew Bible or its Christian descendant, Golden admired and perhaps in some way envied the strength that many black churchgoers drew from the imagery depicting a triumphant end to slavery. He respected the power of all such spiritual armor that had been worn by believers throughout history. An understanding of the influence America's churches had on the powerful did not elude him either. He knew, as James "Scotty" Reston once observed when writing about the civil rights movement in the *New York Times*, that "all [members of Congress] want to be re-elected, and all of them know the political power of the church, even if they never go there except for votes."[55]

Golden's readership was always predominantly white, but he had black fans as well, especially those who felt at home with the language and ideas he borrowed from African American preachers urging listeners to look beyond the fight for desegregated lunch counters to something greater. This righteous work of the black churches first empowered the civil rights movement, followed later by white congregations, and provided the famous and the ordinary folk with the strength to remain active in the fight for years to come. Golden was deliberately provocative, but utterly serious, when he spoke about the role of Christianity in the movement: "The Negroes themselves, in using Christianity as a weapon in their fight for social justice, gave their fellow Christians hope and proof that Christianity still has its uses." It did not save whites from the Depression or the Jews from Hitler, he said, but Christianity was going to save the black man.[56]

Evangelizing as Art Form

Golden was captivated by the charismatic power of many popular evangelists, perhaps recognizing kindred spirits in these men with persuasive, theatrical styles. He had a soft spot for "Daddy Grace," the African American preacher whose mass baptisms (sometimes carried out with a fire hose if full immersion wasn't possible), claims of raising the dead, and glittering jewelry dazzled a huge flock of followers until his death in the 1960s. Golden gave credit where it was due, in this case to a man of God who sold his own brands of coffee, toothpaste, cold cream, and handkerchiefs "moistened with a tear of the Lord"—a man who beat both the IRS and a rap for violating the Mann Act by traveling with a young piano player and who got the Charlotte police to search for and find a missing suitcase stuffed with $25,000 in cash donations.[57]

Golden happily brokered an invitation for his friend Billy Graham to deliver a sermon at Belmont Abbey College in 1963, the first time Graham had been invited to preach before a Roman Catholic church. Golden cackled at the resulting headline in the *Charlotte News*: "Jew Helps Baptist with Catholic Talk." Graham, a Charlotte native, was already well known by the 1950s when the men met. Graham's stance on segregation was mixed but in some ways surprisingly moderate; he had insisted as early as 1944 that an audience be integrated. In the South, however, seating at his crusades was routinely segregated until after 1954. One turning point came when Ralph McGill pressed Graham in a 1953 letter to describe his view of segregation. The preacher wrote back, "In my study of the Bible, I find no verses or chapters to support segregation."[58]

In 1956, Graham wrote an article that was impressive for the time, published by *Life* under the headline "Billy Graham Makes Plea for End to Intolerance." The lengthy piece was both personal reflection and directive sermon, and it accomplished the rare feat of looking at all sides without diluting the central issue of race hate. Graham portrayed southern segregationists with some sympathy and correctly pointed out that prejudice was not all-white or all-southern. But he did not waffle when describing the Christian's duty to avoid prejudice, racism, and violence: "Accept your responsibility. If you are a Christian, you are your Brother's Keeper. It is easier to conform to the crowd, to act with only your own interests in view, to avoid sticking your neck out; but it is our duty to know, to proclaim and to live by the truth."[59]

Critics of Graham, including Morehouse University president Benjamin Mays and editorialists at black-owned newspapers, challenged him to do more for civil rights; opponents of integration labeled him a danger; and moderate-to-liberal writers such as Golden and McGill admired his willingness to question the practices of his church and country. He preached in Little Rock in 1957, and the next year he was barred from the grounds of the South Carolina statehouse by Governor George Bell Timmerman Jr., who called the preacher "a widely known advocate of desegregation." In the 1960s, his staff met with the Reverend Martin Luther King Jr.'s close advisors and provided practical advice on planning and carrying out large-crowd gatherings. In 1964, when a shattered Birmingham mourned the loss of four black children who died when white supremacists bombed a church during Sunday school, a group made up of Jews, Gentiles of all denominations, blacks, and whites asked Graham to come. He did.[60]

In 2002, taped recordings of anti-Semitic remarks in conversations between President Richard Nixon and Graham in 1972 left many people stunned. Jews and Christians castigated the eighty-three-year-old preacher, who issued an apology, saying he did not remember the remarks. The idea that he was responding to Nixon's paranoid anti-Jewish rant got him off a bit easier with those who believed that mere proximity to the disgraced president was unavoidably corrupting.[61]

There is no doubt that Graham cared for and respected Golden. In 1960 Golden wrote, "I believe it would come as a great surprise to many people to know of our close friendship; my deep affection for you and the ample evidence I have that my affection for you is not unrequited." Thirteen years later, within a year of the conversation with Nixon, Graham wrote Golden, thanking him for a Christmas letter and adding, "You too are a good friend—and I love you very much!" A relationship that took place more on paper than in person might not seem as close or loving as the men described it, but to both Golden and Graham, it was obviously important.[62]

When the handsome Graham came to the *Carolina Israelite* office in December 1960, Richard Goldhurst finally met the famous evangelist about whom he had heard so much from his father. "Harry described Billy as looking like a tiger," Goldhurst said. "I would describe him as possessing animal magnetism." When Graham greeted the office staff, the two secretaries "almost collapsed in a welter of admiration." They were deeply impressed to see that the boss was holding off on his bourbon out of respect for Graham's abstemious beliefs.[63]

Graham was there in answer to a pleading letter Golden had sent the month before, seeking help in fighting the imprisonment of a popular North Carolina union official, Boyd E. Payton of the Textile Workers Union of America. "You know I would never 'use' you," Golden began. "But now I do intend to . . . for someone else." He explained that Payton "was accused, tried, and convicted in an atmosphere of prejudice and fear," and then stated twice that he was absolutely convinced of the man's innocence. Golden asked Graham to use his influence with outgoing governor Luther Hodges and governor-elect Terry Sanford to get clemency for Payton. The situation was a political minefield by the time Graham was asked to intervene. It had started back in the fall of 1958, when workers at the Harriet & Henderson Cotton Mills figured that their expiring contract would be re-upped without much fuss, as had been the case the last two times around. But when mill ownership demanded a no-strike clause, 1,038 members of the Textile Workers Union of America walked out.[64]

Golden had a little bit more warning than most. He and Payton talked often about the political and economic clout of local mill owners and the strikes in the 1920s and 1930s that had been marked by violence and few victories for the workers. Even when national union membership swelled after the war, textile workers in North Carolina and elsewhere in the South were harder to sell on the advantages of joining up. Fighting between rival unions and postwar concerns about Communism within organized labor were factors, but perhaps the most significant barrier was cultural. In the mid-1940s, "organizers noted with frustration, anger, and grudging respect the very persuasive social, political and economic authority exercised by management over workers," wrote textile-industry historian Brent D. Glass. The two men couldn't know it yet, but the Harriet & Henderson strike would become what Glass called "a symbol of failed unionism and management resistance."[65]

For now, they spoke of homier things. Payton, busy as he was as union director for the Carolinas, could provide the sort of detail Golden loved to hear about life among the mill workers. The Paytons were the Wentworth neighborhood's go-to folks for help with just about anything: projects at their Baptist church, babysitting, chores, and meals. His wife was "Two-Cake Kitty," always making more food than her three kids could eat and sharing in a way that didn't hint at charity.[66]

The strike dragged on for more than a year, neither side making enough concessions to get the wheels unstuck. In February 1959, mill ownership dropped the hammer: Come get your jobs, they said, but no contract. Only about 5 percent of the workers planned to cross the picket line, and the situation went out of control quickly when strikebreakers and picketers clashed. Hodges, himself a textile mill owner, sent in state troopers and then the North Carolina National Guard, with critics berating him for waiting too long and then allowing troopers to protect scabs but not strikers. Payton was hurt at least twice: attacked and knocked out, then later injured when rocks were thrown at his car. In June, Payton and seven other union men were arrested and charged in an alleged plot to dynamite a power station and mill buildings. The evidence was flimsy, the star witness for the prosecution was untrustworthy and unconvincing, and the trial was awash in prejudice and procedural irregularities. Despite a strong team of defense lawyers and sympathetic news coverage, all eight were convicted. Payton was sentenced to up to ten years in prison. The North Carolina State Supreme Court denied an appeal, and the U.S. Supreme Court would not hear the case.[67]

Golden's connections kept him apprised of the situation, and he prepared a long essay for the July 1959 *Carolina Israelite*, "The Textile Workers and the South." The piece used labor history and the Henderson strike to examine the strengths and weaknesses of the textile union in a dispassionate fashion. He held it until the last minute, then appended a paragraph to note the late-breaking news of Payton's sentencing. The effect was much stronger than his usual short editorial style, which relied so heavily on anecdote and the more liberal use of the personal pronoun. He sent the clip and a detailed timeline of the case to reporters around the country, to state politicians, and to the powerful Billy Graham.[68]

Daily newspapers covered the case closely, including detailed pieces by Charles Clay in the *Raleigh News and Observer* and Kays Gary in the *Charlotte Observer*. There were others working behind the scenes, and Golden was personally encouraged by high-ranking state officials, perhaps even Hodges himself, to find a way to make the focus shift from the legal to the religious. A call for Christian charity, as Golden so often noted, was an excellent weapon. He knew a public request by Graham could be hung out in front of people only once, so when Payton was tricked into taking a lie-detector test in prison and supposedly failed, Golden reined in the plan until he could quietly spread the word of the unreliability of the test. A few months later, Graham came in on cue. The preacher wrote to Sanford as "My Dear Governor" and vouched for Payton's "exemplary personal life . . . devotion to family life, and his participation in religious activities [that have] made him beloved by all who know him."[69]

Payton's sentence was soon shortened, and he was released on parole in August 1961. He received a full pardon in 1964. The Textile Workers Union declared the strike officially over. Graham and Golden congratulated each other. The preacher wrote his friend, "I always thought we needed a Rabbi on the team, and I think you would be a good one."[70]

The Reverend Martin Luther King Jr.

The pastoral leader who became most identified with the movement was a figure in Golden's life as well, although in a much different way than Graham was. "I did not know Martin Luther King well," wrote Golden in his autobiography. "I met him several times, usually at meetings where we spoke to raise money for the Freedom Riders or the NAACP Legal Defense Fund, and I talked with him on the occasion of the March on Washington in 1963." (Golden did once brag that he was the only lecturer who could accurately claim to have introduced King at an NAACP event in Charlotte and then gone on in the same week to be keynoter at the city's Junior Chamber of Commerce.)[71]

Anyone familiar with Golden's style might be surprised that he did not make much more of this relationship. But while he spoke and wrote about

King many times, Golden did not overstate their connection. His accounts were sincerely respectful but not always paeans. His highest praise for King placed him alongside Robert F. Kennedy, who *was* a friend and whom Golden deeply admired. Golden did not appear to know just how much the two men disliked each other. As Kennedy biographer Evan Thomas wrote, Robert Kennedy and King "*should* have been mutual admirers" but were not. Despite some common traits—admiration of courage and perhaps a similar kind of self-consciousness from growing up in privilege—the two men were culturally miles apart. "Because of small, seemingly superficial differences, matters of taste and humor and style, Bobby Kennedy and Martin Luther King passed by without ever really understanding, or liking, each other," wrote Thomas.[72]

Golden seems to have assumed, as many Americans did (and some Kennedy history buffs probably still do), that an incident in which both John and Robert Kennedy reached out to King came out of their strong regard and concern for the minister. At the start of the 1960 presidential campaign, King was arrested and jailed in Georgia during a protest. John Kennedy called Coretta Scott King, who was pregnant, to express his concern, and Robert Kennedy called the Georgia judge to push for King's release. Both Kennedys saw the calls as the decent and expedient thing to do, but the call to Coretta King would not have happened without a lot of maneuverings, manipulation, and nail biting by their staff and advisors. It was good advice. The senior Martin Luther King told a crowd that he was so impressed by Kennedy's courage in calling his daughter-in-law Coretta that he was changing his vote. "I had expected to vote against Senator Kennedy because of his religion," the elder King said bluntly, "but now he can be my President, Catholic or whatever he is." He added the kicker: "I've got all my votes and I've got a suitcase, and I'm going to take them up there and dump them in his lap."[73]

Golden, regardless of how aware he was of the currents between the men, got to the heart of the matter. He regarded King as a black man able to "think white" and frame the civil rights issue as a morality question understandable to the majority culture. Kennedy was a man who could "think black" and be listened to by African Americans. "Martin Luther King and Robert Kennedy were equally important heroes," he wrote. "They were heroes because they were leaders to whom all of us, white and black, could relate."[74]

Some of the reasons for Golden's reserve in writing about King are clear. Since the stressful days of doing business with the infamous Bishop Cannon, Golden was generally more careful when quoting and describing encounters with Christian clergy. (He showed less restraint when describing his interactions with rabbis.) And it was true that meetings with King were brief, always taking place in the company of people in the minister's inner circle. The most significant tie between the two men—and it was a big one—was the complimentary reference King made to Golden in his famous *Letter from Birmingham Jail*, written while King was locked in a cell after his arrest in that city in 1963.

Golden was respected by grassroots organizers at Highlander, as well as by the movers and shakers of the NAACP, with whom King's Southern Christian Leadership Conference had an uneasy relationship. As more divisions grew in the black-activist community, Golden's support of King's positions was more valued by the minister's inner circle, who showed their approval by inviting Golden personally to marches and other scheduled events. When invited to demonstrations in Selma in 1965, Golden answered King directly: "Bless you for the telegram. You yourself once told me, stay there and write the words. . . . I have a scheduled address . . . at Drake University. . . . I will discuss Martin Luther King, America's Gandhi. All my love to you. You may wind up making Christians out of us all, Gentiles included."[75]

Golden was proud of the connection, and in this instance he reprinted the telegrams in the *Carolina Israelite*. Yet behind his positive observations of King there was some small doubt or disagreement, criticism, or old resentment that one picks up from a close study of Golden's writings and correspondence. Perhaps it was the mix of awe and resentment that so often follows a charismatic leader. It is also true that by the mid-1960s, King and Golden had staked out different positions on the Vietnam War. King was pushing hard for American withdrawal and suggested that he would be the right person to broach a discussion with Ho Chi Minh and others. Golden, at this time, believed the "domino theory," which argued that leaving Vietnam without a clear victory would put the larger region at risk for full Communist takeover. These differences may have influenced Golden's writings about King. The exact nature of his true feelings about King remains unclear, and whatever its ingredients, Golden put it aside.

Time for All

There was a noticeable increase in popular-magazine coverage of both Golden and King by the end of the 1950s. Flattering profiles surfaced in *Time* magazine. Golden was featured in an article in 1957, and King appeared on the cover in the same year. King was praised lavishly. "Negro leaders look toward Montgomery," said *Time*. "The man whose word they seek is not a judge, or a lawyer, or a political strategist or a flaming orator. He is a scholarly, 28-year-old Negro Baptist minister . . . who in little more than a year has risen from nowhere to become one of the nation's remarkable leaders of men." The "risen from nowhere" line betrays either ignorance of the black-church royalty of the South or a desire to romanticize the facts, or both.[76]

The *Time* article did give a sense of King's unique strengths: "He can draw within himself for long, single-minded concentration on his people's problems, and then exert the force of personality and conviction that makes him a public leader." The editors no doubt considered this line to be the highest of compliments: "Personally humble, articulate, and of high educational attainment, Martin Luther King Jr. is, in fact, what many a Negro—and, were it not for his color, many a white—would like to be."[77]

Of Golden, *Time* said, "While Southerners . . . have become increasingly impatient of Northern reporters who write stories criticizing segregation in Dixie, one of North Carolina's most influential citizens is a sharp-tongued Yankee newspaperman who unabashedly derides discrimination in any form." Golden, the unsigned profile continued, is "consulted constantly by Southern officials concerned with racial issues, many of whom have even learned to treasure his irrepressible wisecracks." "Consulted constantly" was not far off the mark. As the 1960s commenced, Golden was settled in comfortably as cultural translator for middle-class white America and beyond. He was an expert witness on behalf of the civil rights movement, sought out by politicians of both parties, church leaders, Jews, and blacks at the forefront of organized protests.[78]

His ability to speak to both liberals and states' rights segregationists was most appreciated. Tensions in Washington had been steadily rising in the years since a document known as the "Southern Manifesto" was signed by most of the southern Democrats in the spring of 1956. In it they vowed to fight *Brown*: "We pledge ourselves to use all lawful means to bring about a reversal of this decision which is contrary to the Constitution and to prevent the use of force in its implementation. In this trying period, as we all seek to right this wrong, we appeal to our people not to be provoked by the agitators and troublemakers invading our States and to scrupulously refrain from disorder and lawless acts."[79]

As Lyndon Johnson's biographer Robert A. Caro put it, this was "nothing less than an outright call by one hundred elected legislators in the national government for massive, unified, defiance of an order from the nation's highest court." The divide between segregationist southern Democrats and the rest of the party had been smoothed over somewhat in recent years, largely due to the tireless efforts and expert arm-twisting by Senator Lyndon Johnson and the more dignified but equally determined Sam Rayburn, Speaker of the House. Now the gap was greatly widened, and the dialogue that had once flowed across aisles and delegations was stilted.[80]

Golden and his writing could defuse tension when few others could. Democrats and Republicans, moderates, liberals, and conservatives all had constituents who knew about Harry Golden. *Time, Saturday Evening Post, Life, Ebony, Jet*, the NAACP's *Crisis*, and others ran his work, sometimes putting his byline on the cover, and published a stream of stories about him written by others. His speeches were covered by mainstream media regularly, such as the sermon he delivered Thanksgiving week in the beautiful St. Paul's Chapel on the Columbia University campus in 1960, where he processed in behind "faculty deans, chaplains, and religious counselors, followed by the Verger and the learned Episcopalian rector."[81]

News of Golden's writing and speeches also appeared more often in the black press, such as the quote in the *Chicago Daily Defender* in the fall of 1962: "Gradualism is a good word. Each of us develops gradually, and so do our children, our families and our cultures. . . . But what is wrong with 'gradually' in relation to the racial segregation of the South is that it never happened. In a sense it has indeed been 'gradually'—three hundred and forty years of 'gradually.'"[82]

By 1961–62, five of his books were selling well: *Only in America, For 2 Cents Plain, Enjoy, Enjoy!, You're Entitle'*, and the latest one, *Carl Sandburg*, a collection of anecdotes and short essays about his dear friend. (As Golden put it, "I am now up to Moses—five books.") A British publisher brought out a handsome volume, *The Harry Golden Omnibus*, a selection of pieces from the first three books. His newspaper columns for the Bell-McClure syndicate reached all corners of the country. The page count of the *Carolina Israelite* was climbing, as was its mailing list.[83]

A photograph taken for one of his early book jackets was used so widely in advertising that it barely needed a caption: a grinning Golden, cigar clamped in the side of his mouth as he leaned back in his rocking chair, short legs stretched straight out in front of him. It became the heart of an effective circulation campaign promoting the *Carolina Israelite* between publication of his books. "WHY WAIT A YEAR FOR HARRY GOLDEN'S NEXT BOOK?" blared the headline.[84]

In between his usual speaking tours to places like Wichita and Cleveland, Golden received many other requests to appear or contribute. Some of the requests for his time were more gratifying than others. The U.S. Army sent

Golden to talk to troops in Korea. North Carolina's Belmont Abbey College gave him an honorary doctorate in 1962. At that occasion, Golden happily noted that conservative William F. Buckley Jr., a staunch Roman Catholic whom he disliked for his conservative views and to-the-manor-born affect, would certainly "look with less than enthusiasm upon this honor." At best, Golden thought Buckley pompous. At worst, he saw Buckley as an anti-Semite who, in the context of Israel's trial of Nazi Adolf Eichmann, referred to the Jewish people as a "mythical legal entity" and asserted that Holocaust deaths numbered in the "hundreds of thousands," rather than the millions known to be accurate. Buckley disagreed with many of Golden's simple prescriptions for social betterment. And like many intellectuals of the day, Buckley was annoyed by Golden's popularity. But he understood the breadth of that audience, so he was quick to respond when Golden wrote or said something disparaging about him. Golden once called Buckley "rhetorically impenetrable" and was soundly rebuked by Buckley's representative at the George Matthews Adams Service, which syndicated Buckley's column.[85]

Golden was appearing more often now at colleges and universities, along with the usual fundraisers and entertainment venues. He had been a proud supporter of SNCC since 1960 and appreciated that students, even at smaller, quieter campuses, were stirred by the sit-ins in Greensboro and then Nashville that began to get national press coverage in 1961. When African American James Meredith fought to gain admission to the University of Mississippi that year, the campus energy ramped up rapidly.[86]

Golden was struck by how the questions asked of him by these students differed from those raised by his other audiences. The usual inquiries of "What are those people up to?" gave way to the most-often-asked question: "What can one person do?" His standard answer was a quiet and motivating moment for many of the listeners: "The next time someone uses the word 'nigger,' put your hand on his wrist and say, 'Please, not in front of me.' And perhaps he will never use this word again in front of anyone. That is something."[87]

These audiences reflected a generation that was coming of age having been exposed to the idea of interfaith cooperation at a level that many of their parents had not imagined. It's fair to say that Golden's popularity was both contributing cause and effect of this broad trend toward interfaith activities within and outside the civil rights movement. He liked to tell these groups about the time in the early 1940s when he'd enlisted Charlotte women to sell memberships in a nascent chapter of the National Conference of Christians and Jews. The woman who widely outsold her peers was a Presbyterian who told her prospects about a wonderful group called the National Conference of Christians—simply dropping the part of the title that added "and Jews." Back then, Golden joked, this was the only surefire way to do successful interfaith work.[88]

As his public was drawing closer, some Jewish intellectuals pointedly distanced themselves. Writing in *Commentary* in 1961, Theodore Solotaroff was baffled and annoyed that *Life* had asked Golden to travel to Israel, having handpicked him to cover the trial of Nazi Adolf Eichmann. Golden was somehow chosen from "all the Jewish intellectuals and leaders in the country to stamp its publication of the Eichmann confession as kosher," complained Solotaroff. Golden had been largely ignored by this group; now he came under their harsh scrutiny and was criticized for, among other things, the very traits most liked by his vast readership: his humor, nostalgic tales, and decidedly unintellectual views. Another characteristic that annoyed the intellectuals was something politicians in Washington valued about Golden: his cordial communication with The Enemy—white southerners, including segregationists, conservative lawmakers, and clergy. The tough piece by Solotaroff was seconded by the young Philip Roth, who chimed in to agree from the pages of *American Judaism*.[89]

Solotaroff, with encouragement from his editor Norman Podhoretz, set out to dissect Golden's popularity with critics and his huge appeal to book buyers. Solotaroff read hundreds of reviews of *Only in America* and found that the affection for Golden transcended geography, politics, and intellect. "On the far left, the Communist *Worker* rejoiced in Golden's 'lusty' way of 'ridiculing Jim Crow hypocrisy and know-nothingism,' while on the far right, the Chicago *Tribune* was delighted by the 'sympathy and humor' with which Golden handled minority group problems. . . . He was praised as fulsomely by the *Nation* as by Hearst's Chicago *American*, just as he later charmed the skeptics both of *Time* and of the *New Yorker*," wrote a disgruntled Solotaroff.[90]

More than 8,000 words later, he managed only to make the Golden conundrum more baffling. Golden, he concluded, is sentimental; he's an apologist for the poverty of the Lower East Side and southern segregationists. His most popular tales—such as the long-winded account of a Lower East Side family bargaining for a son's first suit in the garment district—are silly, not funny. He is unduly optimistic about social progress, linking the Triangle factory fire to improved safety laws and anticipating better things for American blacks in a time when racism still flourishes. He contradicts himself continually: "Here he tells us that our society is in trouble—it is bored, materialistic, frivolous, apathetic; there he tells us that this or that sturdy accomplishment of democracy or social progress could happen only in America."[91]

As Golden wrote in the *Carolina Israelite* a few months later, "There have been critics who complained of my writings that I depend upon nostalgia and sentiment too much. I do not wish here to present a defense to such a charge, because it is probably true and, moreover, the critics are not legion." As for Golden's optimistic belief that social progress can grow from misery, Solotaroff's disdain has been proved wrong more often than not. He chided Golden's "up-beat moralizing," such as his claim that improvements in workplace safety resulted from the Triangle fire. Several accounts of the fire, including centennial coverage of the tragedy in the *New York Times* in 2011, make the same point that Golden declared: Thanks to union officials and activists, fire laws *did* change after the death of the trapped workers, most of whom were young women.[92]

Golden's readers got a pasting from Solotaroff too. "But what is most disheartening about the Golden case is not the books themselves nor the mindless praise of them but rather the actuality of American life which these books and their success reflect," wrote Solotaroff. "For Golden is not just another folksy Jewish humorist who has hit on a bestseller formula; he represents with depressing clarity certain very real problems and conditions of our society in the past decade—a society characterized by its well-intentioned but soft, sloppy, equivocal thinking about itself."[93]

One of the pieces defending Golden appeared in *Congress Bi-weekly*, published by the American Jewish Congress, which rightly pointed out that *Commentary* itself had run Golden's work often in the 1950s. The piece also reminded readers of Golden's breadth of connections: He wrote a civil rights pamphlet for the Jewish Labor Committee and spoke at President Kennedy's Civil Rights Conference on the suggestion of Eleanor Roosevelt and Senators Herbert Lehman and Hubert Humphrey.[94]

Asked about Solotaroff's indictment of his friendships with southern segregationists, Golden got in the small quote that, in his fans eyes at least, outweighed Solotaroff's thirteen pages: "Of course they are my friends because I do not dehumanize them. They are my neighbors and to dehumanize them, while fighting for humanity for someone else, is no gain. You are right back where you started from. And furthermore, it is the Southerners, these white Protestant neighbors of mine, who must solve the problem."[95]

Golden was less sanguine about Roth's piece titled "The New Jewish Stereotypes" in *American Judaism*. Roth was already a well-known literary figure, and his observations about Golden cut deeper. He lumped Golden in with Leon Uris, author of the blockbuster novel made into a film the year before—*Exodus*. He did not intend the comparison as a compliment. Roth declared that his friend Solotaroff's analysis of Golden was "thoroughly and brilliantly" carried out, which it certainly was when compared with the sprawling article by Roth himself. He was correct when he suggested that some of the appeal of Golden's work for Gentiles was its guilt-reducing properties: "If the victim [of anti-Semitism] is not a victim, then the victimizer is not a victimizer either." His fuming about what he saw as ignorant and damaging stereotypes of Jews created by Golden and Uris, however, did not noticeably affect either Uris's or Golden's popularity.[96]

Three years later when Roth felt forced to defend himself against some of the criticism of Jewish stereotypes in his own fiction, Golden all but patted the author on the head in a letter to the editor of *Commentary*. "I'm afraid Philip Roth takes himself too seriously," he began. He dismissed Roth as immature, a *pisher* who didn't know from real enemies. He continued: "I am certain that many writers, reading Roth's defense against his critics, will smile at the minor-league stuff Roth complains about. . . . How would Roth feel if he had to send half his mail to the FBI to check for fingerprints?"[97]

Golden described the novelist with pitying observations along the lines of "Roth is merciless in blotting from his work every touch of softness." He was not alone in that view; some respected critics agreed. Historian and social critic Irving Howe declared the same thing a few years later in a famously tough piece in *Commentary* in 1972. Roth, he wrote, "is an exceedingly joyless writer, even when being very funny." Howe surely hit a nerve for both Roth and Golden when he wrote in the same article that "[Roth's] *Portnoy's Complaint*, for all its scrim of sophistication, is spiritually linked with the usual sentimental treatment of Jewish life in the work of popular and middlebrow writers. Between *Portnoy's Complaint* and [Golden's] *Two Cents Plain* there is finally no great difference of sensibility."[98]

None of these criticisms affected Roth's prolificacy a whit, of course. Roth was already too successful and gifted a writer to be hurt by such criticism. Nor, for that matter, did the very negative reactions among Conservative and Orthodox Jews affect his popularity. Golden might have enjoyed an unintentionally ironic line by scholar Hermione Lee in her 1982 analysis of Roth's work: "To have been attacked by the Jewish establishment was nothing unusual for a Jewish writer if he was not Leon Uris or Harry Golden." Golden dined out on these squabbles for a long time in the *Carolina Israelite* and by crowing to listeners that Philip Roth tried to pick on him.[99]

The observations of Solotaroff and Roth did not diminish Golden in the eyes of most of his readers, but their writings opened the door to further critical comments on Golden's work. When historian and novelist J. Saunders Redding reviewed the autobiographical *Echo in My Soul* by Septima Poinsette Clark for the *New York Times* in the fall of 1961, he took Golden to task for the foreword he wrote focusing on Clark's bravery after her arrest at Highlander Folk School, rather than her wider contributions as a teacher and activist. Those social facts and attitudes were "stale" revelations that "pall in the light of the truth of Mrs. Clark's character and her personal story," wrote Redding.[100]

Coming from a venerable black historian and critic, this stung. Golden was proud that Clark had asked him to write the foreword. "I plead guilty," Golden wrote in the *Carolina Israelite*. "I cannot tell the story Septima Clark knows. . . . I can but agitate for legislation to help register Negro voters. . . . The human story, the dramatic story of the Negroes emerging from the darkness of prejudice, bigotry, and discrimination I leave to Mrs. Clark and to Negro novelists such as Saunders Redding."[101]

CHAPTER SIX

Ghosts and Great Men

The early 1960s were a heady time for Golden. He was famous—as one of America's most popular Jewish figures looked to for editorial comment as civil rights events increasingly occupied newspaper columns and TV airtime, as a commentator for *Life* magazine on one of the century's most watched international events, and as an acquaintance of the charismatic Kennedy clan. The early years of this decade saw him, quite literally, all over the map.

In 1960, Golden and much of the rest of the world were riveted by the news that "veterans of the Jewish underground," as *Life* put it, had captured Nazi war criminal Otto Adolf Eichmann in Argentina and he was to be tried in Israel on charges of engineering the deaths of 6 million Jews. Eichmann, a high-ranking member of the Nazi's intelligence-gathering unit, would be described as the "executive arm for the extermination of the Jewish people," by the prosecutor in his trial. Details of the manhunt continue to be debated, but the motivation for the dogged tracking effort was never in doubt. Eichmann was indicted on fifteen charges of crimes against humanity and the Jewish people.[1]

Life plunged into this sensational story, running Eichmann's so-called confession in two installments in the fall of 1960. He admitted his part in the butchery, adding, "In fact, I was just a little cog in the machinery that carried out the orders of the German Reich." In his day, Eichmann said, "an order was an order." The magazine asked Golden to reflect on the confessions for a "teaser" page that ran the week before the first installment. Included in his brief rumination was Golden's observation, "It is a service to bring this memoir to the public precisely because it awakens the terror, the shock, and the disbelief that mass murders of such magnitude could have populated our own generation."[2]

It was this short bit of writing, and the plan to send Golden to the trial, that so upset Solotaroff, prompting his *Commentary* attack on Golden as an unsuitable spokesman for such a serious subject. The *New Yorker*, after all, sent Hannah Arendt, whose controversial probing about what she considered complicity and appeasement of the Nazis by some Jewish leaders was incendiary, and whose signature phrase, "the banality of evil," would become part of the vernacular. Golden was critical of Arendt, sounding more bewildered than angry. Arendt, he wrote "condemned the very actions that had worked wonders for the Jews for nearly a thousand years in a hostile Europe—total nonviolence, some bribery, and lots of Uncle Tomism." His observation was typically lacking in nuance, but he had a great deal of company in his basic antipathy for Arendt's writings on the subject. Historian Stephen J. Whitfield put it this way: "No dozen pages Arendt ever wrote generated so much controversy, or required such a combination of historical knowledge and moral poise to evaluate."[3]

Life's assignment editors clearly set out to hire the most popular mainstream Jewish writer they knew, and Golden filled that bill. The magazine was not looking for a new angle on the story; it joined most other mainstream publications in portraying Eichmann as the worst rotten fruit of a totalitarian state. As David Cesarani later pointed out in *Becoming Eichmann*, that view resonated with the suspicion and fears about the Soviet Union at the time.[4]

Life also assigned Golden to write about the first days of the trial, which followed in the spring of 1961. The resulting essay gave him huge international exposure, a result of the shocking subject and *Life*'s popularity, not the quality of the writing. For fourteen weeks Eichmann sat or stood in a glass booth in the courtroom in Jerusalem. Close to a hundred witnesses testified; the majority were survivors of extermination camps. Found guilty on all counts, Eichmann was hanged in Israel on 31 May 1962.[5]

"What is so remarkable about Adolf Eichmann, sitting in his booth of bulletproof glass, is that he is so ordinary looking," Golden began. "He might be a waiter, window washer, perhaps, or an insurance agent." To Golden, one of the most remarkable aspects of the proceedings was that "it was the first time in centuries that the Jews themselves have tried a man for persecuting and killing Jews." Golden cabled his notes to Richard Goldhurst with instructions on crafting the essay. Much of the resulting piece reads like a more polished version of Golden's usual *Carolina Israelite* fare: a mix of small moments observed in the present alongside loosely cited history of the distant past. Golden imagined the defendant in his protective box as surrounded by ghosts, "godfathers of Auschwitz," from as far back as ancient Rome and its decrees restricting Jews. Golden included a warning about painful revelations to come in the trial. "The defense will most certainly try to claim that a year before the war ended, Eichmann had offered to let hundreds of thousands of Jews out . . . but (as the story goes) all the doors were shut tight."[6]

After the first piece, *Life* decided against using Golden for further coverage of the trial. The original plan called for him to write multiple articles on Eichmann, and before the trip to Israel he had traveled to Germany, where he gathered material with the idea of writing about reactions to the upcoming trial and other aspects of German life, especially within the small Jewish population. But after the first Eichmann article, his editor contacted him with a change in plans. The trial was "dragging on too long and being reported too exhaustively, both in newspapers and TV," the letter explained, so the magazine would use photos and long captions instead of full-length pieces.[7]

The editor's explanation for limiting Golden's coverage was true as far as it went. The magazine had already published a long piece about the hunting of Eichmann in February, and there was an absence of fresh material in Golden's dispatches. The *Life* copyeditors, at least, got the benefit of the off-the-record bulletins he sent for their edification during his trip to Germany: "On the Sunday afternoon at the Grasse Freiheit [he meant the street named Grosse Freiheit, literally Big Freedom, and Hamburg's red-light district] I saw two prostitutes passing three nuns on the street and the prostitutes lifted their skirts up—they had no panties on—and they said, 'Look at this, sisters.' The master race. I had never seen this even when I was a clerk at the Hotel Markwell on 49th Street."[8]

Golden wrote a longer piece on the reactions to Eichmann's trial based on interviews with what he termed the "pathetic remnant" of Jews left in Germany, but *Life* rejected it. Instead he ran a lengthy article, "The Jews in Germany—1961," in the *Carolina Israelite*, peppered with interviews and opinions about the small Diaspora. Golden groused to a friend that the magazine's editors rejected it after they had "sent it to van Dam, the boss of the Jews," a reference to Hendrik George van Dam, then secretary general of the Central Council of Jews in Germany, which had been formed soon after the end of the war. Van Dam "hit the ceiling" over his story, Golden said.[9]

Golden's account of van Dam's reaction might be true. Van Dam could have found Golden too irreverent when he cracked a joke about two Jews coming out of the movie *Mein Kampf*, with one saying, "I liked the book better," or when he quoted an unnamed Jewish leader saying, "If the Germans lose their prosperity, we may catch hell again." Maybe someone sent van Dam a clipping from the *Carolina Israelite* in which Golden proposed forming a "Society of Half-Jews" in America as a way to outnumber the Christians. There was also the rumor that Golden, on discovering that he looked a great deal like one of Eichmann's legal team, would cut to the front of the line and breeze past the police instead of waiting to get into the courtroom. Most likely, the magazine's editors simply decided that the sprawling Germany piece needed too much work to fit into *Life*'s formulaic style. Whatever the truth of the matter, Golden made sure to give van Dam a shove in his paper: "A day with Dr. van Dam recalls the memory of the 'Fancy Jews,' as we Eastern European immigrants in New York used to refer to the German Jews who worshiped in the big temple on Fifth Avenue," he wrote. "You do not slap Dr. van Dam on the back nor banter with him, and you write him a letter before you call him on the telephone." Van Dam, Golden continued, "knows how to use both status and power, and he has accomplished several near miracles in the matters of compensation for the Jews. But it is quite apparent that he is not above nourishing the fiction of 'Jewish power,' to the extent that many German officials . . . actually fear him."[10]

The subject of Jews in Germany was not a mainstream topic at the time, in part because, as Golden once said, Americans of the era were generally obsessed by three things: "Communism, calories and deodorant." But in his rambling storyteller's way, he raised important questions about the challenge facing a country and its people—Jews and Gentiles—to move forward after such enormous loss. Along with his jabs and jokes, he soberly revisited anti-Semitic activity that had taken place in Cologne in 1959, which had been the first to be widely publicized since the end of the war. It wasn't just the painting of swastikas on synagogues that was shocking, he wrote. It was the timing, that the defacements happened during relatively prosperous times, when Germany was well into its rebuilding. "It has always been accepted among Jews everywhere that anti-Semitism is triggered by hard times; mass unemployment, economic depression or military defeat. Suddenly this was exposed as folklore, and the Jews were shaken." Golden, always able to catch the small moments that conveyed complex or far-reaching change, quoted an elderly Jewish man in

Germany who told him, "When my wife and I . . . pass a German who looks 38 years old or over . . . either she whispers to me or I whisper to her, 'I wonder what he was doing in Hitler's time?' "[11]

The notes from the Germany and Israel trips also reflect the working relationship that had existed for years between Golden and his son Richard, and which had grown more important by this time. Golden was the reporter who could get anyone to talk, who had a gimlet eye for the absurd, and who habitually filed away any bit of good color for later use. When a story was handed off to his rewrite editor, he was done—no back-and-forth, no revisiting or negotiating. Richard Goldhurst had the enviable skill of being able to assume his father's writer's voice and then to sublimate his own more sophisticated style. Years spent working around theatrical productions gave him a keen ear for the details that defined a speaker's or writer's style. He shared his father's quick wit and his ability to see humor in unlikely moments.[12]

Freedom Riders

On the heels of his Eichmann project came the Freedom Rides, launched by CORE in 1961. Even Golden's harshest critics had no quibble with him covering this news, which played to his strengths and knowledge in a way that international journalism did not. For all his globe-trotting and heightened celebrity, Golden was still most interested in and moved by the people back home who repeatedly put aside their own safety to bring about change.

Segregated seating on interstate transit had been successfully challenged in court six years earlier, but it continued on buses that traveled through the South and the stations that served them. The premise of the protest was simple: Thirteen carefully screened, polite, neatly dressed riders of various ages, white and black, boarded two buses in Washington, D.C., and chose seating that violated the usual practice. The minute they sat down, the riders created "one of those unforeseen tectonic shifts at which history blithely excels," wrote Diane McWhorter in the foreword to *Breach of Peace* by Eric Etheridge, a stirring book crafted of mug shots and photographic portraits, then and now, of Freedom Riders.[13]

Golden credited black churches and Christianity as he marveled at the nonviolent approach of these campaigns. "They beat them with chains and brass knuckles and they bomb their houses," he wrote, and yet the victims didn't raise their fists; they prayed. "Some day all of us everywhere will rise up to cheer this most wonderful story of the American civilization," he declared in an essay written during the first wave of Freedom Rides. (His use of the word "wonderful" when he clearly meant "heroic" was an extremely poor choice. Even those familiar with Golden's strong words against the violence visited on movement protestors would have winced.)[14]

The first trip was tense from the start, with arrests, threats, and at least one rider beaten at a stop in South Carolina. On 14 May, in Anniston, Alabama, about 150 miles northeast of Birmingham, a mob attacked one bus and set it on fire, coming within seconds of killing the riders by holding the door shut as the vehicle burned. At the last moment the passengers escaped, some by clambering out windows. Riders in the second bus were beaten when they arrived in Birmingham. With police commissioner Eugene "Bull" Connor and Ku Klux Klan members masterminding the plan, local police stayed away and let the mob have its way for fifteen bloody minutes.[15]

When riders moved on to Montgomery, rioting broke out at the bus depot on 21 May, and a gathering in the Reverend Ralph Abernathy's First Baptist Church, with the Reverend Martin Luther King Jr. asking his listeners to remain calm and committed to nonviolence, turned into a terrifying scene. The Kennedy administration struggled to control the situation, now rapidly becoming an international embarrassment just as the president was poised to meet with overseas leaders, including the Soviet Union's Premier Nikita Khrushchev. Hundreds of U.S. marshals struggled overnight to hold back an angry crowd of whites outside the church. Within two days of the violence being quelled, another group of Freedom Riders was en route to Jackson, Mississippi, where they were promptly arrested. Others followed. By the end of summer, 328 people were arrested, and most served time in the Mississippi state penitentiary (often called "Parchman Farm"). Many of the jailed protestors refused to post bail.[16]

While the imprisoned women and men sang hymns and protest songs to keep spirits up, the attorney general's office petitioned the Interstate Commerce Commission, which subsequently issued a new order banning segregation on all interstate transportation and facilities as of 1 November 1961. The Freedom Riders had won. CORE organized hundreds more riders to go on test trips, and "to almost everyone's amazement, there was almost complete compliance," historian Raymond Arsenault said in an interview accompanying the Public Broadcasting System's film *Freedom Riders*, based on his book *Freedom Riders: 1961 and the Struggle for Racial Justice*. It was, as Arsenault put it, the first "unambiguous victory" in the long history of the civil rights movement.[17]

There was no levity in Golden's biting criticism about the widely publicized violence that greeted a later wave of Freedom Riders in Alabama. He blamed the state for inciting the mob "and, God help them, many editors and columnists around the country" for failing to lay the blame where it belonged almost a decade after *Brown*: "When you keep saying that you intend to do everything possible to prevent the implementation of the Supreme Court decision against racial segregation, you give the greenlight to hoodlums, gangsters and terrorists. . . . The half-crazed woman who was using her heavy pocketbook to strike blow after blow across the back of a girl, one of the 'white' Freedom Riders, had in effect received 'authority' for her actions from the Capitol House of a sovereign state."[18]

Golden frequently welcomed organizers, protestors, and Freedom Ride reinforcements who needed a place to sleep on the way to or from the South. It became unremarkable for him to come downstairs in the wee hours and step over someone in a sleeping bag on the floor. Golden's oldest friends had to laugh at the poetic justice of him becoming a soft touch. Engaging drifters or dedicated Freedom Riders, Golden turned almost no one away. He admitted as much: "I get everybody—Presbyterians, ministers, Negroes, Catholics, Jews. When they call up and say, 'Mr. Golden, I'm at the bus station.' I know I'm in for it. The radicals all come to the bus station. The other guys come to the airport."[19]

An exception to the welcome mat for all was Golden's view of activist Robert Williams, an African American former Marine who formed a breakaway chapter of the NAACP in Monroe, Union County, North Carolina, and advocated armed resistance by blacks against white aggression. His entreaty to "meet violence with violence" in 1959 came ahead of the Black Panther movement, and while it attracted followers in some quarters, it caused Golden and other liberals in the area to renounce him. Golden initially sympathized with the younger man's outrage at some aspects of racism, but he was repelled by his violent rhetoric, finding him to be "often bristling with bitterness." Later Williams fled the country to avoid charges of kidnapping a white couple, living a life on the run in Canada, Mexico, China, Vietnam, and Cuba. He returned to the United States in 1969, and the charges were eventually dropped.[20]

Golden took no little satisfaction in exposing those who used violence or cruel underhandedness to thwart citizen activists. He did so in his own paper as well as by skillfully timing speeches that mainstream media would trumpet to an even larger audience. In 1962 a White Citizens Council president in New Orleans came up with the mockery of "Reverse Freedom Rides," offering poor blacks free one-way bus tickets to northern cities and telling them that good jobs awaited. Golden found a way to turn the joke on the racists. In a speech to the North Carolina Council on Human Relations in Durham that spring, he announced he would provide the means for the black travelers to "return home after their vacations." He made sure the local press had a copy of his speech in time to make morning editions, and an Associated Press story hit the wires immediately. A year later, the story of Golden's revenge was still being told by the *Chicago Daily Defender* and other newspapers, and it continues to surface in stories about the Freedom Riders.[21]

The Kennedys

The same year that the first Freedom Riders braved the buses, Golden, who by now had connections in the Kennedy White House, began to push an idea he had floated in speeches to various NAACP chapters, suggesting that a Second Emancipation Proclamation by a president would do more for the civil rights movement than anything Congress could come up with. The centennial of Lincoln's executive order freeing the slaves would be 1 January 1963. Former broadcast journalist Edward R. Murrow, now director of the United States Information Agency, helped Golden write a memo to Kennedy on the subject in August 1961, then personally delivered the finished document to the White House. He wrote Golden when the task was done, calling himself "your postman." The postman quoted the president's remarks on receiving the letter: "Have read Harry Golden's letter. Be interested to see what you fellows come up with in the way of 'Kennedy Declaration.' "[22]

Golden was heartened that Kennedy had signed Executive Order 10925 a few months before, establishing the Committee on Equal Employment Opportunity with a mandate to study discrimination in federal jobs and contracts and recommend policies to prevent it. Golden's intention was for the proclamation to be a ceremonial follow-up to the order. His six-page draft came down to three of its lines: "Neither the President nor any of his cabinet members nor any Federal official can change the hearts of men. The individual alone, abetted by his belief in God, can change his heart. But the President and his cabinet and the officers of the government can say, 'Obey the law.' "[23]

Golden sent copies of the draft to Roy Wilkins of the NAACP and to the Reverend Martin Luther King Jr., who were also pushing for an executive order to mark the centennial. A staffer for Wilkins wrote to Golden, correcting a line to make clear that both enforcement of existing laws and additional civil rights legislation were needed. Golden also sent a draft to World publisher Ben Zevin and editor William Targ. He ignored their suggestions for tightening the wordy document.[24]

The widening distance between Golden and black activists is evident from this event. Golden believed that a statement making clear that the White House stood for civil rights would carry great weight. To him it was not unlike his father and other immigrants hanging up a copy of a citizenship certificate signed by President Theodore Roosevelt and feeling that they were included in the country's thrilling democracy. King, frustrated at the slow pace of progress in the courts after *Brown* and the need to prove the worthiness of black Americans in the first place, had no interest in this suitable-for-framing idea, no matter how inspiring the language. He wanted the Kennedy administration to effectuate widespread change; he wanted the president to beat down discrimination through executive orders. Black activists who chafed at King's nonviolent approach and what they saw as glacial gradualism had no use for proclamations, orders, or more of the same dialogue.

Golden, of course, had some understanding of the frustration blacks felt at the too-slow pace of change after the exciting promise of *Brown*. He too had expected bigger, faster gains. But to him, Kennedy's inviting of King to the White House for a private meeting in October 1961 was a meaningful step. He did not realize the depth of the suspicion with which the Kennedy circle viewed King. Therefore, Golden was unaware that the private luncheon with the president and First Lady, flattering as it seemed, was contrived to keep the conversation light, avoiding tricky racial issues. As historian Taylor Branch pointed out, King, too, was adept at such social maneuvering. When he and the First Couple walked through the Lincoln room and passed a framed copy of the first Emancipation Proclamation, King brought up the matter to the president.[25]

Golden later described Kennedy's avoidance of a second Emancipation Proclamation in this hollow sentence: "He had come to the conclusion that the Congress and the people, as well as the President, must play appropriate roles in the civil rights struggle." He went on to say that the horrific images of attack dogs loosed on protestors, as well as news of the bombs and the beatings of citizens unprotected by southern police, were what ultimately drove change—not the president or Congress. (Both the president and Robert Kennedy said the same thing on occasion.) After John F. Kennedy's death, Golden made a sad nod to the inadequacy of his proclamation idea: "While the folks might have had something for [hanging on] the wall, this did not open up the avenues of freedom." He did not publicly say what he believed to be true: that Kennedy's popularity and enormous charisma could have sold the civil rights agenda to America had the administration's political caution not blocked it.[26]

People close to the president who tracked the favors done and sacrifices made found Golden useful now, the distraction of the proclamation idea notwithstanding. His ringing praise for the administration, in print and in stump speeches, had a long reach, and the vote counters could track the effects—especially in Jewish blocs. Politicians of any stripe appreciated Golden's able handicapping of political races. He had a memory like flypaper when it came to odd campaign outcomes and voting patterns. Moreover, Golden could see a politician as *a person*, cutting through the haze of opinions, propaganda, and rumor that surrounded him or her. He could easily be dismissed as a dreamer, when in fact he was a dreamer who was also an unusual political creature capable of simultaneous personal devotion and blunt analysis.[27]

Golden, along with much of America, had been immediately enthralled by the energetic glamour of the Kennedy clan. Writing in the *Carolina Israelite*, he was an early critic of the anti-Catholic bias against John F. Kennedy, making the accurate observation that no one worried about Kennedy's religion when he was serving his country during World War II. The more galling issue for Golden was the noise being made by some Catholic leaders who took issue with Kennedy's interview in *Look* magazine in which he said an elected official's religious beliefs did not take precedence over his oath to uphold the Constitution and the separation of church and state. Golden fumed: "I am quite sure if God spoke to him personally while he were President and said, 'I've just told the Pope that there's something wrong with the 21st Amendment; now I'm telling you, and I'm going to tell Bishop Oxnam and Abba Hillel Silver this afternoon.' I am sure Mr. Kennedy would do his best to make God happy, no matter how he had to violate the Constitution. But God, in His Infinite Wisdom did not see fit to talk to any of our Presidents, let alone aspiring nominees."[28]

Golden's introduction to the Kennedy family had not come about through his usual practice of courting the prominent. He first came into the family's orbit in 1957 via the indefatigable Eunice Kennedy Shriver. Golden was already on the record condemning sterilization for the mentally ill, and Shriver discovered he was the father of a son born with what was then called mental retardation. She asked him to deliver a keynote speech at a fundraiser for the Joseph P. Kennedy Jr. Foundation, which focused on the needs and rights of the mentally disabled.[29]

Golden *did* run true to form in 1959 when he sent some of his writings blasting the anti-Catholic naysayers to then-senator John Kennedy, who responded with a friendly note. Golden took this as a signal to initiate a full-blown correspondence. By the 1960 presidential campaign, he was in regular touch with members of the Kennedy entourage. Given the insular nature and fierce devotion of the staffers, it counted that Golden had fans in their ranks. When an assistant wrote to Golden in 1959, inviting him to see Senator Kennedy during an upcoming visit to Washington, the staffer added a postscript about *Only in America*. It was the only book, he said, other than *David Copperfield*, that he, his wife, and his mother-in-law could all agree was good.[30]

By the end of the 1960 campaign, Golden had made more than fifty speeches supporting a Kennedy presidency. When speaking to Jewish audiences in California, Golden was joined by Carl Sandburg, in Hollywood at the time serving as a consultant on a film. The two men on the stump together were a bit of genius. "I played the impresario by keeping him in the wings," Golden explained. He introduced his friend with a flourish: "I brought you a bonus—Carl Sandburg!" Sandburg usually drew a standing ovation. The cheers would break out anew when the older man paused and—as if he'd just thought of the phrase—declared, "We are just a couple of North Carolina boys plugging for a young fellow from Boston who will make us a good President."[31]

Biography of a Friend

That Golden and Sandburg were still so close is a credit to them both. Golden had proposed a book about Sandburg a few years earlier, surely the biggest test of any writerly friendship. The manuscript was in its final stages during the Kennedy campaign, and the book came out in the fall of 1961. The writing of *Carl Sandburg* held Golden to a different standard of truth-telling. Sandburg loved a good tale and could turn a poetic metaphor inside-out like a pants pocket in order to shake out every last cent, but he wasn't an embellisher when it came to his own life. Nor was he about to let his eager friend get away with being one. When Golden proposed a book about Sandburg, it was with the assurance that the latter would have editorial veto power. In the end, Sandburg asked for small factual changes in Golden's draft, but he made an effort not to interfere with the manuscript overall. From the first it was firmly described as a collection of observations, not biography. The description of parameters—a disclaimer, actually—appeared in the foreword of the book and was quoted by Golden to interviewers: "I want to write about Carl Sandburg, but this will not be the definitive biography. To begin with, anyone who wants to write the definitive biography will have to spend six years at the University of Illinois perusing and cataloguing the Sandburg papers. . . . I am too old and too fat and perhaps too impatient to spend time with all those sources."[32]

Reviewer Herbert Mitgang of the *New York Times* was grateful for the new insights and irritated by Golden's writing. He had "assembled a wonderful and yet exasperating jumble of facts, opinions, excerpts, reviews, plugs, knocks, Sandburgisms and Goldenisms," Mitgang wrote. It was "a chaotically organized memoir and appreciation whose original material, nevertheless, is fascinating." Golden's friend Julian Scheer at the *Charlotte News* gave it a rave, observing the many similarities between the men, most notably that "they both are talkers." One did not visit either man's home and expect to get a word in, wrote Scheer. The review by Kays Gary in the *Charlotte Observer* included this insight: "One does get the impression that Golden takes it mostly off the top and that Sandburg has managed to keep much of himself to himself." In context, it is clear that Gary's criticism of Golden's style was less the point than bowing to Sandburg's ability to give much of himself while still remaining a private man.[33]

Golden, as always, deeply admired Sandburg's genuine humility and the humor that often accompanied it. When he described his friend's handling of reader mail, Golden found a way to sum this trait up in a snippet. "In answer to those 'hate' letters or those of strong criticism, Carl sends a form," wrote Golden. " 'Dear Mrs. Jones: Thank you for your letter. I shall try to do better.' "[34]

Few of the writers who have profiled Sandburg mention Golden; their omissions are in line with those who wrote about Stevenson, Robert Kennedy, and others without noting his role. His friendship was not considered influential in the poet's life, and his decidedly unscholarly background kept him below the radar of academic writers. Golden's respect (and veracity) while ruminating on Sandburg makes for a somewhat less lively collection of essays than some of his other books. But those writings create a view of Sandburg more intimate than that produced by some skilled biographers and critics.

Golden was with Sandburg when an early review came out on the latter's poetry collection, *Honey and Salt*, published in 1963. The reviewer asked, "Where is the Sandburg who talked of picket lines? Where is the Sandburg who sang of whores?" Golden described his friend's reaction: "Carl put the review down and said, 'I'm eighty-five years old. I am not going to talk about whores at my age. As far as the union boys are concerned, they are playing the dog races in Miami. The romantic days are over. Now you put that in your *Carolina Israelite*.' I did."[35]

One skill Golden failed to absorb from Sandburg was that of being a gentle mentor to younger writers. He encouraged them, but when it came to constructive editorial criticism, Golden typically fell short. "Unfortunately for a male poet to make any money at all he must be eighty years old at least, and give out philosophy on the side," he wrote a fledgling composer of verse. "A female must wear pants, smoke cigars, and go to bed with itinerant truck drivers." Friends didn't get much more in the way of editorial guidance. "Sometime in the 1960s I gave Harry the draft of a novel I'd written," recalls Charlotte attorney Mark Bernstein. "Naturally—unfortunately!—it was about a young trial lawyer handling an anti-trust case. I went over to the house, and he was sitting there in his rocking chair, cigar in hand, glass of bourbon nearby. He looked up at me and said 'Mark, it's an interesting story, but there's no fucking in it. So there is no possibility that this book would sell.' "[36]

"As Old as the Scriptures"

Golden and Sandburg watched and listened with full hearts to the president's historic televised address to the country about civil rights on 11 June 1963. This was the speech in which Kennedy made the point that the morality of civil rights and the American tradition were ineluctably connected. "We are confronted primarily with a moral issue," said Kennedy. "It is as old as the Scriptures and is as clear as the American Constitution." Or as Golden had written in his proclamation memo to the president, "It is not possible that Americans are or can be intimidated by the moral idea of equality . . . for America itself is the first moral idea among the nations of the world."[37]

Golden would not have been surprised to know—and perhaps he *did* know—that the speech's reference to morality came from Robert Kennedy. Nor had the younger Kennedy missed Golden's similar expression; his personal note to Golden praised his writing of the "stirring and eloquent declaration" that contained it. Kennedy and Golden took a liking to each other quite quickly; their correspondence was wide ranging and warm. Golden more than once wrote that he "loved Robert Kennedy like a brother."[38]

One of the more accurate descriptions of the relationship appears in Golden's autobiography: "I was pretty close to Bobby Kennedy, at least as close as an older man and an editor can be to a younger man who could become the political leader of the free world." This almost certainly was written by Richard Goldhurst, who worked closely with his father on *The Right Time*, more as ghostwriter than editor.[39]

Kennedy sent Golden a fan letter in 1959. At the time he was chief counsel for the Senate's ominously titled Senate Select Committee on Improper Activities in the Labor or Management Field, also known as the McClellan Committee or the Rackets Committee. Kennedy enclosed one of Golden's books (most likely *For 2 Cents Plain*) and wrote, "I have always been a great admirer of yours and what you have stood for. I would be highly honored indeed if you would take the time to autograph a copy of your book for me." Golden responded warmly and added a reference to the committee's dogged efforts to bring down teamster union leader Jimmy Hoffa. "As an old trade-unionist, I cannot help but admire the people who are keeping after Mr. Hoffa. I just do not believe he has the education, the character, and the responsibility, to run the United States of America of Benjamin Franklin." Kennedy wrote back to Golden ten days later, a casual handwritten note of unusual candor, thanking him for the inscription. "As for Mr. Hoffa, he is interested only in himself," Kennedy wrote. "This of course cannot be for a union official and the result has been that he has continually betrayed his membership." In a democracy, Kennedy wrote, when such information is known, a man like Hoffa "cannot long survive." He signed the note "Bob Kennedy."[40]

The letters grew more personal: "I was wondering how you have been doing since I saw you last in New York," Kennedy wrote. "I would like to see you sometime again, so I hope you will be coming to Washington and that we can get together." The two men could not have been more different in background, but they shared certain values. Robert Kennedy "loved America in a deep and sentimental way," as biographer Evan Thomas observed, and so did Golden. Kennedy could be fearless in assailing anti-Semitism and racism. As an undergraduate at Harvard, he shocked his family by castigating a Roman Catholic priest for making anti-Jewish remarks, and at the University of Virginia Law School in 1951, he called his fellow students "gutless" for hesitating to organize an integrated forum to host United Nations peace negotiator Ralph Bunche as speaker.[41]

Kennedy, appointed U.S. attorney general by his brother in 1961, came to his public advocacy of civil rights somewhat slowly, but from a direction similar to Golden's. Their basic natures deplored racism; they felt the strongest sympathy for the underdog in any battle. More than one biographer has linked Kennedy's empathy to his own childhood struggle to hold his own among the boisterous, accomplished elders in his large family and his willingness to take on a fight—or just as often start one—even when the odds were not in his favor.[42]

On 6 May 1961, the new attorney general delivered his first formal address at the University of Georgia Law School in Athens. He opened by poking fun at his own northern roots with a Jewish joke straight out of Golden's repertoire: A bearded Hassidic Jew is followed down a southern street by a growing crowd of children curious about his long coat, side curls, and hat. Finally the annoyed man turns around to ask, "Haven't you ever seen a Yankee?"[43]

Halfway through his address, Kennedy took up the subject of civil rights and school desegregation: "Our position is quite clear. We are upholding the law. Our action does not threaten local control. The federal government would not be running the schools in Prince Edward County any more than it is running the University of Georgia or the schools in my state of Massachusetts. In this case, in all cases, I say to you today that if the orders of the court are circumvented, the Department of Justice will act. We will not stand by and be aloof—we will move."[44]

The younger Kennedy's personal pledge, unique and heartfelt, did not mean he gave unfettered support to the civil rights movement. His devotion to his brother's success was fervent. As Nicholas Lemann put it, at the start of the 1960s, Robert Kennedy's "overriding moral crusade at that moment was getting his brother elected president." During the campaign and the years of his brother's presidency, Robert Kennedy, with no experience talking with or listening to black Americans, was frustrated by what he saw as a lack of gratitude for the administration's attentions. But he was a man able to learn and change through contact with more African Americans and closer proximity to the problems of discrimination—another way in which he resembled his friend Golden. In a few years, he would put these hard-won lessons to work as a candidate for the presidency, endearing himself to many Americans in the civil rights fight.[45]

The work of managing civil rights protests was new ground for the Kennedys, despite their vast experience with manipulating public opinion. News coverage of violent white crowds preying on high school kids trying to go to school in Little Rock had played around the world, to the detriment of Kennedy's predecessor in the White House. When violence erupted in 1962 over James Meredith's attempt to register at the University of Mississippi, President Kennedy got a much clearer sense of how difficult it was to control civil rights battles. Meredith, who had served nine years in the U.S. Air Force before applying to Ole Miss, was represented by the NAACP legal defense team and attorney Constance Baker Motley. They took his fight all the way to the Supreme Court and won. Governor Ross Barnett himself literally barred Meredith's way into the registration hall and urged his constituents to resist the tyranny of the federal government. Ten days later, on 30 September, Oxford, Mississippi, was a battleground.[46]

When the violence subsided, Meredith walked into the registrar's office and became the first African American enrolled at Ole Miss. He and his supporters had "crushed forever the Southern strategy of 'massive resistance' to integration," wrote William Doyle, author of *American Insurrection: The Battle of Oxford, Mississippi, 1962*. It would have been inconceivable to those who watched this that by the twenty-first century, Meredith would no longer be a well-known figure in America. It became, wrote Doyle, "a turning point in history that was almost invisible."[47]

A Line in the Dust

While the battle of Oxford has slipped away in American memories, the word "Birmingham" seems to have stayed. The city's name remains a synonym for something cataclysmic at the intersection of race and violence. The state of Alabama became a regular target for Golden and other editorialists after the Freedom Rides and the election of George Wallace in 1962. "It seems to me I have met George Wallace somewhere before," wrote Golden. "The scowl, the laugh that reminds one of the victorious Neanderthal, the disguised act of the combative underdog." Wallace, he added, was like a Huey Long and a Joe McCarthy tailored for the 1960s.[48]

Wallace ultimately served as governor for three terms, providing quotable bombast nearly every time he opened his mouth. During his January 1963 swearing in, Wallace secured his place in history by declaring, "I draw the line in the dust and toss the gauntlet down before the feet of tyranny. And I say 'Segregation now! Segregation tomorrow! Segregation forever!'"[49]

Some of the biggest spectacles in the civil rights era took place in Wallace's state, in particular the Birmingham campaign in the spring of 1963. "Brooding Birmingham" as *New York Times* reporter Harrison Salisbury dubbed it, was an industrial steel-and-coal city. Segregation was maintained in much more menacing ways than it was in Golden's Charlotte, and threats to the status quo were treated swiftly. Salisbury, later an influential editor and prolific author who argued against the war in Vietnam, set the stage for *Times* readers back in 1960. His language was dramatic, his sense of impending doom prescient. Observing the separate worlds of blacks and whites in Birmingham, he wrote what would become a much-quoted piece under the front-page headline, "Fear and Hatred

Grip Birmingham." In this city, Salisbury wrote, "Every channel of communication, every medium of mutual interest, every reasoned approach, every inch of middle ground has been fragmented by the emotional dynamite of racism, reinforced by the whip, the razor, the gun, the bomb, the torch, the club, the knife, the mob, the police and any branches of the state's apparatus."[50]

Among members of the press, the Birmingham unrest and change had special meaning. Salisbury's coverage in 1960 had infuriated local officials, who filed multimillion-dollar lawsuits against him and his newspaper, and the long legal battle prompted the *Times* to cautiously keep reporters out of Alabama to prevent them from being served. The case dragged on for years, eventually going to the Supreme Court and leading to a crucial win for the *New York Times* and freedom of the press. Without *Sullivan v. New York Times Co.*, the civil rights movement (and many other events since) quite simply could not have been covered widely by the press. "This was the contribution of Alabama to the rights of the American press," wrote Salisbury later. "By invoking the libel laws to inhibit free reporting the Alabama officials produced the opposite effect. . . . It stripped [public figures] of the ability to intimidate the press through the power of the purse and the libel law."[51]

Birmingham: Where It's At

One thing Birmingham *did* have going for it was the energy of the Reverend Fred Lee Shuttlesworth. An early force in the Southern Christian Leadership Conference, this Baptist minister could not be deterred. Shuttlesworth had a temper, and his peers worried about his impetuousness; but no one doubted his tireless commitment. When the state's NAACP chapter was nixed, he promptly started the Alabama Christian Movement for Human Rights. He was arrested repeatedly for "vagrancy" and other trumped-up charges—on one occasion, twice in the same day. He was beaten, his home and church were bombed, and his closest comrades were murdered. More than forty years after his Birmingham home was dynamited, Shuttlesworth serenely explained his staying power: "They were going to blow me to heaven that night. It had my name on it. . . . But I heard [Him] say: 'Be still! God is here. Wherever you are I will be with you.'"[52]

Shuttlesworth, whom historian S. Jonathan Bass called "the perfect foil for Bull Connor," was convinced that if progress was made in Birmingham, then the civil rights cause would be lifted up, a case he made forcefully to King and Abernathy ("Birmingham is where it's at, gentleman"). They agreed. King believed the way to make a Birmingham campaign a success was to goad Commissioner of Public Safety Theophilus Eugene "Bull" Connor into violence. It worked: The protestors' nonviolent actions blew up into rioting in the city's streets in the spring of 1963. During the upheaval, King spent eight days in the Birmingham jail in April and produced one of the most-often referenced writings from the civil rights movement, *Letter from Birmingham Jail.*[53]

King's passionate words, written on scraps of paper and smuggled out, responded to an open letter signed by several clergymen published in the *Birmingham News.* King was responding to the second in a pair of letters. The first one came from eleven clerics, including a rabbi, and asked for tolerance of anticipated court decisions ordering desegregation of schools. The clerics acknowledged that "many sincere people oppose this change and are deeply troubled by it. As southerners we understand this. We nonetheless feel that defiance is neither the right answer nor the solution." They went on to cite their belief that "no person's freedom is safe unless every person's is equally protected," and they spoke against hatred and violence, urging patience and obedience to court decisions on all sides.[54]

The second letter ran three months later in the newspaper and was signed by eight of the clerics, again including the rabbi. The editors ran the letter adjacent to a photograph of King, Abernathy, and other demonstrators. This time they expressed worries that "some of our Negro citizens, directed and led in part by outsiders"—such as King—were holding demonstrations that were "unwise and untimely." This letter also praised the calm manner in which local law enforcement had handled such unrest. The clerics were stung by King's denunciation of them; they did not disagree with King on fundamentals; the divisive differences came over their beliefs about which approaches (and at what speed) would bring about civil rights for blacks. That gulf between them, though, was wide.[55]

King's *Letter* was not a spontaneous outpouring. He had long considered writing such an open letter but knew that unless it was carefully timed, it would not have the desired effect. His words, when they did come, were stunning. He "established a kind of universal voice, beyond time, beyond race," as historian Taylor Branch put it. He wrote as a prisoner, a prophet, a father, a traveler, and a leader with his back against the wall, said Branch. King's letter poured out his frustration at what he saw as hypocrisy: "You deplore the demonstrations taking place in Birmingham. But your statement, I am sorry to say, fails to express a similar concern for the conditions that brought about the demonstrations." He refuted the ministers' criticisms one by one. King took "moderates" to task as well as those who argued against civil disobedience. "We should never forget that everything Adolf Hitler did in Germany was 'legal,'" he wrote.[56]

While "gravely disappointed" with the white moderates—Jews and Gentiles alike—he singled out a few people for praise, including Golden: "I am thankful, however, that some of our white brothers in the South have grasped the meaning of this social revolution and committed themselves to it. They are still too few in quantity, but they are big in quality. Some—such as Ralph McGill, Lillian Smith, Harry Golden, James McBride Dabbs, Ann Braden and Sarah Patton Boyle—have written about our struggle in eloquent and prophetic terms."[57]

Golden was flattered and grateful to be mentioned in this good company, although he did not comment widely on his inclusion in the famous letter. In the months following King's letter, he was bolder in his dismissive comments about the Birmingham clergy than he might have been at any earlier point. If the city's clergy speak for anything, he declared, "they speak for the status quo."[58]

All of the others mentioned in King's Birmingham letter were brave writers who challenged segregation at risk to themselves and their careers. Smith was a southern novelist who explored the forbidden topic of interracial relationships in *Strange Fruit* and was an outspoken foe of racism and segregation. Dabbs probed the psychological reasons for southern resistance to civil rights in *The Southern Heritage*. He believed the race issue was the glue used by politicians to "keep the South solid." His measured prose carried considerable weight, given his place in southern society as a plantation owner and elder of the Presbyterian Church. Boyle, a Virginian, wrote boldly on the subject of integration in the 1950s for national magazines. Braden, also a southerner, started her career at the *Courier-Journal* in Louisville and then was blacklisted for years over her Leftist activism and outspoken opposition to segregation. She may not have been thrilled to be sharing such billing with Golden. Activist Virginia Foster Durr was close friends with Braden, and in one of her letters Durr noted their shared view that Golden was "a phony." Braden could not know it at the time, but Golden's name was in the original text of *Letter from Birmingham Jail*, whereas hers and Boyle's were added in the polishing of the manuscript that followed.[59]

As it turned out, Golden and King were thinking about each other that week. Two days before *Letter* was written, Golden wrote King's assistant, the Reverend Wyatt Tee Walker, enclosing a check for "the purpose of buying the boys there some little comforts" in Birmingham.[60]

To Golden, Birmingham turned up the lights to a painful brightness. He saw "evidence of a growing loud-mouthed anti-Semitism" in the city. When Jewish merchants tried to break ranks with the segregationists in the business community, they were avoided or threatened. He tried a bit of his old humor: "But as I've always told my Jewish audiences, 'Gurnisht helfen,' Nothing helps. So you may as well be humanitarians." Around the same time he delivered the commencement speech at Miles College, just outside Birmingham, where he announced with mock seriousness to the predominantly black audience his creation of the "Bull Connor Award." All high school seniors in Birmingham would be eligible, white and black. It would, Golden said, carry a one-year scholarship and "a bronze medallion showing Bull Connor directing the police dogs." On the other side, the medal would say, "We Shall Overcome, Alabama 1963." Golden planned, he said, to have his friends newsmen Ralph McGill, Bill Baggs of the *Miami News*, and Harry Ashmore to act as judges. The medallion, he added, "will be suspended by a piece of hose rather than the usual ribbon."[61]

But Golden had hoped for so long that blacks would gain a real voice in the South, and now that it was happening, he suddenly felt more keenly the long-standing shortage of liberal white leaders to take race relations to the next level. "One of the terrors in Birmingham is the realization that there is no voice of real substance, save that of the Negroes, on this side of the United States of America," he wrote.[62]

Success . . . and the Seeds of Disfavor

Leading up to and during the Birmingham violence, contradictions were taking place in Golden's work. His presence as a commentator was solid, and the *Carolina Israelite* subscription list was stable at close to 22,000 true subscribers. (The departure of the "curiosity seekers" who had pushed the circulation to 55,000 in the early 1960s did not worry Golden.) Ads bracketed every page: for dry cleaners, music stores, coal and ice, lumberyards, and seemingly every church for miles. Even the Baptist Book Store in Raleigh took a good-sized spot. Golden's comfortable place on Jack Paar's *Tonight Show* went away when the host left in 1962, but he soon made the move to Johnny Carson's late-night couch. His books were selling very well. "Why Not Make It Five Million and Three?" asked a house ad in the *Carolina Israelite*: "The publishers say five million copies [hardcover and paperback] have been sold of 'Carl Sandburg,' 'You're Entitle" and 'For 2-cents Plain.' . . . Ken Robertson, circulation manager of *The Carolina Israelite*, would like you to make it 5,000,003. Here's how."[63]

Yet there was evidence that Golden's ear was not as finely tuned to the cause as it had been. A 1963 essay, "Looking for Work and How to Find It," was the sort of slice-of-life approach that had worked so well to acquaint white readers with the issue of civil rights in his early writings. It came from Golden's sense that if he showed white readers and listeners that the civil rights fight was about regular Americans just like themselves who were trying to protect, feed, and shelter their families, there was a chance to foster understanding and avoid more violence. But now that race issues were front and center, the "small moment" style could sometimes oversimplify the very problems he wanted to highlight. He quoted a "wandering Negro" saying, "When I go in to another town . . . I get in there early in the morning and look up a garbage truck or station around the town dump. If the helper on the garbage truck is a Negro, I figure I will stay a while. If he is white, I get out of town. There is no job there for me."[64]

Golden was not blind to change within the movement. But he did not yet fully realize all the ramifications of activist Bayard Rustin's observation: "The Negro community is now fighting for total freedom. . . . Tokenism is finished." At the same time, private correspondence and conversations with acquaintances in the NAACP and other black organizations made Golden well aware of the tensions and rifts between black leaders, and he didn't hesitate to talk about it. He attacked the Black Muslims (meaning the Nation of Islam and Malcolm X) for having "racial policies [that] differ in no way from the Ku Klux Klan or, for that matter, differ in no way from the policies of Apartheid laid down by the South African whites." He heartily seconded his friend Ralph McGill, who wrote, "If a real hater—a Black Muslim—had come along with Dr. King's power of speech and personality, the South long ago would have been bloodstained. The South is lucky to have Dr. King."[65]

Quiet Desegregation, "A Jubilee Day" . . . and Anarchy

What did lighten the dark feelings about Birmingham and radical shifts were the quiet desegregation efforts going on at home. Golden got the inside dope on efforts by editor Pete McKnight at the *Charlotte Observer* and other North Carolina newsmen who were working behind the scenes to move the issue forward. It was a plan after his own heart.

"Indeed, one of the most striking aspects of desegregation in Charlotte during the 1950s and 1960s was the active role played by the city's journalists," wrote civil rights historian and law professor Davison M. Douglas. "Rather than simply report on desegregation initiatives, they helped shape those initiatives through their personal involvement." In 1963, McKnight was called upon by the influential Chamber of Commerce to draft a resolution that all Charlotte businesses be open to patrons regardless of race, creed, or color. He did so, later writing an editorial on the subject as well. McKnight wasn't new to this; in the late 1950s he and other North Carolina newspaper editors worked behind the scenes with school boards in order to move a small number of black students into public schools. Such partisanship by newspapers of record would be considered flatly unethical in later years, and some journalists balked at it back then as well.[66]

The resolution was put in motion in May of that year, when white and black leaders in the community met in heretofore segregated hotel dining rooms around the city for three days of carefully orchestrated lunches, breaking long tradition and attracting national publicity. Author and *Charlotte Observer* writer Fannie Flono, reflecting on the fiftieth anniversary of these events, wrote that the "strategy offered by restaurateur Slug Claiborne and cobbled together by [Mayor Stan] Brookshire and the Charlotte Chamber of Commerce did keep violence at bay. More importantly, the move started the dismantling of segregation in hotels, theaters and restaurants in the city. That action helped define Charlotte as a progressive New South city, and propelled its reputation for working across racial lines to get things done."[67]

The interracial dining strategy, for all the notice it brought to the city, did not do away with the practice of segregation, and it would not erase the long history of a color line; but Charlotte avoided the sort of violent standoffs that other southern cities experienced over segregated restaurants and other businesses. To Golden, especially after Birmingham, that was something to cling to.

Near summer's end came a few days that lifted his spirits even more. One hundred years after the Emancipation Proclamation, a "Great March on Washington for Jobs and Freedom" was set for 28 August 1963. At least 200,000 people—some sources said 300,000—gathered on the hot day. "It was the last happy moment of the movement," Golden wrote. He left Charlotte the day before, brandishing a letter from King requesting that he be on hand for the march. His happiness flagged a bit when he didn't see any other white people leaving for the event from the Charlotte airport. Why this should surprise him, he couldn't say.[68]

Once in Washington, he checked into the Mayflower Hotel. He shared a room with writer and six-time Socialist Party presidential candidate Norman Thomas, whom he admired and corresponded with for years, particularly around the successful efforts to commute the sentence of Junius Scales, the only American to be sent to prison for membership in the Communist Party. As Golden later put it, "All his life . . . Thomas preached the need for the reform of American economic life—for social security, old-age pensions, Medicare, low-cost housing . . . but what the American people were willing to accept from [Franklin Roosevelt] the senior warden of the Hyde Park Episcopal Church who wore a Navy cape they could not accept from a Socialist."[69]

The next morning Golden chatted about the march with a reporter from Voice of America radio. Then he walked from the Washington Monument to the Lincoln Memorial with Thomas, Tom Wicker of the *New York Times*, and Harold Stassen, the former governor of Minnesota.[70]

The political tension behind the event was strong, despite the conventional historical account that makes it seem as though the March on Washington was the work of a seamless black entity. This tension was inevitable; the leadership of the event was a powerful group of strong egos, men with conflicting convictions about the best way to press for equal rights. Roy Wilkins of the NAACP had ruthlessly reduced the list of speakers allowed to share the platform with King and Randolph. It included himself; John Lewis of SNCC, who was forced into cutting some strong criticism of Kennedy from his speech; James Farmer of CORE; and Whitney Young Jr. of the National Urban League. Some activists regarded the march as a protest against the lack of action by the Kennedy administration. Others, like Golden, wanted the world to see that Americans of both races, of all religions and backgrounds, and from all parts of the country were marching away and leaving the old, evil legacy of racism behind.[71]

Rabbi Joachim Prinz, head of the American Jewish Congress, made this point with an authority no other speaker could claim that day. Prinz had been expelled from Germany in 1937 for opposing Nazism and came to America under the wing of another Jewish leader, Rabbi Stephen Wise. "When I was the rabbi of the Jewish community in Berlin under the Hitler regime, I learned many things," Prinz told the crowd. "The most important thing that I learned under those tragic circumstances was that bigotry and hatred are not the most urgent problem. The most urgent, the most disgraceful, the most shameful and the most tragic problem is silence. . . . America must not become a nation of onlookers." Prinz spoke right before King, and for understandable reasons his words have been referred to as the "least remembered great speech in American civil rights history."[72]

Regardless of motive or expectations, political infighting, feelings of optimism or anger, it was a transcendent moment when the great gospel singer Mahalia Jackson took the podium and sang the first grave words of "I Been 'Buked and I Been Scorned." When she next raised up the huge crowd with "How We Got Over," it was a joyful noise indeed:

> Had a mighty hard time coming on over
> You know my soul look back and wonder
> How did we make it over?[73]

It was, Golden said, "a jubilee morning. . . . Black militancy was still in the ground. No city had been razed by rioters. The March was the high-water mark of liberalism. Not until we finish this fight will we know another day with the stirring excitement of Martin Luther King Jr.'s speech 'I Have a Dream.' "[74]

Golden was right about the stirring nature of the speech, although not accurate in assuming its immediate impact. That brilliant oratory by King has over time been separated from the rest of the day, played and replayed, quoted and parsed. It has come to be regarded as representative of what was heard and felt by participants and onlookers that day. In fact, because of the political maneuvering around the timing and order of earlier speeches, King's remarks came well into the warm day. "At 1:59 the official speaking began. For those who listened it was full of noble statement about democracy and religious sincerity, but the crowd was dissolving fast now," wrote Russell Baker in the *New York Times* in a lengthy, thoughtful description of the march. Before King spoke, "huge portions of the crowd had drifted out of earshot." The "I Have a Dream" speech gained its power and importance after the fact, when America realized what it had missed that day.[75]

More Heartbreak: Birmingham and Dallas

The triumph of the March on Washington lasted less than a month. The weeks and months until the end of 1963 were a blur of shock, grief, and anger. On 15 September, four African American girls were killed in the bombing of the Sixteenth Street Baptist Church in Birmingham. *Newsweek* reported that there been some fifty bombings in the city since World War II, many not making news outside the city. This one, of course, was different. The church was ostensibly chosen by white supremacists because it was a meeting place for civil rights activities. The bomb went off during Sunday school; it killed Denise McNair, 11, and Carole Robertson, Cynthia Wesley, and Addie Mae Collins, all 14, and caused Collins's younger sister, Sarah, to lose an eye. Frantic rescuers dug with their bare hands and found shattered bodies in Sunday-best dresses. Offers of help and money for rebuilding the church came flooding in.[76]

Once Golden might have written about that show of support. Now all he could convey was hopelessness and deep anger: "After that bitter Sunday . . . the usual calm settled over the city. Violence was contained. The white Chamber of Commerce talked about its shame and the white ministers talked about His Peace and the white citizens' council talked about 'outside agitators.'" He continued, "In the aftermath of this terrible tragedy we are witnessing the complete reversal of Anglo-Saxon law. It is obvious that there is no law in Birmingham, just long periods when anarchy is under control."[77]

Golden simply could not tolerate politicians who were still blaming blacks for demanding equality or claims that "outside agitators" had stirred up the violence. He struggled to put the matter into a context so simple that any reader could understand it:

> On a dark street you are assaulted. The thief splits your skull and leaves you huddled on the curb badly bleeding. When the policeman discovers you, instead of calling the station house, he sits you up and says rationally, calmly, and dispassionately, "The thing we've got to do now is reason this thing out." Anarchy is the state wherein the victim becomes negotiable. . . . To convince themselves this peace is real, they will invent even more myths . . . that [the victim] is content with his lot [and] if only the outside agitators would go away he would indeed sit down with the policeman and discuss his cracked skull with patience and forbearance.[78]

Death of a President

Then came 22 November 1963.

"John F. Kennedy was an *idea* to the people of the United States," a weary Golden told a Miami audience in the month after the president's assassination. "More than the man he was, and the office he held, was an idea of what we could become; what we could be, what we could achieve." As he haltingly memorialized Kennedy, Golden was also talking about the civil rights movement. It too was an idea of what we could become, what could be achieved once America's long racist history began to change. He did not want to believe that the leader he admired and the cause that had become his life could be so suddenly taken. He did what a writer does at such a time: He wrote out his grief.[79]

Mr. Kennedy and the Negroes, Golden's seventh book, was half written when the president was assassinated. Suddenly there was a different pressure to complete it. What would have been a conversational collection of stories resembling the Sandburg book became a narrative, a plainspoken telling of civil rights progress since Reconstruction. Although it was not published under a co-byline, without Richard Goldhurst's writing and editing the book would not have been completed.

The brilliant *New York Times* journalist Anthony Lewis, not an easy sell despite his personal fondness for Kennedy, found the book "important and fascinating." Lewis, who at the time covered the Supreme Court and wrote regularly about civil rights, saw that Golden could lay aside his usual bantering to write "seriously, though not heavily about the excruciating subject of race" and still make good use of his storyteller's gift: "Mr. Golden's anecdotal style brings out as well as anything could the cruelty of racism." Lewis guessed that Golden tapped into a readership much broader than even top newspaper reporters, himself included, could reach.[80]

Golden was obviously biased; his admiration for the Kennedy family was clear. He emphasized the moral victory behind the civil rights gains spawned in the Kennedy years, as did countless others close to the administration who needed to focus on the heroism in order to assuage their grief. But Golden was not blind to Kennedy the political animal. He knew the administration's involvement in civil rights issues was strategic, and each move was carefully weighed for political fallout. "Whether he was a civil rights President because of political expediency, or because he could not avoid being a civil rights President, or because he believed in this cause with all his intellectual fervor and being—all this is irrelevant," wrote Golden. "He remains the civil rights President."[81]

After Kennedy was in the White House, his severest critics on civil rights issues were not "political enemies or segregationists the New Frontier had written off," observed Golden, but "Democratic liberals and Negroes who complained that President Kennedy had wasted two years before he ended housing segregation in government-financed units; and that when the President did end it by his celebrated promise of 'a stroke of the pen' it was not half as strong as they hoped it would be."[82]

The segregationist enemy camp was more astute, Golden thought. "The segregationist politicians knew what was going on and it alarmed them. . . . President John F. Kennedy, the Attorney General and his civil rights staff were slowly but surely cutting the heart out of the racial *status*

quo of the South. . . . Kennedy had accepted the challenge of the segregationists to fight the battle, county by county, school by school, Negro by
Negro. He was using laws that were there all the time—for over two and
a half years of President Eisenhower's second term—but they were laws
which had not been made into effective legal weapons."[83]

The book would not stand up to the coming deluge of Kennedy books
by administration insiders, historians, and biographers. For a time it
appeared in the occasional bibliography, but it is rarely cited today. Yet
in its era it was, as respected critics such as Lewis recognized, welcomed
and valued by those who admired Kennedy and were already trying to fit
his presidency into the larger view of American history. Not to be under-
estimated, in the book's pre-Internet era, is the value of keeping historic
speeches in circulation among general readers, including the address by
Kennedy to Congress on 28 February 1963, the centennial of the Emancipation Proclamation, and his 11 June 1963 televised speech on civil rights.
Golden knew that the things Kennedy said had tremendous influence in
a time of change and turmoil and would be studied far into the future for
that reason.

Many writers, Golden included, have likened Kennedy to Abraham
Lincoln. But in Golden's mind the two were brothers for reasons beyond
their roles in the emancipation of black Americans. Both possessed the
gift for causing the common people to rethink their own sphere and
abilities in the darkest hours, and their power outlived them by generations, growing stronger with time. "Kennedy's significance in the Negro's
advance was not so much that he helped him along, as that he understood this revolution was important and that it must succeed, not only in
the cause of justice for the Negro but more important, for the welfare of
America," wrote Golden.[84]

Kennedy had ushered in a new media age, and now Golden and
movement activists were no longer alone in their grasp of the depth and
effects of American racism. Television meant that violence against blacks
in the South played out in living rooms across the country and showed
the rest of the world how America's democratic experiment was faring
in the twentieth century. Television also enlarged the country's base of
consumers. "American business and industry has invited the Negro into
this vast open society by making him a customer," Golden wrote in *Mr.
Kennedy and the Negroes*. "To the marginal man television and the movies are a window on the affluent society. Any man exposed often enough
to the luxuries and comforts presented on 'Father Knows Best' or 'I Love
Lucy' will want them." Recalling the circumstances of the poorest of

southern blacks, Golden wrote with bald sarcasm, "Watching television, the unemployed segregated Negro sees that what really concerns Americans, judging by the time devoted to it, is how they smell. Every blonde on television worries about deodorants and here he is—the Negro—living in a dirt-filled yard in a house on stilts without an inside toilet."[85]

There is a great sadness in this book, and it goes beyond Golden's grieving for the slain president. Golden was now in his sixties, thinking about his own mortality. He openly regretted that the mantra of gradualism had lasted as long as it had and that he had played a part in prolonging it. Earlier that year he had written that the main accomplishment of "so-called moderates" was to "prove we live in a world in which it is necessary to summon mass protest to attain elemental justice." It was not the first time he had voiced these sentiments, but this was a more personal indictment and a dramatic change from his years of focusing on the heroism of those very protests. Now, with the death of Kennedy, his observations grew darker: "In his earliest campaigns for simple justice, the Negro, perhaps mistakenly, relied upon the leadership of whites who were sympathetic, who tried to help him by telling him to wait," he wrote in *Mr. Kennedy and the Negroes*.[86]

Golden now resembled a career diplomat who realizes that there is dwindling need for a once-valuable skill at interpreting events for a group of warring factions. He was shaken that rising black activists did not want or need him to fight on their behalf. Moments of bitterness surfaced occasionally in his speeches and writing. One came over remarks made by writer and activist James Baldwin following Kennedy's murder. Baldwin had clashed memorably with Robert Kennedy earlier that year at a private meeting of black leaders and artists and the attorney general, and after the president's death, he told an audience at a SNCC event, "Let us not be so pious now as to say that President Kennedy was a great civil-rights fighter." The tense meeting between Baldwin; Robert Kennedy; Kenneth Clark, whose research with black schoolchildren had been cited in the *Brown* decision; Jerome Smith, one of the first CORE volunteers on the Freedom Rides in Alabama; singer Harry Belafonte; and others became a legend. As described in an arresting account by journalist Carol Polsgrove, the meeting was a watershed in Baldwin's life, an upheaval in Kennedy's life, and an important factor in Vice President Lyndon Johnson's taking up the civil rights fight.[87]

At another time, Golden would probably have used Baldwin's observation to make a point about the movement, perhaps reminding readers that there was a time not long ago when such a remark would have put a black man in great danger. Or he might have disagreed with Baldwin's view but agreed that there was still much more to be done by the country's leaders to enable civil rights. But with the pain of Kennedy's death so fresh, Golden's response was simply angry and defeated: "He missed the whole point. But Mr. Baldwin is not the only Negro intellectual who has been cynical about the racial activities of the late President."[88]

Grief, Hope, and Black Power

Even in his grief, Golden was not moved to make a martyr of John Kennedy. He did not mourn the romantic "Camelot" image promoted so aggressively by Jacqueline Kennedy and others in the inner circle. Nor did he disdain Lyndon Baines Johnson, as did his friend Robert Kennedy and many other loyalists. Golden had not lost his knack for enjoying friendships with people outside his political circle. His compeers naturally included rivals such as Lyndon Johnson and Robert Kennedy.[1]

Golden was among those political writers who watched with close interest Johnson's positioning of himself on civil rights issues. Six months before Kennedy's murder, Johnson had turned a stock Memorial Day speech at Gettysburg into an object lesson on racism in America, where despite a century of freedom, "the Negro remains in bondage to the color of his skin." A popular view held that Johnson came later to leadership on civil rights, picking up the fallen president's mantle. In fact, Johnson was already strongly identified with the issue, in this case by disapproving southern lawmakers and savvy black leaders when this speech (delivered to the *Washington Post* in advance) hit the wires.[2]

Now Golden's pragmatism was ascendant; the powerful Senate majority leader from Texas had been wisely chosen to add southern strength to John Kennedy's run for the White House in 1960. He did not have the panache of Kennedy, but no one could match Johnson's ability to mastermind, cajole, and bully others into giving needed support and votes. He had been a crucial force behind the compromise 1957 Civil Rights Act, which lacked muscle but opened the door for the long-overdue civil rights changes. It also freed Johnson from the burden of a segregationist political machine, allowing him to run for national office. In 1964, Golden wrote, "They called him a 'wheeler dealer.' Well, a man with the reputation of a wheeler dealer is a man who keeps his word and owns up to his bargains. . . . The wheeler dealer is a man who understands the *quid pro quo* of politics. Franklin D. Roosevelt and Dwight D. Eisenhower were masters of the devious move. Some of the tricks they played would have left Lyndon B. Johnson in a state of stupefied moral outrage. But no one ever particularly wanted to hang the charge of deceit on F.D.R. or Ike. They hung it on Lyndon Johnson."[3]

Writing a few years later as the war in Vietnam was defining and crippling Johnson's presidency, Golden said, "Lyndon B. Johnson remembers when cotton sold for five cents a pound, and he keeps thinking of the poverty and the illiteracy of a rural and mountain America lost in the industrial age of the twentieth century. A war President is a role which appeals to him hardly at all."[4]

Golden was not bothered by the things that dismayed Washington's elite and many of his friends about Johnson. The beautiful young Kennedy couple in the White House had ushered in an era of art, celebrities, fine food, and fashion that was in sharp contrast to the administrations before and after. The energy that came with them galvanized young America, and a good many of the not-so-young, all of whom were caught up in the "ask not what your country can do for you . . ." rallying cry. Johnson could not compete with Jack Kennedy's charisma; Lady Bird and the Johnson daughters were not the photogenic Kennedy wife and toddlers. Golden's love for the Kennedys was rooted in other things—most of all Robert Kennedy's friendship—and he understood that the country now needed Johnson's steely resolve, his many established relationships, and political acumen to get civil rights legislation passed.[5]

Johnson had risen to power in the Senate while opposing or avoiding civil rights measures, always taking the shrewd, big-picture view, at which he was so skilled. He had not signed the shameful so-called Southern Manifesto that vowed to defy *Brown*, and he managed to stay above the fray as majority leader without alienating the rest of the southern delegation. Now he took up the lonely work of a true leader, beat back the southern delegation's record-breaking filibuster, and horse-traded to get the Civil Rights Act of 1964 through. The first southern president since the Civil War did what he did best: He plotted, he planned, and he didn't rest until he made it happen. As Roy Wilkins of the NAACP wrote, "I came away from the conversations I had with L.B.J feeling that he was not only with us but often ahead of us."[6]

Six months after Johnson's landslide victory in 1964, the law said, among other things, that public facilities could no longer be segregated and that employers could no longer legally hire, fire, or manage employees based on race or sex. The federal government had the tools to enforce these and other rights that made Americans equal. Now, as Johnson told the country, at long last "those who are equal before God" would also be equal in the voting booth, the classroom, the factories, and the restaurants. Golden was neither disrespectful nor facetious when he said that history would show that "Kennedy's finest achievement was Johnson."[7]

1964 and Freedom Summer

Important groundwork was already in place when Johnson took office. Kennedy's team had started dismantling practices of intimidation and red tape that kept blacks from registering to vote in the South. The limp gestures of the Eisenhower years had given way to swarms of lawyers and investigators "tramping dusty roads in Mississippi, Alabama, and Louisiana, knocking on the doors of Negro shacks, asking 'Did you ever try to register? When? What happened?'" wrote Golden. "For the first time in a century, blacks in the South could actually believe a white man who promised action." As momentous as this was in a historical sense and as inspiring as it was to a generation of young Americans, immense pressure from Johnson and bold on-the-ground action would still be needed to propel the civil rights cause ahead.[8]

Although there was serious disagreement among black organizations about how best to proceed, they came together to register voters in Mississippi in the "Freedom Summer" campaign of 1964. The NAACP, CORE, and SNCC collaborated and created the Council of Federated Organizations. Freedom Summer was ground zero for the worst intimidation of black would-be voters, and hundreds of volunteers were ready to go. A triumphant campaign would send a message across the country, and Golden applauded the determination and bravery of the plan. Proof of the need for a Freedom Summer, he thought, could be summed up by quoting the stark advice given to black volunteers on their way into rural areas of the South to register voters: "Always make sure you travel with a white civil rights worker. . . . They *look* for white bodies."[9]

By the Freedom Summer months, the hand-wringing of the 1950s by southern Jews—those who worried about Golden drawing unwanted attention—seemed almost quaint. He no longer stood out as a Jew criticizing segregation and racism. Influential Jewish organizations had been involved in the civil rights movement from its beginning, and now the mainstream press reported regularly on actions of the AJC, the ADL, and the American Jewish Congress. Before Kennedy was killed, one of the most stirring voices on behalf of civil rights was Rabbi Abraham Joshua Heschel, who, like King, drew on the messages of the Hebrew prophets when exhorting others that bringing about peace and social justice was the duty of all, not a few. Heschel's telegram to Kennedy on 13 June 1963, sent right before a meeting of religious leaders and others in the White House, was lyrical and forceful: "We forfeit the right to worship God as long as we continue to humiliate Negroes. . . . Ask of religious leaders to call for national repentance and personal sacrifice. Let religious leaders donate one month's salary toward fund for Negro housing and education. . . . I propose that you Mr. President declare state of moral emergency. . . . The hour calls for high moral grandeur and spiritual audacity."[10]

Many of the foot soldiers in the movement were Jews. About a third of the white Freedom Riders were Jewish. A majority of the New York lawyers who volunteered or held paid positions on the side of the movement were Jewish. (The old accusations that used "Jew" as a synonym for "Communist" were still hurled by segregationists. When the National Lawyers Guild opened an office in Jackson, Mississippi, its Communist connections frightened "establishment" Jewish lawyers into drafting more of their own crowd into the cause.) The most notorious story of that summer, the murders of volunteers Michael Schwerner, Andrew Goodman, and James Chaney, was told and retold. That Schwerner and Goodman were Jewish is still almost always noted when this case is written about. It did not matter how religiously observant they were; their Jewishness was noted from the first.[11]

Meanwhile, friction was growing between Golden and some leaders of national Jewish organizations. His relationship with the AJC in particular was strained that same summer. In June, Morris Abram, AJC president, sent Golden a three-page, single-spaced letter taking him to task for misrepresenting the agency's stand on race issues in *Mr. Kennedy and the Negroes*. The offending passages, according to Abram, downplayed or misstated the AJC's stand on race issues.[12]

Golden's response was fast and overwrought; he called the critical letter "cold, callous and unreasoning," which it was not, and sputtered that the small details cited as incorrect were insignificant. Abram was right; Golden did indeed leave the impression that Irving Engel, former director of the AJC, was less than aggressive earlier in the movement as he positioned the organization as an opponent of segregation. As for Golden's overreaction, it was in part due to his strong feelings about the book's subject—President Kennedy—for whom he still grieved. It was also related to the uncomfortable memory of Engel as one of his saviors back in 1953; Engel had sent $5,000 when frightened advertisers were jumping ship from the *Carolina Israelite*. Golden could be defensive when patrons or lenders from the past surfaced, and he seemed to go out of his way to make the point that he would not give past benefactors special treatment in his writings and speeches.[13]

Engel, now an honorary director of the AJC, received copies of the heated correspondence. He let two weeks pass and then wrote a measured letter to his old friend, walking him through the passages in question and taking him to task for his emotional outburst. A chastised Golden apologized for the tone of his letter to Abram, then proffered a joking defense that essentially retracted his apology: "But I recall reading a Heywood Broun interview with the pitcher Christy Mathewson. The great ballplayer had lost a game and by way of explanation said; 'It was too cold today—I can only pitch when I'm hot.'" Golden did not change the text of the Kennedy book in later printings as Abram and Engel had hoped, and while the correspondence smoothed things between them, the relationship of Golden to the AJC leadership remained somewhat rocky. The world of the Jewish organizations was small, and the days in which Golden was asked by AJC leaders to provide on-the-ground intelligence about the Ku Klux Klan and other groups in the South were over. He had long been regarded as a maverick; now he was seen more as a loose cannon, a perception helped along by the sharper tone in some of his writing.[14]

Just a few months before the Abram-Engel matter, Golden had shrugged off the Second Vatican Council's ongoing discussions of Jews in what would eventually become *Nostra Aetate*, a declaration on the relation of the Church to non-Christian religions, issued by Pope Paul VI. The Roman Catholic effort to do away with the "Christ-killer" epithet hurled at Jews for centuries was hailed by many Jewish leaders as a great breakthrough for Christian-Jewish relations. Golden, in direct disagreement with an AJC statement on the matter, questioned whether it would do much to roll back anti-Semitism. He emphasized his point in a *Carolina Israelite* essay by suggesting—not entirely in jest—that Jews hold their own ecumenical council and "forgive the Christians for the Inquisition, the Crusades, the ghettoes, and the expulsions." He compounded this offense the next year by reprinting the essay and sending it out as a holiday season promotional piece.[15]

Work, Deadlines, and More Work

Golden was clearly aggravated by a workload that was too large. He had been finishing his sixth book, *Forgotten Pioneer*, published in 1963, when the pressure came to accelerate the writing of *Mr. Kennedy and the Negroes*. *Forgotten Pioneer* was the first to break out of his pattern of collected essays, much to the relief of his editor, who continued to worry about Golden strip-mining the subjects covered in the *Carolina Israelite*. This was a happy coincidence, as Golden was not heeding Targ's advice; he had his own reasons for writing *Forgotten Pioneer* when he did. "With the race issue hot . . . and Berlin and all the other crises, I thought maybe it would be well to put out just a small book about a bit of Americana," Golden told columnist Lewis Nichols of the *New York Times*. "I can remember the peddlers, but they're dying, they deserve a tribute."[16]

Golden wrote in the introduction, "The pack peddler practiced free enterprise in its purest form. He had no help from anyone, except perhaps an initial loan from a relative who had preceded him to America—a loan of forty dollars at the most. . . . I smile today when I read the enthusiastic editorials and speeches which proclaim the wonders of free enterprise even as the city fathers give a manufacturer a tax-free plant or make him a gift of a parking lot."[17]

Forgotten Pioneer details the lives of three Jewish peddlers, two fictional composites told in the first person and a biographical sketch of Levi Strauss, the man who made blue jeans an American uniform. As is so often the case for fiction writers, the characters, intentionally or not, share qualities with their creator. For years Golden suggested that all of his family name changes occurred at Ellis Island, when in fact they came later and for various reasons. When one of the fictional peddlers explains his name change, he gives an account that is close to Golden's actual experience: "The first thing I discovered was that to tell a customer my name was Morris H. Witcowsky was out of the question. . . . So I just said, 'My name is Morris.' Years later . . . every customer called me Morris and some of the ladies called me Mr. Morris, so I left it that way. I've forgotten whether I ever did this legally or not."[18]

A goodly number of the reviewers—Nichols included—described the book's content without rendering an opinion as to its merit. The departure from Golden's successful formula seemed to baffle critics. Even though it dealt with Jewish America, *Forgotten Pioneer* had no snappy one-liners or anything resembling a Golden Plan. It was a fraction of the size of his previous books, just 157 pages, including the rich pen-and-ink illustrations by artist Leonard Vosburgh. *Time* magazine's take was typical: "Harry (*Only in America*) Golden, whose brother Jake had peddled to support his family, tells the story of the peddlers and, in a leisurely introduction, offers insights into life on the road." A reviewer in *Christian Century* was not impressed; Golden was "out of his usual groove." Another critic wished the book had been longer and more detailed. In a kind of irony visited on many a successful, prolific writer, Golden now ran the risk of being criticized for being formulaic—or for disappointing readers when he broke out of that mold.[19]

By 1964 Golden had published a book a year for six years. He had never heeded publisher Zevin's warnings about putting his books out too fast, and after the first three (*Only in America*, *For 2 Cents Plain*, and *Enjoy, Enjoy!*), Golden pushed them to press even faster. After *Carl Sandburg* in 1961, he published another essay collection, *You're Entitle'*, in 1962. The title came from a favorite expression of Leib Goldhirsch's. "He was enamored of the phrase," Golden wrote in the book's early pages. "In my youth, I told him over and over again that the phrase was . . . 'you're entitled.'" Leib Goldhirsch never did learn to pronounce the d on the end of the word. "It was the expression of a free man. . . . No one was entitled in Eastern Europe. You served in the army for ten years and it entitled you to nothing. . . . But in America men were free and *entitled*, or as my father insisted, 'You're Entitle.'" Also that year came *Five Boyhoods*, in which Golden's chapter shared billing with those of Walt Kelly, creator of the iconic Pogo comic strip; playwright Howard Lindsay; novelist John Updike; and journalist William Zinsser. In 1963, *Forgotten Pioneer* was released. In 1964 Golden published both *Mr. Kennedy and the Negroes* and another book of essays, *So What Else is New?* He would crank out ten new books in the next eleven years.[20]

He was also stumping for his friend Robert Kennedy, who was running for the U.S. Senate in 1964 against Kenneth Keating in New York. Kennedy wanted to be sure he got the Jewish vote, and Golden did several radio interviews in his hit-and-miss Yiddish as well as delivering speeches at any Jewish organization event that would have him. He worked Kennedy into nearly every speech, column, or essay that was remotely connected to politics. In an appearance on Johnny Carson's *Tonight Show* in August, he gently chided the host for getting laughs in a previous monologue that poked fun at Kennedy's carpetbagger status. Police chiefs and city managers are hired from outside posts all the time, Golden pointed out, adding, "New York would be lucky to get him." Golden also lived up to his billing as a funny guy by throwing in a well-voiced rendition of "She's Only a Bird in a Gilded Cage" (with "bird" pronounced "boid") and set Carson up for a good laugh when he likened the host to King Lear. The quick-witted Carson rejoined, "Well, *his* show's not on any more."[21]

Kennedy insiders Arthur Schlesinger, Edwin Guthman, and Theodore White—all Pulitzer Prize winners—wrote warm letters praising campaign efforts by Golden. After Kennedy's victory, Golden stayed with the cause, writing a piece for *Esquire*, "The Bobby Twins Revisited," in which he praised the senator's civil rights record and character. He recalled that during the campaign, there was always someone in the audience asking about Kennedy's reputed ruthlessness. Golden wrote, "I finally found the answer. . . . 'His wife and eight kids don't think he's ruthless.'" The *Esquire* piece got enormous exposure—it didn't hurt that Sean Connery as James Bond was on the cover—and several people in Kennedy's close circle wrote Golden to thank him. "I remember reading it and knocking my fist on the table and saying, 'That's it, that's it.' I wish I had written that myself," wrote White.[22]

Hot Dogs and the Borscht Belt

Golden continued to find humor in unlikely places and to rise to the occasion when a snappy comeback was needed in matters less controversial than race. A seemingly innocent column about the waning popularity of the frankfurter drew considerable mail, including anguished protests from the National Livestock and Meat Board in Chicago. Golden wrote the group's spokesman a soothing note, explaining that he was simply pointing out that the hamburger had cut into the hot dog's market share. "I have heard from a great number of people and I intend to write a big article about my love of the hot dog and all it has meant to me in my life," Golden wrote the spokesman. "As St. Paul said, 'Let not your heart be troubled.' St. Paul was a man who ate kosher food long before he had any idea that he would be made into an un-kosher symbol." He fared less well a few years later when he angered the swimming pool industry. An offhand remark in a syndicated column about aggressive and "wily" pool salesmen was met with a furious response from an industry representative. Months later Golden was still trying to placate the offended parties—who were apparently less forgiving than the hot dog folks—and so gamely agreed to serve as a judge in the trade group's annual Swimming Pool Design Competition.[23]

He was deeply moved by the reception he received at the Sixth National Conference of Cursillos in Christianity attended by some 1,000 Catholic clerics and laity. He spoke about the positive changes he had seen in Catholic-Jewish relationships, and this time he avoided any politically incorrect remarks about the pope putting an official end to the "Christ-killer" label. But he was not exactly easy on the Church. He recalled for his listeners a time when local priests could not sign a "petition of any kind having to do with Negroes" without permission. And, he added dryly, that permission took a very long time to obtain. When he finished, a group of clergy and laypeople stood, clasped hands, and sang:

He's got Harry Golden in His hand,
He's got Harry Golden in His hand,
He's got the whole world in His hand.[24]

He was met by an appreciative audience of a different sort when he played the so-called Borscht Belt in 1964 at the popular Concord resort ninety minutes outside New York City in the Catskills region. The fact that he had not previously been active in this busy world of Jewish resort entertainment points up his changed stature. By now Golden was no longer the dangerously controversial speaker whose appearances had often been preceded by anonymous, threatening calls to event managers.[25]

At the Concord, one of the female guests put a question to Golden after a dinner speech. All this civil rights talk is well and good, she said, "but what have the Negroes ever done for us?" Golden looked around the room with its swarming waiters and tables groaning under platters of food, then leveled his gaze on his questioner. "Madam," he said, pausing for a beat or two to be sure he had everyone's full attention, "the minute the Negroes get themselves a Concord Hotel we will ask them to do something for us, and not a moment sooner." He was invited back for the next year's special Passover-week show.[26]

Despite the enjoyment Golden drew from this busy, varied round of appearances, the work of preparing speeches and producing columns and books was exhausting. The murders—of President Kennedy, NAACP's Mississippi field secretary Medgar Evers earlier in 1963, the four little girls in a Birmingham Sunday school, and the three young volunteers in Mississippi—took their toll. Golden felt every day of his six decades. Even before the worst of the losses had happened, he had felt moved to ask Gabriel Cohen, friend and editor of the *National Jewish Post* in Indianapolis, if he would agree to assist his son Richard as a literary executor of the *Carolina Israelite*, should that be necessary. "It would be a comfort to know that Dickie will have this kind of advice at a time when he will need it badly," wrote Golden.[27]

A Prize and a Gift

There were bright spots. The Reverend Martin Luther King Jr. was awarded the Nobel Peace Prize, only the second African American to receive it and, at thirty-five, the youngest since the award's founding in 1901. (The first African American was United Nations mediator Ralph J. Bunche, who had won in 1950 for his work in peace talks between Arabs and Jews.) *Time* had named him Man of the Year earlier in 1964.[28]

Reactions ranged from Pope Paul VI expressing his pleasure to Bull Connor blustering that the Nobel people "scraped the bottom of the barrel." One prominent segregationist quoted in the *New York Times* declared that this award proved just how powerful the Communist influence was in the world, and he added in frustration, "Shame on somebody."[29]

But the biggest upside and most fertile source of editorial material for Golden was the candidacy of Republican senator Barry Goldwater of Arizona, who challenged Johnson in the 1964 presidential race. Goldwater was even more worthy of lampooning than Eisenhower. "Barry Goldwater's nomination for President of the United States is God's greatest gift to the essayist and social historian," Golden wrote. His pleasure grew greater when the *Charleston News and Courier* wrote of Goldwater, "At last a white man's candidate." The nicest thing this newspaper, sympathetic as it was to segregationists, ever published about Golden was to suggest that he "go back to the garment district." Golden found that simply listing the endorsements for Goldwater was fun: "Calvin F. Craig, a Grand-Dragon of the Ku Klux Klan, formally announced, 'It's Goldwater all the way,' at a Klan Convention in Atlanta. . . . Then there is that familiar, middle aged woman in our own community [who] has spent the last five years trying to purge the public library of books by Steinbeck, Justice Douglas, and other foreigners, telling her group of vigilantes, 'Barry Goldwater is the only man who can save America.' "[30]

Goldwater was raised in his mother's Episcopal faith, but his grandfather was Jewish; the family name had made the journey from Goldwasser in the late nineteenth century. Its newer incarnation graced the family's successful department stores in Arizona. Golden seized on the situation when stories began to mention Goldwater's background; Golden called him an "amateur Gentile" and coined a one-liner that became the most quoted of all his ripostes: "I always knew the first Jewish President would be an Episcopalian."[31]

Golden had not always treated Goldwater with a light touch. When the senator's book, *The Conscience of a Conservative*, came out in 1960, Golden was coldly critical, lumping Goldwater with the southern segregationist who was all too willing to set aside his insistence on states' rights when it came time for the federal government to provide him with electricity via the Tennessee Valley Authority dams of the New Deal. He wrote, "The conscience of a conservative is no more than a dream, the same sort of dream that nourishes the segregationist, a dream of a past that cannot, and should not be recalled." Golden grew tougher on the candidate close to the 1964 election when he wrote a long essay for the *New York Post* stating flatly that Goldwater was "more dangerous than Joe McCarthy ever was. . . . McCarthy never believed half the stuff he charged, while Goldwater is sincere in everything he says."[32]

Selma

Enjoyable jabs at the Arizona Republican offered a respite from other news of the day, but by the early days of 1965, Golden and much of America were riveted as they watched valiant protestors and marchers make history in Selma, Alabama. A group called the Dallas County Voters League had been working there for some time to combat the efforts of whites keeping blacks from registering to vote. Only 300 of the 15,000 blacks eligible to vote were registered in the county. Now the ministers of the Southern Christian Leadership Conference and the younger activists of SNCC joined the effort. The Reverend Martin Luther King Jr. made national headlines in January when he announced plans for a voter-registration effort that would test the Civil Rights Act of 1964. It would be, King said, "Selma's opportunity to repent."[33]

By 3 February, more than 2,000 people had been arrested in and around Selma, including King, who had deliberately put himself in a position to be jailed to bring attention to the demonstrations. News footage and photographs seen around the world showed lines of black students, some of them more child than adult, backs straight, holding hands and singing or praying. These images were enormously effective. "Selma pierced people's consciousness as nothing had done before," wrote a *New York Times* reporter years later. The young men and women in their neatly pressed slacks and skirts were a bleak reminder that another generation of African Americans had grown up without the equality promised by law.[34]

President Johnson, speaking to a White House press conference on farm subsidies on 4 February 1965, switched topics suddenly: "On another matter, I should like to say that all Americans should be indignant when one American is denied the right to vote. The loss of that right to a single citizen undermines the freedom of every citizen. This is why all of us should be concerned with the efforts of our fellow Americans to register to vote in Alabama." Johnson's charismatic style was replaced with the wooden delivery that often took over when he spoke from prepared remarks, especially on television. One line, though, had a flash of the aggressive style that his friends and opponents knew brooked no argument: "*I* intend to see that *that right* is secured for all of our citizens," Johnson declared.[35]

Images of the 7 March "Bloody Sunday" demonstrations in which Wallace ordered police to club and gas demonstrators shocked America when the film hit the TV news. Then, on 15 March, Johnson spoke to Congress and the country in a televised address about the proposed Voting Rights Act he was putting forward. "We cannot, we must not, refuse to protect the right of every American to vote in every election," Johnson told his audience. "And we ought not, and we cannot, and we must not wait another eight months before we get a bill. We have already waited one hundred years and more and the time for waiting is gone." The cause "must be our cause too," he said, "because it is not just Negroes, but really it is all of us, who must overcome the crippling legacy of bigotry and injustice." Johnson looked up and into the camera and told America, "And we *shall* overcome." It was perhaps his finest public hour. It was, wrote Johnson biographer Robert A. Caro, the only time in all their years together that King's aides had seen King cry.[36]

The sacrifices and courage of thousands of demonstrators and supporters and the determination of Lyndon Johnson spawned a victory: On 6 August, the president signed the Voting Rights Act of 1965. The humiliating "literacy tests" and other Jim Crow tricks used to keep blacks from voting were now against the law of the land. Lyndon Johnson was a flawed leader who had avoided or opposed many efforts to grant civil rights to black Americans, yet he was responsible for the biggest victory yet. As Golden wrote a few months later, Johnson was "a Southerner who wants to be remembered as the President who finally smashed the last vestiges of racial segregation. He is the poor boy turned millionaire who wants to help the poverty-stricken unemployed and those who live in slums and ghettos." During the Vietnam War, Golden was a rare liberal who reminded his readers that the same man had pushed effectively for civil rights and voting laws.[37]

Abraham Lincoln freed black Americans, wrote Johnson's biographer Robert Caro, "but it was Lyndon Johnson who led them into voting booths, closed democracy's sacred curtain behind them, placed their hands upon the lever that gave them a hold on their own destiny, made them, at last and forever, a true part of American political life."[38]

Black Power

Golden would never have imagined that anything could temper the joy of seeing voting rights signed into law. Yet within weeks of that milestone, his happiness was overshadowed by his fear that hard-fought gains were being destroyed by black militancy. When race riots broke out in various cities in 1964, Golden had at first viewed the unrest as hoodlums seizing the spotlight. But when the poor, black Watts neighborhood in central Los Angeles erupted in August, just five days after Johnson signed the new voting rights legislation, the scale of the violence could not be minimized. The six-day riot started on a hot August night when a white police officer pulled over a black driver suspected of being drunk. The routine stop turned ugly; the crowd and the police ranks grew. Efforts to defuse the situation in a public meeting the next day failed, and full-scale rioting broke out. Before the riot was quashed, 34 people died, 1,000 were hospitalized, and as many as 4,000 were arrested. Some 14,000 national guardsmen and more than 1,000 local police were called in to deal with the burnings, lootings, and assaults. Leaders of the country and the civil rights movement were severely shaken.[39]

"For Johnson and King, and for their countrymen, Watts was a defining moment—an ominous one," wrote journalist Nick Kotz in *Judgment Days*. Both of these proud men had come to believe their efforts were more effective, more widely embraced and appreciated, than was actually the case. When writing about these "grand assumptions," Kotz could have been speaking about Golden as well. As Watts burned, Golden watched in horror. Then, in June 1966, activist Stokely Carmichael told a crowd in a Mississippi park, "We been saying 'Freedom' for six years. . . . What we are going to start saying now is 'Black Power!'" Golden heard it as a loud, clear call to arms that was "bringing the entire civil rights movement to a halt." An intelligent, charismatic activist, Carmichael had led protests and voter-registration campaigns as a young man, and in 1966 he became head of SNCC. He moved to a black-nationalist view and was described as an "honorary prime minister" of the Black Panthers. Carmichael didn't invent the "Black Power!" cry, but he uttered it at a time and place that caused it, in today's parlance, to go viral. "Black power was just a slogan, loaded words, not a real program," wrote NAACP leader Roy Wilkins in his memoir, "but it crystallized resentments that had been building for years, the frustrations of black folks on one hand—and all the animosity of the white backlash on the other." The phrase, Wilkins believed, played right into the hands of racists. Golden was in full, grim agreement with this view.[40]

Golden had made the charge before that radical black activism could undo progress. Three years after comparing Black Muslims and Malcolm X to the Ku Klux Klan, he now broadened the indictment to include any blacks not pursuing the nonviolent-protest model, adding, "The only difference is that any three Ku Kluxers know more about violence than all the 22 million Negroes together." Rhetoric that urged blacks to move away from nonviolent activists and away from any whites in the move-ment fueled arch-segregationists, Golden said. The worst, he said, was Malcolm X's "ballot or bullet" school of speechmaking, which had created new and public opponents to the civil rights cause. "Whites who did not find it 'decent' to speak out against the Negro during the past ten years have found their tongues . . . and their influence," he wrote. Surely, he said, these militants should see that using Christianity and nonviolent civil dis-obedience was more effective than violence? Racists were racists, Golden reasoned, but over the past decade the specter of "a group of Negroes kneeling on the sidewalk in front of Woolworth's praying to be allowed to eat hot dogs" had forced (or shamed) regular folks into paying attention to the problems of segregation. Golden had written thousands of column inches demonstrating that he understood that asking for one's basic rights on bended knee was exhausting, demoralizing, and infuriating, but now he was frightened by the cumulative fury behind the call for a move away from nonviolent tactics.[41]

He did know, all too well, that even blacks who were highly visible business and civic figures still lived under the threat of white violence. In relatively quiet Charlotte, dynamite had exploded in 1965 at the homes, offices, and churches of his friends Kelly and Fred Alexander, attorney Julius Chambers, and Reginald Hawkins, a dentist, minister, and activist. "It was as if a compressed coil of racial hatred suddenly sprang forward," wrote Charlotte historian Dan L. Morrill. These men and others, despite professional and educational success, were still vulnerable in their own communities.[42]

Golden met Chambers soon after the young lawyer arrived in 1964 and set up practice in a small office on East Trade Street. After attending segre-gated schools near Charlotte and graduating first in his class at the University of North Carolina Law School, Chambers emerged from the NAACP's Legal

Defense Fund trained to fight civil rights cases back home. Golden firmly believed that *Swann v. Charlotte-Mecklenburg School Board*, the lawsuit Chambers filed on behalf of black parents in Charlotte, was crucial to bringing about the desegregation of public schools beyond token gestures and ineffective approaches. (The case went to the Supreme Court in 1971.) He knew but was less close to Hawkins, whose approach was more confrontational than that of his peers in the state NAACP who chose to work through the courts and push for voter registration among blacks to bring about change.[43]

Perhaps his own success prevented Golden from fully acknowledging the validity of such deep anger. If the civil rights gains were indeed Pyrrhic victories, his life's work became hollow comedy. Golden had made his name by extolling nonviolent sit-ins, boycotts, and marches; the bravery of black families sending children off to white schools; and the courage it took for whites to go against the status quo in their communities. He did not shrink from pushing for ambitious solutions. In the fall of 1966 he had given lengthy testimony in front of a Senate subcommittee, supporting passage of open housing and fair-employment legislation, as well as a "$100 billion indemnity" for blacks, arguing that only such large-scale remuneration would begin to level the playing field for all races. "We must say to ourselves . . . that we will provide an adequate living for those who became adults in the segregated society and who may not be able to compete in the industrial world of today," he said. His promulgation of this idea, first promoted as the "Freedom Budget," by A. Philip Randolph, did not redeem Golden in the eyes of this new breed of black activist. His work was now part of a poisoned gradualism that must be left behind.[44]

Slipping from Favor

As Golden's role in civil rights dialogues was changing, so was his place in the publishing world. His relationships with editors had been limited to contact with a few tolerant types during his career, and more often than not he ignored their suggestions. Even Richard Goldhurst, who had steadily taken on more rewriting duties and in some cases was a full-on ghostwriter, steered away from full-scale editing of his father's copy. "I didn't rewrite him unless he made some excruciatingly miserable mistake," said Goldhurst. Golden had never really developed the ability to benefit from editing. He wrote what he wrote and moved on, confident he was the best judge of his work. Targ continued to push Golden to take advantage of the professional editing available to him, but he rarely succeeded. As time passed, he also tried to impress on Golden the need to deliver on deadline and stick to production schedules. His writer could usually sidestep him: "I am not going to give an absolute date about the manuscript for fear of the Evil Eye," Golden once wrote Targ.[45]

By the mid-1960s, this long-standing pattern of editorial tolerance had changed. Earlier editors of Golden's magazine articles had occasionally rejected or severely cut his work, but usually under some other guise—such as when *Life* cited the saturation of coverage on the Eichmann trial, saying it was wiser to use text blocks and photographs instead of a second narrative piece by Golden. The *Saturday Evening Post* was one of the first major publications to come down hard on Golden. In the fall of 1965, a senior editor sent back Golden's piece titled "The Negro Intellectuals Who Need to Be Carefully Taught" intended for the magazine's "Speaking Out" column. The article lumped together and criticized New York congressman Adam Clayton Powell, novelist James Baldwin, and poet/playwright LeRoi Jones (who later took the name Amiri Baraka). As the unhappy editor pointed out, Golden failed to make a convincing case for grouping the three before his somewhat shrill attack. He listed stalwart white southern liberals who fought for civil rights as if their efforts should exempt all white activists from any criticism. Of Baldwin and Jones, Golden wrote in his draft, "They are going the wrong way on a one way street . . . heaping sarcasm, scorn, and contempt on the white society generally, and on the white liberals particularly. . . . They are both original, aggressive men, and they probably feel it is no participation at all to follow the lead of the NAACP which concentrates on winning moral and practical successes in the courtroom." He ended on a sarcastic note: "Both writers are also super-sophisticates and nothing terrifies the super-sophisticate like simplicity." The editor wrote Golden that "when all is said and done, and in complete candor, it would take a lot to get this piece printed here." He offered Golden the standard kill fee of $250, adding that it was with "real regrets."[46]

That spring, an article Golden wrote for *Playboy* came back with similar criticisms and less tact. "While there is much merit to it in its present form, there are also a number of serious problems. There seems to be a noticeable lack of the wry, sardonic humor which we have come to expect from a Harry Golden piece," wrote a senior editor. The piece rambled and generalized about Jewish-Gentile relations and relied on recycled material well known to Golden's readers. He made some changes suggested by the *Playboy* editors, and the piece ran in December 1966, still lacking the voice Golden's editors wanted.[47]

Even some publishers who were directly promoting Golden's work seemed less enthusiastic. In 1966, the ADL put out a booklet of photographs and dialogue with Golden. The foreword written by Dore Schary, ADL's national chairman, piled on the caveats: "There are some controversial items. . . . While one may disagree with some of his views . . . Mr. Golden may be charged with some over-simplification or for a few hasty conclusions."[48]

The booklet preserves much of Golden's personality and style as a speaker, and the photographs are some of the best taken of him. The writer-photographer who interviewed Golden was Solomon Littman, who was working in the ADL's New York office. Forty-five years later, when asked about this seeming ambivalence by Schary and others, Littman characterized their concerns about Golden as common at the time. Many Jewish leaders were not confident of what Golden described as significant progress on racial issues in the South, he said. "It's that old Jewish saying, 'If everything is so good, why I am I so worried?' " Littman added, "Golden was not an apologist for the South, but perhaps at this point he had too benign a view. While he personally found a great respite there, other Jews and blacks had not found the Nirvana that he had."[49]

That same year, Golden's sixth book of collected essays came out. *Ess, Ess, Mein Kindt (Eat, Eat, My Child)* finally granted his long-standing wish for a Yiddish title—at the time not generally regarded as a smart marketing move. The more attentive among the reviewers put the changes in his work into context: "He may be more bitter than he was, but he keeps his sense of humor," wrote a reviewer in the *New York Times*.[50]

However, most missed the larger point of the book's title. Literally, the expression "Eat, eat, my child" was both endearment and command. Food was love and survival. Anyone who dismissed the book as too sentimental never had home-baked, dark-rye bread spread with chicken fat as an afternoon snack, Golden figured. He was used to critics twitting him about his dreamy recollections on food, and he ignored them. Golden had found that observing a community's food and related customs was one of the most useful ways to frame cultural differences and assimilation. As historian Marcie Cohen Ferris wrote in the delightful *Matzoh Ball Gumbo: Culinary Tales of the Jewish South*, "The act of eating in the Jewish South reflects how Jews balanced their Jewishness in a world dominated by white and black Christian southerners."[51]

Dueling Headlines

Magazine editors still wanted Golden's pieces, but as criticism or rejection became more common, the appeal of doing the work faded for him. His syndicated column wasn't safe from criticism either; in fact, it was the vehicle for an especially awkward blunder that began in the fall of 1965 and continued into the next year. It grew out of correspondence with labor leader David Dubinsky. Dubbed "King of the Garment District," Dubinsky was president of the International Ladies' Garment Workers' Union, and over three decades he had brought the union from a backroom to a place of considerable power, with 350,000 members and, at its peak, coffers of close to $500 million. Dubinsky was even more colorful than Golden. When he wasn't riding around the city on his bicycle, a beret atop his gray crew cut, he was an arm-waving, argumentative, charming, and utterly inexhaustible fighter for the workers who revered him. Born in what was then Polish Russia, Dubinsky left school at thirteen and had already headed a local bakers union, led a strike, and served hard time in a Russian prison when he immigrated to New York City in 1911 at nineteen. He spoke Polish, Russian, and Yiddish and, much to Golden's delight, never lost his heavy accent when he yelled in English. His success at bringing living wages, safer workplaces, and a thirty-five-hour workweek to the sweatshop world made him a hero to thousands of workers and endeared him to Golden. They had much in common: a cause, circles of loyal friends, and strong affection for questioning authority and settling down to a stiff drink served with a side of pastrami, herring, and pickles. Their occasional meetings were companionable events.[52]

By 1965, Dubinsky was on his way out. The union bosses wanted him gone, and his endorsement of Republican John Lindsay for mayor of New York City flew in the face of their support of Democrat Abraham Beame. In October, Golden wrote Dubinsky a chatty letter: "I was watching the visit of Pope Paul on television and I thought the only man who could bring out more New Yorkers was—David Dubinsky." He went on to explain that he would be making a few speeches on behalf of Beame. Golden conceded that Lindsay was actually "to the Left" of his opponent but said that he felt electing a member of the GOP would send the wrong message across the country, enabling rampant election of *more* Republicans. Dubinsky wrote back, arguing for his candidate.[53]

Richard Goldhurst remembered it this way: "Dubinsky, in a private letter to Harry, asked his opinion about the election. Harry wrote a two-paragraph reply. He praised Lindsay as an honest man, who though rich, was devoted to the city's welfare. But—and this is an important 'but'— Harry was endorsing Beame, equally devoted to the city, who grew up poor and presumably better understood the needs of blacks, Puerto Ricans, and those who did not quite make a living. Dubinsky deleted the second paragraph and published the first."[54]

Dubinsky did indeed reproduce an edited version of Golden's letter and his own response in huge ads in the *New York Times* and the *New York Post*. The exact changes Dubinsky made to Golden's letter aren't clear, but it is fair to say that he made Golden sound wishy-washy on the mayoral race. The matter might have faded away had Golden not then run his own full-page ad, headlined "Harry Golden's open letter to David Dubinsky." There he got tougher on Lindsay, accusing the candidate of making references to "crime in the streets"—which Golden declared was "nothing more than a euphemism for 'Negro.'" Golden had essentially been goaded by Dubinsky into overstating his position on Lindsay. When Golden tried to use some of the content from his ad in his syndicated column, the *New York Post*, which had endorsed Lindsay, refused to run it. A ferocious unsigned editorial followed on 29 October. It called Golden a "front-man" for a pitiful effort by the Beame campaign and blasted him for implying that Lindsay was a racist, adding, "in the immortal words . . . spoken in a fateful confrontation with Sen. McCarthy, we ask Golden 'Have you no shame, sir?' "[55]

Golden scrambled to soothe the powers-that-be at the *Post*, including Dorothy Schiff, the formidable publisher, and editor Max Lerner. Golden was unsuccessful, and so he began to spread the word that the *Post* had dropped him because of his political beliefs. The ads made Golden and Dubinsky look like two old circus lions batting at each other in a contrived and desultory fight. Golden came across as out of touch, his involvement ending up more as a distraction from the issues than the source of a meaningful political argument. He grandly assured *Post* editor Lerner that he would "make certain that as far as I am concerned no one will use this to heap scorn on the paper for which I have a deep affection." The entire incident was left out of his autobiography.[56]

The Brethren

Feeling less confident of his reception by editors, Golden was thankful for his long friendships with other newsmen. He wrote letters to the old crowd, "the Brethren," often. He bantered with Harry Ashmore, now at the Center for the Study of Democratic Institutions in Santa Barbara; Bill Baggs; and Ralph McGill. After the Dubinsky mess, he began to plan a trip with Ashmore and Baggs, along with Claude Sitton, national editor of the *New York Times*; newscaster David Brinkley of NBC; and Paul Anthony of the Southern Regional Council for a few days of food, drink, and talk in Atlanta. The plan was to meet informally to talk about education and the civil rights movement, "if we can manage it . . . without any publicity," Golden wrote Brinkley beforehand.[57]

They could *not* manage it, as it turned out. The October 1966 gathering made news when Anthony was quoted in the *Los Angeles Times* saying that the "group of distinguished editors and officials of foundations" had agreed that the election of an "apartheid President" resembling a premier of South Africa could happen "if the nation's racist trend is not reversed." After the story came out, an annoyed Golden wrote Ashmore that "one of the free-est-wheeling-est editors, with tongue hanging out"—meaning himself—had kept quiet about the group's discussion, only to discover that Anthony was quoted in the national press as if he spoke for the group. The incident would not have bothered Golden a few years earlier. Now, coming as it did while he dealt with critical editors and other writers garnering more headlines for movement activities, it did. The good news, he wrote Ashmore, was that such news stories faded fast.[58]

The depth of Golden's friendships with newsmen is evident in the ripple effect of the connections. It was not unusual for him to correspond with members of a friend's family, as he did with the elderly father of CBS Washington correspondent Martin Agronsky. In a wonderfully written letter, Isador N. Agrons (members of his family variously used Agrons, Agron, and Agronsky) introduced himself; sketched his own immigrant experience, challenges, and regrets; and then asked Golden what his thoughts were on the "existence of a hereafter," a question that was obviously plaguing him. Golden answered thoughtfully and at length, ending with some gentle humor: "Let me put it this way: when mankind is finally led up Mount Sinai, mankind will be led by either Jesus, Karl Marx, Sigmund Freud, or Albert Einstein. This is hardly a coincidence, and this should be enough for any Jew to gather the strength he needs in the twilight of his years. I hope it will be enough for me, but you can never be sure." Golden shared the letter with Martin Agronsky, who replied with a note of gratitude: "It is strange about fathers and sons," Agronsky wrote. "It seems Pop could not bring himself to discuss with me the problems he presented to you. He could not have made a wiser choice."[59]

A Little Girl Is Dead

Even as Golden's popularity as a writer and stature as a civil rights fighter were fading, another phoenix-like moment was rising. Finally his longest-held literary hope had come true, and he glowed with the satisfaction of publishing *A Little Girl Is Dead*, about the Leo Frank lynching case. The book was so different from Golden's usual work that many critics and readers evaluated it as separate from the rest of his writing. In *A Little Girl Is Dead*, Golden moved away from his usual essay form and built the longer narrative on more careful research.[60]

When an idea for a book follows a writer for much of his or her life, it is a protean being: It grows, shrinks, inspires, and depresses the author. It might start as an altruistic mission to set a record straight, grow into activism, and become a competitive bar to hurdle or a wistful dream. For Golden, the Frank story was this sort of changeable creature. By the time he wrote it, his goals were clear in his mind: to make the case for Frank's innocence, which he never seems to have doubted, and to explore the "factors and forces" that led to the mob violence that took Frank's life.[61]

"I always thought this would be my first book," he told his newspaper readers when *A Little Girl Is Dead* was published by World in 1965. "I've thought about it for 25 years, but now I am glad that it will be my tenth book. I have a vast audience in America." His readership, despite the decline in popularity of his books, *was* still large, and more important, he had not lost his skill at using mainstream media for self-promotion. He made sure his many news contacts were alerted to the imminent publication.[62]

The Leo Frank story Golden told was a gripping tragedy that started with a mysterious murder half a century earlier and anti-Semitic mob justice that shook the country and left many southern Jews fearful for decades. It required more work than anything else Golden had done, and Richard Goldhurst was vital to the project. Neither was experienced in analyzing a lengthy court case, but Goldhurst's gift for shaping history into compelling narrative and his father's many years of gathering string on the Frank case served the project well.

Leo Frank was a college graduate from New York, a German-American Jew who married into a prominent Atlanta family after moving south to run his uncle's factory, the National Pencil Company. "In 1913 it was not too difficult to call a man a pervert on the evidence that he had gone to college," Golden cracked. When thirteen-year-old Mary Phagan, one of the factory's many young workers, was found strangled to death in the basement of the building, evidence soon pointed to a black janitor named Jim Conley. But Conley told a tale that was more appealing to the locals: A Jewish monster in their midst had assaulted and killed one of their own. Frank was arrested, charged, and tried for thirty days in an atmosphere thick with prejudice and perjury.[63]

Convicted and sentenced to death by hanging, he appealed the case, which grew messier and more sensational, all the way to the U.S. Supreme

Court. For a time the Frank trial shoved all other news, including the war in Europe, out of the headlines. It was, as Golden pointed out, the rarest of events: A white man was convicted of a crime in Atlanta due to the testimony of a black man. Georgia governor John M. Slayton commuted Frank's sentence and was nearly lynched himself. A mob broke into Frank's cell, dragged him out, and hanged him from a tree. An enterprising photographer got a few shots of the body dangling from the lynch-rope, and postcards of the sight were available in local stores for a long time to come. It was, wrote Golden, a European-style pogrom in America.[64]

Golden found the evidence to solidify his belief that Frank was innocent, as have nearly all the serious writers who have considered the case over the years. He focused on what he saw as the larger point: the lethal results of a situation in which institutionalized discrimination and an ailing economy come together. Today it might be called a "perfect storm," one that left a disaster in its wake. At the time, "there was an economic depression among the farmers of Georgia," wrote Golden. "The banks could no longer finance the seed. Thousands of them poured into the city, hoping for some work, so they could eat. . . . Into that cauldron of frustration and poverty there was thrust a diversion. A little girl was murdered."[65]

The mob needed a suspect they could vilify, and desperate times made it easier for anti-Semitic forces to whip up anger at that old canard that "Jews have all the money" and are capable of all manner of evil deeds, including getting away with child murder. Golden was most fascinated by Thomas E. Watson, the Georgia political boss who had once championed the rights of the poor and oppressed and served in the U.S. House of Representatives, but who, by Frank's time, was a bitter, racist hatemonger. "Tom Watson thrived upon the ignorance and prejudices of rural Georgians," wrote historian Leonard Dinnerstein. Watson's weekly newspaper, *The Jeffersonian*, and his monthly, *Watson's Magazine*, circulated throughout the state and provided many Georgians their only contact with the outside world. Watson's newspapers were popular among poor illiterates who listened to others read the venom-filled content aloud, said Dinnerstein, and his following was rabidly loyal.[66]

However, Watson's power came not only from the ignorant and isolated. As historian Oscar Handlin and others have pointed out, Watson tapped into the swelling anger of frustrated rural southerners of a Populist stripe who included the Jews among those they blamed for their failures to bring about positive change for farmers. (In this sense, Watson's methods would be familiar to today's listeners of certain bloviating radio-show hosts.) The Leo Frank case made Watson a star with an extremely profitable newspaper franchise. He railed against the "typical young libertine Jew" and painted a picture of a perverted monster. He provided the rallying cry of "Hang the Jew!" to the combustible atmosphere, which was literally yelled out in the courtroom when Frank's attorney opened his mouth to speak. Watson's hate campaign was so popular that after the Frank lynching, he rose from his political obscurity to serve briefly in the Senate.[67]

As insidious and unhinged as Watson's anti-Semitic rants were, his earlier efforts on behalf of the struggling farmer still mired in the poverty that descended in the post-Reconstruction South added to Golden's curiosity about the man. Watson's battling in Congress during the early 1890s for Rural Free Delivery to the mailboxes of isolated farmers was just the sort of odd struggle that Golden appreciated.[68]

In the years since the publication of *A Little Girl Is Dead*, other books have overtaken it. The first was Dinnerstein's *The Leo Frank Case*, which came out three years later and has remained a respected classic, reissued in 2008. In 2003 came the 645-page wonderfully vivid *And the Dead Shall Rise: The Murder of Mary Phagan and the Lynching of Leo Frank*, by Steve Oney. Golden's work did not have the foundation of scholarship of Dinnerstein's book, and Oney's book benefited from its exhaustive detail, the author's skill as a storyteller, and the passage of time, with its discoveries about the case and technological advances enabling more in-depth reporting. Yet *A Little Girl Is Dead* tells the story well, convincingly recreating the courtroom scenes and key players so that readers can grasp many of the legal complexities and understand the dramatic manipulation of public opinion in Georgia by the press.[69]

"It is a prodigious job," wrote Eleanor Kask Friede, the expert publicist who guided Golden through the prison scandal in 1958, "thorough, beautifully organized, and continually fascinating." Most critics agreed. *Newsweek* zeroed in on the book's strength: "Not only has he written a crisp, engrossing narrative . . . he has also carefully set the tragedy against the background of Southern Populism and Nativism which renders it intelligible." *Saturday Review* clipped Golden for being too glib in explaining the roots of southern racism but allowed that it was "an otherwise excellent work." Golden grinned around his cigar upon reading that a *New York Times* critic was listing it along with Truman Capote's *In Cold Blood* as one of the year's best true-crime books.[70]

To young Hershel the newsboy, Frank's murder in the distant South had sounded like the stories told by his immigrant parents about Cossacks and pogroms that drove them to America. During Golden's prison time, the story haunted him; he could clearly imagine Frank's time as a prisoner and knew that the line that separated a free man from a convicted one was thin indeed. Once in the South and as he grew more involved with the civil rights movement, Golden began to understand the legacy of lynching. He wrote, "Only once in this country has a Jewish community feared for its livelihood and the lives of its members. . . . That fearful instant came in 1915 in Atlanta, Georgia, an instant in American history which involved not only the Jew and anti-Semitism but also the South, the black man, hard times, mob rule, and the mystery of who murdered a pretty girl in the basement of the factory in which she worked."[71]

When Frank's widow died in 1957, Golden told a brief version of the terrible story, then he wrote, "For a long time the young housewife, Lucile Frank, stood 'alone' beside her husband, and she acquitted herself with wisdom and dignity throughout the ordeal. . . . I say 'alone' because, contrary to the stereotype of 'sticking together,' the real truth of the matter is that the Jewish people are highly sensitive to a situation of this kind—where a member of their community gets in trouble." Eight years later he offered a more accurate and nuanced view of the situation when he acknowledged that there was, in fact, extraordinary support from prominent Jews who worked behind the scenes to raise money and awareness of the case. His earlier observation was accurate in one sense: During Frank's trial these supporters eschewed public stands, and when Frank was murdered, his frightened Jewish supporters in Atlanta left the city or essentially went underground and shed any signs of their religion.[72]

In 1913 when AJC president Louis Marshall was made aware of the case, he warned that appearing to rally behind Frank could lead to damaging claims of northern-Jewish interference. But doing nothing was, of course, wildly at odds with the AJC's mission. (And Marshall was certainly not one to shrink from a fight. He would later argue Frank's appeal before the Supreme Court and had already made a name for himself as a forceful opponent to proposed immigration restrictions on Eastern European Jews.) So the organization navigated with care, decided against taking public action, and instead encouraged powerful individuals to quietly support Frank's cause. Many did.

Key figures were Albert D. Lasker and Adolph Ochs. Lasker was an advertising agency magnate from Chicago who made the name "Quaker Oats" part of the American lexicon. He put enormous amounts of energy and money toward the effort to prove Frank's innocence, building a coalition of influential Jews, along with icons such as settlement house pioneer Jane Addams and inventor Thomas Edison. Ochs was the Jewish owner of the *New York Times* who was born and raised in Tennessee and had founded the *Chattanooga Times*, launched a campaign of editorial support for Frank, and organized a national group that fought to exonerate him, a role that was very much out of character. "Like other ambitious Jews fearful of anti-Semitism, Ochs assumed the protective coloration of the gentile world and distanced himself from Judaism," wrote reporter Ron Chernow in the *New York Times* in 1999. But "with uncharacteristic fervor, he took up the case of Leo Frank." When the *Times* editorialized in protest of Frank's lynching, Ochs's fears were realized. He was, wrote Chernow, "horrified by the anti-Semitic letters that swamped the mail room."[73]

When *A Little Girl Is Dead* was done, Golden wrote a friend that he was satisfied that he had made "a good case for Frank's innocence." He did not find a satisfactory answer for himself as to whether such a thing could happen again in twentieth-century America. In the book's introduction he wrote that he doubted anyone would be convicted in the 1960s on the evidence and testimony put forward in the Frank trial. But he was less confident about the country's resistance to a charismatic demagogue and a powerful propaganda machine skillfully engendering such monumental hatred and mob violence. He never stopped wrestling with his old question: "Could a Tom Watson make any headway today? I cannot answer."[74]

CHAPTER EIGHT

The Real Iron Curtain

For a man whose exercise consisted of rolling his desk chair to a file drawer four feet away and who remained hydrated mostly by bourbon, Golden was surprisingly healthy. His gallbladder fought back now and then, he had two prostate cancer scares, and he suffered the usual irritants of one's later sixties; but when he collapsed late one night in December 1966, it was the first life-threatening illness Golden faced. It was nearly his last. His friend, physician Raymond Wheeler, rushed him to Charlotte Memorial Hospital and was at his side when he went into surgery. Wheeler was a comforting presence. He was, in Golden's opinion, as close to a saint as anyone he knew. Wheeler was in the trenches of the civil rights battle, methodically gathering facts and pushing to end hunger and malnutrition among poor children, both black and white. He was not deterred from this Sisyphean task by chilly indifference from peers and those in power or by threats from racists.[1]

During surgery Golden went into cardiac arrest and stopped breathing; a tracheotomy was performed. He remained in a coma for four days and resurfaced wondering how a gallbladder attack had landed him in such a spot. "When I came out of it . . . I thought: *What a prosaic way to die.* An infected gallbladder is an unromantic killer, but it would make me as dead as the next man. . . . [It] could have proved the most ruthless of all censors," he wrote.[2]

"When Harry came home, he was wounded and slow," said Richard Goldhurst. That did not stop Golden from yanking his newspaper back from his son and helpers who had put out the first two issues of 1967. He was grateful, but barely. The twenty-four-page January–February *Carolina Israelite* was a bit funereal, filled with reminisces by friends of Golden's, with past tense implied if not actually employed. An essay headlined "Welcome Home Thoreau" by Richard Goldhurst in the April–May issue was clever and affectionate, but it was unmistakably the story of a horse being led out to pasture. His son noted that Golden's doctor had ordered him to "live in a regularly run home, a home that included routine naps in the afternoon, shopping budgets, and a doorbell people have to ring before they enter." Hearing this directive, Golden insisted there was no need to change anything; he could live that way in his office. No, Goldhurst countered, you cannot. The housekeeper was no longer going to move a file cabinet in order to get to the refrigerator.[3]

The coverage Golden's illness got in the mainstream press mollified him somewhat. As newsman Joe Wershba wrote him, the nightly news anchors were all over the story: "I was with Carl and Mrs. Sandburg on the Thursday and Friday of your operation. As the bulletins kept tumbling over Cronkite, Huntley-Brinkley, the North Carolina stations, the South Carolina stations . . . Paula [Sandburg's wife] reacted as if flesh and blood were being wrested from her: 'No, no . . . Harry's got to come through.' "[4]

An editorial run by the *Winston-Salem Journal* after the surgery was similar to columns that appeared in papers across the country: "North Carolina needs you, Harry Golden. The South needs you. America needs you. We need your unfailing wit, your spirit of tolerance and understanding, your rollicking sense of humor and infinite capacity to make discrimination look absurd. . . . Get well, Harry Golden. Everybody needs you."[5]

Norma Leveton, daughter of Golden's brother Jake, heard the news about her Uncle Harry on the car radio and hurried home to listen for updates with her family. "When he got out, they told him he could have only one cigar a day and one drink a day," Leveton said, pausing a few seconds before delivering a drawn-out line worthy of her uncle: "So he found the *longest* cigar and the *tallest* glass he could find, and that's how he got through it."[6]

To Golden, the most striking thing about his illness was not its frightening suddenness or even the near-death experience. It was the moment in the hospital when he realized a black man was recuperating nearby. Nearly thirty years earlier he had watched, perplexed and then angry, when black men stepped off Charlotte sidewalks to let him pass. Back then a black child could die waiting for a black ambulance when the whites-only service was close by. Now, he said, the "real American dream" was taking place in his hospital room. Two men, one black and one white, both with good health insurance created by the federal government, were getting better side by side. It didn't matter that this had been happening for some time. Now it was real to him.[7]

A Sister, Found and Lost Again

When death comes so close, remembering people who are loved and lost is not far behind. Golden had long ago accepted his sister Matilda's estrangement, but now he was newly inspired to try to find her. He remembered her as a young woman sewing in a Lower East Side factory for nine hours a day, six days a week. The usual explanation given by her family was that Matilda was heartbroken when forbidden to marry a cousin she loved, and so she left home in rebellion and moved to Hollywood around 1935, where she supported herself designing and sewing clothes. The romance was indeed thwarted years before, but it is more likely that other issues were to blame. Perhaps she resented her brother's marriage to an Irish Catholic while her own relationship was forbidden. The grim prospects for her in New York City during the Depression economy and the humiliation of being rounded up in brother Harry's mail-fraud trials no doubt helped motivate her to distance herself from the family. Other than occasional letters to Clara, she cut off communication with her siblings.[8]

In his autobiography, Golden wrote, "I never saw Matilda after she left home, but I was reminded of her sadness when I was autographing books in a Los Angeles department store forty years later. A reporter handed me a penciled note which read, 'Herschele, always thinking of you, Matty.' Try as we might, that reporter and I with a phalanx of clerks and even the store detective could not track down Matilda." That account was a romanticized and wildly misdated conflation of two incidents in 1959: A May Department Store manager who knew Matilda told Golden that his sister had asked about him, and a short time later Matilda sent her brother a warm telegram—obviously her first communication in many years—telling him "the sales on your book are about to increase by one" as she prepared to get his new book, *For 2 Cents Plain*. The two apparently communicated very rarely until 1966.[9]

Golden omitted the bitter exchange of letters that started when Matilda let him know how furious she was over his depiction of her in his writings. "You, an avowed anti-segregationist segregated your sisters from the rest of the human race by telling your public that we are spinsters; that you were born in 1902 and that we were both older than you, as if there were not already enough vaudeville and parlor jokes about 'old maids.' "[10]

A dismayed Clara tried to patch things up, but Matilda was through with her brother. (For that matter, she appeared to be through with her brother Max, too. When the youngest sibling went to California to visit her, Matilda apparently moved before he arrived at her door.) The letters Golden sent to her post office box henceforth came back marked "Return to Sender." His efforts to track her down after his illness were unsuccessful. Matilda died in 1993 at age ninety-seven, having outlived her siblings, cousins, friends, and probably most of the young women who long ago had happily worn affordable, stylish dresses made by her capable hands.[11]

Looking Back

By the summer of 1967 Golden was back in the saddle. He would never regain his former level of energy and sharpness, but he was not incapacitated. "He carried on, which displays his courage, or actually, his nerve," said Goldhurst. Golden now relied even more heavily on his son to put out the paper, as well as shape his articles and books. The illness had convinced Golden that he needed to get on with his autobiography. Goldhurst pulled together dictation and folders full of his father's notes for the long-planned book, wove in material from the voluminous correspondence files, and added his own and Tiny's recollections to craft *The Right Time*, which was published in 1969.[12]

It was pushed ahead of a book on Israel for which Golden had already received an advance of $10,000 from Putnam and which was at least a year late. *The Israelis: Portrait of a People*, published in 1971, was Goldhurst's work, a collection of bits and pieces drawn from his father's notes and articles about the country. Had Golden written the book on schedule and by himself, it would certainly have been weaker. A careful reader familiar with both men's styles can enjoy tracking their voices in the narrative. It was not greeted with much excitement. The *New York Times* dismissed the book with just a mention in a list of new titles: "The humorist and homespun philosopher in Israel following a tediously familiar trail. There are some fresh and lighthearted moments, but not enough."[13]

The Israelis is a good window into Golden's Zionism, which by this time in his life was a relatively clear-eyed admiration for the people who had carved a thriving country out of the desert. As the introduction noted, "Israelis feel they offer the world the first chance to see if a people can overcome a long and pitiless history." Golden's long-held belief that health care was a basic right, and one that reflects the core values of a government, was woven into his Zionism. In his notes for *The Israelis*, he marveled at the large number of clinics, hospitals, and child-care centers. The country was largely free of that haunting monster from his childhood, tuberculosis.

Earlier essays about Israel were a bit more romantic. An article he wrote for *Holiday* in 1967 extolled the Israelis as the hardest workers among international teams of technicians sent to build infrastructure in Africa. But for the most part, he saw the country as an imperfect experiment succeeding against the odds of history. "Perhaps the true miracle of Israel's survival is that the people have let time and events change them as time and events should. They have not outgrown their first purpose, because they have always found new ones." He and Goldhurst were prescient about the future interest and need for the field of Holocaust studies, at the time not the specialty it is today. The book quotes Baal Shem Tov, the Polish Jew who founded the Hassidic movement: "The secret of redemption is remembering and exile is the price of forgetting," to which Golden added, "That is the succinct reason for Holocaust studies."[14]

Any disappointment in the reception for *The Israelis* was probably softened by the ongoing success of *The Right Time*, which editor Bill Targ called "a humanist epic with a dozen motion picture plots in it" after reading the manuscript in 1968. A year later it was a strong seller. The *New York Times Book Review* recommended it, and it was a Book-of-the-Month Club selection touted with attractive full-page ads in major magazines and newspapers. The book's more than 400 pages definitely embodied Golden's strengths and weaknesses, often on the same page. Peppered with inaccuracies of fact and wandering in its chronology, it mined his earlier work to an extreme degree. "The popular and garrulous raconteur has set down a turbulent life which has heretofore been exploited before in many folksy books, articles and musings," began the *Kirkus Reviews* summary, which ended with the accurate observation that "Golden is hard put to it to step outside his genial image but the self-exposure that does slip through is newsworthy." Wry asides and connective tissue made the book hang together in spite of itself and resulted in a work both entertaining and touching. In the end, it managed to be a picaresque portrait more true to its subject than not.[15]

Quieter Days

The *Carolina Israelite* was in a state of health similar to that of its publisher: shaky, yet game. The business side of the newspaper was in flux even before Golden fell ill, dating back to the death from lung cancer of longtime advertising manager Ken Robertson in 1964. Golden had hired Robertson in 1948 as an ad salesman. He was a bachelor who "was fond of lifting a stein or two" and, as Golden put it, was so obsessed with baseball that he could barely get his mind off St. Louis Cardinals second-baseman Red Schoendienst long enough to talk about the cataclysmic *Brown* decision in 1954. "Ken was a good man, a loyal employee and faithful friend. He did his job, he hated no one, and I testify to the best of my knowledge he was incapable of an unkind act," Golden wrote the week of the memorial service.[16]

Now Golden had plenty of opportunities to fret over finances, had he been so inclined. The *Carolina Israelite*'s balance sheet had looked healthy through the early 1960s, but ad sales and subscriptions had since steadily declined. Several of Golden's paid appearances had been canceled as he recovered. He was still in demand: Tax returns for 1967–68 showed close to $20,000 in "other income," which was mostly from speeches, but in his heyday he had earned more than twice that for such appearances. His early books and columns had healthy paydays, helped by *Reader's Digest*, Book-of-the-Month Club, bulk military purchases, and leading periodicals, but those coffers had dwindled dramatically. World Publishing's bean counters waited until he was back on his feet, then wrote to report that sales of the Sandburg book had dropped to below 1,000 copies that year, suggesting a lower cover price to keep it in print. Golden, however, was more worried about the *subject* of that book; Sandburg was frail, and Golden knew his friend might leave him soon. It happened on 22 July 1967.[17]

The funeral was held in a small church near Sandburg's home, and Golden attended with Ralph McGill. The latter wrote to the Brethren crowd of newsmen—Bill Baggs, John Popham, and Harry Ashmore (all still using the made-up honorifics of "My Esteemed Bishop," "Colonel," "Doctor," and "Brother")—informing them that "Dr. Golden and I have the distinction of having sung 'John Brown's Body' in a church built by a former treasurer of the Confederate states." Golden looked well and had lost weight but was quieter, McGill reported. This group of friends knew that Golden's heart was very heavy, and they understood why. Golden had many heroes in his life, but Sandburg was the one who returned the admiration in like measure, who loved him and believed in him as a writer.[18]

Quitting the Student Non-Violent Coordinating Committee

Golden was yanked from his reverie a month later when SNCC issued a shocking public statement. In its August 1967 newsletter, SNCC accused "the Zionists" of murdering Arabs and published a crude, anti-Semitic cartoon of Israel's defense minister Moshe Dayan wearing a uniform branded with a dollar sign. The Jewish Telegraphic Agency wire service wrote, "Ralph Featherstone, SNCC program director, told newsmen at his headquarters in Atlanta that the SNCC attack against Zionism and Israel is not anti-Semitic but is directed against 'Jewish oppression.' Among the oppressors, he said, were 'those Jews in the little Jew shops in the ghettos.' "[19]

Golden was angry but not stunned, as many of his comrades were. Anti-Semitism never shocked him. He agreed with a view once voiced by Bayard Rustin, that when times get bad, the blame doesn't seem to be placed on the worst oppressors but on those who were in the trenches trying to help but failing. The "little Jew shops" slur was a reference to the fact that so many of the hundreds of race-related incidents and riots in American cities since 1964 had involved Jewish-owned stores in the poorest neighborhoods. Golden wrote eloquently and toughly on the subject beginning in 1965, reminding his readers that the relationship between Jewish merchants and black customers was one of long interdependence, and arguing that focusing on the so-called anti-Semitism behind the destruction instead of the generations of poverty suffered by urban blacks was to miss the point. "The truly surprising thing is that we do not have riots every day of the week," he wrote, adding, "to make of this anti-Semitism is not only fruitless but in a way cruel. Nothing should obscure our vision of why these riots take place."[20]

Now he was dismayed for other, more personal reasons: Golden had for so long nurtured his image as a person who was simpatico with national Jewish groups yet able to maintain a distance as a sort of heroic loner, unbound by any institution. He felt that the naked antipathy of the SNCC statement lumped him in with an amorphous Jewish crowd, and that association wounded almost as much as the hateful words. He used all of his well-honed media-manipulating skills to be sure the resignation letter he sent Featherstone on 18 August 1967 was widely publicized. He was quoted far and wide as comparing the SNCC action to tactics of the Ku Klux Klan and the American Nazi Party. "Negroes have been victims of racism for too long to indulge in group stereotype and racial hate themselves," he wrote. He found the attack especially sickening, he said, given that "this comes in ill grace from an organization from which two Jewish boys, [Michael] Schwerner and [Andrew] Goodman, along with Mississippi Negro [James Earl] Chaney were murdered while doing field work for S.N.C.C."[21]

Golden's resignation attracted a great deal of mail, including some of the more frothing-at-the-mouth hate letters in his large collection. A self-declared Confederate from Nokomis, Florida, wrote, "After watching your antics and garish jewish crudities as an intruder into a social order in which you have had no qualification to join, and certainly not to criticize, it gives me deep satisfaction to see your convulsive reactions when YOUR bull is being gored by SNCC. . . . For a sheenie who found harbor and safety from pogroms, you and your people have ill-repaid the White Americans in the South."[22]

Leaders in both the African American and Jewish activist communities loudly decried the SNCC remarks; both sides insisted that a very small and radical group led by H. Rap Brown (then head of SNCC and, later, a leader of the Black Panthers) was responsible. The Reverend Martin Luther King Jr. issued a statement pledging to "do my utmost to uphold the fair name of the Jews," declaring, "It would be impossible to record the contribution that Jewish people have made toward the Negro's struggle for freedom—it has been so great." As historian Milton R. Konvitz observed, "The fact that Dr. King felt it necessary to make this statement is itself some proof of the emergence of Negro-Jewish tensions as a problem for both groups." The damage was done, and it would not be fully repaired. Many Jewish supporters of SNCC pulled away, taking funding with them. For that and myriad other reasons, SNCC would soon collapse.[23]

Finding humor, even the dark variety, in this was a struggle. But within a few days, Golden found a way, uttering a line that was quoted widely for a long time: "When I resigned from the Student Nonviolent Coordinating Committee, the black power organization, I received almost one hundred letters from arch-segregationists who said they didn't know what SNCC stood for, but if I was against it, it had to be good."[24]

The "Real Iron Curtain"

The year 1967 would prove to be a demarcation in Golden's life. On one side fell the twenty-three-plus years that he had been the voice of the feisty *Carolina Israelite*; he had been the witty observer who could be counted on to stand up to the hateful, the hypocritical, the windbag, and the enemy of the little guy and to bring on belly laughs while doing it. For ten of those years he had been a real celebrity. On the other side of this divide, Golden's life moved out of the public arena. His popularity did not decline overnight, of course, but as 1968 commenced, Golden's life changed decidedly. He announced at the beginning of the year that he would close down the *Carolina Israelite*.[25]

Years later, when friends of Golden's were asked about his life, many understandably described his emergency surgery and illness as the turning point. But as his personal correspondence and writings make clear, however debilitating the health situation, it was the closing of the paper, the deaths of heroes and friends, and the upheaval in the movement that were by far the greater blows. He could still hold court and would publish books for another eight years, but in 1968, Harry Golden became an old man.

"I am back on the lecture circuit. More and more of my dates are at colleges. . . . My lectures are always well-attended and that is not, I hasten to say, because of my own personality," he wrote in the last issue of his paper. "The students come to hear out everyone from politicians aiming at the Presidency to black power militants aiming for anarchy." In years past, students in his audience had been hungry to talk about literature, journalism, and the complex intransigence of the South. Now, he wrote, black students wanted to talk about the need for separate dorms and a black-culture curriculum, and white dissidents wanted to hear antiwar sentiments: "They only ask me about Viet Nam. What kind of answers or nostrums can I provide: a more than middle aged journalist with no connections in Washington or the Pentagon?" Worse, he added, was that "I get the distinct impression they suspect I, Harry Golden, somehow conspired to commit Marines and infantry to Viet Nam. . . . The real Iron Curtain is between adults and kids."[26]

Golden could have pushed that curtain aside; his Leftist credentials, irreverence, and ability to pillory establishment types made him a natural to attract younger fans. But his outspoken support of Lyndon Johnson was, quite simply, intolerable to these young Americans. He was regularly booed when he spoke to young crowds—a new experience for someone who had been listened to with such obvious admiration for so long. Even harder was the gap that was forming between him and longtime liberal friends who were bitterly opposed to the war. Golden saw the Vietnam War as the inevitable result of America's rabid fear of Communism, tamped down since the 1950s but now smoldering under the surface of the free-love 1960s, kept in motion by a president with no other choice. Leaving the fight without being able to say the objective—*any* objective—had been achieved would be a diplomatic disaster for the United States, Golden believed. The American Left would be satisfied if Johnson pulled troops out, Golden wrote in 1965, but the conservatives and hawks would then make sure the next president was Goldwater, or worse. As it turned out, Johnson kept the war going *and* Richard Nixon was elected—the worst of both worlds, as far as Golden was concerned.[27]

From Rage to Despair

Then the shots were fired. The Reverend Martin Luther King Jr. was murdered on a Memphis motel balcony the night of 4 April 1968. King had been preparing for a march on behalf of striking sanitation workers in the city. Golden was debating Senator Strom Thurmond of South Carolina in an auditorium at Virginia Polytechnic Institute when the news was announced by a school official. Golden told the students it was "a sad day for the world and a sadder day for Americans," adding that King "borrowed an idea from Gandhi and transformed that idea of nonviolence into an American and Christian tradition." Golden later noted with satisfaction that the students took it upon themselves to lower the flags of the state and nation, despite being denied permission by a school official. Golden ended his column, "Dr. King's life was too short, but maybe it made ours fuller. I hope so."[28]

Two months later, on 5 June, Robert F. Kennedy was murdered as he passed through a hotel kitchen in Los Angeles. Kennedy had just won the California and South Dakota primaries for the Democratic nomination for president. "When President John Kennedy was murdered in Dallas, I remember the rage that consumed me," wrote Golden. "But we are living, as the Reverend Ralph Abernathy says, in a decade of assassination, and the rage has passed into aching loneliness and despair."[29]

Robert Kennedy's family sent Golden a telegram with the numbers of a train car and a church pew reserved for him at the funeral, a gesture that meant a great deal to him. He did not go, he said, because his son Billy was getting married. Even without that excuse, he might not have gone. He was not sure he could watch another Kennedy being laid to rest. The deaths of King and Kennedy were unfathomable; the passing of author John Steinbeck at the end of the year seemed to close a literary era. Within months newspaper buddies Bill Baggs and Ralph McGill would be gone. Having already lost Sandburg in 1967, Golden felt unmoored. "An old man has fewer and fewer friends each year," he wrote.[30]

The closing of the *Carolina Israelite* prompted an avalanche of press coverage, and this would be the last one of such size in Golden's life. The *New York Times* ran an articulate question-and-answer interview with Golden, and wire services, magazines, newspapers, and broadcasters picked up the news. He vowed to keep writing for the *Nation* and assured his readers that the magazine would also pick up his mailing list. Dismayed readers sent piles of letters and telegrams. Comrades (and even some detractors) from seemingly every national civil rights and Jewish organization wrote to him. Former Kennedy aides and conservative pundits alike recalled past battles. Editors and publishers with whom Golden had worked over the years got in touch. More than one newsman admitted to shedding a tear—and to lifting a glass in mourning. Frank P. Graham, now retired from the United Nations and back in Chapel Hill, wrote to say he felt he had "lost a dear, long-time friend" with the closing of the paper. Many of the letters proudly quoted back Golden's words about themselves. Advice columnist Ann Landers said she doubted that she was the "brilliant newspaperwoman" he had once claimed, but "I accept, I accept!"[31]

One of the most treasured letters in the piles of mail that followed the announcement came from Vice President Hubert Humphrey, who would serve one more year at Johnson's side, seek the presidency himself, and lose to Richard Nixon. "What's this I hear about you closing down the *Carolina Israelite*?" Humphrey wrote. "This whole world of ours will never be the same if you do that, but I can well understand that there comes a time when a fellow wants to take it a little easier; in fact I am beginning to feel that way myself. . . . You are like a spring tonic to me. I always feel better when I think of you and read what you have to say. God bless you."[32]

Golden liked and respected Humphrey, who with another longtime correspondent, Senator Paul Douglas of Illinois, was an inspiring liberal voice dating back to the Truman years. Humphrey was one of the few famous folks who reached out to Golden first, in his case responding to a typo in a 1959 *Carolina Israelite* piece on how oddball names could penalize presidential candidates. Golden wrote that one Paul V. McNutt would have been Franklin Roosevelt's running mate in 1944 if he had had a different last name. He went on: "People just won't vote for a man named McNutt. . . . 'Adlai' though an uncommon name, is still in the Bible. The fellow who is in real bad trouble is Hubert Humphries [*sic*]. His name is not in the Bible and taxi drivers usually make jokes about the name 'Hubert.' [He] would do well to change his name to 'Joe.' . . . Jack Kennedy is in the best shape, but he'd be in even better shape if he anglicized his name to Goldberg."[33]

Humphrey promptly wrote to Golden: "I read with enjoyment your editorial. . . . I do not know who Hubert or Joe Humphries is, but I do know a Humphrey who will give them a run for their money." They traded letters and visited when their paths crossed during campaign seasons or when Golden was in Washington, D.C.[34]

Golden stumped for Humphrey as he successfully sought the Democratic nomination for president in 1968, and again in 1972, when he lost to George McGovern. A 1972 letter from Humphrey thanked Golden for "pinch-hitting" during the campaign season when he was unable to make one of his scheduled speeches. Humphrey also sent his condolences on the passing of Golden's brother Jake, who had died just a few days earlier. Golden found he was no longer hungry to collect praise from famous men; it was Humphrey's kind mention of Jake that mattered to him, and he underlined that phrase with the bold, wide-tipped black pen he favored, before carefully putting the letter aside to save.[35]

The New Jewry

Along with the rise of Black Power and differences over the Vietnam War, there was another development thwarting the possibility of Golden gaining and keeping a younger audience: the changing focus of the American Jewish community. The Nazis, Golden often said, had made him embrace his Jewishness anew as a young man, and he was most definitely a Zionist; but it was the Six-Day War in 1967 that made him actively attentive to Israel now. He had this in common with the majority of those American Jews now focused on the Jewish state. But in the process many of these Jews were also moving away from civil rights and, to some extent, from interfaith efforts. "The Six Day War made us all Zionists, if not literally than psychologically," wrote Abraham Foxman of the ADL, looking back in a 2007 editorial. "The American Jewish connection to Israel was sealed."[36]

This greater cultural bonding with Israel also led more baby-boomer American Jews to turn their energies toward building a community that reflected their contemporary needs and views. As historian Jonathan D. Sarna put it, "Influenced by the same 'anti-establishment' restiveness . . . and expressions of minority group liberation and pride that suffused America as a whole during this time, Jews—especially baby boomers . . . channeled their feelings of rebelliousness, assertiveness, and alienation into domestic programs aimed at transforming and strengthening American Jewish life." Golden's hymns to a romanticized Lower East Side didn't resonate with this generation; he was part of the American Jewish past they had left behind.[37]

Still, Golden was not quite out of the game. A fat volume titled *The Best of Harry Golden* had come out in 1967, impressive for its heft and well designed to show off his wide-ranging subjects. He was enough of a household name that Volkswagen asked him to contribute to *Think Small*, a clever little collector's item of a book filled with cartoons and blurbs by William Steig, Charles Addams, and other popular writers and cartoonists. The *New York Times* listed his autobiography, *The Right Time*, as one of the best books of the year in 1969. When his name was worked into one of the newspaper's crossword puzzles, editor Targ wrote him: "You are now indeed an immortal." In 1970, yet another collection of essays came out, *So Long as You're Healthy (Abee gezunt)*. An early, influential review damned it with faint praise, saying, "This concoction of brief articles and commentary has more content than much of Golden's East-Side-boyhood fizz which seems to have lost its effervescence." The approbation buried in that sentence is accurate; *So Long as You're Healthy* did indeed have a lot of material *not* about the Lower East Side, and it is one of Golden's most enjoyable collections.[38]

Next came *The Israelis* and a string of coffee table books that kept royalties flowing but showed little of Golden's activist past. *The Greatest Jewish City in the World* was mildly entertaining for its photographs and tidbits, but it was not the valuable trove of Judaica it might have been. *The Golden Book of Humor* in 1971 was a sloppy joke book that borrowed from too many other similar books. In fact, Golden had to pay a share of the small royalties to one annoyed comedy writer who challenged the blatant lifting of his work.[39]

Travels through Jewish America in 1973 was more in the vein of the *Greatest Jewish City in the World*, a once-over-lightly travelogue. These books were published by Doubleday, a departure for Golden, and the absence of Targ's skillful hand was evident. Golden had followed Targ from World to G. P. Putnam's Sons in 1966, and after the two Doubleday books, they worked together for the rest of Golden's writing life. *Our Southern Landsman*, out in 1974, is doubtless more engaging to a biographer of Golden than to other readers, with its snippets hinting at his old adventures. Read alone, it would leave one with a puzzling impression of Golden's work, as it veers between solid fact and opinion and extols Jewish leaders, only to add sweeping inaccuracies about them, such as "The Jews of Charlotte remained silent during the entire black struggle for civil rights." Golden also availed himself of numerous questionable opportunities for recognition: Acting as a "panelist" advising in the creation of silver commemorative medals marking the ten-year anniversary of John F. Kennedy's inauguration and sold through *The Rotarian* magazine was one such activity. Serving as a judge for the Miss Nude America Contest was another.[40]

Golden's correspondence dropped off from the days when he wrote dozens of letters a month, sometimes exchanging three or four with a single person in the same week, but he could still pack a zinger into a one-page missive. Racism was alive and well in the South, he wrote to Supreme

Court Justice William O. Douglas, but now the paramount issue was the "government is getting too big" prejudice. "They would elect Mohammed Ali mayor of Charlotte if he somehow promised no collective bargaining and no minimum wage for minority workers," Golden wrote. An occasional speech and a series of lectures at Charlotte's Piedmont Community College kept him busy as well and earned modest amounts. (The college system gave with one hand and took away with the other; in 1973 his Elizabeth Avenue home and office was sacrificed so that a new parking lot might live.) His companion, Anita Stewart Brown, offered him a home nearby, at 1701 East Eighth Street, which he accepted, and he lived in the yellow stucco English-cottage-style house for the rest of his life.[41]

He could, when inspired, still hold forth with gusto. Charlotte historian Dan L. Morrill remembered sharing a 4 July radio broadcast late in Golden's life. "He had lost a lot of capacity," said Morrill, "but when they asked him questions about the Constitution, it was *amazing*—almost like a switch was turned on. He was right on top of it."[42]

Golden would publish one more book, and one more Yiddish book title, or to be precise, a parenthetical subtitle, with *Long Live Columbus (Leben Zul Columbus)*. This book, as one review put it, was predictable with "all sorts of pleasant, inaccurate statements" about famous people. In the contrary conclusions so common among those evaluating Golden's work, the same review referred to "Golden's always essentially valuable convictions about civil rights."[43]

He hoped to see another title in print and pitched several possibilities to editor Bill Targ during the 1970s, including biographies of Ted Kennedy, Senator Henry "Scoop" Jackson, and Senator Jacob Javits. None of the projects got any traction. Neither did his draft of a book tentatively titled *America, I Love You*. "It is not easy, Harry, saying no to you, someone we have loved and respected for so many years," wrote Bill Targ. Golden was turned down by several other trade publishers. At one point he had at least three agents trying to place it, but there were no takers. Harry Jr. sent his father two bluntly worded letters taking him to task for ignoring his suggestions for editing and organizing the jumbled material. Golden was disappointed, but he still had one more cause near to his heart to take up, and this one he would win.[44]

Unfinished Business

During the Johnson administration, Golden had filed a federal "Petition for Pardon after Completion of Sentence" in which he cited an interest in running for local office. In truth, he just wanted the old prison shame expunged before he died. The White House had not gotten around to his request, and fortunately, his habit of poking fun at Richard Nixon did not derail the process. He was further fortunate that Ronald Reagan would not take over the White House for another twelve years. Golden had made an enemy when he attacked Reagan with vigor in the *Carolina Israelite* in 1962 for an antitax speech made to the North Carolina Trade Fair. Reagan, then a spokesman for General Electric, had moved to the Right in recent years, was a voice for big business, and had an obvious bead on public office. He was also quite thin-skinned and responded at length in a wounded tone to Golden. "I do regret one thing about my article," Golden wrote back. "I could have handled it with humor and not in anger. . . . The article should have been completely humorous, a description of the guys [at the Trade Fair] shouting themselves hoarse for you in your arguments against 'Government spending,' and the same guys clawing at the Government for that half-billion a year they get down here—in Government money. A joke, is it not?" Golden's newspaper buddies were tickled about this exchange. "The correspondence between you and Ronny is good stuff," wrote editor Bill Baggs from Miami. "Your response to his letter has nailed him to the cross he obviously wishes to carry."[45]

Such pardons require a current FBI investigation, and Golden had also written disparagingly about J. Edgar Hoover and his fiefdom, a fact noted in his FBI file years earlier. The accounts of Golden's memberships and civil rights activities were chronicled at the specific request of "the Director" as scribbled on a 1959 note in his file. Later newspaper clips in which Golden criticized Hoover were collected in the file as well; one of the last was labeled "typical" in a comment added by an unnamed bureau reader. In his pardon application, Golden minimized his Wall Street crimes, describing them as a single charge. He made no mention of the 1943 check-kiting spree in Birmingham, Alabama, that landed him back in court and on probation. The passing of time and loss of his celebrity worked in Golden's favor; no one cared about Golden's subversive tendencies now.[46]

The pardon was granted the first week of December 1973. Sister Clara lived long enough to see her little brother, now seventy, forgiven for the crimes that had caused them both so much pain. She died in 1974, the last person who had known Harry Golden when he was Chaim Goldhirsch and the only one who never wavered in her adoration and firm belief that he was meant to do big things.[47]

"Thank you and may you live to be 120, like Moses," Golden wrote Nixon's general counsel Leonard Garment when he got word of the pardon. A *Washington Post* writer called for an interview and teased him about the irony of Nixon being the gracious and forgiving leader. At first Golden responded with rare circumspection: "I wouldn't criticize him today after what he has done for me." But when the reporter pressed him, asking how he would characterize the Nixon *presidency*, if not the man himself, Golden clearly could not resist this opportunity for editorial comment. Nixon's tenure, he whispered, was, so far, "a disaster."[48]

It was one of the last irreverent Goldenesque quotes to run in a major newspaper. Harry Golden died in 1981, his body wearing out before he ran out of questions. "He wanted to understand everyone and write about them all," said his friend Walter Klein. "He almost made it."[49]

Only in America

Back in Golden's heyday, who could have imagined that the daily news sources of choice for millions of people in the twenty-first century would be niche cable channels with clear political biases or comedian-commentators serving up the latest happenings in Washington? Or that blogs and YouTube would exist and make politicians' fumbles impossible to sweep under the carpet? The seriously wounded newspaper business and a world in which anyone with a cell phone can become a broadcaster combined to dig up and replant the playing field in ways unthinkable in Golden's era. As he would have said, in his raspy drawl, "Only in America . . . *yeahhhh.*"

A pop writer's legacy is hard to trace. It is too simple to say that Golden begat this or that later pundit or style, but a look back at the evolution of his ideas and energy, and the writing that made him stand out in the 1950s and 1960, is revealing. In fact, Golden pioneered much of what is right with this New Media world. Here was a smart and accessible writer, a master of the short form, refusing to go fully or quietly into any pigeonhole; he was simultaneously a humorist, a Jewish writer, a civil rights agitator, and a storyteller. He was a troublemaker, a personality who both participated in and reported on the momentous civil rights story, rejecting many of the rules of engagement for traditional journalists. He forced vitally important issues into the public dialogue. He was a blogger, even if the term had yet to exist and even if the extinction of big, glass, rubber-cement bottles with sticky brushes sitting on newsroom desks, thundering printing presses, and the deaths of so many venerable newspapers would have broken his heart.

Golden collected stories all his life and kept them close at hand. He toted countless contradictions throughout his life as well: He tricked people out of money and reneged on promises. Yet the people Golden wronged continued to give to him and forgive him. He revered his pious Jewish mother, who spoke only a few words of English, and married a quick-witted Irish Catholic at a time when "mixed marriages" were discussed in whispers, as if such unions were serious illnesses. He found fame, was discovered for the ex-felon he was, and found bigger fame. Women were drawn to him, a not-handsome, short, fat, cigar-smoking, bourbon-drinking know-it-all. He loved the ethics of the great journalists and eschewed objectivity. He was a Jew who believed the black Christian clergy would lead America out of its racist past. He was a blatant self-promoter who loved nothing more than a quiet hero. He was a cool pragmatist and sharp political handicapper with a wide sentimental streak.

He was also a success, by all manner of measures.

The poverty of the teeming Lower East Side did not defeat Golden; instead it imprinted the ideas and images that became his byword. Among his friends were members of Congress and White House insiders, sweatshop workers, anti-Semites, movie stars, literary giants, Communists, segregationists, labor-union kingpins, cab drivers, black ministers, white priests, journalists, prison inmates, Quakers, white supremacists, Zionists, holy rollers, typesetters, prostitutes, poets, and talk-show hosts. His detractors were a much smaller group, and it was not uncommon for *them* to be charmed by the man, even as they deplored his politics or wished he would just go away and be quiet.

The often-tardy *Carolina Israelite*, saddled with a name that no branding expert would ever endorse, delighted tens of thousands of readers for a quarter of a century and brought a stream of speaking invitations, from Hadassah luncheons to the U.S. Congress, and assignments from top national magazines and newspapers. He sold millions of hardcover and paperback books around the world; the first five of them made the *New York Times* bestseller list (two at the same time), and even the later, less-popular books kept royalty checks rolling in for the rest of his life and then some.

It helped that Golden's lifespan and circumstances covered so many of the most fascinating happenings in twentieth-century American history.

With his sharp curiosity, pushy confidence, and a sophistication that often surprised new acquaintances, Golden made the most of the time in which he lived. An opportunist by nature, he was ever alert for any chance to move from outside looking in right into the catbird seat. Once he sniffed out a story, he made it his own.

At first glance the most unlikely aspect of Golden's many resurrections was his move to the South, which welcomed and nurtured him in ways that no other place could have. "The South made me a writer," Golden liked to say. In his view, the "greatest domestic news story of the twentieth century" was the reason for his success. He firmly believed that the changing of the South and the upheaval of its social order in the 1950s and 1960s made the entire country a better place. He relished the chance to chronicle the national reverberations of the South's boycotts, lunch-counter sit-ins, Freedom Rides, voter-registration drives, marches, and pickets.[1]

There was more to his southern-bred success than the milestones of the movement. Golden became a big fish in a small southern pond. He may not have traveled in the circles of the "first" families, those successful Jews and Gentiles with the deepest roots in Charlotte, but their genteel societies tolerated him and in many instances made him feel welcome even when they resented his outrageous pronouncements. Every person I interviewed who knew him in Charlotte made the same observation: Golden was never fully accepted, but he said the things that many others thought and could not say at the time—and his speaking out made a difference. A minister from nearby Winston-Salem wrote Golden a letter in 1968 and put it as well as anyone could: "Your stand in Dixie has enabled others to stand."[2]

A "Free Ride"

If Golden had had his way, American Jews would have declared war against racial segregation in a splashier manner. "In 1955 I urged the B'nai B'rith to organize help for the Negro. I said for the first time in 1,500 years we had an opportunity to fight for democracy in a situation where we are not the target of oppression, and that when you fight for others, you build a wall of security around yourself," he wrote in the *Nation* in 1968. All of the national Jewish organizations did, in fact, take up the fight for rights of minorities. But he believed that they needed to make much more noise—or perhaps a different kind of noise that would be heard in all corners—a revolutionary idea in 1955.

"I urged them to put an ad in all the big papers of America saying that we Jews, as a community, would use our funds and our energies, and our social-action know-how in the fight for the Negro, because the Negro has indeed given the Jews a free ride, the biggest free ride in history," he declared. "They have gone into the courts of America and proved that the Constitution means what it says." He did not deny that these Jewish groups pushed the cause with energy and success, but the untethered Occupy Wall Street uprisings in 2012 would have delighted him. This was the disingenuous side to Golden's activism. Even he did not really expect crowds of Jewish Americans to rise up and call out the rest of the country on the race question. What he *did* think was possible, and sorely needed, was for any group with a big platform or individual with clout to speak more loudly and to tirelessly needle those in power.[3]

Truth be told, whether Golden admitted it to himself or not, a lot of fun would have gone out of his life had everyone he nagged joined him in his noisemaking. By the early 1950s, Golden had figured out the best way to get attention, and he was from then on an independent operator, writing and speaking out about race, class, and religion in ways guaranteed to annoy or frighten many of his Jewish neighbors in the South and entertain people everywhere. He so clearly relished that role, and did it with such originality, that even a great many of the people he annoyed or frightened could not hold it against him.

He did a lot of preaching to the choir, of course. Then, as now, colorful commentators who challenge embedded behaviors and beliefs do not lack followers or outlets. But Golden's reach as a speaker and writer was large enough that the particles of his civil rights campaign got into the water and the air breathed by millions of Americans of all stripes. As Ralph McGill wrote, the visibility of black Americans made their lot a much harder one, and change came only after a bright spotlight was trained on the bigots too. Golden was among the country's most effective wielder of bright lights; humor, as it turns out, illuminates things so thoroughly that few hiding places remain.[4]

The Roots of Activism

As a child, Golden was exposed to many injustices, most of which were things only visited on the poor: friends who had to leave grade school in order to keep the family fed; the few dollars paid for his sisters' and older brother's long hours of work, first in firetrap factories and later in offices with six-day weeks; the common dread of a breadwinner getting "Jewish asthma," or tuberculosis. Later, when young Harry went to Wall Street, Senator Carter Glass taught him well about the long reach of a powerful person with a grudge. He saw firsthand the deprivations and humiliations of prison. He watched helplessly as the same system lock up a talented young arts writer because of his supposed sexual orientation and a labor leader because he challenged the bosses.

But the injustice that never went away was the reality of being "the other"—the Jew in a Gentile majority, who despite appreciating the impressive acculturation and success of Jews in the United States by the mid-twentieth century, did not forget the long, harsh history and innumerable small cuts that go with that status. In one of the most insightful observations yet made of Golden, historian Leonard Rogoff wrote, "Antisemitism was important to Golden's worldview and sense of himself. . . . He wrote of antsemitism as a 'constant of western culture,' and it validated his own marginality and fellowship with the oppressed and persecuted." Furthermore, Golden did not see himself as a victim, but as a *comrade*—to the poor, the immigrant with no English, the exhausted mill worker or miner, a black man called "boy," and a poor woman sterilized against her will. He did not confuse this bond with being inside their spheres, an insulting tendency of some do-gooders. He had black friends, but he was not of their world and did not presume honorary membership. He found his life's work in being "the other."[5]

Forgotten Pioneer

Golden's writing is not well known today, and this, too, is not unusual for popular-culture commentators and pundits of any era. Generally speaking, what remains well known are the writings or utterances of individuals who were revolutionary thinkers or martyred through violence or both, such as the Reverend Martin Luther King Jr., or those who were legendary opponents who personified racial hatred, such as George Wallace and Bull Connor. The work of many of Golden's contemporaries who were more gifted writers and journalists has also receded into history. A particularly relevant example is Rabbi Joshua Loth Liebman, one of the most famous Jews in twentieth-century mainstream culture, a charismatic speaker and a man who was almost as unlikely a celebrity as Golden. An "outspoken Zionist and fighter for racial equality as well as an interfaith activist," Liebman wrote a surprise bestseller, *Peace of Mind*, which brought religion and psychology together in a discussion of human nature and self-acceptance in a form that grabbed a wide audience. The book was a bestseller for over a year, and his radio broadcasts from Boston drew an interfaith audience in the millions. Liebman's fame seems to have faded even faster than Golden's.[6]

It is commonplace to decry the death of newspapers and respected broadcast news and the proliferation of online aggregation machines that serve as sources of information today. The losses are real. But among the key characteristics that make the Web so different from its paper ante-cedents is its apparently infinite shelf space and odd egalitarian nature. Anyone determined enough can ascend in this online environment. If Golden wrote today, with his prolific production and flair for showman-ship, he might be less likely to disappear as fast as he did in his own time.

But disappear he did, and the neglect of Golden's work has deprived historians and their readers of a useful tool for comprehending the arc of the civil rights movement. Golden's essays, including the much-quoted Golden Plans to solve segregation (and the reaction to them), reflect the dramatic divide between blacks and whites of the time, and the absurd or violent lengths many Americans and their government went to in order to preserve that status quo.

As the movement gathered steam, Golden accurately credited the Afri-can American churches for much of the progress; he placed the major events of the day in historical context and drew attention to individuals who advanced or stalled the cause. He emphasized the need for better education and health care for blacks and the poor. He alerted his audience to the very real economic penalties of segregation. When the changes and militancy of the later years pushed him aside, he wrote about the confu-sion and pain of that shift, shared by many others, black and white, who had devoted years to the movement. He was not remotely objective on this subject, coming as it did when he was facing his own mortality. Golden's optimistic, forward-looking view was no longer his default setting; he accurately predicted the losses that would result from the polarization. There are lessons for today's activists in the rise and fall of his influence in the fight.

As had been the case so often in his life, Golden's timing was in an odd way fortuitous—at least for the country, if not for himself. When America most needed Golden, he was onstage. His unlikely arrival in the South in the early 1940s came as both the place and the man were poised for dramatic change. In the 1950s, when "brotherhood became a civil religion," as historian Rogoff put it, Golden was positioned to be a fitting representative. By the 1970s, when Golden's original, clever mind faltered and his body declined, and as his writer's voice no longer carried, the South had cleaved to the rest of the country with a lasting firmness, and the momentum of the civil rights movement would not be stopped.[7]

Golden's work provides a needed reminder that this movement was not a unified effort but a complicated convergence of old hatreds, postwar changes in the economy, and new expectations by African Americans. The carefully preserved speeches, legislation, and manifestos of politicians and movement leaders give a partial view of the upheaval of the time. Golden's straightforward editorializing expands and colors the picture. His ability to communicate the everyday injustices and common needs faced by African Americans was a bridge that brought many white Americans into sympathy with, or at least some understanding of, the civil rights fight. When delivering speeches to regular folks around the country, Golden used his stories to convey a simple message: One's everyday acts of bravery or cowardice were of real consequence. He never wavered in his conviction that an individual could force change in his or her own lifetime by standing up and speaking out against acts of hatred or ignorance. It wasn't easy, he said, but it was the only way out. He was living proof.

Remembering Golden's work has another value, one that is vitally important but harder to articulate than the others. As I write this, almost half a century after the passage of the Voting Rights Act and more than thirty years after Golden's death, the protections put in place to ensure equal voting rights have been attacked, allowing districts to be redrawn and obstacles to be put between poor and minority citizens and their voting booths. Editorialists on all sides of the issue continue to hold forth on what it means to give states more latitude on these matters.

One of Golden's last long essays for a national magazine contained an observation that reminds us that civil rights are not static: "Those of us who are, for want of a better word, co-revolutionists see now that the road toward absolute equality is longer and more treacherous than we thought. We cannot traverse it with song and enthusiasm; we have to hack our way through prejudice, distortion, ignorance, and plain intransigence. Hard work and patience are the only blades we have."[8]

NOTES

A Note to the Reader

Golden's essays, speeches, predictions, and memorable one-liners often appeared in multiple places, much changed, slightly altered, or identical. The decisions on which sources to cite were made case by case. In some instances the first-known publication date was the deciding factor; in citing humorous anecdotes, the version deemed most entertaining by the author was cited. The process was far from a perfect science, which Golden would have appreciated.

All *Carolina Israelite* articles cited were authored by Golden unless otherwise indicated.

All correspondence cited is from and to Golden unless otherwise indicated.

Abbreviations Used in the Notes

UNCC-HG   The Harry Golden Papers (UNCC Mss 20, pts. 1 and 2), J. Murrey Atkins Library Special Collections, University of North Carolina at Charlotte

UNCC-MS   Morris Speizman Papers, J. Murrey Atkins Library Special Collections, University of North Carolina at Charlotte

DOCSOUTH   Documenting the American South, digital publishing initiative sponsored by University Library, University of North Carolina, Chapel Hill

UVA-CG   Papers of Carter Glass, Accession #2913, Special Collections, University of Virginia Library, Charlottesville

CI   *Carolina Israelite*

NYT   *New York Times*

Introduction

1. *Letter from Birmingham Jail*, written by King in 1963, was published that year by various periodicals, in some cases without permission or in an edited form. King included it in his book *Why We Can't Wait* in 1964. See also the Martin Luther King Jr. Research and Education Institute and the King Papers Project, Stanford, Calif., http://mlk-kpp01.stanford.edu/, and the Martin Luther King Jr. Center for Nonviolent Social Change, Atlanta, Ga., http://www.thekingcenter.org/.

2. Golden, *Right Time*, 54.

3. Ibid., 280–81.

4. Branch, *Parting the Waters*, 306–8, 360. Had the two men discussed civil rights that night, it would have been an illuminating conversation. Stevenson's position on race issues was mixed, and his critics faulted him for not taking a firm stand against Jim Crow. Yet Stevenson also had strong supporters among the ranks of those most concerned with race issues throughout the 1960s. Branch describes situations in which these supporters recognized Stevenson's discomfort around African Americans and avoidance of the political issues. One was Kennedy campaign advisor Harris Wofford, who was appointed in 1961 as a special assistant on civil rights. Wofford once commended Stevenson in a confidential letter to King.

5. Established in 1975, the Ada Comstock Scholars Program is for women of "nontraditional college age."

6. Joseph Wershba, "A Post Portrait: Harry Golden," *New York Post Daily Magazine*, first of five parts, 30 January 1961. The full quote was "We sold 250,000 copies of 'Only in America,' and 2,000,000 in paperback. 'For 2-cents Plain' has sold 160,000 hardcover and 1,000,000 paperback. 'Enjoy, Enjoy' is now close to 90,000 and still on the bestseller list. Altogether half a million hardcover books for $4 each and 3 million paperbacks for 50 cents—without using any four-letter words or pictures of naked women." A word about the number of Golden's books: His first book was *Jews in American History: Their Contributions to the United States of America*, co-authored with Martin Rywell and published in 1950; it was rarely mentioned by Golden and typically not counted in the total of his published works. Eighteen were trade books under his byline, beginning with *Only in America* in 1958. *Travels through Jewish America* shared a byline with his son Richard Goldhurst. Golden wrote a number of forewords and introductions and contributed chapters to other books, but two often included in his bibliography (by him and others) are *The Spirit of the Ghetto* and a chapter in *Five Boyhoods: Howard Lindsay, Harry Golden, Walt Kelly, William K. Zinsser, and John Updike*. Two compilations of his work, *The Harry Golden Omnibus* and *The Best of Harry Golden*, were published as well, bringing the number to twenty-three. He was anthologized many times. His first two books, *Only in America* and *For 2 Cents Plain*, hit the top slot on the *New York Times* bestseller list, and his next three books made the list as well—*Enjoy, Enjoy!*, *Carl Sandburg*, and *You're Entitle'*. The Sandburg book appeared as a bestseller on just one week's list, which did not stop Golden from crowing about it.

7. "America on a Huge Breast Binge," *CI*, June 1954.

8. Whitfield, "'Golden' Era of Civil Rights," 29.

9. Diner, *Lower East Side Memories*, 27–28.

10. A case in point about Golden being accepted as an author of serious topics: In 1955 Golden proposed a book about the Leo Frank lynching. His agent shopped the idea around, including a pitch to J. B. Lippincott and Co. The publisher passed, citing *Night Fell on Georgia* by Charles and Louise Samuels, just out as a 25-cent Dell paperback. That was likely just a more tactful way to reject his proposal, as the market would surely have been able to support a book on the subject along the more detailed lines proposed by Golden. Several years after he became famous, Golden was able to sell the idea that became *A Little Girl Is Dead* with no difficulty. See John A. S. Cushman, Curtis Brown, Ltd., 19 January 1956, UNCC-HG, pt. 1, box 5:55.

11. Undated letter to Richard Goldhurst about attending NASA event with friend Julian Scheer, UNCC-HG, pt. 2, box 11:37. As Golden later noted, "Julian and I were close; we

collaborated on several articles, and we used to boast we were the only poor Jews in Charlotte" (*Right Time*, 353). Scheer left daily news and went to work for NASA in 1962. His mix of journalistic talent and promotional skill made him a natural compatriot for Golden. See "Julian Scheer, 75, a Leader in Selling the Space Program," *NYT*, 5 September 2001.

12. As will become clear, Golden was especially adept at making sure mainstream media reported on his utterances and writings, a very useful ability and one that successful writers now employ as a matter of course but that was less usual in his day.

13. Manchester, *The Glory and the Dream*, 899. Manchester observed about the America of 1954, "Negroes still did not exist as people for mainstream America. In popular entertainment, they were more like pets. Stepin Fetchit, Hattie McDaniel, Butterfly McQueen, and Eddie Anderson—these were good for the nudge and the guffaw but weren't looked at as human beings."

14. Hall, "Long Civil Rights Movement and the Political Uses of the Past," 1232. As Hall put it: "By confining the civil rights struggle to the South, to bowdlerized heroes, to a single halcyon decade, and to limited, noneconomic objectives, the master narrative simultaneously elevates and diminishes the movement" (1234).

15. Golden's belief that academics were terrified of allowing charm or accessibility to seep into their writing was expressed often. One example appeared in his letter to friend George Geiger, 26 April 1963, UNCC-HG, pt. 2, box 6:32.

16. Golden, "Gradual Integration," in *You're Entitle'*, 218.

Chapter 1

1. The anecdote about the shoe polishing (which he may well have co-opted from another storyteller) appears in many places in Golden's work, including *Right Time*, 33.

2. Ibid., 20, and Sorin, *Tradition Transformed*, 48. The FBI began collecting information on Golden in the 1950s and later carried out interviews and checked records when Golden applied for a presidential pardon. Many people who knew Golden did not realize the variations of surname within his family. His parents, older brother Jake, and youngest brother Max remained Goldhirsch; Harry and his sisters used Goldhurst. In his autobiography, *The Right Time*, Golden simplified matters in the index by listing all his immediate family members as "Goldhurst" rather than bothering with sorting out the surnames they actually used.

3. The trail of documents revealing the changes was not easily available in his lifetime—in fact, the first digital public archiving of the SS *Graf Waldersee*'s manifest garbled the spelling of "Goldhirsch" so that it was hidden even after the lists were published on an Ellis Island commemorative website.

4. Golden, *For 2 Cents Plain*, 121. The state of California death certificate for Matilda Goldhurst lists her as born in 1896 in Austria, daughter of Louis Goldhurst and Naomi Zonis. The siblings often used "Louis" on official documents when referring to their father.

5. Golden, *Right Time*, 19; Handlin, *Adventure in Freedom*, 80–84; Sarna, *American Judaism*, 151–54. See also UNCC-HG, pt. 2, box 42:11, and Group 85, Records of the Immigration and Naturalization Service, Microfilm Serial M1464, microfilm roll 25, line 15, and "New York Passenger Lists, 1820–1957," Ancestry.com (1 November 2014).

6. Author's interview with Jake's daughter Norma Leveton, 2006. U.S. census, ship manifests, and family records show contradictory times for Jake's arrival. His descendants believed Jake arrived with his father, but it appears that Leib entered first, through Canada, and Jake came in aboard the *Amerika* in February 1906 and was detained briefly until released to his father. Jake's arrival year is variously noted as 1906 or 1908 in official records. See Certificate of Naturalization for Leib Goldhirsch, 6 August 1916, Certificate No. 757095, Petition Vol. 238, No. 58900, National Archives and Records Administration, Washington, D.C., and "Manifests of Passengers Arriving at St. Albans, VT, District through Canadian Pacific and Atlantic Ports, 1895–1954," Record Group 85, Records of the Immigration and Naturalization Service, Microfilm Serial M1464, microfilm roll 25, line 15, and "New York Passenger Lists, 1820–1957," Ancestry.com (1 November 2014).

7. Jackson, *Encyclopedia of New York*, 696–97. The family lived in more than one apartment on Eldridge and also resided at 216 East Houston Street, the address listed on Leib Goldhirsch's citizenship paperwork.

8. Golden, *Right Time*, 20–22; "I Visit the Lower East Side," *CI*, July–August 1958.

9. This story appears in several places in Golden's work; this version was the first at this length, and the phrase "the story of the immigrant . . . who . . . had his head beaten in on the picket line" was later changed to ". . . died on the picket line" ("The Story of My Father," *CI*, May–June 1959). See also "The Status Wanderer—The Story of My Father," in *Enjoy, Enjoy!* 226. A "cloaks operator" refers to a factory job in which a worker ran a sewing machine in the making of women's coats.

10. Golden, *Right Time*, 22.

11. Golden revisited the tea ritual among immigrants in essays and worked it into speeches throughout his life; see *Right Time*, 21, and *Enjoy, Enjoy!* 118. This version is borrowed; the name "Dudja Silverberg" appears in an editor's response to a letter that ran in the *Jewish Daily Forward* in 1908. As Richard Goldhurst said when asked about this anecdote, like a lot of Golden's polished routines, the gist of it was true, but "Harry wasn't above stealing someone else's telling of a similar tale and making it his."

12. *Right Time*, 24–25; Metzger, *Bintel Brief*, 70. See preceding note; Golden lifted his response from a letter written to the *Jewish Daily Forward* in which the editor responded by describing an interaction with *his* father: "Once when I chided him about his piety in view of the fact that he was a freethinker, he answered me . . . Dudja Silverberg goes to shul to speak with God, I go to shul to speak with Dudja."

13. Sarna, *American Judaism*, 158–59; Howe and Libo, *World of Our Fathers*, 16; Sorin, *Tradition Transformed*, 34–35.

14. Golden, *Right Time*, 24; Sorin, *Tradition Transformed*, 81. By 1910 there were more than 2,000 such organizations known as *Landsmanshaftn* in New York City. Matteawan State Hospital was established in Beacon, New York, in 1893 as a hospital for insane criminals. See New York State Archives, http://www.archives.nysed.gov/a/research/res_topics_health_mh_hist.pdf (1 November 2014).

15. Letter to Leon Toback, 11 July 1960, UNCC-HG, pt. 1, box 9:46. Golden met Toback at a B'rith Abraham convention and asked to borrow Tobak's marriage certificate in order to copy it. The document had been signed by Leib Goldhirsch as the officiant.

16. Golden, "The Status Wanderer—The Story of My Father," in *Enjoy, Enjoy!* 232. The judge whom Golden cites as delivering the eulogy was Herman Hoffman, grand master of the B'rith Abraham Order and a former Special Sessions judge.

17. Golden, *Growing up Jewish*, 190; Joseph Wershba, "A Post Portrait: Harry Golden," *New York Post Daily Magazine*, third of five parts, 1 February 1961. Wershba and Golden became friends in the early 1950s while the former was a CBS News reporter and producer working with Edward R. Murrow. Wershba wrote the foreword to an edition of Golden's book *Carl Sandburg*.

18. Golden, *Right Time*, 28–35.

19. Ibid., 32.

20. Ibid., 30; Glazer and Moynihan, *Beyond the Melting Pot*, 155.

21. Golden, *Right Time*, 37. Golden liked to recall that the restaurant near Jake's hotel was for a time called Offer's and boasted this slogan: "No One Offers What Offer's Offers."

22. Goldhurst, "Locating the Deity," 113; author's interview with Richard Goldhurst, Westport, Conn., 2001.

23. "About the Convert to Christianity," *CI*, November–December 1962.

24. "Buying a Suit or an Overcoat for the Winter," *CI*, March–April 1955. The version quoted appeared in Golden, "Buying a Suit on the East Side," in *Only in America*, 54.

25. Golden, "Buying a Suit on the East Side," in *Only in America*, 54. Most often "*mayvinn*" is now spelled "maven" and is used to denote an expert on some subject(s).

26. Golden, "How's That Again?" in *Enjoy, Enjoy!* 112.

27. Golden was, as he usually did, referring to the total number of Leib Goldhirsch's children, not just Anna's offspring.

28. Golden, "The Poets Were Paid," in *Only in America*, 53.

29. *The Greatest Jewish City in the World* aired on WNBC, 9–13 April 1973. The film won Golden an Emmy in the Seventeenth Annual New York Emmy competition; see www .nyemmys.org (1 November 2014). See also Golden, "The 'Eleanor Club,'" in *So What Else Is New?* 233, and Eleanor Roosevelt Papers Project, George Washington University, http:// www.gwu.edu/~erpapers/ (1 November 2014). Eleanor Roosevelt taught dance and calisthenics in University Settlement House beginning in 1902 until sometime prior to her marriage to Franklin Roosevelt in 1905.

30. Golden, "The East Side Revisited," in *Best of Harry Golden*, 131; Dollinger, *Quest for Inclusion*, 19–22.

31. Sorin, *Tradition Transformed*, 50; Rose, *Ghetto and Beyond*, 6; Glazer, *American Judaism*, 67.

32. Ascoli, *Julius Rosenwald*, chaps. 3 and 4; Sorin, *Tradition Transformed*, 56.

33. Diner, *In the Almost Promised Land*, 119; Konvitz, "Jews and Civil Rights," 278.

34. Letter from Hermann E. Cohen, 6 April 1962, UNCC-HG, pt. 1, box 5:41.

35. The Social Security database lists 1888 and 1972 as Jake's birth and death dates, as do other documents more reliable than the U.S. Census information provided by his sister.

36. Golden, *Right Time*, 40–42.

37. Author's interview with Norma Leveton, 2006; "The Tales of Poverty," *CI*, July–August 1962; Telushkin, *Golden Land*, 9.

38. Author's interview with Norma Leveton, 2006.

39. Letter to Alfred A. Gross, executive secretary, George W. Henry Foundation, 31 July 1956, UNCC-HG, pt. 1, box 6:45.

40. Jake Goldhirsch at various times owned the Union Square Hotel, Cadillac Hotel, Alpine Hotel, and Markwell Hotel in New York. Norma Leveton confirmed that her father lost all four hotels by the 1940s and took pride in paying off all the tradespeople to whom he owed money. "He always had Shane the painter or Louis the plumber, people who were starving. He hired them, gave them a room and they'd work all week and go home on the weekend," she said.

41. Letter to Jack Shuttleworth, 19 August 1965, UNCC-HG, pt. 2, box 12:29.

42. Golden, *Right Time*, 54–55.

43. Ibid., 39. *A Little Girl Is Dead* was published in 1965.

44. "The Influence of Sex," *CI*, January–February 1959. Acquaintances who knew Golden well, when asked about the likelihood of his frequenting prostitutes himself, responded in various colorful ways, but all agreed that he had little need to seek paid companionship.

45. Golden, *Right Time*, 49. Golden included an essay on "cockalization" in *The Golden Book of Jewish Humor*, in the essay "God Bless the Gentiles," 118. Even he could not make a funny story out of this memory. It was indeed a well-known ritual. In his redolent description of life on the Lower East Side, Samuel Chotzinoff describes a narrow escape from such a threat, in *Lost Paradise*, 87; see also Riis, *How the Other Half Lives*. Riis was born in Denmark and immigrated to America in 1870. He became a muckraking reporter for the *New York Tribune* and, later, the *New York Sun*. While he proved to be a remarkable force for change through his documentation of the squalid lives of the urban poor, Riis had what Howe characterized as "a reformer's zeal but only a limited capacity for seeing the people he proposed to help" (Howe and Libo, *World of Our Fathers*, 396–97).

46. Golden, "Notes for an Autobiography," in *You're Entitle'*, 291.

47. Letter to *Coronet* magazine researcher Gwenn Hutchins, 8 May 1958, UNCC-HG, pt. 1, box 5:52.

48. Golden, *Right Time*, 60–81.

49. Ibid.

50. Howe and Libo, *World of Our Fathers*, 366–67.

51. Golden, "How Tammany Hall Did It," in *Only in America*, 206–7; Sorin, *Tradition Transformed*, 208; author's interview with Richard Goldhurst, email, 2013.

52. Golden, *Right Time*, 66–69. Golden and the rest of the Round Table would have known that black intellectual W. E. B. Du Bois had expressed decidedly anti-Semitic sentiments in the 1903 edition of his important book *The Souls of Black Folk*. See Diner, "Between Words and Deeds," 99. Golden apparently did not let that get in the way of his admiration for the man.

53. Joseph Berger, "100 Years Later, the Roll of the Dead in a Factory Fire Is Complete," *NYT*, 20 February 2011. The names of 6 of the 146 people killed in the fire remained unknown until 2011.

54. "Triangle Fire," *CI*, January 1956 and May–June 1961. Golden's comment came after the 25 March 1961 memorial service marking the fiftieth anniversary of the tragedy.

55. Golden, *Right Time*, 65.

56. Ibid., 97–102.

57. Goldhurst, "Locating the Deity," 6, 112, 116. Tiny, wrote Goldhurst, was a "champion swimmer" in her girlhood, a talented musician, and a practical sort who mowed the lawn after her husband retired to their suburban house with the Sunday newspapers, baffled by the mechanics of a push-mower. Richard Goldhurst was born in 1927. Harry Jr. lived from 1927 to 1988; William, 1929 to 2010; and Peter, 1938 to 1957.

58. Golden, "God Bless the Irish," in *Enjoy, Enjoy!* 278–79. Attorney Fallon, who died in 1927, was a larger-than-life character whose defense of various mobsters and criminals was as effective as it was flamboyant.

59. Golden, *Right Time*, 252–55

60. Ibid., 67–68, 252–55; Golden's foreword in Mordell, *World of Haldeman-Julius*, 5–7. Golden claimed he had contributed a few Little Blue Books, but there is no reliable record of his doing so.

61. The quote from Haldeman-Julius (1889–1951) appears on a website designed for collectors and scholars of Little Blue Books, http://www.haldeman-julius.org (1 November 2014). In 1953, Golden corresponded with Oxford University Press about writing a biography of Haldeman-Julius. The editor's vision of a scholarly 75,000 to 80,000 word chronological biography was probably enough to scare Golden off, and the press no doubt quickly realized that this assignment would not be a good fit. See letter from Carroll G. Bowen, 23 December 1953, UNCC-HG, pt. 1, box 5:14.

62. Unsigned, "Cannon's Broker Gets 5-Year Term," *NYT*, 17 October 1929.

63. Golden, *Right Time*, 124.

64. Dabney, *Dry Messiah*, viii.

65. Golden, *Right Time*, 124; Horowitz, *Rereading Sex*, 368–69, 398–403. Cannon's education was far superior to Comstock's, and the bishop did not rely on crude or shocking vignettes to sell his arguments against alcohol, as Comstock sometimes did in his rhetoric and writings; but Cannon's sweeping statements about the universally damaging effects of a particular vice borrowed directly from the earlier crusader's style.

66. Hohner, *Prohibition and Politics*, 19; Golden, *Right Time*, 130.

67. Hohner, *Prohibition and Politics*, 90–93; Golden, *Right Time*, 129.

68. Cannon and Watson, *Bishop Cannon's Own Story*, 335.

69. Ibid., 205; unsigned, "Declares Women Flout Old Morals," *NYT*, 15 May 1924.

70. Golden, *Right Time*, 131; Hobson, *Mencken*, 345, 386. References to Cannon's character often quote the brilliant, irascible Baltimore scribe H. L. Mencken, who initially loathed then came to admire the cleric.

71. Hohner, *Prohibition and Politics*, 244–56, 295.

72. Unsigned, "Dark Horse Days," *Time*, 9 June 1924.

73. Hohner, *Prohibition and Politics*, 83.

74. Dabney, *Dry Messiah*, 192–93; Patterson, "Fall of a Bishop," 493–518.

75. Golden, *Right Time*, 125, 131; unsigned, "Cannon Explains His Stock Dealings," *NYT*, 21 June 1929, 3. The timing of the first meeting between Cannon and Goldhurst is unclear. Golden and news accounts place it variously from 1924 to 1928.

76. Golden, *Right Time*, 88, 114; unsigned, "Goldhurst Accused in New Stock Case," *NYT*, 24 July 1929.

77. Unsigned, "Business Records," *NYT*, 25 May 1928; Golden, *Right Time*, 131.

78. Unsigned, "Cannon's Broker Gets 5-Year Term," *NYT*, 17 October 1929, 29; Patterson, "Fall of a Bishop," 493–518. Goldhurst and the others working for Kable & Co. reportedly took $77,753 in salaries and commissions over ten months. Telephone and telegraph costs topped $48,000 for ten months. Postage expenses for that period were listed at a hefty $27,579.

79. Unsigned, "Cannon Explains His Stock Dealings," *NYT*, 21 June 1929; unsigned, "Says Cannon Deals Were Speculative," *NYT*, 26 June 1929; testimony of Harry L. Goldhurst, 24 June 1929, UVA-CG, box 263, Correspondence-Cannon case. F. Vesta Lee Gordon of Charlottesville, Virginia, provided research assistance with the Glass papers.

80. Unsigned, "Raided as Tipsters in Motors Building," *NYT*, 28 August 1929.

81. Unsigned, "Women Broker Sued by Investor," *NYT*, August 1928; unsigned, "Woman Broker Put Out of Business," *NYT*, 4 May 1929; notary records of partnership between Clara Goldhurst and Celia Manasse, *New York Herald Tribune*, 18 February 1921. The 1929 news story notes that Clara Goldhurst's daily market newsletter called "From 10 to 3 in Wall Street" was probably written by brother Harry. As independent and difficult as Clara could be, her father was especially protective of her. Leib, and most likely Harry, knew that the unmarried Clara had given birth to a baby in September 1926, while at sea aboard the new steamship *Andania*. Clara and her father were returning from a visit to their hometown, Mikulintsy, in Galicia. What became of the child is unknown. See "Passenger Lists of Vessels Arriving at New York, New York, 1820–1897," National Archives Microfilm Publication M237, and Records of the U.S. Customs Service, Record Group 36, Passenger and Crew Lists of Vessels Arriving at New York, New York, 1897–1957, National Archives Microfilm Publication T715, Records of the Immigration and Naturalization Service.

82. Golden, *Right Time,* 137; unsigned, "Bishop Cannon out of Kable Inquiry," *NYT*, 9 July 1929.

83. Unsigned, "Stock Tipster Loot Put at $5,000,000," *NYT*, 14 August 1929; unsigned, "Goldhurst Indicted Again in Stock Case," *NYT*, 24 September 1929. Both articles mentioned Matilda Goldhurst. She may have simply been visiting his office at the wrong time, was working as a stenographer, or was just a figurehead listed as a company officer. See Golden, *Right Time*, 145–47.

84. Unsigned, "Cannon's Broker Gets 5-Year Term," *NYT*, 17 October 1929.

85. Golden, *Right Time*, 143; Patterson, "Fall of a Bishop," 515; Okrent, *Last Call*, 326–27.

86. Unsigned, "Bribery Is Charged in Prison Transfers," *NYT*, 10 July 1931; unsigned, "Says Convicts Paid $35,000 to Be Moved," *NYT*, 11 July 1931; "Report of the Hearing of Harry Goldhurst," 21 May 1931, UVA-CG, 260, Goldhurst Parole Hearing folder.

87. Letter to H. C. Heckman, Executive Secretary, U.S. Board of Parole, 19 October 1931, and "Report of the Hearing of Harry Goldhurst," 21 May 1931, UVA-CG, 260, Goldhurst Parole Hearing folder.

88. Golden, *Right Time*, 157; unsigned, "Cannon's Broker Loses His Parole," *NYT*, 11 December 1931. Dates of Golden's prison time noted in several places in FBI Bureau file 73-16547.

89. Golden, *Right Time*, 162–63.

90. Ibid., 167–68; Okrent, *Last Call*, 326; Dabney, *Dry Messiah*, 337–40.

91. Unsigned, "Carter Glass, 88, Dies in Capital," *NYT*, 29 May 1946; Associated Press reports in late editions of various newspapers, 28 May 1946.

92. Unsigned, "Glass, Nearing 79, Hopes to Live to 80," *NYT*, 3 January 1937.

93. FBI Bureau file 73-16547 and Charlotte field office file 73-432, 15 April 1969.

94. Joseph Wershba, "Pages from a Writer's Life: Harry Golden," *Forward*, 17 January 1982; "The Story of My Past," *CI*, October–November 1958.

95. Goldhurst, "Locating the Deity," 100.

96. Golden, *Right Time*, 213–14; "Growing Up between Two Worlds: Reflections of the Child of a Mixed Marriage," *Commentary*, July 1953, 30–35. Richard Goldhurst intended to use a pen name for this, his first magazine article, but through an editorial miscommunication, the piece was bylined with his real name. Tiny was angry enough to write or call everyone in the family and denounce her son.

97. Golden, *Right Time*, 210–11; Ellwood, *1950*, 37; author's interview with William Goldhurst, telephone, June 2006. Father Coughlin was a Catholic priest, the Reverend Charles E. Coughlin, whose radio program reached millions each week in the 1930s.

98. Golden, *Right Time*, 217.

99. Golden, "How about Whiskey?" in *You're Entitle'*, 33.

100. Author's interview with Richard Goldhurst, 2001.

101. Golden, *Right Time*, 371; author's interview with Richard Goldhurst, email, 2012; "Daily Closeup: Harry Golden," *New York Post*, 28 November 1958. Wershba described Golden as short, round, cigar-smoking, and bourbon-drinking, recalling, "Harry looks down at the empty glass and joyously calls out to no one in particular, 'Where is it? Where is it? Make it a double!'"

102. Goldhurst, "Locating the Deity," 127; Golden, *Right Time*, 178.

103. Golden, *Right Time*, 172–74, 181; author's interview with Norma Leveton, 2006.

104. Goldhurst, "Locating the Deity," 136.

105. Golden, "I Was a $300 Angel," in *For 2 Cents Plain*, 105–7; Golden, *Right Time*, 188; author's interview with Norma Leveton, 2006; unsigned, "Mistake Minute," *NYT*, 26 December 1933. The timing of this reference to a midget production of the same melodrama that appeared in the *New York Times* matches Golden's story. Golden's niece remembered her parents talking about her uncle's short-lived production with specific detail. Harry Goldhurst did not invent this tasteless genre. Plays with midget casts had been performed previously in New York City, and as early as 1905 Coney Island proudly promoted its Midget City. See "Great New Dreamland at Coney This Year," *NYT*, 25 April 1905. He did, however, continue to promote stories on the topic. A *Life* editor wrote Golden in 1956 thanking him for suggesting that the magazine do a photo shoot at "the midget wedding" (UNCC-HG, pt. 2, box 10:33).

106. "The Death of a Newspaper," *CI*, November–December 1963; Golden, *Right Time*, 216–17, 225. Peter Goldhurst stayed at home until his teens and, according to Richard Goldhurst, was often cared for by his brothers while Tiny worked. Eventually he moved to an institution run by the State of New York Department of Mental Hygiene in Wassaic. See UNCC-HG, pt. 1, box 6:35.

107. Albin Krebs, "Clarence Norris, the Last Survivor of 'Scottsboro Boys,' Dies at 76," *NYT*, 26 January 1989; Alan Blinder, "Alabama Pardons 3 'Scottsboro Boys' after 80 Years," *NYT*, 20 November 2013. See also Carter, *Scottsboro*.

108. Golden, "The New York World's Fair," in *Enjoy, Enjoy!* 113–16.

109. Author's interview with Richard Goldhurst, 2001; Kirsten Fermaglich, "'This Too Is Partly Hitler's Doing': American Jewish Name Changing in the Wake of the Holocaust,

1939–57," in Cesarani and Sundquist, *After the Holocaust*. As Fermaglich demonstrated with her study of thousands of New York City's official name-change petitions, the reasons for changes were varied, complex, and largely unexplored. The mixed choices of the Goldhirschs illustrate that the very freedom to change one's name in the United States was a valued right sometimes exercised for various reasons within one family.

Chapter 2

1. Golden, *Right Time*, 224; Goldhurst, "Locating the Deity," 137; author's interview with Richard Goldhurst, email, 2010. A source identified as a former employer of Golden's at the *Norfolk (Va.) Times-Advocate* told an FBI field agent that Golden still owed him $180; see FBI Bureau file 73-16547 and Norfolk field office file 73-106, 24 April 1969.

2. Golden, *Right Time*, 225; "Was It the Presbyterians or Charlotte Russe?" *CI*, September–October 1964; Goldhurst, "Locating the Deity," 154.

3. Golden, *Right Time*, 234.

4. "A Pulpit in the South," *Commentary*, December 1953. In this story about the southern city of "Elizabeth," Golden cast himself as the Jewish outsider and described the firing of a rabbi who failed to "mix" socially.

5. Golden, *Right Time*, 250.

6. Ibid., 237; Polsgrove, *Divided Minds*, 97.

7. *American Dilemma* is a staggeringly detailed, still relevant, and revealing 1,400-page study that was funded by the Carnegie Corporation and carried out by Swedish scholar Gunnar Myrdal. The text and notes were written with assistance from economist Richard Sterner and sociologist Arnold Rose. U.S. Census figures report 8.8 million blacks in the United States in 1900, with 89.7 percent living in the South. See also Hobbs and Stoops, *Demographic Trends in the 20th Century*, November 2002, 73–74, 83.

8. Glass, *Textile Industry in North Carolina*, xiii, 18–19, 35; Ready, *Tar Heel State*, 286–87.

9. Goldfield, *Cotton Fields and Skyscrapers*, 124–25.

10. Glass, *Textile Industry in North Carolina*, 30–33; Ready, *Tar Heel State*, 266–67.

11. Ready, *Tar Heel State*, 277–78, 281.

12. Cash, *Mind of the South*, 175.

13. "Why the Resistance?" *CI*, April–May 1962.

14. Ayers, *Promise of the New South*, 114–16.

15. Glass, *Textile Industry in North Carolina*, 84–85; Golden, "I Am Now Kosher," in *Only in America*, 36–37, a particular favorite of this author.

16. Crow, Escott, and Hatley, *History of African Americans in North Carolina*, 130.

17. Roberts and Klibanoff, *Race Beat*, 8; Hall et al., *Like a Family*, 66

18. Roberts and Klibanoff, *Race Beat*, 9.

19. Ready, *Tar Heel State*, 269–73.

20. Goldfield, *Cotton Fields and Skyscrapers*, 6.

21. Ready, *Tar Heel State*, 333–39.

22. Golden was a firm believer in following the money, and it tickled him that his new city had its own mint, which had opened in 1837 when southern gold prospectors got weary of lugging their nuggets elsewhere; see Morrill, *Historic Charlotte*, 124. See also

Fannie Flono, "Helping Charlotte Find Its Way—50 Years Ago," *Charlotte Observer*, 30 May 2013, http://www.charlotteobserver.com/2013/05/30/4076378/helping-charlotte-find-its-way.html#.U3fpti8gmHk (1 November 2014).

23. Claiborne, *"Charlotte Observer,"* 207–8; Douglas, *Reading, Writing, and Race,* 55.

24. Golden, *Right Time,* 236.

25. "Harry Golden," *Nation,* 19 August 1968.

26. Golden, "Highway 85 and I," in *So Long as You're Healthy,* 94; "The Post Office Trash-Cans," *CI,* May–June 1955.

27. Golden and Goldhurst, *Travels through Jewish America,* 9; Golden, *Right Time,* 239–40.

28. Golden, *Right Time,* 227–28, 239.

29. Ibid. Sometimes in the telling of this story about Witter, Golden claimed there was another newspaperman with him for this under-the-viaduct cocktail hour. If that was the case, there was a good chance it was Golden himself

30. Golden, *Right Time,* 240.

31. "What Are the World's Greatest Books?" *Charlotte Labor Journal,* 12 November 1942; "Culture and Books," *Charlotte Labor Journal,* 25 June 1942.

32. Golden, *Right Time,* 227–28. The year and location of Witter's famous bullet wound shifted, depending on the storyteller and the audience. Sometimes it was 1929, sometimes a decade later. It was in Gastonia, Shelby, or High Point. Mrs. Witter's explanation is the most plausible.

33. Speizman, *Jews of Charlotte;* UNCC-MS 1:2.

34. Poetry snippet, undated, UNCC-HG, pt. 1, box 5:41; author's interview with J. E. Cohen, nephew of H. E. Cohen, telephone, 2007.

35. Speizman, *Jews of Charlotte,* 72–76; letter from Speizman, including a copy of H. E. Cohen's transcribed remarks asking for any errors to be noted, 17 November 1976, UNCC-HG, pt. 2, box 4:45. Golden's margin gloss appears on his own file copy and includes his notation "Mostly Bull." Golden added that his friendship with Cohen "far outweighed any discrepancies" in the transcript. Cohen got the last word in about their friendship, and it was kind. He dictated a letter 13 October 1977 to Rabbi Richard Rocklin of Temple Israel in Charlotte, urging the creation of an honorary life membership for Golden; see UNCC-HG, pt. 2, box 4:45. In a detailed oral history interview, Hilbert Fuerstmann, a businessman who moved to Charlotte in 1941, mentions his admiration of both Golden and Cohen. His assessment of their relationship was accurate: "[Hermann] Cohen was one of the characters in town and in fact . . . kept [Golden] in food and shelter. And if it wasn't for Hermann Cohen . . . Harry Golden would have probably left Charlotte" (New South Voices, interview by Steven Haas, 26 February 1989, http://newsouthvoices .uncc.edu/interview/jcfu0003 [1 November 2014]).

36. Golden, *Right Time,* 257–58; "The Carolina Israelite," *Charlotte Labor Journal,* 14 February 1944; Claiborne, *"Charlotte Observer,"* 189, 210; letter to Cohen, 12 July 1959, UNCC-HG, pt. 1, box 5:41; author's interviews with Jack Claiborne, 2000, 2006. The interruption after the initial launching of the *Carolina Israelite* was puzzling to those who later tried to reconstruct the paper's history and reconcile conflicting start dates. Golden's first attempt to publish the paper was a trial run, and he resumed publication when he had financial backing, in 1944, with volume 1, number 1.

37. Harry Ashmore, "Gentle Iconoclast," *Nation*, 6 September 1958, 117. The first of Davis's books was the 1949 work *Whisper My Name*, a novel about a Jewish businessman "passing" as a Gentile. According to several residents interviewed, the book shocked Charlotte with its close resemblance to a local retailer. The story about Angela Davis, daughter of Burke and Evangeline Davis, is from author's interview with Jack Claiborne, email, October 2011.

38. "Harry Ashmore," *CI*, August 1946; Golden, "Those Sexy Novels," syndicated column, "Only in America," 22 August 1959, UNCC-HG, pt. 1, box 32:1; Myrna Oliver, "Harry Ashmore; Arkansas Editor Fought Segregation," *Los Angeles Times*, 22 January 1998. Ashmore had a gift for a pithy phrase that rivaled Golden's. He made famous a line saying that the white South told blacks, "Come close, but don't go too high," while the white North said, "Go high, but don't come too close." See Roberts and Klibanoff, *Race Beat*, 194–95. Reston's remark from UPI interview, *Stars and Stripes*, 23 October 1959.

39. W. B. Silverman, "The Fighting Jew," *CI*, February 1944.

40. Front page of *CI*, February 1944.

41. "The Editor's 'Financial Statement,'" *CI*, July 1946; "The Carolina Israelite Will Be Issued on the 26th of Each Month," *CI*, August 1946. The number of copies of the paper printed varied between 2,000 and 3,500 during this time, perhaps affected by how large a press run Golden could afford in a given month. See also "Rabbi Fineberg Lectures on Crucifixion of Jesus," *CI*, March 1946, and "The Carolina Israelite Resumes Publication," *CI*, December 1947.

42. Letter from Cohen, 11 July 1959, and response from Golden, 12 July 1959, UNCC-HG, pt. 1, box 5:41.

43. Documents in UNCC-HG pertaining to financial affairs with Goodman and Blumenthal include Southland Publishing meeting minutes, 12 June 1945, pt. 1, box 9:27; letter from Charlotte attorney Maurice Weinstein re Southland Publishing dissolution, 28 August 1946, pt. 1, box 9:27; Southland meeting minutes, 1 October and 10 December 1946, pt. 1, box 9:27; "Statement of Earnings for Golden Advertising Agency earnings and expenses, December 1945–1947," pt. 1, box 6:34; arbitration-session minutes, with Blumenthal, Goodman, and local businessmen Leo Gottheimer and J. H. Goldstein, 19 December 1948, pt. 2, box 3:16, and 22 December 1948, pt. 1, box 5:11; letter to Charlotte attorney W. H. Abernathy re Southland reorganization and formation of the Henry Lewis Martin Company, named for Golden, printer Henry Stalls, and writer Martin Rywell, 13 October 1949, pt. 1, box 9:27; letter from I. D. Blumenthal regarding unpaid debts, 16 April 1968, and Golden's responses, 18 April and 9 May 1968, pt. 1, box 5:11. Golden went out of his way to publish flattering mentions of his benefactors in the early years, especially in the case of Goodman, who served in the North Carolina legislature. Documents in UNCC-MS, 6:30, include correspondence and documents detailing the disagreement between Blumenthal and Golden.

44. The Birmingham arrest is noted in a report in FBI Bureau files 73-16547 and HQ 62-105851, 18 November 1959, and attached to a copy of Golden's fingerprint report from the arrest. See Goldhurst, "Locating the Deity," 151–53. After the probationary period, the Birmingham case was "closed by special order," according to the FBI report, possibly an intervention by a highly placed friend of Golden's in later years.

45. The envelopes are mentioned in an affidavit written by Golden defending his relationship with IRS agents Vincent Tangari and Darrell Kaiser in Charlotte, 14 October 1960, UNCC-HG, pt. 1, box 9:42.

46. Author's interview with Richard Goldhurst, email, 2011; letter from Ruth Allman, UNCC-HG, pt. 1, box 4:9. See previous note for affidavit by Golden.

47. Author's interview with Philip Blumenthal, nephew of I. D. Blumenthal, telephone, March 2009. I. D. Blumenthal twice married women who converted to Judaism, and his second wife, Madolyn Carpenter Blumenthal, joined him as an enthusiastic supporter of Wildacres, a 1,400-acre mountaintop retreat near Ashville that he bought in 1936 and developed for interfaith gatherings beginning in the 1940s. See also the Blumenthal Foundation's account of I. D. Blumenthal's business history, www.blumenthalfoundation.org (1 November 2014).

48. Letter to Russell Cain of the "Therapeutic Research Foundation" in Philadelphia on "Golden Advertising Agency" letterhead, concerning asthma cure, 27 November 1948, UNCC-HG, pt. 1, box 5:21; "Our Father Who Art in Charlotte," *CI*, January–February 1967; author's interviews with Richard Goldhurst, email, 2006, and with William Goldhurst, telephone, 2006. The secretary featured in the Midas water cooler photographs was Monty Graham, this author's mother. See letter from Charlotte attorney M. A. Weinstein, regarding certificate registering Midas Mineral Water, 28 August 1946, UNCC-HG, pt. 1, box 9:27. Golden had already tried and failed to run an ad business with a partner, hiring E. Scott Kalitz to handle telephone sales. Kalitz fell ill, and the partnership was dissolved in May 1945. Golden's jumbled, single-spaced letters to Kalitz and his wife discuss back wages and reflect the panic he apparently felt. See UNCC-IIG, 21 and 27 April 1945, pt. 1, box 7:14.

49. Revenue for the *Carolina Israelite* in the 1940s is listed in an accountant's summary document, UNCC-HG, pt. 2, box 41:8. During interviews in 2000, Charlotte acquaintances of both men noted that Goodman was the one person in on the formation of the *Carolina Israelite* who concerned himself with Golden's ability as a writer, and he was impressed with Golden's skill. A reference to this is found in Herman Cohen's dictation discussed in this chapter. It is also quoted in Kratt, *Charlotte, North Carolina*, 138. In 1969, when Golden applied for a presidential pardon of his prison sentence, the required FBI investigation revisited the arbitration of Golden's handling of Blumenthal's funds. The FBI report referred to the three-person group as a "Beth Din," meaning the traditional Jewish court of three judges. See FBI Bureau file 73-16547 and Charlotte field office file 73-432, 8 May 1969.

50. Golden, "They Never Met a Payroll," in *Only in America*, 202; letter to Bernstein, 24 February 1949, UNCC-HG, pt. 1, box 5:4.

51. Letters from Blumenthal, 16 April and 8 May 1968, and Golden's responses, 19 April and 9 May 1968, UNCC-HG, pt. 1, box 5:11. The total cited by Blumenthal as the amount owed by Golden was $1,500 higher than the arbitration paperwork stated, indicating other debt was involved after the men had signed the arbitration agreement in 1948.

52. Author's interview with Walter Klein, 2000; letter to Cohen, 12 July 1959, UNCC-HG, pt. 1, box 5:41. According to a 1956 summary by Charlotte CPA George Hall containing a retrospective of the *Carolina Israelite*'s taxable earnings back to 1946, the newspaper was run as an "individual enterprise" from 1946 to 1953, then as the Carolina Israelite, Inc. The

summary is included on p. 2 of an untitled document beginning, "The Carolina Israelite, Incorporated . . . was chartered on September 4, 1953" (UNCC-HG, pt. 2, box 41:8).

53. Klein, *Bridge Table*, 48.

54. Author's interview with Jack Claiborne, 2000.

55. Golden, "Singing with the Salvation Army," in *Enjoy, Enjoy!* 41–42. "The Messiah is the successful melding of art and religion," wrote Golden in "Easter Holiday Offers Best in World's Music," syndicated column, "Only in America," 19 April 1960, UNCC-HG, pt. 1, box 32:1. Klein was an appreciative listener of these hymn sings. "I was invited to join them and the bottle they shared," he wrote. "But I was in uniform, not all that familiar with the words, and recent corn liquor was not my first choice. Pity. They could have used a baritone" (Klein, *Bridge Table*, 48).

56. Golden and Goldhurst, *Travels through Jewish America*, 9. Invoice from Ed Mellon Co. shows the sale on 6 October 1947, which Golden did not pay for until the end of November; see UNCC-HG, pt. 1, box 6:34.

57. Author's interview with Jack Claiborne, in Charlotte, 2000. Claiborne worked for the *Charlotte Observer* from 1949 to 1990 as an award-winning reporter, editor, columnist, and Washington correspondent.

58. Broughton was elected to the U.S. Senate in 1948 but died within the first year in office.

59. American Jewish Committee, *American Jewish Yearbook, 1944–45*, 46:144; Speizman, *Jews of Charlotte*, 73; author's interview with Jack Claiborne, 2000.

60. Program for "Annual Brotherhood Week Meeting, 1946," honoring Josephus Daniels, UNCC-HG, pt. 2, box 4:74; Peters, *Tilting at Windmills*, 51–52. As a young man, Peters rented a room in New York in 1946 from Tiny, subsequently became friends with Richard Goldhurst, and met Harry Golden a short time later. In "Bernard M. Baruch," *CI*, January–February 1965, Golden proudly remembered that he had not given in to the impulse to ask for an $800 loan from Baruch. "I wouldn't in a million years. We met as elder statesman and reporter."

61. Golden, *Right Time*, 11; Golden, "A Speech to the Presbyterians," in *Long Live Columbus*, 260; Douglas Robinson, "Harry Golden on Things Remembered," *NYT*, 26 February 1968; Annual Brotherhood Week Meeting program for 1946, UNCC-HG, pt. 2, box 4:74. Golden's story about the intervention by Graham appears in several places in his work. Cited here is "Harry Golden's Twentieth Anniversary: Last of the Personal Journalists," *Saturday Review*, 12 January 1963. Golden dedicated his second book, *For 2 Cents Plain*, "To the late James Street, Tar Heel writer, and the late Noel Houston, teacher of Tar Heel writers. My champions, my friends."

62. Tom Wicker, "Dr. Frank's Legacy Was Love," *Charlotte Observer*, 22 February 1972; Egerton, *Speak Now against the Day*, 130–34. Egerton notes that one "principal beneficiary" of the protected and stimulating environment created by Graham was Howard Odum, a sociologist whose 1936 work *Southern Regions* influenced leading progressives, including editorialists such as Ralph McGill. See also Sosna, *In Search of the Silent South*, 42–59.

63. Programs and correspondence for "Third Annual Brotherhood Week, 1947," honoring Frank P. Graham, UNCC-HG, pt. 2, box 6:59–63. A year after the HUAC accusations,

Graham was given full security clearance as president of the Oak Ridge Institute of Nuclear Energy; see "Graham Cleared by Atomic Board . . . Is Held Loyal Despite Former Association with Reds," *NYT*, 21 December 1948, and Walter Gellhorn, "HUAC: Report on a Report of the House Committee on Un-American Activities," 1193–1234. See also Sosna, *In Search of the Silent South*, 165; Pleasants and Burns, *Frank Porter Graham and the 1950 Senate Race in North Carolina*; Robert Williams, "Rise of a Liberal in North Carolina," *NYT*, 29 June 1930; and "Dr. Frank Graham Dies at 85, Civil Rights Leader in the South," *NYT*, 17 February 1972.

64. A summary of the *Carolina Israelite* Gold Medal Award winners appears as "Editorial Comment: Judge John J. Parker," *CI*, January 1949. See also Crow, Escott, and Hatley, *History of African Americans in North Carolina*, 145; Golden, *Right Time*, 291–99; "The Greatest Republican in America," *CI*, January 1949. Some of the same material on Parker appeared in "The Greatest Republican in America: Judge Parker of Charlotte . . . The Greatest Democrat in America—Dr. Frank P. Graham of Charlotte," *CI*, April 1961. Golden was in good company defending Parker. In introducing the proposed Civil Rights Act of 1958, the influential Democrat Senator Paul H. Douglas of Illinois quoted a speech by Parker in which he said, "[If liberty is to continue . . .] no man must be prejudiced by reason of race or color or creed in his standing before the law or in his enjoyment of benefits conferred by the State" (*Congressional Record*, 10 February 1958).

65. Pleasants and Burns, *Frank Porter Graham and the 1950 Senate Race in North Carolina*, 6; unsigned, "W. Kerr Scott, 61, Senator Is Dead," *NYT*, 17 April 1958; Christensen, *Paradox of Tar Heel Politics*, 110, 115.

66. The bed frame clue was provided by Richard Goldhurst. The comments on Golden's womanizing are from sources too numerous to list here (and too many speakers desire anonymity). Golden's FBI file includes an interview with an unnamed neighbor in connection with Golden's request for a presidential pardon. The individual noted that Golden was known to pinch women, but he added helpfully that this was probably "his manner of showing affection without intending to show any disrespect" (FBI Bureau file 73-16547 and Charlotte field office file 73432, 28 April 1969).

67. Author's interview with Richard Goldhurst, email, 2006, and with Marc and Ruth Ben-Joseph, telephone, 2006.

68. Kuralt, *Life on the Road*, 250.

69. "At Last! 'Jews In American History'—Their Contribution to the United States Is Told in Print," *CI*, January 1949. The uneven style of the newspaper's capitalization in headlines smoothed out eventually, most often using a single uppercase letter at the start of the phrase. See Frankel, "Bookends: Chronicle of Jews in America," *Charlotte News*, 13 April 1950, and Wittke, "Review of *Jews in American History*." See also related business documents and correspondence with Rywell in UNCC-HG, pt. 1, boxes 7:55, 8:79, and 9:27.

70. Typical of Golden's ability to get others to promote his work, a section of *Jews in American History* discussing Charleston, S.C., was read into the *Congressional Record* by Senator Burnet R. Maybank (D-S.C.), 24 July 1950. That honor was then duly reported by Golden in "Jews in American History in Congressional Record," *CI*, September 1950. Golden and Rywell went their separate ways, but the latter surfaced periodically to suggest reissuing their book, to berate Golden for cheating him out of editorial credit, or to

request publicity for his own work. Among other projects, Rywell produced a newsletter with the brave name of *Hillbilly Israelite*.

71. Sandburg shared the Pulitzer Prize for poetry in 1919 with Margaret Widdemer, author of *Old Road to Paradise*; see http://www.pulitzer.org/awards/1919 (1 November 2014). The line "Sometime they'll give a war . . ." appears in Sandburg's book-length poem about America, "The People, Yes," in *Complete Poems*, 464.

72. "A Day with Carl Sandburg," *CI*, March–April 1956; Golden, *Right Time*, 319–36.

73. Golden, *Right Time*, 319–36; letter to Simmons Fentriss, editorial writer at the *Charlotte Observer*, 23 August 1958, UNCC-HG, pt. 1, box 5:32.

74. Sandburg's "Home Fires" was first published in *Smoke and Steel* in 1920.

75. Author's interview with Richard Goldhurst, telephone, 2001. Paula Sandburg raised prize-winning goats, and her husband often insisted that visiting reporters try a glass of goat milk. Golden was on hand more than once for this ritual and enjoyed watching the polite visitors gamely choke down the stuff.

76. Letter to Simmons Fentriss, editorial writer at the *Charlotte Observer*, 23 August 1958, UNCC-HG, pt. 1, box 5:32.

77. Letter from Sandburg to Allan Nevins, 3 February 1949, in *Letters of Carl Sandburg*, 455.

78. Letter from Sandburg to Ralph McGill, 25 June 1952, in *Letters of Carl Sandburg*, 483. Leonard Ray Teel, "The Brethren," in *Ralph Emerson McGill*, 274–95, describes the friendly circle of newsmen and writers that included Golden, Sandburg, Ashmore, and others. It also chronicles McGill's quiet courting of J. Edgar Hoover over the years, a pastime he almost certainly did not discuss with Golden. See letter from attorney Maurice C. Greenbaum regarding Golden's role as Sandburg executor, 26 February 1974, and Golden's response, 28 February 1974, UNCC-HG, pt. 2, box 41:11. The attorney gently explained that the aging Golden was no longer the best person to serve as executor.

79. Sandburg, "Singing Nigger," in *Cornhuskers*, 108; "The Lawyers Know Too Much," in *Smoke and Steel*, 189; Herbert Mitgang, "Sandburg, Champion of the Powerless," *NYT*, 12 August 1991.

80. Golden, *Carl Sandburg*, 265–66.

81. Brian O'Doherty, "Sandburg Feted at Youthful 85," *NYT*, 8 January 1963.

Chapter 3

1. Golden, "Segregation at Sundown," *Commentary*, November 1955; "A Bit of Philosophy: Thoughts on Communal Living," *CI*, December 1953; Golden, "How's Abe Greenberg," in *For 2 Cents Plain*, 41.

2. Later Golden would sometimes place this event in Christ Episcopal Church when telling the tale, as on his album titled *Harry Golden*, released by Vanguard in 1962. However, the version used here is accurate, as told to reporter Douglas Robinson, "Harry Golden on Things Remembered," *NYT*, 26 February 1968. Golden loved to collect bits and pieces for his church audiences. When a new translation of the Bible came out, he complained, "No one ever asks us . . . we're just the *authors*, that's all" ("The New English Bible," *CI*, March–April 1961).

3. Golden, "The Church Kitchen," in *For 2 Cents Plain*, 295.

4. Whitfield, "Declarations of Independence," 390; Handlin, *Adventure in Freedom*, 256.

5. Sarna, *American Judaism*, 274–75; Sarna, "Cult of Synthesis in American Jewish Culture," 52–79; Rogoff, *Homelands*, 209. Herberg has since been criticized for ignoring nonbelievers, blacks, and other Americans who did not neatly fit into his "triparte scheme," but his work undeniably helped change how mainstream religion and its role in American life was understood.

6. "About 25,000 Readers," *CI*, October 1953. On the microfilm copies that preserve the *Carolina Israelite*, reminders of Golden's far-flung mailing-list strategy fly by occasionally, such as the mailing label clinging to a December 1952 issue addressed to a rabbi in Capetown. Regarding circulation at other times: The *Carolina Israelite* was "taken" by between 2,365 and 3,481 families by 1946–47. The number of those subscriptions that were paid is unknown. The paper's circulation crept up until it was approximately 5,000 in 1952 and 12,161 in 1957, the year before *Only in America* was published. Within two years it would reach 15,000 and was 53,000 to 55,000 in 1960–61. In a year it began to decline, settling around 22,000 until the late 1960s, when it dropped below 8,000. Circulation numbers are drawn from printing bills and a house ad with promotional statistics. See "The Carolina Israelite Printing," *CI*, January–February 1957; "Publisher's Statement," 1 July 1957, UNCC-HG, pt. 2, box 41:8; "Circulation Distribution," *CI*, July–August 1959; summary by Charlotte CPA George Hall in 1956, UNCC-HG, pt. 2, box 41:8; letters to and from J. E. Dowd, general manager of the *Charlotte Observer* and *Charlotte News*, which discuss past and present circulation figures, 10 December 1965, UNCC-HG, pt. 2, box 4:13.

7. Klein, *Bridge Table*, 48–49. According to Klein, ad salesman Ken Robertson talked enough customers into parting with $5 or $10 for ads to keep Golden, printer Henry Stahls, and himself eating for years.

8. "National Conference of Editorial Writers Honors Carolina Israelite," *CI*, April 1952; letter from Maureen Titlow to Maurice Greenbaum, 3 October 1961, in which she notes her start date as Golden's secretary, UNCC-HG, pt. 2, box 31:13; Mamie Hill quote from "A Word to the Wise for the Goniffs," *CI*, January–February 1967.

9. "National Conference of Editorial Writers Honors Carolina Israelite," *CI*, April 1952.

10. Jay Jenkins, "Around the USA: It Glitters and It's Golden, Too," *Nation*, 10 March 1956.

11. Pfeffer, *A. Philip Randolph*, 45–88; "John F. Kennedy," *CI*, January–February 1964; L. M. Meriwether, "The Negro: Half a Man in a White World," *Negro Digest*, October 1965, 4–13. See also the Martin Luther King Jr. Research and Education Institute and the King Papers Project, Stanford, Calif., http://mlk-kpp01.stanford.edu/, and the Martin Luther King Jr. Center for Nonviolent Social Change, Atlanta, Ga., http://www.thekingcenter .org/. The name of the Army Air Corps became Army Air Forces in 1941, then in 1947, the United States Air Force.

12. "Progress for Negroes Reported for 1941," *NYT*, 6 January 1942; unsigned, "Walter White, 61, Dies in Home Here," *NYT*, 22 March 1955; Sosna, *In Search of the Silent South*, 105–6. The *Pittsburgh Courier* is credited with starting the "Double V Campaign" in 1942; see Gilmore, *Defying Dixie*, 364.

13. Martin Meyer, "The Lone Wolf of Politics," *Saturday Evening Post*, 11 July 1964; Arsenault, *Freedom Riders*, 24–28.

14. Golden, "1312 Elizabeth Avenue," in *Ess, Ess*, 278; "Happy Birthday, F.O.R.," *CI*, March–April 1967; "Two Speeches," *CI*, July–August 1962. Accountants' worksheets for Golden's taxes do not show cash or in-kind donations to the NAACP or other black rights groups that came later, yet his files have many pieces of correspondence acknowledging his gifts. His lists of donations do, however, include many Jewish organizations and social programs serving the poor. Most likely the 1959 donation of $100 to the "Alcoholism Information Center," was Tiny's gift. See "Harry L. & Genevieve Golden, Charlotte, N.C., Contributions 1959," UNCC-HG, pt. 2, box 41:27.

15. "Adam Clayton Powell" *CI*, March–April 1963; Golden, "Harlem's Adam Clayton Powell," in *So Long as You're Healthy*, 224.

16. "Was It the Law or a Book?" *CI*, January–February 1959; syndicated column, "Only in America," 22 November 1959.

17. *Jet* ran the shocking photographs of Till's corpse in the edition of 15 September 1955.

18. Roberts and Klibanoff, *Race Beat*, 2–13, 78. In one example the authors note that the *Pittsburgh Courier* hit a circulation high of 358,000 in 1948 and was down by half in 1955; see Crow, Escott, and Hatley, *History of African Americans in North Carolina*, 131.

19. Author's interview with Richard Goldhurst, email, 2001; Enoc P. Waters Jr., "Adventures in Race Relations," *Chicago Defender*, 15 April 1957, 10. The columnist points out that Golden "has noted as no one else has, that racial segregation is never practiced as long as people stand up." Golden's syndicated column appeared in the *Chicago Daily Defender* for the first time on 9 December 1963. The subject was the death of President Kennedy.

20. Roberts and Klibanoff, *Race Beat*, 34; McAlpin reference in entry for John H. Sengstacke, a prominent black newspaper publisher, in Vaughn, *Encyclopedia of American Journalism*, 478.

21. Golden, "Long Life to Harry Truman," in *Ess, Ess*, 239–41; "Eleanor Roosevelt and Gladys Tillett," *CI*, March–April 1961; Golden, "Winner by a Mule," in *So What Else Is New?* 23. The taxi driver story appeared in many places in Golden's work, including "The Poverty Stalemate," in *So Long as You're Healthy*, 160, and in Golden's column in the *Nation*, 20 May 1968.

22. McCullough, "Unexpected Harry Truman," 40.

23. The 21 July 1947 Truman diary entry appears on the Harry S. Truman Library and Museum website: http://www.trumanlibrary.org/diary/transcript.htm (1 November 2014).

24. Truman speech, 29 June 1947, at convention of NAACP, americanrhetoric.com/speeches/harrystrumannaacp.htm (1 November 2014); Branch, *Parting the Waters*, 66.

25. Friedman, with Binzen, *What Went Wrong?* 147–48. Text of *To Secure These Rights* appears on the Harry S. Truman Library and Museum website, http://trumanlibrary.org/civilrights/srights1.htm (1 November 2014). On distribution and impact of *To Secure These Rights*, see Sullivan, *Lift Every Voice*, 353.

26. *To Secure These Rights*, chap. 1, http://trumanlibrary.org/civilrights/srights1.htm (1 November 2014).

27. Frick's quote appears in ibid., chap. 2. More often remembered by dedicated baseball fans is the colorful and crude retort by Dodgers manager Leo Durocher, who let his players know, beyond any doubt, that they would play alongside Robinson or not play at all. See Simons, *Cooperstown Symposium*, 38.

28. Ashmore, *Hearts and Minds*, 178; Sullivan, *Lift Every Voice*, 395. It took five years for the desegregation of the military to be "virtually complete." The navy, air force, and some army units went first, with the rest of the army following suit.

29. Branch, *Parting the Waters*, 13.

30. *To Secure These Rights*, chap. 1, http://trumanlibrary.org/civilrights/srights1.htm (1 November 2014). On lynching, see Giddings, *Ida*; White, *Rope and Faggot*; Dray, *At the Hands of Persons Unknown*; and Raper, *Tragedy of Lynching*.

31. White, *Rope and Faggot*, 9; Myrdal, with Sterner and Rose, *American Dilemma*, 560–69. Mencken wrote with great passion about lynching and the failure to prevent it. See Marion Elizabeth Rodgers, *H. L. Mencken: Courage in a Time of Lynching*, on the website of the Nieman Foundation for Journalism at Harvard, http://www.nieman.harvard.edu/reports/article/100441/HL-Mencken-Courage-in-a-Time-of-Lynching.aspx (1 November 2014).

32. "Lynching: The American Fever," *CI*, June–July 1967.

33. Golden, "Lynching in America," in *So Long as You're Healthy*, 81–93.

34. Cook, *Eleanor Roosevelt*, 2:178–81. The story about Truman's reaction is recorded in many accounts, with slight variations in his quote. This is cited from Wilkins and Mathews, *Standing Fast*, 193.

35. Golden, *Mr. Kennedy and the Negroes*, 65. Even the moderate and liberal journalists of Golden's acquaintance often held back on this issue. Editor Ralph McGill believed the matter should be kept at the state level. He pointed to the decline in lynchings as progress and proof that federal intervention wasn't necessary. He argued that the violence was carried out by a small number of thugs and decried by most southerners. McGill declined Truman's request to serve on the Commission on Civil Rights. See Teel, *Ralph Emerson McGill*, 234–36. It was not until 2005 that the U.S. Senate apologized for its failure to pass an antilynching law despite the requests of seven presidents—and even then the gesture was not unanimously supported by the members of the Senate. See Avis Thomas-Lester, "A Senate Apology for History on Lynching," *Washington Post*, 14 June 2005.

36. "Eisenhower in Columbia, S.C." *CI*, September 1954. Eisenhower told the audience that having a mother from Virginia and being born in Texas himself allowed him to be one of the privileged number who could "stand up when they play Dixie." This bit of history was buried until Bruce H. Kalk found it for *Origins of the Southern Strategy*, 7.

37. "Shakespeare's 400th Anniversary" *CI*, March–April 1964.

38. Golden, *Carl Sandburg*, 107; letter from Roosevelt to Golden, 29 July 1960, UNCC-HG, pt. 2, box 13:37. Stevenson's remarks appear in Theroux, *Book of Eulogies*, 103.

39. Author's interview with Newton Minow, email, 2009; letter from Stevenson, 10 January 1955, UNCC-HG, pt. 2, box 15:1.

40. "Adlai E. Stevenson," *CI*, July–August 1965.

41. Golden, "Are Ghost Writers Necessary?" in *Enjoy, Enjoy!* 261–62; "The Story of the Ghost-Writer, *CI*, November–December 1956; Golden, *Right Time*, 275.

42. "Adlai E. Stevenson," *CI*, July–August 1965. Golden was probably tapped for help during Stevenson's 1956 campaign at the urging of Harry Ashmore. The latter had left newspaper work for a year to work for Stevenson. See Roberts and Klibanoff, *Race Beat*, 145.

43. Martin, *Adlai Stevenson of Illinois*, 49, 74–75, 78.

44. Ibid., 105, 482. In 1964 Golden dedicated his book *So What Else Is New?* to Stevenson and later remembered when the two happily celebrated a two-man Passover Seder at the former's home in Illinois in 1966; see "Passover with Adlai Stevenson," *CI*, January–February 1966. Stevenson, unlike most politicians who corresponded with Golden, did not immediately move to a first-name basis, sticking to "Mr. Golden" for some years. See early letter to Golden, 10 January 1955, UNCC-HG, pt. 2, box 15:1. Goodwin on Stevenson is in Theroux, *Book of Eulogies*, 83.

45. "KKK," *CI*, November 1951; speech by King to Montgomery Improvement Association (MIA) Mass Meeting at Holt Street Baptist Church, Montgomery, Alabama, 5 December 1955. For transcripts and audio of the speech, see also the Martin Luther King Jr. Research and Education Institute and the King Papers Project, Stanford, Calif., http://mlk-kpp01.stanford.edu/, and the Martin Luther King Jr. Center for Nonviolent Social Change, Atlanta, Ga., http://www.thekingcenter.org/.

46. Goldhurst, "Locating the Deity," 202; Golden, "For Anonymous Callers," in *Best of Harry Golden*, 74; Golden, "P. D. East," in *So Long as You're Healthy*, 239; East, *Magnolia Jungle*, 181; author's interviews with Anita Stewart Brown, 2000, and Walter Klein, email, 2011. Golden wrote once that he was about to celebrate his tenth anniversary of "taking the telephone off the hook every night before going to bed, an act which I have had to do as automatically as most people put out the cat" (letter to the editor, *Commentary*, April 1964). A native of Mississippi, East was an extraordinary character, a brave misfit with a gift for writing darkly hilarious material. He, like Golden, believed the way to eradicate segregation and racism was to get everyone laughing at the haters. He risked his life to put out his newspaper, *The Petal Paper*, with lines such as "We've lived for years off the labor of the Negro and now we're just plain scared out of our wits. Some of us might have to go to work for a living. Some of us right now don't know where our next mint julep is coming from" ("Letter to 'friends,' " 21 October 1962, P. D. East Collection, Manuscripts Collection of the University of Southern Mississippi Libraries Digital Collection, no. M324, http://www.lib.usm.edu/legacy/archives/m324.htm [1 November 2014]).

47. Bayley, *Joe McCarthy and the Press,* 17, 20–25, 51. Within a day or two of the Wheeling speech, McCarthy changed the number of Communists on his list—205, 207, and 57 were variously cited in news stories quoting him.

48. "Senator McCarthy Uses an Old Tammany Trick," *CI*, October 1951; "Senator McCarthy Has Won a Great Victory—No More 'Letters to the Editor,' " *CI*, June 1951.

49. Author's interview with Richard Goldhurst, email, 2006; financial aid application for care of Peter Goldhurst, State of New York Department of Mental Hygiene, 1955–56, UNCC-HG, pt. 1, box 6:35.

50. Letter from Tiny, 3 June 1959, UNCC-HG, pt. 2, box 42:18; author's interviews with Richard Goldhurst, 2001, and email, 2012.

51. Claiborne, *"Charlotte Observer,"* 221. Golden's second son used the name "Harry Golden Jr." when he came to Charlotte, making it official when he registered for the

military draft at age eighteen. See US WWII Draft Registration Card, Serial No. 1054, Order No. 14440, Records of the Selective Service System, 1926–1975, National Archives, Atlanta, Ga.

52. Author's interview with Richard Goldhurst, email, 2011. Richard Goldhurst enlisted in the army at age eighteen on 12 March 1945. See World War II Army Enlistment Records, National Archives, College Park, Md. See also Goldhurst's essay "Our Father Who Art in Charlotte," *CI*, January–February 1967. (This issue of the paper was put out by Goldhurst and other *CI* staff while Golden was ill.) Goldhurst borrowed his mother's irreverent dinner-table prayer for this headline.

53. Peters, *Tilting at Windmills*, 49–54; Goldhurst, "Locating the Deity," 107–8; author's interview with Norma Leveton, 2006.

54. Golden and Goldhurst, "Religion, Mixed Marriage, and Fears among the Jews of the South," in *Our Southern Landsman*, 100.

55. Golden, "From the American Scene: 'Hebrew-Christian' Evangelist: Southern Style," *Commentary*, December 1950; author's interviews with Walter Klein in Charlotte, 2000; with Mark Bernstein, telephone, 2006; and with Leona Lefkowitz, Charlotte, 2001, and email, 2001. The subject of Jewish communities in the South and in Charlotte was discussed at length with Lefkowitz, among others cited in these notes. Lefkowitz, then eighty-two, had lived for many years in Shreveport, Louisiana, where her husband, Rabbi David Lefkowitz, served a Reform congregation. She moved to Charlotte after his death.

56. Golden, "From the American Scene: 'Hebrew-Christian' Evangelist: Southern Style," *Commentary*, December 1950.

57. Author's interview with Mark Bernstein, telephone, 2006; Rogoff, "Harry Golden, New Yorker," 44; Rogoff, *Down Home*, Kindle location 3545.

58. Golden, "On the Horizon: A Son of the South, and Some Daughters," *Commentary*, October 1951.

59. Ibid.

60. Golden, "A Pulpit in the South," *Commentary*, December 1953.

61. Speizman's letter appeared in *Commentary*, March 1954. The letter was edited for publication; for the original, see 23 December 1953, UNCC-HG, pt. 1, box 9:28. Leonard Rogoff notes occasions when Speizman wrote or spoke out to make clear that Golden was not representing the Jewish community. One such occasion was in 1969, when Golden wrote a letter to the *Charlotte Observer* in which he took a country club to task for not allowing Jews and blacks to join. Speizman then wrote a letter to the president of the club using the "Harry Golden does not speak for me," line. See Rogoff, "Harry Golden, New Yorker," 44.

62. "What I've Done for the Jews of the South," *CI*, January 1955; "It's Wonderful to Be a Gentile," *CI*, March–April 1961.

63. Evans, *Provincials*, 38; Cash, *Mind of the South*, 333–34; Goldstein, "'Now Is the Time to Show Your True Colors,'" 150. Dixon's quote appeared in an unsigned article about his speech to a group of booksellers, "The Negro a Menace," *NYT*, 9 June 1903.

64. Whitfield, "'Golden' Era of Civil Rights"; Friedman, with Binzen, *What Went Wrong?* 22; Olmsted, *Journey in the Seaboard Slave States*, 440, http://docsouth.unc.edu/nc/olmsted/olmsted.html#p439 (1 November 2014). One of the very few influential voices speaking out against the bigotry against Jews was North Carolinian Zebulon B. Vance, a

Charlotte attorney respected for his measured leadership as governor during and after the war. In 1874 Vance began traveling and delivering a speech of his own writing, "A Scattered Nation," a dramatic sermon tracing the Judaic roots of Christianity, extolling the Jewish people, and calling for present-day tolerance. See Adler, "Zebulon B. Vance and the 'Scattered Nation,' " 362.

65. Diner, "Entering the Mainstream," 104; Sorin, *Tradition Transformed*, 23. Other Jewish peddlers and merchants who made retail history were Adam Gimbel, Benjamin Bloomingdale, Edward Filene, Benjamin Altman, and the Rosenwald and Straus families behind Sears and Macy's.

66. Golden, *Forgotten Pioneer*, 16–17. Golden continued, "Theodore Roosevelt, John Hay, Sinclair Lewis, F. Scott Fitzgerald, Henry Adams, Brooks Adams, and Henry James expressed contempt for the businessman, his energies, and his values." See also Rogoff, "Harry Golden, New Yorker," 57.

67. Diner, "Entering the Mainstream," 99.

68. Golden, "A Book on the Schwartzes," in *Enjoy, Enjoy!* 197–98.

69. Webb, "Tangled Web," 193; "Jewish Store in the Negro Ghetto," *CI*, September–October 1963.

70. Dollinger, *Quest for Inclusion*, 166; Greene, *Temple Bombing*, 40.

71. Webb, "Tangled Web," 196; letter from I. H. Madilia, Federation of Jewish Charities, Charlotte, to "Gentlemen" of the American Jewish Congress, 7 May 1953, UNCC-HG, pt. 1, box 7:6; letter from David Petegorsky, Executive Director, American Jewish Congress, 21 January 1954, UNCC-HG, pt. 1, box 4:15; Speizman, *Jews of Charlotte*, 90; Rogoff, *Down Home*, Kindle location 3403.

72. Golden, "Jew and Gentile in the New South: Segregation at Sundown," *Commentary*, November 1955.

73. Golden's reprint was titled "Unease in Dixie: Caught in the Middle," UNCC-HG, pt. 2, box 27:8–9. *Midstream*, Summer-Autumn 1956, 16–22, published the piece under "Negro and Jew—Encounter in America" and ran it with articles by Leslie A. Fiedler and Albert Vorspan.

74. Golden, "The Negro and Jew in Dixie," in *Only in America*, 139. Golden said in his autobiography that there were 16,000 subscribers at this point. The number of paid subscribers was closer to 11,000. Based on printing invoices from the time, it appears likely that the 16,000 figure is close to the total number of papers actually printed, not the number of subscribers. See Golden, *Right Time*, 310.

75. Webb, "Tangled Web," 197.

76. Anyone reading Golden's essays today would do well to have as a companion volume Bauman and Kalin's *Quiet Voices*, which includes Janice Rothschild Blumberg's piece on her late husband. The exceptions to his indictments about boat-rockers are writ large. The introduction to this collection, written by coeditor Mark K. Bauman, is a cogent account of the southern rabbinical response to race issues. One of the many telling and painful recollections in Blumberg's essay is the account of the evening King and his wife, Coretta Scott King, came to dinner. Unfamiliar with the neighborhood, the Kings stopped to ask a neighbor for directions to the Rothschild home. To avoid spreading the word that the Rothschilds were entertaining a black couple, Mrs. King, rather than her husband, went to the door to ask so that residents would

assume she was on her way to serve at a white family's dinner party. See also Greene, *Temple Bombing*, 255–57.

77. Krause, "Rabbis and Negro Rights in the South," 40–42.

78. Rogoff, *Homelands*, 225–26; Rogoff, *Down Home*, Kindle location 3420. In *Down Home*, Rogoff cites several other examples of southern rabbis who spoke up against racism; see Kindle location 3414–39.

79. Webb, *Fight against Fear*, 55–64; Golden, "A Rabbi in Montgomery," *Congress Bi-Weekly*, May 1957. A letter from Mantinband said, "How I wish we could sit down over twenty cups of tea and have a good long schmoos [*sic*]. Of course we could put a stick in the tea" (1 September 1963, UNCC-HG, pt. 2, box 10:52).

80. Webb, *Fight against Fear*, 55–64; "The Dynamiting and Attempted Dynamiting of Southern Synagogues and Temples," *CI*, January–February 1958.

81. Golden, *Right Time*, 310–11.

82. On Engel, see UNCC-HG, pt. 1, box 4:14, and pt. 2, box 5:52. On Kaplan, see pt. 1, box 7:15–16, and pt. 2, boxes 9:14–16, and 61:9. Golden's tax records reveal that some loans made to the *Carolina Israelite* during this period were carried through at least 1968 and perhaps were never paid. See UNCC-HG, pt. 2, box 41:8, and unsigned, "Kivie Kaplan Reveals Why He Fights Racism," *The Afro-American*, 8 April 1972. See also biographical sketch of Kaplan in the digital finding aid for his papers at the American Jewish Archives, http://americanjewisharchives.org/collections/ms0026/ (1 January 2015), and Whitfield, "'Golden' Era of Civil Rights," 34.

83. Branch, *Pillar of Fire*, 31. The brilliant Warsaw-born Heschel was a compelling teacher, writer, and speaker and would figure prominently in the movement. Heschel and King met on 14 January 1963 at the National Conference on Religion and Race in Chicago, and their passionate views of hate and racism as affronts to God revealed their common ground, as did their ability to move listeners in ways that few speakers could. In 1965, a photograph of the white-bearded rabbi walking abreast with King; Ralph Bunche, undersecretary of the United Nations; and the Reverend Fred Shuttlesworth at a march in Selma was reprinted around the world.

84. Konvitz, "Jews and Civil Rights," 270, 272–75.

85. Sarna, *American Judaism*, 251.

86. Svonkin, *Jews against Prejudice*, 12–13, 22; Weiss, "Long-Distance Runners of the Civil Rights Movement," 129–38; Dollinger, *Quest for Inclusion*, 13; Sarna, *American Judaism*, 308; Friedman, with Binzen, *What Went Wrong?* 45, 56–57, 106. Friedman described this early connection as "upper-class German Jews and WASP reformers inspired by the philanthropic and political ideals of the Progressive Era and a black group led by W. E. B. Du Bois."

87. Friedman also offered a pithy summarizing of historians' revisionist views: "Adolph L. Reed Jr. has argued that the push for civil rights was undertaken to mobilize black support to advance a Jewish agenda. David Levering Lewis declared that the formation of the NAACP and other racial justice efforts . . . was an effort by a German-Jewish elite to curry favor with upper-class liberal WASPs as well as to fight anti-Semitism by remote control" (*What Went Wrong?* 146).

88. Svonkin, *Jews against Prejudice*, 192–93; Konvitz, "Jews and Civil Rights," 285. Translations vary, but the essence of the commandment, from Leviticus 19:16, is that a

Jew is not to stand idly by if someone's life is in danger or to profit by the blood of one's neighbor.

89. Golden spoke and wrote very often about this aspect of Jewish-black relations, most often in a way that seemed curt compared with his usual expansive style. In interviews and speeches, it was often a point at which he suddenly became deadly serious. Joseph Wershba noted one such occasion during an interview at Golden's home. Golden said, "I give it to you straight. The fight for the black man is a fight for the Jews' own security" ("A Post Portrait: Harry Golden," *New York Post Daily Magazine*, first of five parts, 30 January 1961; Golden's version quoted here is from "Anti-Semitism," in *Enjoy, Enjoy!* 217).

Chapter 4

1. Golden, *Right Time*, 304; Douglas, *Reading, Writing, and Race*, 40–41, 70–71.

2. Golden, *Right Time*, 304.

3. Jay Walz, "Negroes Hold Rally on Rights in Capital," *NYT*, 17 May 1957, 1. The remark came in a speech King made at a Prayer Pilgrimage for Freedom in Washington. The speech was printed in the *Congressional Record* 103 (28 May 1957): 7822–24. Full text of the speech was reprinted in the *New York Times* on 28 August 1983. See also the Martin Luther King Jr. Research and Education Institute and the King Papers Project, Stanford, Calif., http://mlk-kpp01.stanford.edu/, and the Martin Luther King Jr. Center for Nonviolent Social Change, Atlanta, Ga., http://www.thekingcenter.org/.

4. Golden, *Right Time*, 309; Douglas, *Reading, Writing, and Race*, 32–39, 42–46.

5. Asch, *Senator and the Sharecropper*, 206.

6. Unsigned editorial, "Thurgood Marshall," *NYT*, 5 March 2011, 9.

7. Along with the seventeen southern and border states were Arizona, Kansas, New Mexico, and Wyoming, in which local districts could choose to segregate. See Patterson, Brown v. Board of Education, xiv–xvi; Kluger, *Simple Justice*, 326–28; Ravitch, *Troubled Crusade*, 12; Balkin, *What* Brown v. Board of Education *Should Have Said*, 31.

8. Diner, *Jews of the United States*, 267; Patterson, Brown v. Board of Education, 44–45.

9. Motley, *Equal Justice under Law*, 106, 108. Motley was a member of the Legal Defense Fund's team of lawyers that worked on *Brown*. She went on to be the first black woman elected to New York's state senate in 1964 and the first to serve as a federal judge in 1966. See Douglas Martin, "Constance Baker Motley, Civil Rights Trailblazer, Dies at 84," *NYT*, 29 September 2005.

10. Webb, "Closing Ranks," 467; Diner, *Jews of the United States*, 267.

11. Gilmore, *Defying Dixie*, 10.

12. "The South Has Exported Its Brains," *CI*, November–December 1963; "Senator Russell's Proposal," *CI*, March–April 1964; "The South's Final Breakthrough," *CI*, May–June 1965.

13. Lemann, *Promised Land*, 6; Wilkerson, *Warmth of Other Suns*, 9; Kimberly Marlowe Hartnett, review of *The Warmth of Other Suns*, *Seattle Times*, 18 September 2010.

14. Teel, *Ralph Emerson McGill*, 259; Roberts and Klibanoff, *Race Beat*, 48–49, 59.

15. Roberts and Klibanoff, *Race Beat*, 50, 57–60.

16. Ashmore, *Epitaph for Dixie*, 162, 203–4, 215; Roberts and Klibanoff, *Race Beat*, 59.

17. Roberts and Klibanoff, *Race Beat*, 57–60.

18. Horowitz, *Consuming Pleasures*, 273.

19. "The Interesting James Jackson Kilpatrick," *CI*, November–December 1962; Elaine Woo, "James J. Kilpatrick Dies at 89; Newspaper Columnist and Arbiter of Language," *Los Angeles Times*, 17 August 2010.

20. Golden, "Rejoicing in Richmond," in *You're Entitle'*, 112; letter from Cecil Prince, 19 May 1958, UNCC-HG, pt. 1, box 8:25; letter from Kilpatrick, date unknown, UNCC-HG, pt. 2, box 9:41; "Mr. Sulzberger, Mr. Howard, Mr. Bingham, Mr. Hills, Mr. Bryan, Mr. Kilpatrick," *CI*, March–April 1959. Several correspondents of Golden's expressed the same sentiment over the years. As historian Leonard Rogoff quoted from a 1978 *Charlotte Observer* article on Golden, "Charlie Cannon, the textile magnate, wrote to him, 'Dear Golden: Enclosed is $3 for renewal. Half your paper stinks, but the other half gives us all lots of pleasure' " (Rogoff, "Harry Golden, New Yorker," 48). Kilpatrick softened on the issue of desegregation over the years, but when he met and became friends with Golden, he was, in his own words, "ten miles to the right of Ivan the Terrible." Kilpatrick went on to become a well-known columnist and commentator on *60 Minutes*, as well as the author of several books. See Elaine Woo, "James J. Kilpatrick Dies at 89; Newspaper Columnist and Arbiter of Language," *Los Angeles Times*, 17 August 2010.

21. Golden, *Right Time*, 305–6.

22. Webb, *Rabble Rousers*, 132, 103–4. Webb was discussing John G. Crommelin, an Alabama racist and anti-Semite who ran for public office in the 1960s on a promise to "Safeguard the White Race and the Nation's Security." In 2003 when Crommelin was honored posthumously for his half-century of military service, a protest erupted over whether his bigoted past should negate his heroism.

23. Kluger, *Simple Justice*, 745–47; "Did the Governors of the South Guess Wrong?" *CI*, September–October 1955, 11.

24. Golden wrote frequently about the misuse of the term "social equality," including an essay titled with that phrase in *For 2 Cents Plain*, 277.

25. Letter from Harry S. Jones, North Carolina Council on Human Relations, with prospective membership list for Charlotte chapter, 25 August 1955, UNCC-HG, pt. 1, boxes 5:33 and 8:24; Douglas, *Reading, Writing, and Race*, 61–62.

26. Golden, *Right Time*, 295–96.

27. Letter to R. F. Leinbach, M.D., 8 February 1955, and Leinbach letter to Dr. O. Ross, 8 February 1955, UNCC-HG, pt. 1, box 8:46; "The Philosophy Club of Charlotte," *CI*, May–June 1963.

28. "The Philosophy Club of Charlotte," *CI*, May–June 1963.

29. Douglas, *Reading, Writing, and Race*, 79; author's interview with Anita Stewart Brown, 2000, and her obituary notice in the *Charlotte Observer*, 24 October 2003; author's interview with Richard Goldhurst, 2000, and email, 2011. Goldhurst described his father's relationship with Marion Cannon as long-standing. Cannon backed many civil rights causes, served as a trustee of Johnson C. Smith University, and financed lawsuits challenging school segregation.

30. Golden's partnership with Brown lasted until the end of his life—and beyond. Letters to Golden's heirs from the attorney handling his estate noted that Brown wanted to pay for the monument to be placed on his grave. See letter from Sol Levine, 25 August 1982, UNCC-HG, pt. 2, box 42:9.

31. Ibid.

32. Author's interview with Jonathan Wallas, son of David and Beatrice Wallas, telephone, 2011.

33. Letter from David Wallas, 31 July 1951, UNCC-HG, pt. 2, box 16:20–23. Angela Bickham of Charlotte provided research assistance with these materials.

34. Author's interviews with Dan Locklair, nephew of the late Wriston Locklair, telephone and email, 2011, 2012.

35. Letter to Locklair, c/o the County Jail, Charlotte, 21 May 1955, UNCC-HG, pt. 1, box 7:41; Golden, *Right Time*, 298.

36. Letter to Alfred A. Gross, 31 July 1956, UNCC-HG, pt. 1, box 6:45; letter to Dr. C. H. Patrick, Raleigh, N.C., 16 January 1956, UNCC-HG, pt. 1, box 7:41. Golden copied Locklair on this letter, which described the job he was offering to ensure parole.

37. Letter from Locklair, 12 August 1955; "Report—as of April 14, 1956—Wriston Locklair"; and letter from Locklair, 23 August 1956, all in UNCC-HG, pt. 1, box 7:41; unsigned obituary, "Wriston Locklair, 59, Is Dead; Led Juilliard Public Relations," *NYT*, 5 March 1984. Golden gave other parolees help in the form of money, work, and supportive letters. One of the first was labor organizer Fred Beal of the National Textile Workers Union in the early 1940s. See Golden, "Revelations of a Strike," in *Long Live Columbus*, 180.

38. Letter to Littlejohn, 15 January 1956, UNCC-HG, pt. 1, box 7:41.

39. Letter from Locklair, 5 February 1959, UNCC-HG, pt. 1, box 7:41; letter from Locklair, 5 September 1961, UNCC-HG, pt. 1, box 7:41.

40. Golden, "Mary, Mary Quite Contrary," in *Ess Ess*, 123.

41. "The Sins of Oscar Wilde," *CI*, February 1955; "What to Do about Homosexuality," *CI*, July–August 1960; "Tea and Sympathy," *CI*, September–October 1956.

42. Unsigned editorial, "Rosa Parks, Zeitgeist Warrior," *NYT*, 1 September 1994.

43. Rosellen Brown, "Book Review: The Wellborn Maverick: The Autobiography of Virginia Foster Durr," *NYT*, 22 December 1985.

44. Arsenault, *Freedom Riders*, 215. Durr's comments about Golden came in letters to close friend Clark Forman, a founder of the Southern Conference for Human Welfare, in 1959, and writer Jessica Mitford, also a close friend, in 1961. See *Freedom Writer: Virginia Foster Durr*, 194, 241.

45. Branch, *Parting the Waters*, 128–42

46. King's speech appears in Gottheimer, *Ripples of Hope*, 210–15. See also the Martin Luther King Jr. Research and Education Institute and the King Papers Project, Stanford, Calif., http://mlk-kpp01.stanford.edu/, and the Martin Luther King Jr. Center for Nonviolent Social Change, Atlanta, Ga., http://www.thekingcenter.org/.

47. Roberts and Klibanoff, *Race Beat*, 119–25; "Segregation on the Busses," *CI*, May 1954; Golden, *Right Time*, 238–39; Branch, *Parting the Waters*, 144.

48. Highlander Research and Education Center website, http://highlandercenter.org/ (1 November 2014).

49. Moyers, "Adventures of a Radical Hillbilly"; Egerton, *Speak Now against the Day*, 78.

50. Charron and Cline, " 'I Train the People to Do Their Own Talking,' " 31. The authors drew on an oral history interview of Clark by Jacquelyn Dowd Hall. See interview with

Clark, 25 July 1976, Interview G-0016, Southern Oral History Program Collection (#4007), http://docsouth.unc.edu/sohp/G-0016/menu.html (1 November 2014).

51. Clark's handwritten letter on Citizenship Education Program letterhead, 6 January 1964, and draft of Golden's foreword for the book, UNCC-HG, pt. 2, box 4:38. Remark about "slave narratives" from Charron, *Freedom's Teacher*, n. 86 for pp. 286–94. The Yiddish expression is more often spelled *gornisht helfen* and can also translate as "it's beyond help."

52. Schmidt-Pirro and McCurdy, "Employing Music in the Cause of Social Justice."

53. "A Ride with Eleanor Roosevelt," *CI*, May–June 1964; letter from Kirkpatrick, 2 June 1958; Golden's answer, 9 June 1958; and Golden's draft telegram to Oscar Cohen at Anti-Defamation League, 6 June 1958, all in UNCC-HG, pt. 2, 7:38–39; "I Shall Never Do This Again," *CI*, May–June 1956.

54. Popham left the *New York Times* and moved to the top editor's job at the *Chattanooga Times* (owned by the Times company until 1999) the same year of this Highlander gathering. See Douglas Martin, "John Popham, 89, Dies; Journalist Was Noted for Perceptive Coverage of South," *NYT*, 14 December 1999. Popham headed the team that put together "A Report on the South," the 50,000-word package of articles examining how southern states were dealing with the race issue after *Brown*. The articles ran 13 March 1956. See Roberts and Klibanoff, *Race Beat*, 109–12, and Salisbury, *Without Fear or Favor*, 352–63. Horton letters about the visit: 28 March 1959, 2 May 1959, 29 May 1958; letter from Golden about flight plans, 12 June 1958, all in UNCC-HG, pt. 2, 7:38. Horton clearly knew Golden quite well. When describing the schedule for the Highlander workshop, he wrote in the 28 March 1959 letter, "I took the liberty of suggesting that you, being an old timer and a rather independent cuss, might prefer to make your contributions in your own way. . . . Consequently you will notice on page 2 that you are scheduled to speak on 'The Golden Rules.' This should give you plenty of leeway."

55. Golden, "The 'Eleanor Club,'" in *So What Else Is New?* 234; letter to Horton, 12 June 1958, and undated notes marked "Eleanor Roosevelt and I," pt. 2, 7:38–39; John N. Popham, "Leaders Defend School in South," *NYT*, 22 December 1957; Roosevelt, *My Day*, 17 June 1958, Eleanor Roosevelt Papers Project, George Washington University, http://www.gwu.edu/~erpapers/myday/displaydoc.cfm?_y=1958&_f=md004147 (1 November 2014). The FBI noted in a report on Highlander Folk School that Eleanor Roosevelt had visited and made financial contributions to the school in 1942; see FBI Bureau file 61–7511, letter to Director J. Edgar Hoover from Herbert K. Moss, special agent in charge, Louisville, Ky., 12 February 1943. The report also includes an unsigned clipping headlined, "Mrs. Roosevelt Presents $100 to Folk School," *Chattanooga News-Free Press*, 2 February 1942.

56. "Highlander Reports, October 1, 1957–September 30, 1958," UNCC-HG, pt. 2, 7:38.

57. The Highlander Research and Education Center continues in New Market, Tenn.

58. Golden, "Leaderless Decency," *Nation*, 29 August 1958, 84–87. This column is misdated in some database references.

59. Golden, *Mr. Kennedy and the Negroes*, 82.

60. "Negro Mortality in North Carolina," *CI*, September–October 1953; "Negro Health in the South," *CI*, January–February 1960; "Tuberculosis and the Negro," *CI*, January–February 1961; Singh and Yu, "Infant Mortality in the United States."

61. "We'll Solve This Our Own Way" *CI*, May–June 1962. A half-century later when the American Medical Association finally issued an apology for abetting discrimination against black physicians, the history of banning African American doctors from professional groups was still not widely known. Writing for the AMA's journal in 2008, Charlotte cardiologist Yele Aluko described the same marginalization of black doctors that Golden had decried. Aluko added that until the late 1990s, virtually no referrals took place between white and black physicians in Charlotte, further hampering the opportunities of African American medical providers. See Aluko, "American Medical Association Apologizes for Racism in Medicine," 1246–47.

62. "The Next Sit-in Protest," *CI*, March–April 1961. King encouraged student activists to form their own arm of the Southern Christian Leadership Committee. But the leadership of the NAACP worried about too much competition between the groups, and a desire for autonomy led the students, black and white, to form SNCC (usually called "snick") on 15 April 1960 at Shaw University in Raleigh, N.C. See Kotz, *Judgment Days*, 50–51.

63. "Tuberculosis and The Negro," *CI*, January–February 1961; Frank L. Stanley, "Being Frank," *Chicago Defender*, 30 April 1960.

64. The original *Winston-Salem Journal* series and subsequent developments are at http://www.journalnow.com/specialreports/againsttheirwill and http://www.doa .nc.gov/ncjsvf (1 November 2014).

65. Ibid.

66. "The Sterilizing Legislators" *CI*, July–August 1962. Historian Johanna Schoen, who shared her years of research on the subject with the *Winston-Salem Journal* reporters, places the North Carolina program into a larger context in *Choice and Coercion*. Not surprisingly, as discussion on the series spread in ever-widening media circles, it often focused on the Nazi-like eugenics aspect and assumed all the women were sterilized against their will, when in fact some elected to control the size of their families. But as Schoen pointed out, the question of women's reproductive rights, specifically the rights of poor women, is less examined. "I would suggest that the public discussion . . . centered on race at the expense of reproductive rights because a great many people in this country continue to believe that women should not have children while they are receiving public assistance" (Kindle location 3374).

67. Some eighty African American students had applied for the right to attend the white school; interviews with school officials and changes of heart winnowed the group to Melba Pattillo, Ernest Green, Elizabeth Eckford, Jefferson Thomas, Terrence Roberts, Carlotta Walls, Minnijean Brown, Gloria Ray, and Thelma Mothershed. See "Land of (Un)Equal Opportunity: Documenting the Civil Rights Struggle in Arkansas," University of Arkansas Digital Collection, http://scipio.uark.edu/cdm4/index_Civilrights.php? CISOROOT=/Civilrights (1 November 2014).

68. The Eckford photo and other powerful images from the civil rights movement were taken by Will Counts, then a staff photographer for the *Arkansas Gazette* and the *Arkansas-Democrat*.

69. See Beals, *Warriors Don't Cry*.

70. Harry Ashmore, "Reflections in a Hurricane's Eye," *Arkansas Gazette*, 9 September 1957; Webb, *Fight against Fear*, 155. Webb was referencing Golden's 1956 piece "Unease in Dixie/Negro and Jew—Encounter in America," in *Midstream*, Summer–Autumn 1956,

16–22. It was followed the next year by "A Rabbi in Montgomery," *Congress Bi-Weekly*, May 1957, on the dismissal of Rabbi Seymour Atlas in Montgomery, which Golden claimed was the result of the rabbi's outspoken views on desegregation.

71. Unsigned, "Upstart Printer," *Time*, 24 December 1945.

72. As circulation grew, Golden's earlier mail-fraud charges did not scare him away from creative accounting when reporting to the U.S. Postal Service. He erred on both ends: low-balling if it got him better postage rates and printing estimates, exaggerating to make the paper appear more successful. A 14,000-circulation figure cited by Sandburg in the foreword of *Only in America* was supplied by Golden, but the actual number was closer to 12,000. "Why They Don't Hate Harry," a profile of Golden by John Kobler in the *Saturday Evening Post*, 27 September 1958, 125, used the 14,000 figure as well and listed Golden's net profit on the paper at $8,000 a year, with another couple of thousand in speaking fees. The income figure was accurate, or close to it. Golden's tax return for 1957 listed his earnings at $11,766. See UNCC-HG, pt. 2, box 41:8

73. Unsigned, "The Press: Golden Rule," *Time*, April 1, 1957.

74. Golden, *Right Time*, 337–38; letter from Zevin, 12 June 1957, UNCC-HG, pt. 2, box 35:33–36.

75. Targ, *Indecent Pleasures*, 278, 280. William Grimes, "Eleanor Friede, 87, Is Dead," *NYT*, 25 July 2008. Targ praised Friede lavishly, and many echoed his sentiments. Friede's ability to turn on a dime and handle just about anything was tested often during her years working with Golden.

76. Golden, *Right Time*, 339; Targ, *Indecent Pleasures*, 277–81. Dollar valuation here and throughout the book is calculated using the CPI calculator of the Bureau of Labor Statistics within the U.S. Department of Labor, http://www.bls.gov/data/inflation_calculator .htm (1 November 2014).

77. William Targ's family name was spelled Torgownik or Turgownik. The first spelling appears in "William Targ, Godfather Editor, Dies at 92," *NYT*, 25 July 1999. That obituary describes him as one of the best editors of his era.

78. Golden, "Why I Never Bawl Out a Waitress," in *Only in America*, 21; Targ, *Indecent Pleasures*, 278.

79. Letter from Targ, 20 December 1957, and letter to Targ about Sandburg and the foreword, 20 December 1957, UNCC-HG, pt. 2, box 35:33–36. There had been a very brief time of a "Harry Golden Sr." byline when Harry Jr. went into the newspaper business. Golden was soundly criticized by Jonathan Daniels, editor of the *Raleigh News and Observer*: "As long as you live—which I hope will be several centuries—you will be Harry Golden. It is up to that junior Harry Golden to add the Jr. Putting the Sr. after your name is not only surplus, it makes you sound senile. Cut it off!" (letter from Daniels, 1 August 1955, UNCC-HG, pt. 2, box 4:74).

80. Foreword by Sandburg in *Only in America*, 13; letter to Targ, 30 December 1957, UNCC-HG, pt. 2, box 35:33–36.

81. "You Can Order My Book," *CI*, September–October 1957; "The Publication of My Book," *CI*, May–June 1958.

82. Unsigned, "Golden's Carolina Israelite Office-Residence Destroyed," *Charlotte News*, 17 February 1958; "The *Carolina Israelite* Fire: An Unlined Flue and the Evil Eye," *CI*, January–February 1958.

83. John York, "Fire Ruins Home of Harry Golden," *Charlotte Observer*, 18 February 1958. This story and other news accounts note the temperature was an unusually low 8 degrees, but historical records of Charlotte temperatures later available list a much higher but still unusual temperature in the 20s. Some close friends of Golden's never did believe the "accidental fire" ruling, but Golden accepted the determination that the chimney, not arsonists, was to blame.

84. Letter to Zevin and Jerome Fried, 18 February 1958, UNCC-HG, pt. 2, box 35:33–36.

85. Unsigned editorial, "The Next Issue Will Be a Little Late," *Charlotte News*, 19 February 1958.

86. Letter to Klein, 2 March 1958, copy from Klein personal papers; author's interview with Klein, email, 2011.

87. Letter from P. D. East, 21 February 1958, UNCC-HG, pt. 1, box 5:69.

88. Letter from Stevenson, 14 March 1958, UNCC-HG, pt. 2, box 15:1.

89. Letter from Kilpatrick, 27 March 1958, UNCC-HG, pt. 2, box 13:26.

90. "The Carolina Israelite Fire," *CI*, January–February 1958.

91. Letter from Littlejohn, 9 January 1956, UNCC-HG, pt. 2, box 7:39.

92. The remarks by Golden were published in Charlotte's newspapers, then reprinted as a one-page essay mailed to subscribers and others in the press. See "Police, Southerners, Clergy, Press, Combine to Save Harry Golden's Paper," UNCC-HG, pt. 1, box 33:9.

93. *Time* magazine staffer Lydia Ratcliff letter to Golden asking for details to add color to the story of the fire, 21 February 1958, and Golden's response, 26 February 1958, UNCC-HG, pt. 1, box 8:60.

94. "The Carolina Israelite Fire: Post No Bills," *CI*, January–February 1958.

95. Letter from Tribble, 3 July 1958, UNCC-HG, pt. 1, box 5:32.

96. Letter from Zevin, 16 July 1958, UNCC-HG, pt. 2, box 35:33.

97. Script for Dave Garroway interview on 24 July 1958, UNCC-HG, pt. 1, box 6:25.

98. Targ, *Indecent Pleasures*, 279.

99. Ibid.

100. Ibid.

101. Ibid.

102. Targ, "A Big Day at World Publishing," *CI*, January–February 1967; Targ, *Indecent Pleasures*, 279.

103. *Only in America* debuted on the *New York Times* list at number 14 in August 1958, then moved to first place in September, where it stayed (with the exception of two weeks in the fall) until February of the next year. Targ must have been delighted to read a quote from M. Lincoln Schuster of Simon and Schuster in a year-end piece in which Schuster said he wished his house had published Golden's *Only in America*. See unsigned, "A Good Thing and Not My Own," *NYT*, 30 November 1958.

104. "Thoughts of a Man with a Best-Seller," *CI*, July–August 1958, 9.

105. Quotes from *Book Review Digest* (1958), 439–40; Harry Ashmore, "Gentle Iconoclast," *Nation*, 5 September 1958; William Du Bois, "Books of the Times," *NYT*, 18 July 1958.

Chapter 5

1. Copy of the anonymous letter from "FRIEND," 13 September 1958, and other materials related to the prison time, UNCC-HG, pt. 1, box 8:54. Golden and those closest to him

had different guesses as to the identity of the writer. One theory had it that an admirer of Tiny's was responsible; another held that an individual cheated during the bucket-shop years was the writer. Others posited that a jealous girlfriend or disgruntled business associate was taking revenge. In this author's opinion there are two possibilities: a childhood friend who abruptly cut off correspondence with Golden without explanation, or a longtime southern acquaintance who clearly moved in a wide arc from admiration to resentment and back again over the years. As Golden himself quickly concluded, it did not matter much in the end.

2. Golden, *Right Time*, 348–58.

3. Judith Crist, "Golden, Best Seller Author, Reveals His Prison Past," *New York Herald Tribune*, 19 September 1958. Crist's front-page story gave Golden a break, allowing him to "confess," and it is also likely that jabs at Sandburg ("in his third childhood") and Stevenson as someone manipulated by Golden made quoting the anonymous rant less appealing. But the real credit for the positive spin goes to publicist Friedo, who talked with Crist and made the case for letting Golden step forward. Crist went on to be one of America's most widely read and broadcast film critics of her time.

4. "Winchell of New York," *New York Mirror*, week of 19 September 1958, UNCC-HG, pt. 1, box 33:12–13; Julian Scheer, "Supporters Rally for Golden after Ex-Convict Story," *Charlotte News*, 19 September 1957.

5. Author's interview with Norma Leveton, 2006. The interview by Murrow aired 3 February 1959.

6. Nicholas Stanford, "Plugging His Book? Golden Saga Publicity," *Charleston News and Courier*, 24 September 1958; unsigned editorial, "Golden's Confession: Strange Reaction," *Charleston News and Courier*, 29 September 1958.

7. Unsigned newspaper editorial-page clip headlined, "Golden—or Sumpin," UNCC-HG, pt. 1, box 33:13. It is not clear where the editorial ran, but its content makes it clear it was a southern newspaper and appeared very soon after the Crist article.

8. Unsigned, "Golden's Confession: Strange Reaction," *Charleston News and Courier*, 29 September 1958.

9. Golden, *Right Time*, 349, 356. When Golden died, one of his obituaries recalled that when the scandal broke, a *Charlotte Observer* editorialist had joked, "Now we can tell Harry what we couldn't tell him before—that most of his friends have known the story for years." While there were surely people who knew of Golden's past and did not tell him, given the competitive nature of newshounds and of Golden's joyful mutual ribbing with friends in the business, it is highly unlikely many of those comrades would have stayed mum. See Dannye Romine, "Activist Writer Harry Golden Dies," *Charlotte Observer*, 3 October 1981, 1.

10. "A True Wall Street Story," *CI*, October 1955.

11. Golden, *Right Time*, 349; letter to Jonathan Daniels about the reaction of his father, Josephus Daniels, to the confession of Golden's involvement with Cannon and the subsequent prison sentence, 19 September 1958, UNCC-HG, pt. 2, box 15:9.

12. Letter to Pete McKnight, 18 September 1958, UNCC-HG, pt. 1, box 8:54.

13. Julian Scheer, "Supporters Rally for Golden after Ex-Convict Story," *Charlotte News*, 19 September 1957.

14. Golden, *Right Time*, 356. Paar's *Tonight Show* was Golden's first real national exposure. He appeared on the show at least eighteen times from 1958 to 1962. "Paar used

vaudeville methods to get a message across," Golden wrote. "He shrugs his shoulders and gives the impression that he is just a boy in these matters. 'Harry, I know nothing about this integration business,' he'd say, 'tell us a little about it' " ("What Is Jack Paar Really Like?" *CI*, January–February 1963). See also letter from Marty Kimmer of MCA Artists Ltd. of New York with copies of the AFTRA engagement contract for the Paar show, 21 October 1959, UNCC-HG, pt. 1, box 8:38. Golden was paid $320 per show that year.

15. McCandlish Phillips, "Golden, Bestselling Author, Reveals He Served Jail Term," *NYT*, 19 September 1958; unsigned, "Author Is Backed after Confession," *NYT*, 20 September 1958; Lewis Nichols, "In and Out of Books," *NYT*, 19 October 1958. Nichols stayed in touch with Golden for years, alerting readers when a new book was about to be published.

16. Letter from Horton, 26 September 1958, UNCC-HG, pt. 2, box 7:38–39.

17. "The Story of My Past," *CI*, October–November 1958.

18. Golden, *Right Time*, 358.

19. Notarized minutes from meeting of the "directors of the *Carolina Israelite*," 4 April 1955, UNCC-HG, pt. 1, box 4:19, stating that Golden had been authorized to seek a loan from American Trust. No signatures save Golden's and the notary public's appear on the document. See also copies of "Statement of Policy Loan" documents for borrowing on a policy from Jefferson Standard Life Insurance Co., August 1955 and March 1956, UNCC-HG, pt. 2, box 8:26.

20. Author's interview with Richard Goldhurst, telephone, 2012; royalty figures from Golden's 1956–60 tax returns and worksheets, UNCC-HG, pt. 2, box 41:27. Worksheets in box 41:8 include lists of people to whom Golden owed money, ranging from U.S. Senator Herbert H. Lehman of New York to various traveling salesmen he likely met as they passed through Charlotte. In 1962, some $14,000 in "goodwill" funds appeared on Golden's balance sheet and remained there for the life of the newspaper. It is not clear where all the funds originated, but some of the money was long-standing debt. On Golden's NAACP membership and Kaplan, see Whitfield, " 'Golden' Era of Civil Rights," 29, 34.

21. Letter from Zevin, 29 August 1958, UNCC-HG, pt. 2, box 35:34.

22. All of the following appeared in *CI*: "My Speech in Denver, Colorado," January 1955; "My Speeches in January 1954," November 1954 and repeated in December 1954; "My Speeches in November," September–October 1957; and "My Speeches in April," March–April 1965.

23. "A Different Speech Every Night," *CI*, May–June 1958.

24. Unsigned, "Detroit Dinner Raises $50,000 for NAACP," *Ebony*, July 1960. The reference to Davis and Golden came from Gerald L. K. Smith, the rabid publisher of the monthly *The Cross and the Flag*. See letter to the editor of *Commentary* from Golden's secretary Maureen Titlow, 1 March 1961. Her letter was responding to a highly critical piece about Golden by Theodore Solotaroff. She was wryly pointing out that *Commentary* and Smith's magazine came the same day. "I am not terribly concerned with Mr. Solotaroff's dissenting opinion (which as a good Presbyterian I can only say—smells)," wrote Mrs. Titlow.

25. "Why I Make Speeches," *CI*, January–February 1959. After one such admonition by his doctor, Golden was hospitalized briefly in 1958, but as Joseph Wershba wrote in the *New York Post* on 28 November that year, it kept Golden from a few speeches, then he was back on the circuit.

26. Letter to editor from Golden, *Congress Biweekly*, 2 January 1960, UNCC-HG, pt. 2, box 4:51. The FBI report makes clear that Golden was of interest before *Only in America* made him famous. In the early and mid-1950s he spoke before several groups—Highlander Folk School among them—that the agency was monitoring as part of its surveillance of possible Communist fronts. The heavily redacted interview describes a speech on 19 September 1957 to the Scholars Gild [*sic*] in Gild Hall, Arden, Del. The informer's report was dated 10 October 1957 and originated from FBI Bureau file 100-401817 and Baltimore field office file 100-15926. The report was copied to Golden's FBI Bureau file 73-16547.

27. "How to Solve the Segregation Problem," *CI*, May–June 1956, and Golden, "The Vertical Negro Plan," in *Only in America*, 121. This essay also appears as "Golden Plans: 1956–58: How to Solve the Segregation Problem," in Carson, Garrow, Kovach, and Polsgrove, *Reporting Civil Rights*, 1:401.

28. "How to Solve the Segregation Problem," *CI*, May–June 1956.

29. Whitfield, "'Golden' Era of Civil Rights," 38–39; Hanchett, "Remembering Harry Golden: Food, Race, and Laughter"; Evans, *Provincials*, 27, 336; author's interview with Evans, son of Mayor E. J. "Mutt" Evans, telephone, 2006. Golden later expanded this plan to include theaters, using "vertical hammocks" instead of seats for long films.

30. "How to Eliminate Anti-Semitism Once and For All," *CI*, May–June 1956.

31. Thomas, with Robinson, *Serious Humor of Harry Golden*. Thomas provides a useful summary of the Golden Plans on pp. 24–36. A media historian, Thomas was the first writer to publish a biography of Golden. Also see "The Golden Bomb Shelter Plan and a Great Religious Revival," *CI*, July–August 1961.

32. One of the times Golden proposed this was in a letter to Vic Reinemer, then an aide to Senator James Murray (D-Mont.). Golden thought arch-segregationist Senator James O. Eastland of Mississippi would be the ideal person to make such a claim. See 16 April 1958, UNCC-HG, pt. 1, box 8:65.

33. "The Golden Vertical Insurance Plan," *CI*, September–October 1964, 15. Also see "The Golden Insurance Plan," in *Ess, Ess*, 164–66.

34. "A Word to the Wise for the Goniffs," *CI*, January–February 1967; "My Favorite Operatic Arias," *CI*, July–August 1955. The bedspread quote was captured by Harry Golden Jr., who wrote a clever piece about the preparation for the Murrow taping at his father's home and office: "Why Murrow's Men Got Slightly Shook," *Detroit Free Press*, 8 February 1959. Golden revealed his ten-cigar-a-day habit when he filled out a biographical questionnaire soon after *Only in America* was published. Under military service he stated, "Too young for World War I, too old for World War II, the lost generation." For physical description he typed, "Brown" (eyes), "Brown-gray" (hair), "5' 6'" (height), and "I refuse to answer" (weight). See UNCC-HG, pt. 1, box 5:54.

35. Author's interview with Richard Goldhurst, 2001, and telephone, 2011.

36. Letter from James P. Cattell, M.D., about Harry Jr.'s health, 19 June 1959, UNCC-HG, pt. 2, box 42:18; letter to Hal Tribble of the *Charlotte Observer* about Harry Jr.'s health, UNCC-HG, 30 June 1959, UNCC-HG, pt. 1, box 5:32; letter from Zevin, 16 July 1958, UNCC-HG, pt. 2, box 35:33. At this point World had the rights to Golden's next two books after *Only in America*, meaning that Zevin was willing to slow the debut of the books with an eye to the bigger picture. See letter from Greenbaum, 19 December 1958, UNCC-HG, pt. 2, box 41:11.

37. Author's interviews with Richard Goldhurst, 2000; Walter Klein, 2000; and William Goldhurst, telephone, 2006.

38. Letter from Targ with copy of Blanck's handwritten notes, 31 July 1958, UNCC-HG, pt. 2, box 35:33–36. Blanck was a former bibliographer of Americana for the Library of Congress, an editor of *Bibliography of American Literature*, and a respected expert on antiquarian books.

39. Lewis Nichols, "In and Out of Books: Plan," *NYT*, 23 August 1959; letter from Levensky, 23 February 1959, UNCC-HG, pt. 2, box 3:30. It didn't matter to Golden that royalty statements from World showed the "Best Selling Books for the Blind" to be tiny amounts; he still loved to use the line against those who tried to slow him down. See "Royalty Report," 25 March 1960, UNCC-HG, pt. 2, box 35:35.

40. Tina Barry, "A Filmmaker's Intimate Portrait, of 'Molly Goldberg,'" *Forward*, 17 July 2009.

41. Samuel T. Williamson, "Another Golden Treasury," *NYT*, 26 July 1959; Lewis Nichols, "In and Out of Books: Hancock," *NYT*, 11 October 1959. The 420,000 figure was not much of an exaggeration. World Publishing's statements to Golden showed 419,365 copies of his first three books sold by the end of June 1961, and most of the sales happened close to the time of Nichols's column. See "Royalty Report," 25 March 1960, UNCC-HG, pt. 2, box 35:35.

42. Mailer, *Spooky Art*, 40. Mailer was referring to the change in public interest from his bestselling first book, *The Naked and The Dead*, in 1948, to *Barbary Shore* in 1951. See also "My Sandburg Book," *CI*, March–April 1961.

43. "Only in America in Paper Back," *CI*, July 1959, 16.

44. "The Broadway Opening of 'Only in America,'" *CI*, November–December 1959; Golden, *Right Time*, 366–68; advertisement, *NYT*, 17 November 1959. Others cast in the play were Shepperd Strudwick and Enid Markey; see unsigned, "Name of O'Neill Adorns Theatre," *NYT*, 19 November 1959.

45. Brooks Atkinson, "Harry Golden Story Is Staged at Cord," *NYT*, 20 November 1959; "The Broadway Opening of 'Only in America,'" *CI*, November–December 1959; Harold Clurman, "Theatre," *Nation*, 5 December 1959.

46. Golden, *Right Time*, 368. Golden's investment in the play was listed as a loss in the couple's 1959 taxes; see UNCC-HG, pt. 2, box 41:27. Also see letter to Cohen, 6 August 1959, responding to the latter's letter inquiring about investing in *Only in America*, UNCC-HG, pt. 1, box 5:41.

47. Golden often wrote forewords and introductions without pay when asked by publishers other than World or Putnam. One such case was his preface for *Spirit of the Ghetto*, a 1965 reissuing of the book about the Lower East Side written in 1902 by journalist Hutchins Hapgood.

48. Letter from Dolores Ziff, J. B. Lippincott Co., 10 February 1960, UNCC-HG, pt. 2, box 10:36. Golden's *Enjoy, Enjoy!* made the *New York Times* bestseller list in July 1960 and stayed there into the first week of January 1961.

49. Letter to Theodore Frederick, personnel director at *Playboy*, 1 December 1961, UNCC-HG, pt. 2, box 27:23–24.

50. Letter from Henry Miller, 24 March 1963, UNCC-HG, pt. 2, box 11:15. Golden's undated response is written on the bottom of the second page of the letter for his secretary

to type and send. Miller might have assumed Golden shared the views of his son about *Tropic of Cancer*. Richard Goldhurst had savaged it on the front page of the July–August 1961 *Carolina Israelite*.

51. Letter and postcard from Steinbeck, 11, 17 July 1963, and Golden's response, 19 June 1963, UNCC-HG, pt. 2, box 14:68. Golden used but did not credit Steinbeck's one-liner in "Causerie on Barry Goldwater," *CI*, July–August 1964. See also letter from Elaine Scott Steinbeck, 1 September 1969, UNCC-HG, pt. 2, box 14:68.

52. "Nobody Knows My Name," *CI*, July–August 1961; letter to "Dave," most likely friend David Wallas of Charlotte, 15 February 1963, UNCC-HG, pt. 2, box 4:46.

53. Golden, "Christianity," in *You're Entitle'*, 259–60.

54. "Unitarians Still Waiting for Their First Negro," *CI*, May–June 1956.

55. James Reston, "Washington: The First Significant Test of the Freedom March," *NYT*, 30 August 1963.

56. The "Christianity still has its uses" line was a Golden standard. He used it in speeches often and in his writings, such as "God Is Dead," in *Ess, Ess*, 295–96; "In Charlotte—the New Pickets," *CI*, April–May 1962; and "White and Negro and 'Social Equality,'" *CI*, January 1955.

57. Golden, "Bishop (Sweet, Sweet Daddy) Grace," in *Enjoy, Enjoy!* 236. Charles Manuel or "Sweet Daddy" Grace was sometimes called "Daddy Grace Divine," not to be confused with his contemporary, "Father Divine," who was the Reverend M. J. Divine of Harlem.

58. "Jew Helps Baptist with Catholic Talk," *Charlotte News*, 14 November 1963; Miller, *Billy Graham*, 25. The first chapter of Miller's book, "No Segregation at the Altar," provides a foundation for understanding Graham's evolution on race issues.

59. Billy Graham, "Billy Graham Makes Plea for End to Intolerance," *Life*, 1 October 1956.

60. Miller, *Billy Graham*, 21; Paul L. Montgomery, "Billy Graham Is Focusing on Rights," *NYT*, 17 April 1965; John Herbers, "Birmingham's Progress Is Slow in Race Relations," *NYT*, 16 March 1964. Taylor Branch notes the meetings between the Graham and King staffs, in *Parting the Waters*, 595. David L. Chappell, in writing about the role of prophetic religion in the movement, puts Graham and the meetings into useful context, in *Stone of Hope*, 97. Jonathan S. Bass writes that the King camp sought advice from one of Graham's public relations experts about a "prison epistle" from King during his Albany campaign in 1962. Graham's expert discouraged the move at that time; a year later, when the timing was deemed more appropriate, King wrote his famous *Letter from Birmingham Jail*. See Bass, *Blessed Are the Peacemakers*, 117.

61. Anti-Defamation League press release following release of Billy Graham/Nixon tapes, 1 March 2002, http://archive.adl.org/presrele/asus_12/4048_12.html (1 November 2014); unsigned article, "Billy Graham Apologizes to Jews for His Remarks on Nixon Tapes," *NYT*, 3 March 2002; staff byline, "Billy Graham, Nixon and Anti-Semitism," *New York Observer*, 11 March 2002.

62. Golden letter to Billy Graham, 16 November 1960, UNCC-HG, pt. 1, box 8:42; letter from Graham, 20 December 1973, UNCC-HG, pt. 2, box 6:58. In 1963 Graham wrote Golden, "You always call me Dr. Graham, and perhaps I should address you as Mr. Golden. If you don't start calling me Billy, then I am going to stop calling you Harry!" (17 October 1963, UNCC-HG, pt. 2, box 6:58).

63. Goldhurst, "Locating the Deity," 234–36.

64. A. H. Raskin, "Textile Union Bid Set Back in South," *NYT*, 25 June 1961; letter to Billy Graham, 16 November 1960, and telegram to Governor Luther Hodges, 14 October 1960, both in UNCC-HG, pt. 1, box 8:42.

65. Glass, *Textile Industry in North Carolina*, 86–87, 90.

66. Kays Gary, "Wentworth . . . Your Street? You Hope Not . . . Not Today," *Charlotte Observer*, 3 November 1960.

67. UPI, "Golden Will Speak at Workers' Rally," *Greensboro Daily News*, 13 November 1959. Golden agreed to speak to a mass rally of workers on the first anniversary of the strike, alongside Payton and other union leaders. See Charles Dunn, "Violence Torn Henderson Strike Began Year Ago Tuesday," *Durham Morning Herald*, 15 November 1959, and Payton, *Scapegoat*, 47, 205–19.

68. "The Textile Workers and the South," *CI*, July–August 1959; unsigned typed notes, "Henderson Conspiracy Case, Arguments Presented by Union Attorneys and Fact Sheet," UNCC-HG, pt. 1, box 8:42.

69. Telegram from Hodges to several attorneys on his reasoning for not granting Payton clemency, 26 October 1960, UNCC-HG, pt. 1, box 8:42. A copy found its way to Golden at the same time. See also letter to Payton, 19 December 1960. Golden wrote to his friend in prison, seeking to comfort him and explain the tactical reasons for a delay in using Graham to push for early release. The letter is copied to Governor Hodges and others, making it clear that the efforts on Payton's behalf were supported by many in high places who felt they could not speak publicly. See letter from Billy Graham to Governor Sanford and Graham's cover letter to Golden, 10 May 1961, UNCC-HG, pt. 1, box 8:42; Charles Clay, four consecutive articles, "A Tug at the Conscience," "The Final Crushing Blow," "What the Climate Meant," and " 'Plot' Marred Clean Slates," *(Raleigh) News and Observer*, 20–23 November 1960; and unsigned editorial, "Will Not Stay Still," *(Raleigh) News and Observer*, 21 November 1960.

70. Letter from Graham, 10 May 1961, UNCC-HG, pt. 1, box 8:42; "The Henderson Strike," *CI*, July–August 1961. On southern cotton mills and related labor actions, see Harriet & Henderson Cotton Mills Records, 1885–1999, Southern Historical Collection, Louis Round Wilson Special Collections Library, University of North Carolina, http://www.lib.unc.edu/mss/inv/h/Harriet_and_Henderson_Cotton_Mills.html (1 November 2014).

71. Golden, *Right Time*, 13–14; "Only in North Carolina," *CI*, September–October 1960.

72. Thomas, *Robert Kennedy*, 128.

73. Branch, *Parting the Waters*, 366; Lemann, *Promised Land*, 115.

74. Golden, *Right Time*, 14.

75. "Two Telegrams Exchanged," *CI*, March–April 1965, UNCC-HG, pt. 2, box 9:43.

76. Unsigned, "The South: Attack on the Conscience," *Time*, 18 February 1957. Clare Boothe Luce, the first woman to serve as a U.S. ambassador and the wife of *Time* founder Henry Luce, may have played a part in the magazine's approving take on King. Foreign, anticapitalist criticism of America's civil rights failures bothered Mrs. Luce, moving her to write King and praise him for his work. See Branch, *Parting the Waters*, 203. King told an NAACP gathering in Atlanta in 1960 that his overseas travels convinced him "that America

is at its lowest ebb in international prestige; and most of this loss of prestige is due to our failure to grapple with the problem of racial injustice" (UPI, "Race Question Costing US Prestige," *Durham (N.C.) Herald*, 26 September 1960).

77. Unsigned, "The South: Attack on the Conscience," *Time*, 18 February 1957.

78. Unsigned, "The Press: Golden Rule," *Time*, 1 April 1957.

79. Badger, "Southerners Who Refused to Sign the Southern Manifesto," 526.

80. Caro, *Years of Lyndon Johnson: Master of the Senate*, 785–87; William S. White, "Manifesto Splits Democrats Again," *NYT*, 13 March 1956.

81. "Only in America," *CI*, January–February 1961.

82. "They Said It," *Chicago Daily Defender*, 11 October 1962.

83. The Moses line was part of an inscription to friend Hermann E. Cohen in the front of a copy of *Five Boyhoods*. It is recalled in a letter from Cohen, 6 April 1962, UNCC-HG, pt. 1, box 5:41. The exact number of newspapers that used Golden's syndicated column, "Only in America," is unclear, but correspondence with the syndicate and notations in more than one file, including the FBI dossier prepared when he sought a presidential pardon, use both numbers 63 and 64, which are most likely low. A letter to Golden from George M. Ivey, president of J. B. Ivey Department Stores, referencing a Christmas column by Golden cited 110 daily papers, which is likely closer to the correct number; see letter from Ivey, 14 October 1960, UNCC-HG, pt. 2, box 8:21. The column was distributed by Bell-McClure from 1958 to 1972; see Letter to John Osenenko, executive vice president of Bell-McClure, 1 January 1969, UNCC-HG, pt. 2, box 34:25. It was distributed by the United Features Syndicate between 1972 and 1975 to a smaller group of newspapers; see UNCC-HG, pt. 2, box 25:1–5. The later columns were not new material but instead drew on Golden's earlier columns and books. Cassell & Company of London published *Omnibus* in 1962.

84. Advertisement for *Carolina Israelite* subscriptions in the *New York Times*, 22 January 1961. The ad ran in publications across the country.

85. Letter from Harry Elmlark of the Syndicate, 31 May 1963, UNCC-HG, pt. 2, box 3:43. Buckley brought Golden on his show, *Firing Line*, on 23 May 1966, to discuss "The Future of States' Rights." Their evaluations of each other held true in the broadcast: Golden skimmed the surface of the topic, and Buckley was indeed pompous. Golden wrote newsman Joe Wershba that he had "smashed old William Buckley," which he most definitely had not, and later added that the camera crew had been cheering him on, which may have been true. See letters to Wershba, 24 May and 25 July 1966, UNCC-HG, pt. 2, boxes 3:43 and 16:37, and Golden, "My Degree at Belmont Abbey," in *So What Else Is New?* 214. In later years Buckley took a very different view, writing at length about the anti-Semitism of his father and condemning that of other conservatives. See Lipstadt, *Eichmann Trial*, 24–25.

86. Roberts and Klibanoff, *Race Beat*, 227. Such sit-ins actually started in 1958 when high school teacher Clara Luper took a group of students into a Katz Drug Store in Oklahoma City. The chain eventually desegregated counters in thirty-eight stores in four states. See Dennis Hevesi, "Clara Luper, a Leader of Civil Rights Sit-Ins, Dies at 88," *NYT*, 11 June 2011.

87. Golden, *Right Time*, 369.

88. Golden, "The Secret of Interfaith Work," in *Enjoy, Enjoy!* 218.

89. Theodore Solotaroff, "Harry Golden and the American Audience," *Commentary*, January 1961; "Commentary's Criticism," *CI*, January–February 1961; Philip Roth, "The New Jewish Stereotypes," *American Judaism*, Winter 1961. For more of Roth's thoughts on his identity as a "Jewish writer," see his article "Writing about Jews," *Commentary*, December 1963. Historian Irving Howe once dryly referred to Solotaroff as an "extreme admirer" of Roth's work, in "Philip Roth Reconsidered," *Commentary*, December 1972. In certain moods Golden was touchier about other people questioning his fitness for covering hard news. His papers include a letter written to *The Day* and *Jewish Morning Journal*, 27 April 1960, in which he complained with uncharacteristic bombast about a letter to the editor that had wondered about the sending of a humorist to postwar Germany. Solotaroff's angle wasn't new, but it caused the biggest splash. See UNCC-HG, pt. 1, box 5:60.

90. "Commentary's Criticism," *CI*, January–February 1961.

91. According to Solotaroff, editor Podhoretz inserted a line in the article about Golden, which was written early in Solotaroff's tenure at *Commentary*. The line was "To be on top is to be on top, which is a wonderful place to be." The line rankled Solotaroff, who understood it to be more about his boss's need to skewer people who dared to enjoy that terribly bourgeois thing—success. See "Adventures in Editing: Ted Solotaroff's 'Commentary' Days," *Nation*, 9 February 2009. In 2000, Podhoretz told a PBS interviewer that "the phrase 'only in America' was invented by a nearly forgotten writer named Harry Golden. . . . It is true that many things are possible or have proved to be possible, only in America. . . . My own life story could only have occurred in America" (http://video.pbs .org/video/1512026816 [1 November 2014]). The story of the suit-buying excursion appears in many places, including Golden, "Buying a Suit on the East Side," in *Best of Harry Golden*, 81–84.

92. "The Triangle Fire," *CI*, January–February 1956; "Is It All Nostalgia and Sentiment?" *CI*, July–August 1961; special coverage of the anniversary of the Triangle fire, in blogs and articles, *NYT*, 26 March 2011. See also Von Drehle, *Triangle*.

93. Theodore Solotaroff, "Harry Golden and the American Audience," *Commentary*, January 1961.

94. Harold Ribalow, "*Commentary* vs. Harry Golden," *Congress Bi-Weekly*, 13 February 1961.

95. Ibid.

96. Roth, "The New Jewish Stereotypes," *American Judaism*, Winter 1961, 49.

97. Letter to the editor about Roth, 10 December 1963, *Commentary*, April 1964; "The Jewish Novelist—Philip Roth," *CI*, July–August 1963. Golden quoted Roth as saying, "My biggest passion in my life is to write fiction, not to be a Jew," a statement he deliberately misconstrued to make his unstated point that Roth was a self-hating Jew.

98. Irving Howe, "Philip Roth Reconsidered," *Commentary*, December 1972.

99. Lee, *Philip Roth*, 33.

100. Golden, "My Critics," in *So What Else Is New?* 205–8; Irving Howe, "Philip Roth Reconsidered," *Commentary*, December 1972; Saunders Redding, review of *Dilemmas of a Negro Educator in the South*, *NYT*, 14 October 1962.

101. "A Great Negro Teacher," *CI*, January–February 1963, 17. Whether Golden intended to be dismissive of Redding by describing him only as a novelist is not clear, but he was

surely aware of Redding's extensive work as a critic and historian of Afro-American studies. See Berry, *Scholar's Conscience*.

Chapter 6

1. Lipstadt, *Eichmann Trial*, 20, 47; "End of a Hunt of Hatred," *Life*, 6 June 1960; Cesarani, *Becoming Eichmann*, 3, 238, 252–53. Mossad agent Peter Z. Malkin participated in the capture of Eichmann, although his role was not disclosed until years later. See Malkin and Stein, *Eichmann in My Hands*, and the unsigned obituary, "Peter Malkin: Israeli Agent Who Caught the Nazi War Criminal Adolf Eichmann," *Guardian*, 7 March 2005.

2. "Eichmann Confesses: Harry Golden Previews an Extraordinary Document to Appear in *Life*," *Life*, 21 November 1960.

3. Theodore Solotaroff, "Harry Golden and the American Audience," *Commentary*, January 1961; Golden, "The War the Nazis Won," in *Ess, Ess*, 170; Whitfield, *Into the Dark*, 186–87.

4. Cesarani, *Becoming Eichmann*, 326–38.

5. "End of a Hunt of Hatred," *Life*, 6 June 1960; Harry Golden, " 'A Stranger to the Human Race,' " *Life*, 21 April 1961; Adolph Eichmann, "I Transported Them to the Butcher," *Life*, 28 November 1960; editorial, "Eichmann and the Duty of Man," *Life*, 5 December 1960; Adolph Eichmann, "To Sum It All Up, I Regret Nothing," *Life*, 5 December 1960. Regarding Golden's popularity at the time: *For 2 Cents Plain* slipped off the bestseller list in February 1960 and *Enjoy, Enjoy!* moved onto the list in July, where it stayed through the first week of January 1961.

6. Harry Golden, " 'A Stranger to the Human Race,' " *Life*, 21 April 1961. In recent years it has become clear that *Life*'s coverage of the Eichmann story was influenced by forces outside the magazine, including the CIA. Declassified documents released in 2006 revealed that the CIA knew of Eichmann's whereabouts in 1958 but did not take action. *Life*'s editors acceded to the agency's request that Eichmann's memoirs be edited so that a Nazi official who went on to serve the government of West Germany would not be mentioned. See Scott Shane, "C.I.A. Knew Where Eichmann Was Hiding, Documents Show," *NYT*, 7 June 2006, and Christopher Lee, "CIA Ties with Ex-Nazis Shown," *Washington Post*, 7 June 2006.

7. Letter from Ralph Graves, articles editor, *Life*, 29 May 1961, UNCC-HG, pt. 2, box 27:4; letter from Graves, 5 January 1961, UNCC-HG, pt. 2, box 5:42. When Golden received the assignment, the nature of the content was left open-ended. Editor Ralph Graves confirmed Golden would be a "byline author" and added, "The nature and extent of your stories, will, of course, be determined by the developments at the trial." Golden interpreted this as carte blanche, but the wording was actually meant to give the magazine the ability to do just what it eventually did—pull the plug on Golden's coverage before the end of the trial. See Tuviah Friedman, "My Search for Vengeance," *Life*, 24 February 1961, and Gjon Mili, photo essay: "Intimate Portrait," *Life*, 14 April 1961. See also "An Arrogant Eichmann Finally Gets on the Stand," *Life*, 30 June 1961. Correspondent Marlin Levin is quoted in the text; British artist Ronald Searle illustrated the article.

8. Letter to Graves, *Life*, 26 May 1960, UNCC-HG, pt. 2, box 27:5.

9. Letter to "Joe," presumably journalist Joe Wershba, 17 March 1961, UNCC-HG, pt. 2, box 5:42.

10. "The Jews In Germany—1961," *CI*, May–June 1961. The idea of a Society of Half-Jews was proposed by Golden at various times, including in "Eleven Notes in Passing," in *You're Entitle'*, 119. Richard Goldhurst recalled the Golden look-alike matter during an interview with the author, 2000.

11. "The Jews In Germany—1961," *CI*, May–June 1961. In the foreword to *The Best of Harry Golden*, published in 1967, Supreme Court Justice William O. Douglas cited Golden's comment about American consumers, a view that "placed in one small capsule a typical reaction of the affluent society to the seething world of discontent around us."

12. Golden more than once noted his surviving sons' accomplishments in the *Carolina Israelite*. Harry Jr. was a reporter of the old-school, *Front Page* type who, after his start in Charlotte, haunted police desks and city hall at the *Detroit Free-Press* and then, later, the *Chicago Sun-Times*. He claimed never to have written a lead paragraph longer than twenty-three words. Golden's youngest son, William, "our F. Scott *Fizgeraldnik*," was an English professor at the University of Puerto Rico and the University of Florida. World published his book on Fitzgerald in 1963.

13. Diane McWhorter's foreword in Etheridge, *Breach of Peace*, 19; James Farmer in Hampton, with Fayer and Flynn, *Voices of Freedom*, 75–76.

14. "The Freedom Riders In Alabama," *CI*, May–June 1961.

15. Arsenault, *Freedom Riders*, 136–39, 144.

16. Ibid., 130, 293; Hampton, with Fayer and Flynn, *Voices of Freedom*, 94–96. A brief film clip inside the church and other materials on the civil rights movement is included in the Civil Rights Digital Library, University of Georgia, http://crdl.usg.edu/ (1 January 2015).

17. Arsenault, *Freedom Riders*, 11–14. Arsenault's book (pp. 533–87) includes a detailed roster of Freedom Riders dating back to the 1947 Journey of Reconciliation. For Arsenault's remarks about the success of the Interstate Commerce Commission's order, see http://video.pbs.org/video/1576287311 (1 November 2014). A digital roster of the Freedom Riders is part of the PBS project at pbs.org/wgbh/americanexperience/freedomriders/people/roster (1 November 2014). See also Kluger, *Simple Justice*, 756.

18. "The Freedom Riders In Alabama," *CI*, May–June 1963.

19. Golden, "Visitors," in *For 2 Cents Plain*, 143.

20. Golden and Williams were of like mind in what was called "the Kissing Case," in which state authorities sent two black boys to reform school for kissing a white girl. Both men were involved with attempts to win release for the boys. See Golden, *Right Time*, 377–84, and Tyson, *Radio Free Dixie*.

21. Arsenault, *Freedom Riders*, 484–86; Associated Press, "Bus Riders Are Offered a Free Trip Back, Too," *NYT*, 1 May 1962; "A Free Ride to Apartheid," *CI*, May–June 1962; unsigned, "What Happened to the Reverse Freedom Riders?" *Chicago Daily Defender*, 18 April 1963; Katy Reckdahl, "Reverse Freedom Rides Sent African Americans out of the South, Some for Good," *New Orleans (La.) Times-Picayune*, 22 May 2011.

22. Golden described the document as being cowritten with Murrow. The final product makes clear that Murrow did not take a significant role in the writing. The following are located in UNCC-HG, pt. 2, box 9:28: draft memo to President Kennedy, 15 August

1961; letter from Murrow, "Message from your 'postman,'" 2 September 1961; letter to John Morsell, assistant to Wilkins, 16 October 1961; letter to Wilkins, 17 October 1961; letter to Murrow, new draft of the Kennedy Declaration, 17 October 1961; "A Memorandum to President John F. Kennedy from Harry Golden, *Carolina Israelite*, Charlotte, North Carolina, with the Help of Edward R. Murrow, Director U.S.I.A.—A Declaration," 20 October 1961. His efforts on behalf of a declaration brought Golden an invitation to the Emancipation Proclamation anniversary reception in the White House. In his thank-you letter, Golden took the opportunity to share observations from recent lecture tours and suggest that Kennedy speak to the people in "fireside chats" on the national debt and on Cuba. See letter to President Kennedy, 9 March 1963, UNCC-HG, pt. 1, box 8:52, and unsigned, "Edward R. Murrow, Broadcaster and Ex-Chief of U.S.I.A., Dies," *NYT*, 28 April 1965.

23. "A Memorandum to President John F. Kennedy from Harry Golden, *Carolina Israelite*, Charlotte, North Carolina, with the help of Edward R. Murrow, Director U.S.I.A.—A Declaration," 20 October 1961, UNCC-HG, pt. 2, box 9:28.

24. Letter from Targ, 24 October 1961, and Golden's response, 25 October 1961, UNCC-HG, pt. 2, box 9:28. While praising the idea and the draft declaration, Targ suggested that since "brevity and absolute clarity are essential here," the document be cut for length, with an eye to clichés that might detract from its impact. Golden thanked the editor for his suggestions, adding that several "were the very ones that Dickie [Richard Goldhurst] and I decided to make." The document, however, was not edited sufficiently to achieve what Targ hoped.

25. Branch, *Parting the Waters*, 517–18.

26. Golden, *Mr. Kennedy and the Negroes*, 167; author's interviews with Richard Goldhurst, 2001, and Anita Stewart Brown, 2000.

27. Golden took a Johnson vs. Goldwater poll of *Carolina Israelite* readers in 1964, running the results in the September–October issue. Johnson was the winner by a mile, an outcome Golden smugly predicted would come to pass in the real race. He rightly imagined that Republican Jews would throw their lot in with Johnson, not Goldwater. Public opinion polls suggested that 90 percent of Jews voting in the 1964 election chose Johnson. See Seymour Martin Lipset, "How Big Is the Bloc Vote?" *NYT Sunday Magazine*, 25 October 1964.

28. "Senator Kennedy and the Catholic Church," *CI*, March–April 1959. On Kennedy as a war hero, see Caro, *Years of Lyndon Johnson: The Passage of Power*, 36–39. See also Carty, "Secular Icon or Catholic Hero?"; "Senator Kennedy and the Catholic Church," *CI*, March–April 1959; Fletcher Knebel, interview with John F. Kennedy, *Look*, 3 March 1959; and "The Bishops vs. Kennedy," *Look*, 23 May 1961. The later article was repudiated by high-level Roman Catholic clergy who took issue with Knebel's claim that they had opposed Kennedy's decision to run for president. Knebel wrote an often-satirical syndicated column called "Potomac Fever." See Bruce Lambert, "Fletcher Knebel, Writer, 81, Dies; Co-Author of 'Seven Days in May,'" *NYT*, 28 February 1993.

29. Author's interview with Richard Goldhurst, 2013. Eunice Kennedy Shriver, the fifth of the Kennedy children in the president's generation, became executive vice president of the foundation in 1957. It was created in 1946 as a memorial for their oldest brother, killed in World War II. Shriver's 1962 magazine article about her sister Rosemary's mental

disabilities, and her work in the field, including her promotion of the Special Olympics, changed the understanding and treatment of the intellectually disabled in America. See Carla Baranauckas, "Eunice Kennedy Shriver, Influential Founder of Special Olympics, Dies at 88," *NYT*, 11 August 2009.

30. This was not the first time Golden raised the Catholic issue; he had explored the issue at some length two years earlier. See "Senator Jack Kennedy and the South," *CI*, November–December 1957, and letter from Myer Feldman, legislative assistant to Senator John Kennedy, 19 March 1959, UNCC-HG, pt. 1, box 8:52. Golden felt that praise from Feldman, a talented and erudite writer, was worth having. In the competitive atmosphere of the Kennedy White House, Feldman and White House colleague Ted Sorensen liked to trade memos in rhymed couplets. See Douglas Martin, "Myer Feldman, 92, Advisor to President Kennedy, Dies," *NYT*, 3 March 2007.

31. "Along the Campaign Trail with Carl Sandburg," *CI*, November–December 1960.

32. Golden, *Carl Sandburg*, 17. In the preface of the University of Illinois Press edition cited here, Sandburg biographer Penelope Niven wrote, "[Golden's] resulting portrait is engaging and human, although not accurate in every detail. Golden did not pretend to do exhaustive research, and he was right about how much time and patience would be exacted of biographers."

33. Herbert Mitgang, "Books of the Times," *NYT*, 21 November 1961; Julian Scheer, "Golden on Sandburg: Like Meeting Shakespeare," *Charlotte News*, 21 November 1961; Kays Gary, "Harry Looks at Sandburg," *Charlotte Observer*, 19 November 1961.

34. Golden, *Carl Sandburg*, 104.

35. Golden, *Right Time*, 336.

36. Letter to member of the Charlotte Writers Club, 5 February 1963, UNCC-HG, pt. 2, box 4:24; author's interviews with Mark Bernstein, by telephone and email, 2006.

37. Thomas, *Robert Kennedy*, 248; "A Memorandum to President John F. Kennedy from Harry Golden, *Carolina Israelite*, Charlotte, North Carolina, with the help of Edward R. Murrow, Director U.S.I.A.—A Declaration," 20 October 1961, UNCC-HG, pt. 2, box 9:28.

38. One of Golden's many mentions of his love for Robert Kennedy came in a letter to California governor Ronald Reagan referencing Robert Kennedy's death, 2 June 1969, UNCC-HG, pt. 2, box 11:17–18. See also letter from Robert Kennedy on Golden's "stirring" declaration, 27 October 1961, UNCC-HG, pt. 2, box 9:28.

39. Golden, *Right Time*, 241.

40. Letter from Robert Kennedy with book to be autographed, 27 May 1959; Golden's response mentioning Hoffa, 10 June 1959; and letter from Robert Kennedy mentioning Hoffa, 20 June 1959, all in UNCC-HG, pt. 2, box 9:31. Golden was biased enough about Kennedy to later wrongly insist, "Jimmy Hoffa manufactured the myth about the vendetta between himself and Kennedy, a blood feud, no less" ("What Is Robert Kennedy Really Like," *CI*, March–April 1964). See Sheridan, *Fall and Rise of Jimmy Hoffa*. Sheridan's 1972 book is not an objective treatment but is important reading in the study of Hoffa's life. Sheridan was a key investigator and assistant to Robert Kennedy during the investigation of Hoffa and years of hearings.

41. Letter from Robert Kennedy regarding visit, 6 November 1959, UNCC-HG, pt. 2, box 9:31; Thomas, *Robert Kennedy*, 47.

42. Caro, *Years of Lyndon Johnson: The Passage of Power*, 63–68.

43. Golden, "You Never Saw a Yenkee?" in *Only in America*, 117. Kennedy wisely did not try to override his Boston brogue to re-create the Yiddish accent on "Yenkee" as Golden did.

44. For speech transcripts, see the U.S. Department of Justice digital collection, http://www.justice.gov/ag/rfk-speeches.html (1 November 2014). See also Kennedy, *RFK*, published by Viking in 1993, with representative speeches from Kennedy's career.

45. Lemann, *Promised Land*, 115.

46. Hundreds of journalists swarmed over the city, and the story played around the globe. Two civilians were killed, and at least 375 were hurt, with more than 200 marshals and troops injured as well. See Doyle, *American Insurrection*, 278–80.

47. Ibid., 295; Reeves, *President Kennedy*, 354–64.

48. Golden, "George Wallace," in *So Long as You're Healthy*, 192.

49. Wallace's speech, digital archives of Alabama Department of Archives and History, 14 January 1963, http://www.archives.alabama.gov/ (1 November 2014). The speech was penned by one Asa Earl Carter, an anti-Semitic racist and Ku Klux Klan member from Alabama and the central character in a bizarre author-outing of the era. A book written by Carter in 1976 titled *The Education of Little Tree* became a bestseller in 1991 under the pen name Forrest Carter. By the time this folksy, culturally sensitive memoir of a backwoods upbringing became popular, Carter was long dead. When a *New York Times* op-ed piece revealed the author's identity and racist past, one of the people left to defend him was his agent, Eleanor Kask Friede, the former publicist who guided Golden through his prison scandal in 1958. See Dana Rubin, "Education of Little Tree," *Texas Monthly*, February 1992.

50. Harrison E. Salisbury, "Fear and Hatred Grip Birmingham," *NYT*, 12 April 1960.

51. Salisbury, *Without Fear or Favor*, 379–82, 390. Damages sought by Montgomery officials suing over a fundraising ad for the Reverend Martin Luther King Jr. along with the damages sought by Birmingham officials over news coverage totaled $6.1 million from the newspaper and $1.5 million from Salisbury.

52. Unsigned, Associated Press, "Colleague of King to Step Down from Pulpit," *NYT*, 20 March 2006.

53. Bass, *Blessed Are the Peacemakers*, 19, 26, 98; unsigned, "Rights Pact Halts Alabama Strife," *NYT*, 12 May 1963; unsigned, Associated Press, "Colleague of King to Step Down from Pulpit," *NYT*, 20 March 2006.

54. Barr, "Rabbi Grafman and Birmingham's Civil Rights Era," 174–75, 177–78; Bass, *Blessed Are the Peacemakers*, 233–34.

55. Bass, *Blessed Are the Peacemakers*, 235–36.

56. Ibid., 19, 26, 110–30, and details of editing changes to *Letter*, 237–56. Bass noted that King's inner circle consulted with evangelist Billy Graham's public relations specialist in 1962 about the wisdom of releasing an open letter; see *Blessed Are the Peacemakers*, 117. See also Branch, *Parting the Waters*, 740.

57. *Letter from Birmingham Jail* has been widely quoted since it appeared. The Martin Luther King Jr. Research and Education Institute and the King Papers Project note that *Letter* was first distributed as a mimeographed copy, then published "as a pamphlet distributed by the American Friends Service Committee . . . and in *Christian Century*, *Christianity and Crisis*, the *New York Post*, and *Ebony*. The first half of the letter was intro-duced into testimony before Congress by Representative William Fitts Ryan (D-NY) and

published in the *Congressional Record*." King included the full text in his 1964 book, *Why We Can't Wait*. See also the Martin Luther King Jr. Center for Nonviolent Social Change, Atlanta, Ga., http://www.thekingcenter.org/.

58. "Unbelievable Birmingham, Alabama!" *CI*, May–June 1963.

59. Bass, *Blessed Are the Peacemakers*, 97, 250; details of editing changes to *Letter*, 237–56; Durr's comments about Golden, *Freedom Writer: Virginia Foster Durr*, 194, 241; Mike Wallace interview of James McBride Dabbs, Harry Ransom Center, University of Texas at Austin, http://www.hrc.utexas.edu/multimedia/video/2008/wallace/dabbs_james_mcbride.html (1 November 2014).

60. Letter to Wyatt Tee Walker, executive assistant to King, 18 April 1963, UNCC-HG, pt. 2, box 9:43. Golden was most likely referring to members of the staff when he said "boys." However, it is possible he had in mind young adults and schoolchildren who were among the Birmingham protestors, having been drafted into a "Children's Crusade" in the first week of May. Connor ordered them arrested, and he called out the fire hoses and the attack dogs. There was no way to explain away these images, and Connor's days were numbered. The children's involvement was not without controversy. As King was encouraging the parents of the young marchers to allow them to participate, Nation of Islam minister Malcolm X was declaring, "Real men don't put their children on the firing line" (M. S. Handler, "Malcolm X Terms Dr. King's Tactics Futile," *NYT*, 11 May 1963).

61. "The Bull Connor Award," *CI*, May–June 1963. The Yiddish expression is more often spelled *gornisht helfen*, meaning "it's beyond help."

62. "Unbelievable Birmingham, Alabama!" *CI*, May–June 1963.

63. Letters to and from Dowd, J. E., general manager of *Charlotte Observer* and *Charlotte News*, both written 10 December 1965, in which past and present circulation figures were discussed, UNCC-HG, pt. 1, box 4:13; "Why Not Make It Five Million and Three?" *CI*, September–October 1963. Golden should have included *Only in America* when he cited the publisher's claim of 5 million copies sold.

64. "Looking for Work and How to Find It," *CI*, January–February 1963, 13.

65. Bayard Rustin, "The Meaning of Birmingham," from a pamphlet, *Civil Rights: The True Frontier*, 18 June 1963. The essay also appears in Rustin, *Down the Line*, 107. See also "The Negro Articulation," *CI*, July–August 1963, 15. Golden's remarks about Malcolm X followed the infamous interview of the Black Muslim leader by Alex Haley in the May issue of *Playboy*. See Ralph McGill, "A Sensitive Southerner's View of a Smoking City," *New York Herald Tribune*, 14 May 1963, and McGill and Logue, *No Place to Hide*, 2: 413–17.

66. Douglas, *Reading, Writing, and Race*, 60, 98–99; Roberts and Klibanoff, *Race Beat*, 146–47.

67. Fannie Flono, "Helping Charlotte Find Its Way—50 Years Ago," *Charlotte Observer*, 30 May 2013, http://www.charlotteobserver.com/2013/05/30/4076378/helping-charlotte-find-its-way.html#.U3fpti8gmHk (1 November 2014).

68. Golden, *Right Time*, 393–94.

69. Alden Whitman, "Norman Thomas, Socialist, Dies; He Ran for President Six Times," *NYT*, 20 December 1968; Golden, "Norman Thomas," in *So Long as You're Healthy*, 220–22. Golden threw himself into the Scales clemency effort, sending letters about the Greensboro, N.C., native to powerful members of the press, politicians, and academics. He helped deliver to President Kennedy an "All Tar-Hell Petition" signed by

Frank Graham and other prominent North Carolinians, as Thomas did the same with a national petition signed by 550 people. See Jude Arnett, "Clemency Plea Sent to JFK," *Charlotte Observer*, 27 April 1962; press release by Thomas on clemency petition, 8 April 1962, UNCC-HG, pt. 1, box 9:2; Ari Goldman, "Junius Scales, Communist Sent to U.S. Prison, Dies at 82," *NYT*, 7 August 2002. President Kennedy commuted Scales's sentence on Christmas Eve 1962.

70. Golden, *Right Time*, 394.

71. "The March on Washington, 1963: They Voted with Their Feet," in Hampton, with Fayer and Flynn, *Voices of Freedom*, 161; Branch, *Parting the Waters*, 847–48.

72. David Suissa, "Before King, It Was Prinz," Jewishjournal.com, 3 September 2008, jewishjournal.com/opinion/article/before_king_it_was_prinz_20080903/ (1 November 2014); text of Prinz speech in Prinz, *Joachim Prinz, Rebellious Rabbi*, appendix B, 261.

73. Ward-Royster, *How I Got Over*, 99.

74. Golden, *Right Time*, 393–94. The famous speech that is so often cited for its inspiring "dream" language, prophetic references, and forward-looking inspiration was a manifesto expressing urgency—"Now is the time to make real the promises of democracy"—and a vow: "We cannot be satisfied as long as a Negro in Mississippi cannot vote and a Negro in New York believes he has nothing for which to vote. . . . We will not be satisfied until justice rolls down like waters and righteousness like a mighty stream." The text of King's "I Have a Dream" speech and a collection of other speeches and reflections on the March on Washington are available on National Public Radio's site, npr.org/news/specials/march40th/index.html (1 November 2014). See also the Martin Luther King Jr. Research and Education Institute and the King Papers Project, Stanford, Calif., http://mlk-kpp01.stanford.edu/, and the Martin Luther King Jr. Center for Nonviolent Social Change, Atlanta, Ga., http://www.thekingcenter.org/.

75. Diner, *Jews of The United States*, 265–70; Russell Baker, "Capital Is Occupied by a Gentle Army," *NYT*, 29 August 1963; F. W. Kenworthy, "200,000 March for Civil Rights in Orderly Washington Rally; President Sees Gains for Negro," *NYT*, 29 August 1963. Evocative pieces by James Reston and Tom Wicker appear in the same issue.

76. Karl Fleming, "Birmingham: 'My God, You're Not Even Safe in Church,'" *Newsweek*, 30 September 1963; this essay also appears in Carson, Garrow, Kovach, and Polsgrove, *Reporting Civil Rights*, 2:26. See also "Civil Rights: The Sunday School Bombing," *Time*, 27 September 1963, and Diane McWhorter, "Civil Rights Justice on the Cheap," *NYT*, 15 September 2013.

77. "The Victim Is Negotiable," *CI*, September–October 1963. Golden took this approach when writing and speaking about anti-Semitism as well. He was often asked by audience members, in effect, "What is there about Jews and Judaism that has produced so much hatred?" He would make the point that Jews are historically the only group asked why a crime has been committed against them. One example appears in a letter to Rabbi Michael Hecht, Temple Israel, Charlotte, 17 March 1966, UNCC-HG, pt. 2, box 7:31.

78. "The Victim Is Negotiable," *CI*, September–October 1963.

79. From Golden's speech delivered to a meeting of the newly formed Associated Organizations for Human Rights in Miami, 22 December 1961. The speech was reprinted in *CI*, January–February 1964. The line quoted had also been used in "The Late President,"

CI, November–December 1963. See also unsigned, "To Salute Kennedy," *Miami News*, 8 December 1963.

80. Anthony Lewis, "A Moral Decision, Weighted with a Sense of History," *NYT*, 10 May 1964; Adam Liptak, "Anthony Lewis, Supreme Court Reporter Who Brought Law to Life, Dies at 85," *NYT*, 25 March 2013.

81. Golden, *Mr. Kennedy and the Negroes*, 29.

82. Ibid., 130, 135; Shogan, *Moral Rhetoric of American Presidents*, 114–15.

83. Golden, *Mr. Kennedy and the Negroes*, 136.

84. Ibid., 262

85. Ibid., 76–77.

86. "The Southern Moderate," *CI*, September–October 1963; Golden, *Mr. Kennedy and the Negroes*, 25; Golden, "A Last Visit with John F. Kennedy," in *So What Else Is New?* 228–29.

87. Polsgrove, *Divided Minds*, 176–86.

88. Golden used the line about Baldwin many times, including in *Mr. Kennedy and the Negroes*, 262.

Chapter 7

1. Golden managed to avoid the cold shoulder usually given by Kennedy insiders to those who consorted with Johnson; in fact, he was asked to provide the first essay in a commemorative book put out about the late president, *A Tribute to John F. Kennedy*, edited by Pierre Salinger and Sander Vanocur and published by *Encyclopaedia Britannica*. His contribution was a brief tribute culled from an earlier piece in the *Carolina Israelite*. The *Negro Digest* recommended the book, despite its sadly accurate statement that "among all the tributes from world and national figures, not a single one is from an African or American Negro" (*Negro Digest*, July 1964, 95). As Robert A. Caro wrote, the bad blood between Johnson and Robert Kennedy went back to Johnson's days as majority leader, when Kennedy was gearing up for battle with the so-called Rackets Committee. Johnson called Kennedy "Sonny boy" and described him as "a snot-nose, but he's bright." Kennedy's strong dislike for the older man worsened during the debating over Johnson's fitness as a running mate for John Kennedy, and it continued throughout Johnson's presidency. See Caro, *Years of Lyndon Johnson: The Passage of Power*, 66.

2. Kotz, *Judgment Days*, 61.

3. Golden, "The Agony Of Lyndon Johnson," in *So Long as You're Healthy*, 213–15.

4. "Johnson and Viet Nam," *CI*, January–February 1966.

5. The significant second line of the Kennedy inaugural address delivered 20 January 1961 is unfortunately not often included when the first line is cited: "And so, my fellow Americans: ask not what your country can do for you—ask what you can do for your country. My fellow citizens of the world: ask not what America will do for you, but what together we can do for the freedom of man." Transcript and video on website of John F. Kennedy Presidential Library and Museum, http://www.jfklibrary.org/JFK/Historic-Speeches.aspx (1 November 2014).

6. Badger, "Southerners Who Refused to Sign the Southern Manifesto"; Wilkins and Mathews, *Standing Fast*, 311.

7. Golden, "Lyndon B. Johnson," in *So What Else is New?* 105; Robert A. Caro, "The Transition," *New Yorker*, 2 April 2012, 32–49. Johnson's speech was broadcast on 2 July 1964.

8. "A Personal Letter from North Carolina about Robert F. Kennedy," on Golden's letterhead, 15 October 1964, sent to multiple recipients, UNCC-HG, pt. 2, box 11:17–18.

9. Golden, "The Attempted Murder of James Meredith," in *Ess, Ess*, 48–49. Golden attributed this advice to Martin Luther King Jr. speaking to volunteers in Savannah in 1956.

10. The telegram is quoted in a collection of Heschel's essays edited by his daughter, scholar Susannah Heschel, *Moral Grandeur and Spiritual Audacity*, vii.

11. Historian Raymond Arsenault noted that of 436 riders, 204 were white and as many as 70 of those were most likely Jewish; author's interview with Arsenault, telephone, 2012. It had been previously reported in many texts, including a statement by historian Murray Friedman, that overall two-thirds of the Freedom Riders were Jews. Friedman wrote, "Jews probably made up two thirds of the white Freedom Riders going into the South in the summer of 1961 and about one third to one half of the Mississippi summer volunteers three years later" (Friedman, with Binzen, *What Went Wrong?* 181–83, 187–88). See Webb, *Fight against Fear*, 79, on the questioning of the "two-thirds" statistic. See also Dollinger, " 'Hamans' and 'Torquemadas,' " 75–77, and Svonkin, *Jews against Prejudice*, 193. Schwerner, Chaney, and Goodman disappeared 21 June 1964. Their bodies were found forty-four days later. All had been shot, and Chaney, who was black, was beaten and mutilated.

12. Letter from Abram, 4 June 1964, UNCC-HG, pt. 1, box 1:35.

13. Ibid.; lists of note-holders, UNCC-HG, pt. 2, box 41:8. Engel contributed a portion of the money himself and coordinated the rest from donors, some of whom stipulated that repayments go to the AJC.

14. Letter from Edwin J. Lukas, director of the AJC civil rights program, 24 June 1957, UNCC-HG, pt. 2, box 1:34. Lukas asked Golden to provide intelligence on the Ku Klux Klan, businesses, and schools in the South. "It will be most helpful in formulating our own plans, as well as those of other agencies with which we have associated ourselves," Lukas wrote. The following are all found in UNCC-HG, pt. 1, box 1:35: letter from Abram to Golden, 4 June 1964, and Golden's response, 8 June 1964; letter from Engel to Golden, 23 June 1964, and Golden's response, 26 June 1964; letter from Abram to Golden, 25 June 1964. Golden and Engel found more occasions after that to tussle over what Engel saw as Golden's "obvious bias against the American Jewish Committee." After a heated letter from Engel taking him to task for an alleged misrepresentation of the AJC's role in the civil rights fight, Golden wryly responded: "In fact I love the American Jewish Committee. Not as much as you do of course, but almost as much." See letter from Engel, 24 October 1974, and Golden to Engel, 28 October 1974, UNCC-HG, pt. 1, box 1:39.

15. "The Ecumenical Council," *CI*, November–December 1963; Golden, "Let Jews Forgive Christians Too," in *Best of Harry Golden*, 264. The promotional piece reprinted from the *Carolina Israelite* was "The Jewish Schema on the Christians," October 1965.

16. Lewis Nichols, "In and Out of Books" *NYT*, 7 July 1963. Golden was referring to the erection of the Berlin Wall in 1961, which was making headlines as he decided to write *Forgotten Pioneer*.

17. Golden, *Forgotten Pioneer*, 27.

18. Ibid., 56.

19. Lewis Nichols, "In and Out of Books," *NYT*, 7 July 1963; unsigned, "Books: The Jew-Wedge-Du-Gish," *Time*, 12 July 1963; unsigned, *Book Review Digest*, 17 July 1963, 388.

20. R. L. Duffus, "Corn but Not Eggplant," *NYT*, 29 July 1962. Duffus, at the time a member of the *New York Times* editorial board, reviewed *You're Entitle'* and other books by Golden. Of *Entitle'* he wrote, "It is more fun to read Mr. Golden than talk about him. He is a native product. He is unique. He is good for all of us." As Golden would have said, *Five Boyhoods* was a hard book *not* to like. Reviewers were in general agreement with Arthur Gelb of the *New York Times*, who wrote, "All five authors are articulate and accomplished reminiscers. The accounts of their boyhoods form a cohesive, vivid and constantly captivating picture of life before the atomic bomb" ("Books of the Times," 20 April 1962). Nothing matched the success of *Only in America*, but sales stayed steady, helped by serialized chapters in magazines, including *Reader's Digest*, and Golden's own tireless promotion on the road and on television.

21. *The Tonight Show* with Johnny Carson, 18 August 1964, Museum of Broadcast Communications collection, Chicago, Ill.

22. Golden, "Aftermath: The Bobby Twins Revisited," *Esquire*, June 1965. The cover teaser for the piece was "What's Right with Bobby Kennedy—by Harry Golden." See also letters from Theodore H. White, 9 August 1965, from Edwin Guthman, 26 January 1965, and from Arthur Schlesinger Jr., 16 October 1964, all UNCC-HG, pt. 2, box 11:17–18. White, an acquaintance of the Kennedy family, won the Pulitzer Prize in 1962 for *The Making of the President, 1960*. He is credited with helping Jacqueline Kennedy create and promote the Camelot image of the era in the days after John F. Kennedy was killed. Guthman won the Pulitzer Prize in 1950 for coverage in the *Seattle Times* that cleared a professor of allegations that he was a Communist supporter. Schlesinger was a special assistant to President Kennedy and a two-time Pulitzer winner for *The Age of Jackson* in 1946 and *A Thousand Days: John F. Kennedy in the White House* in 1964.

23. Golden, "The Vanishing Hot Dog," *New York Post*, 9 September 1963. The piece ran in newspapers across the country as one of Golden's syndicated columns, "Only in America"; see letter to David H. Stroud of the National Livestock and Meat Board, UNCC-HG, pt. 2, box 27:14. See also letters from Sanford Laven, Bel-Aire Pools, Wickliffe, Ohio, 24 May 1967, and Robert Hoffman of Hoffman Publications, 15 December 1967, UNCC-HG, pt. 2, box 7:46.

24. Golden, "A New Spirit among Catholics," *Miami News*, 3 November 1964. The event Golden described in his syndicated column had taken place in East Lansing, Mich.

25. Author's interview with Anita Stewart Brown, 2000.

26. "The Concord and 'Exclusive' Resorts,'" *CI*, September–October 1964, 18; advertisement, "Only at the Concord: World's Greatest Stars," *NYT*, 7 March 1965. Golden's 1965 show was on a double bill with comedian Jackie Mason. The ad also touted "the world's largest artificial outdoor ice rink" and the "April in Paris Singles Weekend." Writing in the *Nation*, 7 October 1968, Golden repeated this story and mistakenly named Grossinger's Catskill Resort Hotel as the place in question.

27. Letter to Gabriel Cohen, 19 February 1963, UNCC-HG, pt. 2, box 4:42.

28. "America's Gandhi: Rev. Martin Luther King Jr.," *Time*, Man of the Year, 3 January 1964. *Time*'s effort to sound in-the-know about black leadership and emphasize King's uniqueness did not come off very well. The profile dwelt on this "unlikely leader" who did not have "the quiet brilliance nor the sharp administrative capabilities of the NAACP's Roy Wilkins." The article went on in this vein for some time, noting the strengths King did *not* have. Furthermore, King "did not make his mark in the entertainment field, where talented Negroes have long been prominent."

29. Unsigned, "Martin Luther King Wins the Nobel Prize for Peace" and "Cheers and Scorn for the Nobel Award," *NYT*, 15 October 1964.

30. Golden, "Barry Goldwater: A Personal View," *New York Post*, 20 September 1964; "Causerie on Barry Goldwater," *CI*, July–August 1964. In "Ralph McGill and Sen. Goldwater," *CI*, January–February 1963, Golden told a story about Goldwater accidentally pledging allegiance to the Confederate flag, then beaming as he said, "But it didn't make any difference."

31. Golden, "Goldwater and a Jewish Secret," in *Long Live Columbus*, 225; "My Thoughts on Goldwater," *CI*, January–February 1964. Golden's friend, *Miami News* editor William C. "Bill" Baggs, wrote him ("Dear cousin . . .") congratulating him on the Goldwater one-liner, saying it was "very tasty and I sucked the juices." He closed with "The note is nothing more than to say I think of you often and miss you" (20 June 1963, UNCC-HG, pt. 2, box 11:12). Golden's "first Jewish president" line has been used hundreds of times in the popular press. A short item in the *Baltimore Sun* summed it up well: "To have a comment he wrote nearly 40 years ago quoted today puts Harry Golden in a club with H. L. Mencken and Will Rogers." The mention of Golden accompanied a column by Theo Lippman Jr., "Striking a Contemporary Note," *Baltimore Sun*, 11 September 2000.

32. Golden, "The Conscience of Mr. Goldwater," in *You're Entitle'*, 167; Golden, "Barry Goldwater: A Personal View," *New York Post*, 20 September 1964, 25.

33. John Herbers, "Negroes Step Up Drive in Alabama; 1,000 More Seized," *NYT*, 3 February 1965; UPI, "Dr. King Will Lead Selma Rights Test," *NYT*, 15 January 1965.

34. Daniel Lewis, "Hosea Williams, 74, Rights Crusader, Dies," *NYT*, 17 November 2000.

35. Johnson's speech to White House Press Corps, 4 February 1965, The American Presidency Project website, http://www.presidency.ucsb.edu/ws/?pid=27196 (1 November 2014). Johnson also spoke with King several times during this period. During the Selma campaign, his White House diary notes that conversations with him and others involved in the situation were a high priority. See digital diary entries for March 1965, Lyndon Baines Johnson Library and Museum, http://www.lbjlib.utexas.edu/johnson/archives .hom/diary/1965/65high.asp (1 November 2014).

36. Roy Reed, "Alabama Police Use Gas and Clubs to Rout Negroes," *NYT*, 8 March 1965; this article also appeared in Carson, Garrow, Kovach, and Polsgrove, *Reporting Civil Rights*, 2:322–26. See also Robert A. Caro, "Johnson's Dream, Obama's Speech," *NYT*, 27 August 2008, and video of Johnson's speech, http://www.lbjlibrary.org/lyndon-baines-johnson/speeches-films/president-johnsons-special-message-to-the-congress-the-american-promise/ (1 November 2014).

37. "Johnson and Vietnam," *CI*, January–February 1966; Golden, "The Agony of Lyndon B. Johnson," in *So Long as You're Healthy*, 213–15. Golden often referred to the obstacles

put in the way of black voters. He addressed the problem in Alabama in "Negro Voting in the South," *CI*, September–October 1959.

38. In a later edition of his book, Caro added this line: "How true a part? Forty-three years later, a mere blink of history's eye, a black American, Barack Obama, was sitting behind the desk in the Oval Office." For Caro's characterization of Johnson's role in history and the Voting Rights Act of 1965, see *Years of Lyndon Johnson: The Passage of Power*, 569. In endnotes, Caro cites his earlier books, *Means of Ascent*, xiii-xxi, and *Master of the Senate*, 715–16. See also the Martin Luther King Jr. Research and Education Institute and the King Papers Project, Stanford, Calif., http://mlk-kpp01.stanford.edu/, and the Martin Luther King Jr. Center for Nonviolent Social Change, Atlanta, Ga., http://www.thekingcenter.org/.

39. John McWhorter, "Burned Baby, Burned," *Washington Post*, 14 August 2005.

40. Kotz, *Judgment Days*, 342–43; "A Hoodlum Is a Hoodlum," *CI*, July–August 1964. In this essay Golden quotes Roy Wilkins of the NAACP saying, "We can help matters by recognizing that a punk is a punk, white or black, and by putting him in his proper place," to which Golden responds, "Amen." See also Michael T. Kaufman, "Stokely Carmichael, Rights Leader Who Coined 'Black Power,' Dies at 57," *NYT*, 16 November 1998; Wilkins and Mathews, *Standing Fast*, 316; and Carmichael, *Ready for Revolution* (note: in some cases, the author is listed as Kwame Ture, the name Carmichael took in 1978).

41. "What Is Black Power?" *CI*, November–December 1966; text of the speech "The Battle or the Bullet," delivered 3 April 1964 in Corey Methodist Church in Cleveland, Ohio, in Breitman, *Malcolm X Speaks*, 23–44. Malcolm X is still remembered by many as the speaker of the phrase "by any means necessary," which has been quoted and misquoted innumerable times. In some contexts it can be understood as a call to violence; in others it is an endorsement of selfless activism. Ironically, two years before Golden's comparison of Malcolm X to the Ku Klux Klan, Malcolm X met secretly with KKK leadership to discuss a possible purchase of land to be developed as a segregated farmland project for blacks. This meeting would arguably be the most controversial move in Malcolm X's career; see Marable, *Malcolm X*, 178–79. See also Malcolm X, *Malcolm X Speaks*.

42. Associated Press, "Workmen Rebuilding Homes of Four Negroes in Charlotte," *NYT*, 25 November 1965. See also historian Dan L. Morrill on roles played by the Alexanders, Hawkinses, Chamberses, and others, http://www.cmhpf.org/educationcivilrights.htm (1 November 2014); Morrill, "The Emergence of Diversity: African Americans," http://www.cmhpf.org/Morrill%20Book/CH12.htm (1 November 2014); and Morrill, *Historic Charlotte*.

43. *Swann v. Charlotte-Mecklenburg School Board* would wend its way through the system to the Supreme Court. In 1971, Chief Justice Warren Burger's historic opinion recognized busing as a "suitable remedial" means to bring about desegregation. See Douglas, *Reading, Writing, and Race*, 107–29. For a sense of how *Swann* was regarded after the Supreme Court ruling, see the North Carolina History website, http://www.northcarolinahistory.org/encyclopedia/296/entry/ (1 November 2014), and David Greenberg, "Swann Song: They Just Killed Busing in the One Place It Really Worked," *Slate*, 23 September 1999. See also Chambers interview, DOCSOUTH, 18 June 1990, Interview L-0127 (#4007), interviewer William Link, http://docsouth.unc.edu/sohp/L-0127/menu.html (1 November 2014).

44. Anderson, *A. Philip Randolph*, xiii; John Goldsmith, UPI report on hearings, 30 November 1966, UNCC-HG, pt. 2, box 13:25; U.S. Senate transcript of hearings on "The Federal Role in Urban Affairs," held by Subcommittee on Executive Reorganization, Committee of Government Operations, November 29–30, 1966, 1529–47, UNCC-HG, pt. 2., box 13:25. The subcommittee was chaired by Senator Abraham Ribicoff of Connecticut and included New York senator Jacob Javits among its members. Golden liked to remind people that he and Javits attended the same public school, P.S. 20.

45. Author's interview with Richard Goldhurst, email, 2001. Targ pushed Golden for a "firm delivery date" for the Sandburg work, and Golden responded by citing the "Evil Eye" excuse, 24 October 1960, UNCC-HG, pt. 2, box 35:34.

46. Draft column, "The Negro Intellectuals Who Need to Be Carefully Taught," attached to Golden's letter to John Hunt, senior editor of the *Saturday Evening Post*, 5 October 1965, UNCC-HG, pt. 2, box 27:35. The headline was a play on the name of a song in the Broadway smash *South Pacific*. The Rodgers and Hammerstein lyrics written in 1949 were controversial; they pointed out that race hatred is learned, not innate, and the subject is introduced in the musical in the context of interracial marriage.

47. Letter from Sheldon Wax, senior editor at *Playboy*, 6 May 1966, UNCC-HG, pt. 2, box 27:23; "God Bless the Gentile," *Playboy*, December 1966, 173.

48. Solomon Littman, *Harry Golden on Anti-Semitism, Jews, Christians, Race Relations, Negros, Whites, Civil Rights, States Rights, the South, the North, Social Action and some other matters, Anti-Defamation League of B'nai B'rith, 1966*. Schary, a filmmaker, producer, and writer, served as ADL national chairman from 1963 to 1969.

49. Author's interview with Solomon Littman, telephone, 2011. Littman, who at the time of the booklet's publication was assistant director of ADL's program division, went on to head the Friends of Simon Wiesenthal Center for Holocaust Studies in Canada.

50. R. I. Duffus, "Carolina Israelite," review of *Ess, Ess, Mein Kindt*, *NYT*, 11 December 1966, 387.

51. Ferris, *Matzoh Ball Gumbo*, 17.

52. Unsigned, "David Dubinsky, 90, Dies; Led Garment Union," *NYT*, 18 September 1982. The membership of the garment workers' union reached as high as 450,000 but had declined to 350,000 by the time of Dubinsky's death, in part because of the shifting base of the garment industry and an increase in imported goods.

53. Advertisement, "A Postscript from David Dubinsky to Harry Golden," *NYT*, 19 October 1965. Conservative writer William F. Buckley Jr. was in the race too. His fluky entry confounded even the candidate himself. Asked what he would do if elected, Buckley famously answered, "Demand a recount" (Sam Tanenhaus, "The Buckley Effect," *NYT*, 2 October 2005).

54. Author's interview with Richard Goldhurst, email, 2011.

55. Advertisement, "An Exchange of Letters from Harry Golden to David Dubinsky," *NYT*, 25 October 1965.

56. All of the following found in UNCC-HG, pt. 2, box 2:12-1: Letter to Dorothy Schiff, *New York Post*, 1 November 1965; letter from John Osenenko, executive vice president of Bell-McClure Newspaper Syndicate, 2 December 1965, telling Golden that the *New York Post* dropped his column because it conflicted with the paper's mayoral endorsement; letter from Paul Sann of *New York Post* to Osenenko, 8 December 1965, correcting that

claim, explaining that Golden's column was pulled because it had run as an ad in the paper and therefore was not appropriate editorial content. Both versions are true. The ad text *was* inappropriate content for a column, and the publisher *was* furious that Golden criticized Lindsay. Also in the same archive: letter to Lerner, 29 December 1965. Golden closed off the mess by writing a letter to Dubinsky on 4 November 1965 with observations about the election results, adding, "Please don't get mad at me, because I love you, and we'll fight again on the same side again." Lindsay didn't hold a grudge. He posed for a photo to be used in a coffee table book Golden put out in 1972, *The Greatest Jewish City in the World*, 58–59.

57. Letters from Golden to Brinkley and others, inviting them to the gathering, 18 August 1966, UNCC-HG, pt. 2, box 2:15.

58. Letter from Ashmore to Griffin, copied to Golden, 29 October 1966, and response from Golden to Ashmore, 2 November 1966, UNCC-HG, pt. 2, box 2:15. A clip of the article was attached to the letter: Jack Nelson, "Election of Apartheid President in U.S. Viewed as Possibility," *Los Angeles Times*, 27 October 1966. It was picked up by wire services and ran across the country.

59. Letters from Isador N. Agrons, 3 April 1966; from Golden to Agrons, 19 April 1966; from Golden to Agronsky, 19 April 1966; and from Agronsky to Golden, 9 May 1966, UNCC-HG, pt. 2, box 2 11:14.

60. This book also brought a $200,000 libel lawsuit, a new experience for Golden. He had referred to a Georgia man as a "legendary liar" and wrote a check for $1,200 to the plaintiff to settle out of court. See FBI Bureau file 73-16547 and Charlotte field office file 73-432, 28 April 1969. Golden referenced the suit later but avoided rehashing the details in print, probably due to intervention by his son Richard Goldhurst; see "Sued for Libel," *CI*, December 1967.

61. Golden referenced his goals in a letter to Morris Abram, 4 August 1965, UNCC-HG, pt. 2, box 1:35.

62. "A Little Girl Is Dead," *CI*, May–June 1965. To reach a total of ten books, Golden was either making a rare reference to his first book, the unfortunate *Jewish Roots in the Carolinas*, or counting his chapter in *Five Boyhoods*, published in 1962.

63. Phagan's age was listed as fourteen by many historians and by Golden. Contemporary experts on the case use thirteen as her age at death, as does the memorial marker for her in Marietta, Ga. See "Causerie on the Death of Mrs. Leo Frank," *CI*, May–April 1957.

64. Oney, *And the Dead Shall Rise*, 16, 340–43; Golden, *A Little Girl Is Dead*, 216.

65. Golden, "A Little Girl Is Dead," *CI*, May–June 1965.

66. Woodward, *Tom Watson*, 377; Dinnerstein, *Leo Frank Case*, 96, 119–20.

67. Golden, *A Little Girl Is Dead*, 210–24, 299; Woodward, *Tom Watson*, 373–89; Ayers, *Promise of the New South*, 229–82; Handlin, "American Views of the Jew at the Opening of the Twentieth Century," 324; Carol Pierannunzi, *The New Georgia Encyclopedia*, http://www.georgiaencyclopedia.org/nge/Article.jsp?id=h-2540 (1 November 2014).

68. Woodward, *Tom Watson*, 211.

69. In his preface to the 2008 revised edition of *The Leo Frank Case*, Dinnerstein recalled that he had been "extremely upset" to learn that Golden was about to publish a book on the same subject. "I thought that I would have difficulty getting my manuscript published. My apprehensions proved to be unfounded," he wrote.

70. Letter from Friede, 4 November 1965, UNCC-HG, pt. 2, box 9:18; "Harry Golden on a Cause Célèbre," *Newsweek*, 29 November 1965; E. M. Yader, "They Hates a Myth, Murdered a Man," *Saturday Review*, 25 December 1965; *Book Review Digest 1965*, 479; Anthony Boucher, "Criminals at Large," *NYT*, 2 January, 1 May 1966. The popular writer-editor-critic Boucher wrote that he "relished" Golden's book, adding, "Golden is as unexpected a fact-crime writer as Truman Capote is. . . . But who is better suited to treat the great Leo Frank case . . . which centers on the position of Jews in the South?" Anita Stewart Brown recalled Golden's reaction to the "true crime" label, in author's interview in Charlotte, 2000.

71. Golden, *Our Southern Landsman*, 80–89.

72. "Causerie on the Death of Mrs. Leo Frank," *CI*, March–April 1957; Golden, *A Little Girl Is Dead*, 257; Oney, *And the Dead Shall Rise*, 607. Mrs. Frank's first name was spelled "Lucille" but appeared in some court documents and newspaper articles as "Lucile," the version Golden used. He may have chosen that version because it appears in a printed version of "The Prisoner's Statement" read by Leo Frank during his trial. An edited version of the statement appears in Golden, *A Little Girl Is Dead*, 155–72. Oney describes the extraordinary statement, which took Frank hours to read aloud in court, in *And the Dead Shall Rise*, 297–305. Golden's old friend Hermann Cohen had dealt with his anger toward Watson in a forthright manner: "I lived through those days, and several years ago I drove by Thomson, Georgia, with my chauffeur and went to the grave where Tom Watson is buried and urinated on it," wrote Cohen in a letter to Golden, 30 June 1965, UNCC-HG, pt. 2, box 4:44–45.

73. Golden, *A Little Girl Is Dead*, 230, 256–57; Oney, *And the Dead Shall Rise*, 346, 366, 375; Sorin, *Tradition Transformed*, 57; Ron Chernow, "Review of *The Trust: The Private and Powerful Family behind the New York Times*, by Susan E. Tifft and Alex S. Jones," *NYT*, 26 September 1999.

74. Golden, "Causerie on the Death of Mrs. Leo Frank," in *Only in America*, 215; letter to Maurice Abram, 4 August 1965, UNCC-HG, pt. 2, box 1:35. Golden never stopped being surprised about the very long reach of the lynch mob. During an interview in Charlotte with an elderly Jewish businessman who had worked with Frank, Golden was incredulous to be asked if he could just let the story lie. "It will only stir things up again," the man pleaded. In this letter Golden made other statements about Jews and Gentiles hesitant to stir up old animosities connected to the Frank case, and he cites one instance in which he believes evidence pointing to Frank's innocence was suppressed.

Chapter 8

1. Golden, *Right Time*, 440–41; letter to Kivie Kaplan about negative prostate biopsy, 2 February 1965, UNCC-HG, pt. 2, box 9:14. An earlier scare happened in 1958. Wheeler joined the Southern Regional Council (founded in 1919 as the Commission on Interracial Cooperation), which worked against racial injustice, and served as its president from 1969 to 1974. See Edward A. Gargan, "Raymond M. Wheeler Dies, Documented Hunger of Poor," *NYT*, 20 February 1982. Dr. Paul Sanger, a well-known heart surgeon who developed the first synthetic arterial graft and a friend of both Wheeler and Golden, was also at the bedside during Golden's emergency.

See Golden, *Right Time*, 440; Heineman Foundation website, http://heineman
.org/about-us/ (1 November 2014). Sanger owned a few shares of *Carolina Israelite* stock,
apparently in return for a loan or loans to Golden; Sanger's children forgave the debt
in 1975. See letter from North Carolina National Bank, 27 January 1975, and undated
letter from Paul Sanger Jr. with response from Golden, 30 January 1975, UNCC-HG,
pt. 2, box 14:2. Golden enjoyed sharing medical humor with Sanger and once
wrote him about a headline in the *Charlotte News* that blared, "Marney Undergoes
Minor Chest Surgery." Golden added, "I'll be a son-of-a-bitch. The next thing we'll
hear about some fellow losing his balls in a minor operation" (letter to Sanger,
6 December 1966, UNCC-HG, pt. 2, box 14:2).

2. Golden, *Right Time*, 440–41.

3. Goldhurst, "Welcome Home Thoreau," *CI*, April–May 1967.

4. Letter from Wershba on an interoffice memo sheet from CBS News, 10 January 1967,
UNCC-HG, pt. 2, box 16:37. The references are to anchormen Walter Cronkite on CBS and
Chet Huntley and David Brinkley on NBC.

5. A copy of the *Winston-Salem Journal*'s unsigned editorial, "A Wish for a Neighbor,"
was sent to Golden by longtime friend Judge J. Braxton Craven, by then serving on the
U.S. Court of Appeals for the Fourth Circuit. Craven scrawled, "It's true, Harry" on his letterhead. Craven played a key role in the *Swann* school desegregation case. See 9 January
1967, UNCC-HG, pt. 2, box 4:64.

6. Author's interview with Norma Leveton, 2006.

7. Golden, *Right Time*, 442.

8. Letter from Dorothy Goldhirsch Fisher (daughter of Jake Goldhirsch), 17 September
1965, UNCC-HG, pt. 2, box 42:23.

9. Golden, *Right Time*, 40–41; Golden, *For 2 Cents Plain*, 213. The spelling of Golden's
first name in childhood varied. See telegram from Matilda Goldhurst, 14 February 1959,
UNCC-HG, pt. 2, box 42:23.

10. Letter from Harry to Matilda, 9 March 1966, and her response, 12 March 1966,
UNCC-HG, pt. 2, box 42:23.

11. Ibid.; letter from Clara Goldhurst to Matilda, 22 March 1966; letters to U.S. Postal
Service, 27 August 1969, and to a private detective in Sherman Oaks, California, 2 April
1965, UNCC-HG, pt. 2, box 42:23. The Los Angeles city and county sheriff's departments
and the city's field office of the FBI had no better luck finding Matilda during a routine
background check of family members when Golden filed for a presidential pardon in
1969. See FBI Bureau file 73-16547 and Los Angeles field office file 73-1889, 24 April 1969.
The California death certificate for Matilda Goldhurst lists her vitals as follows: born 1896
in Austria, daughter of Louis Goldhurst and Naomi Zonis; profession: clothing designer
for forty-five years in the state; died 12 December 1993, at age 97. See California State File
No. 93-218247. Matilda was buried in the Hollywood Forever Cemetery. Regarding the
family legend of Matilda moving before Max arrived, see author's interview with Andrew
Leveton, Golden's great-nephew, telephone, 2014.

12. Author's interview with Richard Goldhurst, email, 2012.

13. List of new titles, *NYT*, 7 March 1971; letter to attorney Maurice Greenbaum, 20
November 1967, UNCC-HG, pt. 2, box 33:8. Golden notes the $10,000 advance already
paid and went through his usual reconfiguring of royalties, which never varied greatly,

and this time gave 20 percent to Richard Goldhurst, 10 percent to Tiny, 15 percent to the *Carolina Israelite*, and the balance to himself.

14. "The Meaning of Israel," *CI*, December 1967, reprinted from *Holiday*; Golden, *The Israelis*, 74–79, 304. Readers interested in glimpsing the Goldhurst/Golden sense of humor would do well to read, in *The Israelis*, "The Generation Gap," 86. "Arbah Arnon," 141–46, a first-person piece that carries Goldhurst's byline, shows the author's enviable ability to find humor and pathos in the same moment and convey both without treacle.

15. Author's interview with Richard Goldhurst, email, 2011. Goldhurst used Virginius Dabney's *Dry Messiah* to check against his parents' recollections of the stock scandal. See *Kirkus Reviews*, 6 June 1969, http://www.kirkusreviews.com/book-reviews/harry-golden-8/the-right-time/#review (1 November 2014). Also see letter from Targ about the manuscript, 3 December 1968, copy from personal papers of Walter Klein, and letter from Targ regarding book's reception, 3 December 1969, UNCC-HG, pt. 2, box 33:8.

16. "Ken Robertson," *CI*, March–April 1964; "Medicare and the Blue Cross," *CI*, January–February 1965; author's interview with Walter Klein, 2000.

17. Golden's tax records and related correspondence are interspersed throughout UNCC-HG, pt. 2, boxes 41:1, 41:6–8, 41:9–14, 41:27, 41:28, 42:1, and 63:9. World Publishing's "Royalty Report" dated 25 March 1960 shows the impressive list of income sources flowing in with Golden's first three books; see UNCC-HG, pt. 2, box 35:35. Letter from Bernard Deeter, 28 March 1967, general manager of World's trade book department, asking Golden to accept a reduced royalty for sales of the Sandburg book, which he reported had sold fewer than 1,000 copies that year, is in UNCC-HG, pt. 2, box 35:35. The University of Illinois published its Prairie State Book imprint editions in 1961 and 1988, which enjoyed stronger sales.

18. Letter from McGill to "Colonel Ashmore" and copied to the "Brethren," 27 July 1967, UNCC-HG, pt. 2, box 2:15.

19. UPI, "Golden Criticizes S.N.C.C. and Quits," *NYT*, 22 August 1967; "Anti-Semitic Attack in Organ of Extremist Negro Organization Evokes Jewish Protests," Jewish Telegraphic Agency, 16 August 1967, http://www.jta.org/1967/08/16/archive/anti-semitic-attack-in-organ-of-extremist-negro-organization-evokes-jewish-protests (1 November 2014). A document in FBI Bureau file 73-464547 and Houston office file 73-464, 25 April 1969, notes Golden's resignation from SNCC and includes the unsigned clipping "Harry Golden Quits SNCC," *Houston Chronicle*, 28 August 1967. The editorial begins, "The only thing we find surprising about Harry Golden's resignation . . . is that it took him so long to do it." The editorial went on to criticize SNCC for forcing whites out and called H. Rap Brown and Stokely Carmichael "among the most active fomenters of racial division and distrust in America." It concluded, "No wonder Harry Golden wants out."

20. "Los Angeles Riots," *CI*, July–August 1965; "Were the Los Angeles Riots Anti-Semitic?" *CI*, September–October 1965.

21. UPI, "Golden Criticizes S.N.C.C. and Quits," *NYT*, 22 August 1967; "Harry Golden Quits SNCC, Calls It Anti-Jew," *Jet*, 7 September 1967; letter to Ralph Featherstone of SNCC, 18 August 1967, UNCC-HG, pt. 2, box 15:6.

22. Typical of the signed hate mail that Golden received, this sender wrote on letterhead for a nonexistent or tiny organization, in this case the "Confederate States Activities, Inc.," 23 August 1967, UNCC-HG, pt. 2, box 15:6–7.

23. Konvitz, "Jews and Civil Rights," 283.

24. Golden repeated this sentiment in letters, essays, and speeches, including this quote from "Vote of Confidence," in *So Long as You're Healthy*, 113, and a slightly different version in *The Right Time*, 395.

25. Golden, *Right Time*, 11–16; letter to Maurice Greenbaum, 17 October 1969, UNCC-HG, pt. 2, box 41:11, requesting that the attorney "terminate" the Caroline Israelite Corporation by the end of the year. Golden spent as much as $60,000 to keep the *Carolina Israelite* afloat for its last three years, which bothered his lawyer and accountant much more than it bothered him.

26. "The Students Ask; I Cannot Answer," *CI*, January–February 1968.

27. "The War in Viet Nam," *CI*, July–August 1965. Golden continued to make news on issues that appealed to those with strong antiwar sentiments, such as his scathing criticism of the National Rifle Association—"a symbol of what a violent nation we are." But his support of Johnson seemed to erase whatever goodwill such pronouncements would have garnered in the past. See "National Rifle Association," *CI*, July–August 1966.

28. "Harry Golden," *Nation*, 29 April 1968; opinion page, *Charleston Gazette*, 4 May 1968. Golden's column in the *Nation* quoted Thurmond calling the slain King "an agitator" immediately after the announcement of the civil rights leader's murder.

29. Golden, *Right Time*, 438.

30. Ibid., 441.

31. A message from James J. Storrow Jr., publisher of the *Nation*, appeared in the last issue of the *Carolina Israelite*. "It is with great pride, then, that *The Nation* announces that, though the *Israelite* may be leaving us, Harry Golden most definitely is not." See letters, all in 1968, from Ann Landers, 5 March; Norman Cousins, 6 March; John P. McKnight, 26 February; Ed Guthman, 21 March; and Frank P. Graham, 22 March, UNCC-HG, pt. 2, box 22:24.

32. Letter from Humphrey, 26 February 1968, UNCC-HG, pt. 2, box 22:24.

33. Golden, *Right Time*, 11–12.

34. Ibid.

35. Letter from Humphrey, 18 February 1972, UNCC-HG, pt. 2, box 7:63.

36. Abraham H. Foxman, "The Six-Day War: 40 Years Later," *New Jersey Jewish Standard*, 25 May 2007.

37. Sarna, *American Judaism*, 318–19.

38. Letter from Targ, 3 December 1969, UNCC-HG, pt. 2, box 33:8; *Kirkus Reviews* review of *So Long as You're Healthy (Abee gezunt)*, July 1970, https://www.kirkusreviews.com/book-reviews/harry-golden-5/so-long-as-youre-healthy-abee-gezunt/ (1 November 2014).

39. The final details of Golden's settlement with the joke writer are unclear. Richard Goldhurst, who refused to have anything to do with the joke book, was relieved that it was dispatched quickly and for a small sum. See author's interview with Richard Goldhurst, email, 2011.

40. Golden, "Charlotte, North Carolina," in *Our Southern Landsman*, 175; advertisement for thirty-five-piece sets of Kennedy medals by the Lincoln Mint in Chicago, *The Rotarian*, February 1971; mailgram from Dick Drost, president, Naked City, regarding Miss Nude America Contest, 30 July 1975, UNCC-HG, pt. 2, box 11:20.

41. Letter to Douglas, 11 November 1974, UNCC-HG, pt. 2, box 5:21. Golden had purchased a house to move to from Elizabeth Avenue but happily took Brown up on her offer of the comfortable Eighth Street house. Brown kept Golden's personal belongings in the house for years following his death. After Brown's passing, a bequest and the house's contents went to the University of North Carolina-Charlotte, and the Harry Golden Fund was formed. Under the direction of curators Robin Brabham and Robert Weiss, Golden's furnishings were incorporated into a permanent exhibit, "The World of Harry Golden," in the J. Murrey Atkins Library, UNCC.

42. Author's interview with Dan L. Morrill, telephone, 2012.

43. *Kirkus Reviews*, review of *Long Live Columbus* dated February 1974, although the book itself lists 1975 as the publishing year.

44. The following are in UNCC-HG, pt. 2: letter to Targ about biographies, 12 July 1974, box 15:15; letter from Perry Knowlton, president of Curtis Brown Ltd., rejecting *America, I Love You*, 12 February 1976, box 4:70; letter from Targ about *America*, 15 September 1977, box 29:4; letters from Harry Jr., one dated 31 July, presumably 1977, and one following a short time later, box 29:4; letters from Julian Back, literary agent, regarding later attempts by Golden to sell *America*, 19 December 1977 and 6 January 1978, box 29:4; Golden's draft manuscript materials, box 29:5–11. Within a month of Golden's death, a literary agent wrote Richard Goldhurst asking to represent the manuscript, which he apparently had not read—an irony Golden would have appreciated. See letter to "Richard Golden" [*sic*] from Scott Meredith, 12 October 1981, box 24:4.

45. "Ronald Reagan of General Electric," *CI*, November–December 1961; letter from Reagan, 11 January 1962, with Golden answering 16 and 18 January 1962, UNCC-HG, pt. 1, box 8:62.

46. Had Golden seen his FBI pardon file, he would have thoroughly enjoyed it, particularly a redacted interview that described him as being "an excellent newspaperman [who] possesses and displays all of the foibles and faults of that trade" (FBI Bureau file 73-16547 and Charlotte field office file 73-432, 28 April 1969).

47. Warrant of Executive Clemency, signed by Richard Nixon, 5 December 1973, UNCC-HG, pt. 2, box 61:32; Clara Goldhurst, April 1895–April 1974, Social Security Death Index.

48. Dan Morgan, "Nixon Signs Pardon for Harry Golden," *Washington Post*, 7 December 1973.

49. Author's interviews with Walter Klein, 2000.

Epilogue

1. One of several instances of the observation "the South made a writer of me" is found in the introduction to Golden, *Mr. Kennedy and the Negroes*, 5–6.

2. Letter from the Reverend William "Bill" Everhart of Hebron United Church of Christ, Winston-Salem, N.C., 23 February 1968, UNCC-HG, pt. 2, box 22:24.

3. "Harry Golden" column, *Nation*, 7 October 1968.

4. McGill's observation appeared in the new introduction for the 1964 edition of his book *South and the Southerner*.

5. Rogoff, "Harry Golden, New Yorker"; Rogoff cites a letter from UNCC-HG to Bob Suritz, 10 February 1965. See also Sorin, *Tradition Transformed*, 1–10.

6. Heinze, *Jews and the American Soul*, 204–6. Heinze quotes a colleague who observed that had the popular rabbi lived longer (he died in 1948, not yet fifty years old), Liebman might have been "a kind of Jewish and more intellectual Billy Graham."

Rabbi Charles E. Shulman, himself a prolific author, noted the similarity of the astonishing sales of books by Liebman and Golden, in "Reviews of Books, *For 2 Cents Plain*," *American Jewish Archives* 12, no. 1 (April 1960): 75–77. It's not uncommon to find old copies of these authors' books inscribed with sentiments like "Merry Christmas, Uncle Joe! Love, Lucy"—amusing reminders of their interfaith appeal.

7. Rogoff, *Homelands*, 209.

8. "What I Have Learned," *Saturday Review of Literature*, 17 June 1967, and *CI*, August–September 1967.

BIBLIOGRAPHY

Archival Collections

Atlanta, Georgia
>The Martin Luther King Jr. Center for Nonviolent Social Change, http://www
>>.thekingcenter.org/. 1 November 2014.

Chapel Hill, North Carolina
>Southern Historical Collection, Louis Round Wilson Special Collections Library,
>>University of North Carolina
>>Harriet & Henderson Cotton Mills Records, 1885–1999

Charlotte, North Carolina
>J. Murrey Atkins Library Special Collections, University of North Carolina at Charlotte
>>Kelly M. Alexander Jr. Papers
>>Kelly M. Alexander Sr. Papers
>>Blumenthal Family Papers
>>Legette Blythe Papers
>>Harry Golden Papers (pts. 1 and 2)
>>C. A. McKnight Papers
>>New South Voices
>>Boyd E. Payton Papers
>>Morris Speizman Papers
>>Kenneth Wilson Whitsett Papers

Charlottesville, Virginia
>Special Collections, University of Virginia Library
>>Papers of Carter Glass, Accession #2913

Hattiesburg, Mississippi
>Manuscripts Collection of the University of Southern Mississippi Libraries Digital
>>Collections
>>P. D. East Collection

Stanford, California
>Stanford University
>>The Martin Luther King Jr. Research and Education Institute and the King Papers
>>Project, http://mlk-kpp01.stanford.edu/. 1 November 2014.

Washington, D.C.
>George Washington University
>>Eleanor Roosevelt Papers Project, Online Documents

327

Government Documents

FBI files for Harry Lewis Golden/Harry Goldhurst/Harry Golden obtained through Freedom of Information Act request are found in Bureau files 73-16547 and HQ 105851. The majority of information contained in these files is the result of investigation following his "Petition for Pardon after Completion of Sentence," filed in 1963 but not finalized until 1969. Other information gathered by the FBI at various times in connection to organizations suspected of Communist ties references Golden and his FBI number, 672835. Other materials also mentioning Golden are housed with the National Archives, file number 36-1357. Also cited is FBI Bureau file 61-7511 on the Highlander Folk School in Monteagle, Tennessee.

Interviews Conducted by the Author

Raymond Arsenault, telephone, 2012
Marc Ben-Joseph, telephone, 2006
Ruth Ben-Joseph, telephone, 2006
Mark Bernstein, telephone and email, 2006
Marion Best, Des Moines, Wash., 2010
Philip Blumenthal, telephone, March 2009
Robin Brabham, Charlotte, N.C., 2000, 2006; email, 2008, 2011, 2013, 2014
Anita Stewart Brown, Charlotte, N.C., 2000
Jack Claiborne, Charlotte, N.C., 2000, 2006; email, October 2011
J. E. Cohen, telephone, 2007
Ruth Easterling, telephone, 2001
John Egerton, email, 2001
Eli N. Evans, telephone, 2006
Susan Gardner, Charlotte, N.C., 2000
Richard Goldhurst, Westport, Conn., 2000; email, 2006, 2008, 2010, 2011, 2013, 2014; email and telephone, 2001, 2011, 2012
William Goldhurst, telephone, 2006
Bruce Kalk, email, 2011
Walter J. Klein, Charlotte, N.C., 2000; email, 2011, 2012; telephone and email, 2013, 2014
Leona Lefkowitz, Charlotte, N.C., 2000; email, 2001
Andrew Leveton, telephone, 2014
Norma Leveton, Longmeadow, Mass., 2006
Solomon Littman, telephone, 2011
Dan Locklair, telephone and email, 2011, 2012
Newton Minow, email, 2009
Dan L. Morrill, telephone, 2012
David Nolan, email, 2010
Charles Peters, telephone, 2008
Peter Ross Range, email and telephone, 2010, 2011
Pearl Taylor, email, 2010

Mary Utting, email, 2009
Jonathan Wallas, telephone, 2011

Newspapers

Agawam (Mass.) Citizen
Atlanta Daily World
Atlanta Journal-
    Constitution
Baltimore Sun
Birmingham News
Boston Globe
Charleston News and
    Courier
Charlotte News
Charlotte Observer
Chicago Daily Defender/
    Chicago Defender
Chicago Daily News
Chicago Tribune
Christian Science Monitor

Detroit Free Press
Durham Morning Herald
Enfield (Conn.) Press
Forward
Greensboro (N.C.) Daily News
Hartford Courant
High Point Enterprise
Los Angeles Times
Louisville Courier-Journal
Miami Herald
Miami News
Montgomery Advertiser
New Jersey Jewish
    Standard
New Orleans
    Times-Picayune

New York Herald Tribune
New York Observer
New York Post Daily
    Magazine
New York Times
North Carolina News and
    Record
Petal Papers
Raleigh News and
    Observer
Richmond Times-Dispatch
Seattle Times
Springfield Union and
    Republican
Washington Post
Winston-Salem Journal

Magazines

American Judaism
Book Review Digest
Carolina Israelite
Charlotte Labor Journal
    and Dixie Farm News
Commentary
Congress Bi-Weekly
Coronet
Crisis
Ebony
Esquire
Family Circle
Holiday

Jet
Jewish Week
Kirkus Reviews
Library Journal
Life
Look
Negro Digest
Nation
Newsweek
New Yorker
Playboy
Publishers Weekly
Reader's Digest

Redbook
Rotarian
Saturday Evening Post
Saturday Review
Slate
Sunday Review of
    Literature
Texas Monthly
Time
TV Guide
Washington Monthly

Works by Harry Golden

Charlotte Labor Journal and Dixie Farm News. 1939–44.
Carolina Israelite. February 1944–January-February 1968.
Jews in American History: Their Contributions to the United States of America. With
    Martin Rywell. Charlotte: Henry Lewis Martin Co., 1950.

Jewish Roots in the Carolinas: A Pattern of American Philo-Semitism. Charlotte: Carolina Israelite, 1955.

Only in America. Cleveland: World Publishing, 1958.

For 2 Cents Plain. Cleveland: World Publishing, 1959.

Enjoy, Enjoy! Cleveland: World Publishing, 1960.

Carl Sandburg. Cleveland: World Publishing, 1961; Urbana-Champaign: University of Illinois Press, 1988.

Five Boyhoods: Howard Lindsay, Harry Golden, Walt Kelly, William Zinsser, and John Updike. Edited by Martin Levin. New York: Doubleday, 1962.

The Harry Golden Omnibus. London: Cassell & Co., 1962. Essays from *Only in America, For 2 Cents Plain,* and *Enjoy, Enjoy!*

You're Entitle'. Cleveland: World Publishing, 1962.

Forgotten Pioneer. With illustrations by Leonard Vosburgh. Cleveland: World Publishing, 1963.

Mr. Kennedy and the Negroes. Cleveland: World Publishing, 1964.

So What Else Is New? New York: Putnam's, 1964.

A Little Girl Is Dead. Cleveland: World Publishing, 1965.

The Spirit of the Ghetto: Studies of the Jewish Quarter. By Hutchins Hapgood. With drawings by Jacob Epstein and preface and notes by Harry Golden. New York: Funk and Wagnalls, 1965.

Ess, Ess, Mein Kindt (Eat, Eat, My Child). New York: Putnam's, 1966.

The Best of Harry Golden. Cleveland: World Publishing, 1967.

The Right Time: An Autobiography. New York: Putnam's, 1969.

So Long as You're Healthy (Abee Gezunt). New York: Putnam's, 1970.

The Israelis: Portrait of a People. New York: Putnam's, 1971.

The Golden Book of Jewish Humor. New York: Putnam's, 1972.

The Greatest Jewish City in the World. New York: Doubleday, 1972.

Travels through Jewish America. With Richard Goldhurst. New York: Doubleday, 1973.

Our Southern Landsman. New York: Putnam's, 1974.

Long Live Columbus. New York: Putnam's, 1975.

Books, Essays, Articles, and Unpublished Manuscripts

Abernathy, Ralph David. *And the Walls Came Tumbling Down: An Autobiography.* New York: HarperCollins, 1990.

Adams, Maurianne, and John Bracey, eds. *Strangers and Neighbors: Relations between Blacks and Jews in the United States.* Amherst: University of Massachusetts Press, 1999.

Adler, Selig. "Zebulon B. Vance and the 'Scattered Nation.'" *Journal of Southern History* 7, no. 3 (August 1941): 362.

Aluko, Yele. "American Medical Association Apologizes for Racism in Medicine." *Journal of the American Medical Association* 100, no. 10 (October 2008): 1116–1256.

Anderson, Jervis. *A. Philip Randolph: A Biographical Portrait.* Berkeley: University of California Press, 1986.

Arsenault, Raymond. *Freedom Riders: 1961 and the Struggle for Racial Justice.* New York: Oxford University Press, 2006.

Asch, Christopher Myers. *The Senator and the Sharecropper: The Freedom Struggles of James O. Eastland and Fannie Lou Hamer*. New York: New Press, 2008.

Ascoli, Peter M. *Julius Rosenwald: The Man Who Built Sears, Roebuck and Advanced the Cause of Black Education in the American South*. Bloomington: Indiana University Press, 2006. Kindle edition.

Ashmore, Harry S. *The Negro and the Schools*. Chapel Hill: University of North Carolina Press, 1954.

———. *An Epitaph for Dixie*. New York: Norton: 1958.

———. *Hearts and Minds: The Anatomy of Racism from Roosevelt to Reagan*. New York: McGraw-Hill, 1982.

Ayers, Edward L. *The Promise of the New South: Life after Reconstruction*. Oxford: Oxford University Press, 2007. Kindle edition.

Badger, Tony. "Southerners Who Refused to Sign the Southern Manifesto." *Historical Journal* 42, no. 2 (June 1999): 517–34.

Balint, Benjamin. *Running Commentary: The Contentious Magazine That Transformed the Jewish Left into the Neoconservative Right*. New York: Public Affairs, 2010.

Balkin, Jack M. *What* Brown v. Board of Education *Should Have Said: The Nation's Top Legal Experts Rewrite America's Landmark Civil Rights Decision*. New York: New York University Press, 2002.

Barr, Terry. "Rabbi Grafman and Birmingham's Civil Rights Era." In *The Quiet Voices: Southern Rabbis and Black Civil Rights, 1880s to 1990s*, edited by Mark K. Bauman and Berkley Kalin, 168–89. Tuscaloosa: University of Alabama Press, 1997.

Bass, Jonathan S. *Blessed Are the Peacemakers: Martin Luther King Jr., Eight White Religious Leaders, and the "Letter from Birmingham Jail."* Baton Rouge: Louisiana State University Press, 2001.

Bauman, Mark K., and Berkley Kalin, eds. *The Quiet Voices: Southern Rabbis and Black Civil Rights, 1880s to 1990s*. Tuscaloosa: University of Alabama Press, 1997.

Bayley, Edwin R. *Joe McCarthy and the Press*. New York: Pantheon, 1981.

Beals, Melba Pattillo. *Warriors Don't Cry: A Searing Memoir of the Battle to Integrate Little Rock's Central High*. New York: Simon Pulse, 2002.

Berry, Faith, ed. *A Scholar's Conscience: Selected Writings of J. Saunders Redding, 1942–1977*. Lexington: University Press of Kentucky, 1992.

Biale, David, ed. *Cultures of the Jews*. Vol. 3, *Modern Encounters*. New York: Schocken Books, 2002.

Blumberg, Janice Rothschild. *One Voice: Rabbi Jacob M. Rothschild and the Troubled South*. Macon, Ga.: Mercer University Press, 1985.

Book Review Digest. New York: H. W. Wilson Company. Editions were consulted for years 1950–80, in both hardbound and digital forms.

Branch, Taylor. *Parting the Waters: America in the King Years, 1954–63*. New York: Simon and Schuster, 1988.

———. *Pillar of Fire: America in the King Years, 1963–65*. New York: Simon and Schuster, 1998.

———. *At Canaan's Edge: America in the King Years, 1965–68*. New York: Simon and Schuster, 2006.

Breitman, George, ed. *Malcolm X Speaks: Selected Speeches and Statements*. New York: Grove Press, 1994.

Bryant, Nick. *The Bystander: John F. Kennedy and the Struggle for Black Equality*. New York: Basic Books, 2006.

Brinkley, Douglas. *Rosa Parks*. New York: Viking, 2000.

Burns, Rebecca. *Burial for a King: Martin Luther King Jr.'s Funeral and the Week That Transformed Atlanta and Rocked the Nation*. New York: Scribner, 2011.

Cannon, James Jr., and Richard L. Watson Jr., eds. *Bishop Cannon's Own Story: Life as I Have Seen It*. Durham: Duke University Press, 1955.

Carmichael, Stokely. *Ready for Revolution: The Life and Struggles of Stokely Carmichael (Kwame Ture)*. New York: Scribner, 2005.

Caro, Robert. *The Years of Lyndon Johnson: The Path to Power*. New York: Knopf, 1982.

———. *The Years of Lyndon Johnson: Means of Ascent*. New York: Knopf, 1990.

———. *The Years of Lyndon Johnson: Master of the Senate*. New York: Knopf, 2002.

———. *The Years of Lyndon Johnson: The Passage of Power*. New York: Knopf, 2012.

Carson, Clayborne. *In struggle: SNCC and the Black Awakening of the 1960s*. Cambridge, Mass.: Harvard University Press, 1981.

Carson, Claiborne, David J. Garrow, Bill Kovach, and Carol Polsgrove, comps. *Reporting Civil Rights*. Pt. 1, *American Journalism, 1941-1963*. Washington, D.C.: Library of America, 2003.

———. *Reporting Civil Rights*. Pt. 2, *American Journalism, 1963-1973*. Washington, D.C.: Library of America, 2003.

Carter, Dan T. *Scottsboro: A Tragedy of the American South*. Baton Rouge: Louisiana State University Press, 1979.

———. *The Politics of Rage: George Wallace, the Origins of the New Conservatism, and the Transformation of American Politics*. Baton Rouge: Louisiana State University Press, 2000.

Carty, Thomas J. "Secular Icon or Catholic Hero? Religion and the Presidency of John F. Kennedy." In *Religion and the American Presidency*, edited by Mark J. Rozell and Gleaves Whitney, 139-56. New York: Palgrave Macmillan, 2012.

Cash, W. J. *The Mind of the South*. New York: Vintage, 1991.

Cesarani, David. *Becoming Eichmann: Rethinking the Life, Crimes and Trial of a "Desk Murderer."* Cambridge, Mass.: Da Capo Press, 2006.

Cesarani, David, and Eric Sundquist, eds. *After the Holocaust: Challenging the Myth of Silence*. New York: Routledge, 2011.

Chappell, David L. *A Stone of Hope: Prophetic Religion and the Death of Jim Crow*. Chapel Hill: University of North Carolina Press, 2004.

Charron, Katherine Mellen. *Freedom's Teacher: The Life of Septima Clark*. Chapel Hill: University of North Carolina Press, 2009.

Charron, Katherine Mellen, and David P. Cline. "'I Train the People to Do Their Own Talking': Septima Clark and Women in the Civil Rights Movement." *Southern Cultures* 16, no. 2 (Summer 2010): 31-52.

Chireau, Yvonne, and Nathaniel Deutsch. *Black Zion: African American Religious Encounters with Judaism*. New York: Oxford University Press, 2000.

Chotzinoff, Samuel. *A Lost Paradise: Early Reminiscences*. New York: Knopf, 1955.

Christensen, Rob. *The Paradox of Tar Heel Politics: The Personalities, Elections, and Events That Shaped Modern North Carolina*. Chapel Hill: University of North Carolina Press, 2008.

Claiborne, Jack. *Jack Claiborne's Charlotte*. Charlotte, N.C.: Charlotte Publishing, 1974.

———. *The "Charlotte Observer": Its Time and Place, 1869–1986*. Chapel Hill: University of North Carolina Press, 1986.

Claiborne, Jack, and William Price, eds. *Discovering North Carolina: A Tar Heel Reader*. Chapel Hill: University of North Carolina Press, 1991.

Clark, Septima Poinsette, and Legette Blythe, eds. *Echo in My Soul*. New York: Dutton, 1962.

Clowse, Barbara Barksdale. *Ralph McGill: A Biography*. Macon, Ga.: Mercer University Press, 1998.

Cook, Blanche Wiesen. *Eleanor Roosevelt*. Vol. 1, *1884–1933*. New York: Viking, 1993.

———. *Eleanor Roosevelt*. Vol. 2, *1933–1938*. New York: Viking, 1999.

Crow, Jeffrey J., Paul D. Escott, and Flora J. Hatley. *A History of African Americans in North Carolina*. Rev. ed. Raleigh: Office of Archives and History, North Carolina Department of Cultural Resources, 2002.

Dabney, Virginius. *Dry Messiah: The Life of Bishop James Cannon, Jr.* New York: Knopf, 1949.

Danish, Max. D. *The World of David Dubinsky*. New York: World Publishing, 1957.

David, Jay, ed. *Growing Up Jewish*. New York: Simon and Schuster/Pocket Books, 1970.

Dershowitz, Alan M. *The Vanishing American Jew: In Search of Jewish Identity for the Next Century*. New York: Touchstone, 1997.

Diner, Hasia R. *In the Almost Promised Land: American Jews and Blacks, 1915–1935*. Baltimore: Johns Hopkins University Press, 1995.

———. "Between Words and Deeds: Jews and Blacks in America, 1880–1935." In *Struggles in the Promised Land: Toward a History of Black-Jewish Relations in the United States*, edited by Jack Salzman, and Cornel West, 87–106. New York: Oxford University Press, 1997.

———. *Lower East Side Memories: A Jewish Place in America*. Princeton: Princeton University Press, 2002.

———. *A New Promised Land: A History of Jews in America*. New York: Oxford University Press, 2003.

———. *The Jews of the United States, 1654–2000*. Berkeley: University of California Press, 2004.

———. "Entering the Mainstream of Modern Jewish History: Peddlers and the American Jewish South." In *Jewish Roots in Southern Soil: A New History*, edited by Marcie Cohen Ferris and Mark I. Greenberg, 86–108. Waltham, Mass.: Brandeis University Press, and Hanover, N.H.: University Press of New England, 2006.

Dinnerstein, Leonard. *Antisemitism in America*. New York: Oxford University Press, 1994.

———. *The Leo Frank Case*. Athens: University of Georgia Press, 2008.

Dinnerstein, Leonard, and Mary Dale Palsson, eds. *Jews in the South*. Baton Rouge: Louisiana State University Press, 1973.

Dollinger, Marc. "'Hamans' and 'Torquemadas': Southern and Northern Jewish Responses to the Civil Rights Movement, 1945–1965." In *The Quiet Voices: Southern Rabbis and Black Civil Rights, 1880s to 1990s*, edited by Mark K. Bauman and Berkley Kalin, 67–94. Tuscaloosa: University of Alabama Press, 1997.

———. *Quest for Inclusion: Jews and Liberalism in Modern America*. Princeton: Princeton University Press, 2000.

Douglas, Davison M. *Reading, Writing, and Race: The Desegregation of the Charlotte Schools*. Chapel Hill: University of North Carolina Press, 1995.

Doyle, William. *An American Insurrection: The Battle of Oxford, Mississippi, 1962*. New York: Doubleday, 2001.

Dray, Philip. *At the Hands of Persons Unknown: The Lynching of Black America*. New York: Modern Library, 2003.

Dubinsky, David, and A. H Raskin. *David Dubinsky: A Life with Labor*. New York: Simon and Schuster, 1977.

East, P. D. *The Magnolia Jungle: The Life, Times, and Education of a Southern Editor*. New York: Simon and Schuster, 1960.

Egerton, John. *Speak Now against the Day: The Generation before the Civil Rights Movement in the South*. New York: Knopf, 1994.

Ellison, Ralph. *Invisible Man*. New York: Vintage International, 1995.

Ellwood, Robert S. *1950: Crossroads of American Jewish Life*. Louisville, Ky.: Westminster John Knox Press, 2000.

Epstein, Joseph. *Essays in Biography*. Mount Jackson, Va.: Axios Press, 2012.

Etheridge, Eric. *Breach of Peace: Portraits of the 1961 Mississippi Freedom Riders*. New York: Atlas and Co., 2008.

Evans, Eli N. *The Lonely Days Were Sundays: Reflections of a Jewish Southerner*. Jackson: University of Mississippi Press, 1993.

———. *The Provincials: A Personal History of Jews in the South*. Chapel Hill: University of North Carolina Press, 2005.

Ferris, Marcie Cohen. *Matzoh Ball Gumbo: Culinary Tales of the Jewish South*. Chapel Hill: University of North Carolina Press, 2005.

Ferris, Marcie Cohen, and Mark I. Greenberg, eds. *Jewish Roots in Southern Soil: A New History*. Waltham, Mass.: Brandeis University Press, and Hanover, N.H.: University Press of New England, 2006.

Flono, Fannie. *Thriving in the Shadows: The Black Experience in Charlotte and Mecklenburg County*. Charlotte: Novello Festival Press, 2006.

Foner, Philip S., ed. *The Black Panthers Speak*. New York: Da Capo Press, 1995.

Franklin, V. P., ed. *African Americans and Jews in the Twentieth Century: Studies in Convergence and Conflict*. Columbia: University of Missouri Press, 1998.

Friedman, Murray, with Peter Binzen. *What Went Wrong: The Creation and Collapse of the Black-Jewish Alliance*. New York: Free Press, 1995.

Gellhorn, Walter. "HUAC: Report on a Report of the House Committee on Un-American Activities." *Harvard Law Review* 60, no. 8 (October 1947): 1193–1234.

Giddings, Paula J. *Ida, a Sword among Lions: Ida B. Wells and the Campaign against Lynching*. New York: Amistad, 2009.

Gilmore, Glenda Elizabeth. *Defying Dixie: The Radical Roots of Civil Rights, 1919–1950*. New York: Norton, 2008.

Glass, Brent D. *The Textile Industry in North Carolina: A History*. Raleigh: Division of Archives and History, North Carolina Department of Cultural Resources, 1999.

Glazer, Nathan. *American Judaism*. Chicago: University of Chicago Press, 1957.

Glazer, Nathan, and Daniel Patrick Moynihan. *Beyond the Melting Pot: The Negroes, Puerto Ricans, Jews, Italians, and Irish of New York City*. Cambridge, Mass.: M.I.T. Press, 1967.

Goldfield, David R. *Cotton Fields and Skyscrapers: Southern City and Region*. Baltimore: Johns Hopkins University Press, 1989.

Goldhurst, Richard. "Locating the Deity: A Memoir Crowded with the Likes of Allen Ginsberg, Harry Golden, and Hubert D. Gallagher." Unpublished manuscript.

Goldstein, Eric L. " 'Now Is the Time to Show Your True Colors': Southern Jews, Whiteness, and the Rise of Jim Crow." In *Jewish Roots in Southern Soil: A New History*, edited by Marcie Cohen Ferris and Mark I. Greenberg, 134–55. Waltham, Mass.: Brandeis University Press, and Hanover, N.H.: University Press of New England, 2006.

Goodman, James. *Stories of Scottsboro*. New York: Pantheon, 1994.

Gottheimer, Josh, ed. *Ripples of Hope: Great American Civil Rights Speeches*. New York: Basic Civitas Books, 2003.

Greene, Melissa Fay. *The Temple Bombing*. Cambridge, Mass.: Da Capo Press, 2006.

Hall, Jacquelyn Dowd. "The Long Civil Rights Movement and the Political Uses of the Past." *Journal of American History* 91, no. 4 (March 2005): 1233–63.

Hall, Jacquelyn Dowd, James Leloudis, Robert Korstad, Mary Murphy, Lu Ann Jones, Christopher B. Daly. *Like a Family: The Making of a Southern Cotton Mill World*, Chapel Hill: University of North Carolina Press, 1987.

Hampton, Henry, compiled with Steve Fayer and Sarah Flynn. *Voices of Freedom: An Oral History of the Civil Rights Movement from the 1950s through the 1980s*. New York: Bantam Books, 1991.

Hanchett, Tom. "Remembering Harry Golden: Food, Race, and Laughter." *Southern Cultures* 11, no. 2 (Summer 2005): 93–97.

Handlin, Oscar. "American Views of the Jew at the Opening of the Twentieth Century." *American Jewish Historical Society* 40 (1950): 323–44.

———. *Adventure in Freedom: Three Hundred Years of Jewish Life in America*. New York: McGraw-Hill, 1954.

Hapgood, Hutchins. *The Spirit of the Ghetto: Studies of the Jewish Quarter of New York*. New York: Funk and Wagnalls, 1965.

Heinze, Andrew R. *Jews and the American Soul*. Princeton: Princeton University Press, 2004.

Hertzberg, Arthur. *A Jew in America: My Life and a People's Struggle for Identity*. San Francisco: HarperSanFrancisco, 2002.

Heschel, Abraham Joshua. *Moral Grandeur and Spiritual Audacity: Essays*. Edited by Susannah Heschel. New York: Farrar, Straus and Giroux, 1996.

Hobbs, Frank, and Nicole Stoops. *Demographic Trends in the Twentieth Century*. U.S. Census Bureau Census 2000 Special Reports, Series CENSR-4, Demographic Trends in the Twentieth Century. Washington, D.C.: U.S. Government Printing Office, 2002.

Hobson, Fred. *Mencken: A Life*. Baltimore: Johns Hopkins University Press, 1994.

Hohner, Robert A. *Prohibition and Politics: The Life of Bishop James Cannon, Jr.* Columbia: University of South Carolina Press, 1999.

Horowitz, Daniel. *Consuming Pleasures: Intellectuals and Popular Culture in the Postwar World*. Philadelphia: University of Pennsylvania Press, 2012.

Horowitz, Helen Lefkowitz. *Rereading Sex: Battles over Sexual Knowledge and Suppression in Nineteenth-Century America*. New York: Knopf, 2002.

Houck, Davis W., and David E. Dixon, eds. *Rhetoric, Religion, and the Civil Rights Movement, 1954–1965*. Waco, Tex.: Baylor University Press, 2006.

Howe, Irving, and Kenneth Libo. *World of Our Fathers*. New York: Harcourt Brace Jovanovich, 1976.

Hunter-Gault, Charlayne. *To the Mountaintop: My Journey through the Civil Rights Movement*. New York: Roaring Book Press, 2012.

Jackson, Kenneth T., ed. *Encyclopedia of New York*. New Haven: Yale University Press, 1995.

Kalk, Bruce H. *The Origins of the Southern Strategy: Two-Party Competition in South Carolina, 1950–1972*. Lanham, Md.: Lexington Books, 2001.

Kennedy, Robert F. *RFK: Collected Speeches*. Edited by Edwin O. Guthman and C. Richard Allen. New York: Viking, 1993.

Kilpatrick, James Jackson. *The Southern Case for School Segregation*. New York: Crowell-Collier Press, 1962.

King, Martin Luther, Jr. *I Have a Dream: Writings and Speeches That Changed the World*. Edited by James Melvin Washington. San Francisco: HarperSanFrancisco, 1992.

Klein, Walter Julian. *The Bridge Table: A Love Story*. Charlotte, N.C.: Temple Beth El, 2007.

Kluger, Richard. *Simple Justice: The History of* Brown v. Board of Education *and Black America's Struggle for Equality*. New York: Viking, 2004.

Konvitz, Milton R. "Jews and Civil Rights." In *The Ghetto and Beyond: Essays on Jewish Life in America*, edited by Peter I. Rose, 270–89. New York: Random House, 1969.

Kotz, Nick. *Judgment Days: Lyndon Baines Johnson, Martin Luther King Jr., and the Laws That Changed America*. Boston: Houghton Mifflin, 2005.

Kratt, Mary. *Charlotte, North Carolina: A Brief History*. Charleston, S.C.: History Press, 2009.

Kratt, Mary Norton. *Charlotte, Spirit of the New South*. Winston-Salem, N.C.: John F. Blair, 1992.

Krause, P. Allen. "Rabbis and Negro Rights in the South, 1954–1967." *American Jewish Archives* 21, no. 1 (1969): 10–47.

Kuralt, Charles. *A Life on the Road*. New York: Putnam's, 1990.

Lee, Hermione. *Philip Roth*. London: Methuen, 1982.

Lemann, Nicholas. *The Promised Land: The Great Black Migration and How It Changed America*. New York: Knopf, 1991.

Lewis, David Levering. *King: A Biography*. Urbana: University of Illinois Press, 1978.

Lipstadt, Deborah E. *The Eichmann Trial*. New York: Schocken Books, 2011.

Mackenzie, G. Calvin, and Robert Weisbrot. *The Liberal Hour: Washington and the Politics of Change in the 1960s*. New York: Penguin Press, 2008.

Mailer, Norman. *The Spooky Art: Thoughts on Writing*. New York: Random House, 2004.

Malcolm X. *Malcolm X Speaks: Selected Speeches and Statements*. New York: Grove Press, 1994.

Malkin, Peter Z., and Harry Stein. *Eichmann in My Hands*. New York: Warner Books, 1990.

Manchester, William. *The Glory and the Dream: A Narrative History of America, 1932–1972*. Boston: Little, Brown, 1974.

Marable, Manning. *Malcolm X: A Life of Reinvention*. New York: Viking, 2011.

Martin, John Bartlow. *Adlai Stevenson of Illinois: The Life of Adlai E. Stevenson*. Garden City: Anchor Press/Doubleday, 1977.

———. *Adlai Stevenson and the World: The Life of Adlai E. Stevenson*. Garden City: Anchor Press/Doubleday, 1978.

McCullough, David G. "The Unexpected Harry Truman." In *Extraordinary Lives: The Art and Craft of American Biography*, edited by William Zissner. Boston: Houghton Mifflin, 1988.

———. *Truman*. New York: Simon and Schuster, 1993.

McGill, Ralph. *The South and the Southerner*. Boston: Little, Brown, 1964.

McGill, Ralph, and Calvin M. Logue, eds. *No Place to Hide: The South and Human Rights*. Vols. 1 and 2. Macon, Ga.: Mercer University Press, 1984.

McGraw, Eliza R. L. *Two Covenants: Representatives of Southern Jewishness*. Baton Rouge: Louisiana State University Press, 2005.

Melnick, Jeffrey. *Black-Jewish Relations on Trial: Leo Frank and Jim Conley in the New South*. Jackson: University Press of Mississippi, 2000.

Mencken, H. L. *On Politics: A Carnival of Buncombe*. Baltimore: Johns Hopkins University Press, 1996.

Metzger, Isaac, ed. *A Bintel Brief: Sixty Years of Letters from the Lower East Side to the Jewish Daily Forward*. New York: Ballantine Books, 1971.

Miller, Steven P. *Billy Graham and the Rise of the Republican South*. Philadelphia: University of Pennsylvania Press, 2009.

Mobley, Joe A., ed. *The Way We Lived in North Carolina*. Chapel Hill: University of North Carolina Press, 2003.

Mordell, Albert, comp. *The World of Haldeman-Julius*. New York: Twayne Publishers, 1960.

Morrill, Dan, L. *Historic Charlotte: An Illustrated History of Charlotte and Mecklenburg County*. Charlotte: Historic Charlotte Inc., 2001.

Motley, Constance Baker. *Equal Justice under Law: An Autobiography*. Farrar, Straus and Giroux, 1998.

Moyers, Bill. "The Adventures of a Radical Hillbilly: An Interview with Myles Horton." *Appalachian Journal* 9, no. 4 (Summer 1982): 248–85.

Myrdal, Gunnar, with Richard Sterner and Arnold Rose. *An American Dilemma: The Negro Problem and Modern Democracy*. New York: Harper and Brothers, 1944.

Niven, David. *The Politics of Injustice: The Kennedys, the Freedom Rides, and the Electoral Consequences of a Moral Compromise*. Knoxville: University of Tennessee Press, 2003.

Niven, Penelope. *Carl Sandburg: A Biography*. New York: Scribner's Sons, 1991.

Norrell, Robert J. *The House I Live In: Race in the American Century*. New York: Oxford University Press, 2005.

Nunnelley, William A. *Bull Connor*. Tuscaloosa: University of Alabama Press, 1990.

O'Connor, Richard. *The German-Americans: An Informal History*. Boston: Little, Brown, 1968.

Okrent, Daniel. *Last Call: The Rise and Fall of Prohibition*. New York: Scribner 2010. Kindle edition.

Olmstead, Frederick Law. *A Journey in the Seaboard Slave States, with remarks on their economy*. New York: Dix & Edwards, 1856.

Oney, Steve. *And the Dead Shall Rise: The Murder of Mary Phagan and the Lynching of Leo Frank*. New York: Pantheon, 2003.

Patterson, James T. Brown v. Board of Education*: A Civil Rights Milestone and Its Troubled Legacy*. New York: Oxford University Press, 2002.

Patterson, Michael S. "The Fall of a Bishop: James Cannon, Jr., versus Carter Glass, 1909-1934." *Journal of Southern History* 39, no. 4 (November 1973): 493-518.

Payton, Boyd E. *Scapegoat: Prejudice/Politics/Prison*. Philadelphia: Whitmore Pub. Co., 1970.

Peters, Charles. *Tilting at Windmills: An Autobiography*. Reading, Mass.: Addison-Wesley, 1988.

Pfeffer, Paula, F. *A. Philip Randolph, Pioneer of the Civil Rights Movement*. Baton Rouge: Louisiana State University Press, 1996.

Pleasants, Julian M., and Augustus M. Burns III. *Frank Porter Graham and the 1950 Senate Race in North Carolina*. Chapel Hill: University of North Carolina Press, 1990.

Polsgrove, Carol. *Divided Minds: Intellectuals and the Civil Rights Movement*. New York: Norton, 2001.

Prinz, Joachim. *Joachim Prinz, Rebellious Rabbi: An Autobiography—the German and Early American Years*. Edited by Michael Meyer. Bloomington: Indiana University Press, 2007.

Raper, Arthur J. *The Tragedy of Lynching*. Mineola, New York: Dover Publications, 2003.

Ravage, M. E. *An American in the Making: The Life Story of an Immigrant*. New York: Harper and Brothers, 1917.

Ravitch, Diane. *The Troubled Crusade: American Education, 1945–1980*. New York: Basic Books, 1983.

Ready, Milton. *The Tar Heel State: A History of North Carolina*. Columbia: University of South Carolina Press, 2005.

Reed, John Shelton. *Southerners: The Social Psychology of Sectionalism*. Chapel Hill: University of North Carolina Press, 1983.

Reeves, Richard. *President Kennedy: Profile of Power*. New York: Simon and Schuster/Touchstone, 1994.

Riis, Jacob A. *How the Other Half Lives: Studies among the Tenements of New York*. New York: Dover Publications, 1971.

Roberts, Gene, and Hank Klibanoff. *The Race Beat: The Press, the Civil Rights Struggle, and the Awakening of a Nation*. New York: Knopf, 2006.

Rogoff, Leonard. *Homelands: Southern Jewish Identity in Durham and Chapel Hill, North Carolina*. Tuscaloosa: University of Alabama Press, 2001.

———. "Harry Golden, New Yorker: I [Love] NC." *Southern Jewish History* 11 (2008): 41–64.

———. *Down Home: Jewish Life in North Carolina*. Chapel Hill: University of North Carolina Press, 2010.

Rose, Peter I., ed. *The Ghetto and Beyond: Essays on Jewish Life in America*. New York: Random House, 1969.

———. *Mainstream and Margins: Jews, Blacks, and Other Americans*. New Brunswick, N.J.: Transaction Books, 1983.

———. *Nation of Nations: The Ethnic Experience and the Racial Crisis*. New York: Random House, 1972.

———. *They and We: Racial and Ethnic Relations in the United States*. New York: Random House, 1974.

Roth, Philip. *Reading Myself and Others*. New York: Vintage, 2001.

Rozell, Mark J., and Gleaves Whitney, eds. *Religion and the American Presidency*. New York: Palgrave Macmillan, 2007.

Rustin, Bayard. *Down the Line: The Collected Writings of Bayard Rustin*. Chicago: Quadrangle Books, 1971.

Salisbury, Harrison E. *Without Fear or Favor: The New York Times and Its Times*. New York: Times Books, 1980.

Salzman, Jack, ed., with Adina Back and Gretchen Sullivan Sorin. *Bridges and Boundaries: African Americans and American Jews*. New York: George Braziller, 1992.

Salzman, Jack, and Cornel West, eds. *Struggles in the Promised Land: Toward a History of Black-Jewish Relations in the United States*. New York: Oxford University Press, 1997.

Sandburg, Carl. *Complete Poems*. New York: Harcourt, Brace and World, 1950.

———. *The Letters of Carl Sandburg*. Edited by Herbert Mitgang. New York: Harcourt, Brace and World, 1968.

Sarna, Jonathan D. "The Cult of Synthesis in American Jewish Culture." *Jewish Social Studies* 5 (Fall/Winter 1998): 52–79.

———. *American Judaism: A History*. New Haven: Yale University Press, 2004.

Schmidt-Pirro, Julia, and Karen M. McCurdy. "Employing Music in the Cause of Social Justice: Ruth Crawford Seeger and Zilphia Horton." *Voices: The Journal of New York Folklore* 31 (Spring–Summer 2005): 32–36.

Schoen, Johanna. *Choice and Coercion: Birth Control, Sterilization, and Abortion in Public Health and Welfare*. Chapel Hill: University of North Carolina Press, 2005. Kindle edition.

Sheridan, Walter. *The Fall and Rise of Jimmy Hoffa*. New York: Saturday Review Press, 1972.

Shogan, Colleen J. *The Moral Rhetoric of American Presidents*. College Station: Texas A&M University Press, 2006.

Simons, William M. ed. *The Cooperstown Symposium on Baseball and American Culture, 2007-2008*. Jefferson, N.C.: McFarland, 2009.

Singh, Gopal K., and Stella Yu. "Infant Mortality in the United States: Trends, Differentials, and Projections, 1950 through 2010." *American Journal of Public Health* 85, no 7 (July 1995): 957–64, and in the digital archives of the National Center for Biotechnology Information, National Institutes of Health, http://www.ncbi.nlm.nih .gov/pmc/articles/PMC1615523. 1 November 2014.

Sorensen, Ted. *Counselor: A Life at the Edge of History*. New York: Harper Perennial, 2008.

Sorin, Gerald. *Tradition Transformed: The Jewish Experience in America*. Baltimore: Johns Hopkins University Press, 1997.

Sosna, Morton. *In Search of the Silent South*. New York: Columbia University Press, 1977.

Speizman, Morris. *The Jews of Charlotte: A Chronicle with Commentary and Conjectures*. Charlotte: McNally and Loftin, 1978.

Sullivan, Patricia. *Lift Every Voice: The NAACP and the Making of the Civil Rights Movement*. New York: New Press, 2009.

———, ed. *Freedom Writer: Virginia Foster Durr, Letters from the Civil Rights Years*. New York: Routledge, 2003.

Svonkin, Stuart, *Jews against Prejudice: American Jews and the Fight for Civil Liberties*. New York: Columbia University Press, 1997.

Targ, William. *Indecent Pleasures: The Life and Colorful Times of William Targ*. New York: Macmillan, 1975.

Teel, Leonard Ray. *Ralph Emerson McGill: Voice of Southern Conscience*. Knoxville: University of Tennessee Press, 2001.

Telushkin, Joseph. *The Golden Land: The Story of Jewish Immigration to America*. New York: Harmony Books, 2002.

Theoharis, Jeanne. *The Rebellious Life of Mrs. Rosa Parks*. Boston: Beacon Press, 2013. Kindle edition.

Theroux, Phyllis, ed. *The Book of Eulogies: A Collection of Memorial Tributes, Poetry, Essays, and Letters of Condolence*. New York: Scribner, 1997.

Thomas, Clarence W., with Shirley Robinson. *The Serious Humor of Harry Golden*. Lanham, Md.: University Press of America, 1997.

Thomas, Evan. *Robert Kennedy: His Life*. New York: Simon and Schuster, 2000.

Tyson, Timothy B. *Radio Free Dixie: Robert F. Williams and the Roots of Black Power*. Chapel Hill: University of North Carolina Press, 1999.

Vance, Zebulon Baird. *The Scattered Nation*. New York: J. J. Little & Co., 1904.

Vaughn, Stephen L., ed. *Encyclopedia of American Journalism*. New York: Routledge, 2008.

Von Drehle, David. *Triangle: The Fire That Changed America*. New York: Atlantic Monthly Press, 2003.

Ward-Royster, Willa. *How I Got Over: Clara Ward and the World-Famous Ward Singers, as Told to Toni Rose*. Philadelphia: Temple University Press, 1997.

Washington, Joseph R., Jr., ed. *Jews in Black Perspectives: A Dialogue*. Lanham, Md.: University Press of America, 1992.

Webb, Clive. "Closing Ranks: Montgomery Jews and Civil Rights, 1954–1967." *Journal of American Studies* 32, no. 3 (December 1998): 463–81.

———. *Fight against Fear: Southern Jews and Black Civil Rights*. Athens: University of Georgia Press, 2001.

———. "A Tangled Web: Black-Jewish Relations in the Twentieth-Century South." In *Jewish Roots in Southern Soil: A New History*, edited by Marcie Cohen Ferris and Mark I. Greenberg, 192–209. Waltham, Mass.: Brandeis University Press, and Hanover, N.H.: University Press of New England, 2006.

———. *Rabble Rousers: The American Far Right in the Civil Rights Era*. Athens: University of Georgia Press, 2010.

Weiss, Nancy, J. "Long-Distance Runners of the Civil Rights Movement: The Contribution of Jews to the NAACP and the National Urban League in the Twentieth Century." In *Struggles in the Promised Land: Toward a History of Black-Jewish Relations in the United States*, edited by Jack Salzman and Cornel West, 128–52. New York: Oxford University Press, 1997.

White, Walter. *Rope and Faggot: A Biography of Judge Lynch*. Notre Dame: University of Notre Dame Press, 2001.

Whitfield, Stephen, J. *Into the Dark: Hannah Arendt and Totalitarianism*. Philadelphia: Temple University Press, 1980.

——. *In Search of American Jewish Culture*. Waltham, Mass.: Brandeis University Press and Hanover, N.H.: University Press of New England, 1999.

——. "Declarations of Independence: American Jewish Culture in the Twentieth Century." In *Cultures of the Jews*, vol. 3, *Modern Encounters*, edited by David Biale, 390. New York: Schocken Books, 2002.

——. "The 'Golden' Era of Civil Rights: Consequences of *The Carolina Israelite*." *Southern Cultures* 14, no. 3 (Fall 2008): 26–51.

Wilkerson, Isabel. *The Warmth of Other Suns: The Epic Story of America's Great Migration*. New York: Random House, 2010.

Wilkins, Roy, and Tom Mathews. *Standing Fast: The Autobiography of Roy Wilkins*. New York: Da Capo Press, 1994.

Wittke, Carl. "Review of *Jews in American History: Their Contributions to the United States of America, 1492–1950*, by Harry L. Golden, with Martin Rywell." *Mississippi Valley Historical Review* 37, no. 4 (March 1951): 689–90.

Woodward, C. Vann. *Origins of the New South, 1877–1913*. Baton Rouge: Louisiana State University Press, 1971.

——. *Tom Watson: Agrarian Rebel*. Savannah, Ga.: Beehive Press, 1973.

——. *The Strange Career of Jim Crow*. New York: Oxford University Press, 1974.

——. *The Burden of Southern History*. Baton Rouge: Louisiana State University Press, 1993.

ACKNOWLEDGMENTS

Timothy Hartnett believed in this book and supported it from start to finish with patience, kindness, pride, and humor. These pages belong to him.

Among the many blessings of my years as an Ada Comstock Scholar at Smith College was the opportunity to study with historians Daniel Horowitz and Helen Lefkowitz Horowitz. Their brilliant work inspires me; their many kindnesses and wise advice sustain me.

Author Richard Goldhurst allowed me unrestricted access to his father's archives and his own memories, answered questions no one else could answer, and stayed with me on this long project, always responding with intelligence and humor. I join him in his deep gratitude for Jeanne Holleman, who was with us all along the way.

Any journalist of my era who takes on a project such as this one faces the challenge of moving from a medium in which her original interviews and discoveries are the most prized things and learning to set those toothsome bits into a deeper context and place them up against the work of historians who went before. In the moments when I succeed at this, it is thanks to the endlessly patient Dan Horowitz and the very generous Leonard Rogoff.

I was aided in great measure by Robin Brabham in his role as curator of the Special Collections Department of the J. Murrey Atkins Library at the University of North Carolina-Charlotte and in the years following his retirement. Librarian Marilyn Schuster of the Special Collections Department, Atkins Library, went above and beyond in helping me find elusive documents and photographs.

I am deeply grateful to the staff of the University of North Carolina Press, especially David Perry, who as editor in chief saw potential in a Golden biography many years ago, and editor Elaine Maisner, without whose wise guidance and tenacity this book would not have happened. Stephanie Wenzel's meticulous copyediting was invaluable. Crucial and kind support came from Caitlin Bell-Butterfield, Gina Mahalek, and Alison Shay.

Walter Klein, writer and advertising man who knew Golden well, enthusiastically supported this effort and shared valuable documents and memories with me, as did Anita Stewart Brown, who responded with grace and candor. Author and former journalist Jack Claiborne shared his wealth of knowledge about Golden and his years in Charlotte.

I am indebted to journalist and photographer Lisa Schnellinger for her inspiring example of an ethical writer's life, her close readings of this manuscript, and assistance with locating rare photographs of Golden. As with all my endeavors, Tanya Jordan Taylor never lost confidence in me, and Kathryn Lyons Egan kept devoted watch over me.

I owe my colleagues at the *Seattle Times* more than I can say for their teaching and support over the years. Melissa Maday picked up where they left off, teaching, editing and encouraging.

Others to whom I owe special thanks include Diane Abt, Angela A. Bickham, Catherine Brewster, Mary Stuart Cosby, Judy Caldwell Culver, Lois Dubin, Martha Gies, Vesta Lee Gordon, Friderike Heuer, Rachel Hitchcock, Carol Isaak, Roberta Jordan, Elizabeth Land, Davia Larson, Leona Lefkowitz, Katie McCormick, Tom Nebbia, B. Ouseafir, Laurie Powers, Helen Reese, Andrew Schneider, Margaret Shirley, Nicole Taylor, Richard Todd, Stephen Whitfield, Susan Luce Williams, and Michael Zielenziger.

Along with the staff at Atkins Library, librarians throughout the country supported me in this work, especially those at the William Allan Neilson Library, Smith College; Lamont Library, Harvard University; Charlotte Mecklenburg Library; Cowles Library, Drake University; and the library systems in Seattle, Washington, and in Multnomah and Washington Counties in Oregon. Members of the Southern Jewish Historical Society provided scholarship and encouragement, including a Kawaler Research/Travel Grant. The Harry Golden Visiting Scholar Program award given to me through the Special Collections Department of the J. Murrey Atkins Library funded important travel and research expenses. The fact that this fund was the bequest of Anita Stewart Brown made it all the more appreciated.

These generous collaborators brought me the best material and the most unflagging support any writer could have; any errors or shortcomings are my own.

Harry Golden was counted out and resurrected many times in his life, and throughout this writing I have held onto the hope that his remarkable luck will hold and his words will come back yet again for a new generation of readers.

INDEX

258; marriage, 29–30, 42, 96–98, 262; memory, 20, 93, 198; messiness, 167–69; musical tastes, 53–54, 68–69, 168, 282 (n. 55); reading, 27–28; self-promotion, 2, 6, 56, 82, 110, 239, 262; sense of direction lack, 57–58; as showman, 4, 72, 141, 266; as "the other," 265; women, 73, 122–23, 258, 262, 283 (n. 66), 325 (n. 41)

Golden, Harry—social activism: attacks on segregation, 50–51, 58–59, 87, 116–17, 120; in Birmingham campaign, 207, 312 (n. 60); black activists' rejection of, 197, 216–17, 233; on black health care, 131–34, 246–47, 266, 296 (n. 61); campaigning for John Kennedy, 6, 77, 93, 199; campaigning for Robert Kennedy, 155, 225–26; campaigning for Stevenson, 93–94, 288 (n. 42); childhood roots of, 24, 46–47, 264–65; hate mail and calls received, 95–96, 159, 251–52, 323 (n. 22); in March on Washington, 179, 210–12; membership in CORE and Fellowship of Reconciliation, 85; NAACP membership and support, 85, 110–11, 162, 164, 286 (n. 14); political savvy of, 198, 309 (n. 27); as political speechwriter, 93; and Scales case, 211, 312–13 (n. 69); and SNCC, 184, 250–52, 323 (n. 19); speaking appearances, 79–80, 163–65, 183–85, 208, 227, 253, 254, 258, 284 (n. 2), 316 (n. 26); support for labor movement, 26, 28, 49, 177–79, 294 (n. 37)

Golden, Harry—writer:
—books: *For 2 Cents Plain*, 170, 183, 270 (n. 6), 302 (n. 41); *America, I Love You*, 258, 325 (n. 44); *The Best of Harry Golden*, 256; *Carl Sandburg*, 199–201, 310 (n. 32); *Enjoy, Enjoy!*, 173, 183, 302 (n. 48), 307 (n. 5); *Ess, Ess, Mein Kindt (Eat, Eat, My Child)*, 235; *Five Boyhoods*, 225, 316 (n. 20); *Forgotten Pioneer*, 103, 224–25; *The Golden Book of Humor*, 257, 324 (n. 39); *The Greatest Jewish City in the World*, 257; *The Israelis: Portrait of a People*, 248–49, 257, 323 (n. 14); *Jewish Roots in the Carolinas*, 74–75, 320 (n. 62); *Jews in American History*, 74–75, 270 (n. 6), 283 (n. 69); *A Little Girl Is Dead*, 238–43, 320 (n. 60), 321 (n. 70); *Long Live Columbus (Leben Zul Columbus)*, 258; *Mr. Kennedy and the Negroes*, 214–16, 222–23; *Only in America*, 3, 18–19, 65, 106, 136–37, 138, 142–44, 162–63, 169–70, 171–72, 199, 270 (n. 6), 298 (n. 103); *Our Southern Landsman*, 257; *The Right Time*, 202, 248, 249, 257; *So Long as You're Healthy (Abee gezunt)*, 257; *So What Else Is New?*, 225, 288 (n. 44); *Think Small*, 256–57; *Travels through Jewish America*, 257, 270 (n. 6); *You're Entitle'*, 43, 183, 225, 316 (n. 20)
—essays and articles: "About the Convert to Christianity," 17–18; "The East Side Revisited," 20; "How about Whiskey?," 43–44; "I'll Write the Entire Paper from Now On," 82; "It's Wonderful to Be a Gentile," 101; "Jew and Gentile in the New South," 105–6; "The Jews in Germany—1961," 191–92; "Looking for Work and How to Find It," 209; "The Negro Intellectuals Who Need to Be Carefully Taught," 234, 319 (n. 46); "The Poets Were Paid," 19; "A Pulpit in the South," 100–101; "A Son of the South and Some Daughters," 100; "A Stranger to the Human Race," 190–91; "Unease in Dixie," 106; "The Wall Street Story," 160; "What Are the World's Greatest Books?," 59; "What I Have Learned," 267; "What I've Done for the Jews of the South," 101
—forewords, introductions, and chapters, 256–57, 270 (n. 6), 302 (n. 47)
—promotional copy, 172–73
—syndicated column, 83, 99, 183, 286 (n. 19), 305 (n. 83); criticisms of,

235–36; *New York Post* dropping of, 237, 319–20 (n. 56)

—writing style, 59, 70, 179–80; as blogger, 1, 95, 261–62; complex social issues boiled down, 6, 95; humor, 4, 31, 43, 59, 77, 80, 85, 95, 100, 143, 144, 185, 193, 208, 226, 235, 238, 246, 252, 259; as storyteller, 4, 9–10, 24, 192, 214, 241, 261

The Golden Book of Humor (Golden), 257, 324 (n. 39)

Golden Plans, 165, 301 (n. 32); Bomb Shelter Plan, 167; Golden Insurance Plan, 167; Plan to Eliminate Anti-Semitism, 166–67; Vertical Negro Plan, 165–66; White Citizens Plan, 167

Goldfield, David R., 52, 55

Goldhirsch, Anna Klein (mother), 10, 11, 15–16, 19, 145, 174

Goldhirsch, Jake (brother), 25, 39, 159, 272 (n. 6); birth and death of, 22, 256, 273 (n. 35); work by, 11, 22–23, 145, 274 (n. 40)

Goldhirsch, Leib (father), 9, 27, 31, 73, 111; about, 12–15; arguing ability of, 13, 145; Talmudic knowledge of, 12, 13, 25, 174; "You're entitle'" as phrase of, 225

Goldhirsch, Lillian (daughter-in-law), 159

Goldhirsch, Max (brother), 11, 22, 147, 248, 271 (n. 2)

Goldhurst, Clara (sister), 10, 15, 22, 25, 159, 259; Wall Street job of, 22, 38, 98, 146, 276 (n. 81)

Goldhurst, Genevieve Alice Marie "Tiny" Gallagher (wife), 29–30, 44, 48, 50, 64, 159, 171, 277 (n. 96); Catholicism of, 42–43, 97, 174; Golden relationship with, 96–98, 148, 162; and Golden's imprisonment, 39, 42; musical ability of, 30, 275 (n. 57)

Goldhurst, Harry Jr. (Buddy) (son), 97, 137, 275 (n. 57); copyediting of Golden's works by, 168–69; name of, 48, 288–89 (n. 51); as reporter, 97, 308 (n. 12)

Goldhurst, Matilda (sister), 10, 11, 14, 15, 21–22, 25, 271 (n. 4); as clothing

designer, 22, 146; death of, 248, 322 (n. 11); Golden relationship to, 247–48; and Golden's stock-market scam, 39, 276 (n. 81)

Goldhurst, Peter (son), 46, 149, 275 (n. 57), 277 (n. 106)

Goldhurst, Richard (son), 48, 177, 227, 275 (n. 57), 324 (n. 39); in Army, 97–98; collaboration with Golden by, 4, 169, 191, 193, 202, 233, 239, 248, 323 (n. 14); recollections of Golden by, 42, 45, 49, 66, 76, 77, 163, 168, 246, 277 (n. 96)

Goldhurst, William (son), 48, 97–98, 254, 308 (n. 12); birth and death of, 39, 275 (n. 57)

Goldwater, Barry, 173, 228–29, 309 (n. 27), 317 (n. 30)

Goodman, Andrew, 222, 251

Goodman, Arthur, 60, 61, 63, 64, 66, 281 (n. 49)

Good Samaritan Hospital, 132

Goodwin, Richard, 94–95

Grace, Daddy, 175

Gradualism, 183, 216, 233

Grady, Henry W., 52

Graham, Billy, 176–77; and Golden, 177, 179, 303 (n. 62); and King, 303 (n. 60), 311 (n. 56)

Graham, Frank Porter, 88, 121, 140, 255, 282–83 (n. 63); *Carolina Israelite* honoring of, 70–72

Graves, Ralph, 307 (n. 7)

The Greatest Jewish City in the World (Golden), 257

Greenbaum, Maurice, 163

Greene, Melissa Faye, 104

Greenville, S.C., 61

Guthman, Edwin, 226, 316 (n. 22)

Guthrie, Woody, 129

Haldeman-Julius, Emanual, 30–31, 76, 275 (n. 61)

Hall, Jacquelyn Dowd, 7, 271 (n. 14)

Hamlet (Shakespeare), 59

Handlin, Oscar, 11, 80–81, 240

The Harry Golden Omnibus, 183
Hawkins, Reginald, 232, 233
Health care, 131–34, 246–47, 266, 296 (n. 61)
Hebrew Benevolent Congregation Temple, 106–7
Hebrew Sheltering and Immigrant Aid Society (HIAS), 20
Hendersonville Times-News, 61
Henry, O., 161
Henry Lewis Martin Company, 74
Herberg, Will, 81
Heschel, Abraham Joshua, 109, 222, 291 (n. 83)
Highlander Folk School, 128–31, 181; Eleanor Roosevelt at, 129–30, 295 (n. 55); Golden at, 130–31, 295 (n. 54), 301 (n. 26)
Hill, Mamie, 83, 168
Hitler, Adolf, 42–43
Hodges, Luther, 107, 136, 177, 178
Hoffa, Jimmy, 202, 310 (n. 40)
Hohner, Robert H., 34
Holiday, 249
Homosexuality, 123, 125–26
Honey and Salt (Sandburg), 200
Hoover, Herbert, 33
Hoover, J. Edgar, 259
Horowitz, Daniel, 118
Horton, Myles, 128, 161–62
Horton, Zilphia, 129, 295 (n. 54)
Hot dogs, 226
Hotel Markwell, 44–45
House Un-American Activities Committee (HUAC), 71
Houston, Noel, 71, 282 (n. 61)
Howe, Irving, 13–14, 187, 306 (n. 89)
Humphrey, Hubert, 186, 255–56
Hurst, Fannie, 162

Infant mortality, 132
Internal Revenue Service (IRS), 64–65, 163
International Ladies' Garment Workers' Union, 236, 319 (n. 52)
Irish, 30
Israel, 248–49, 251, 256

The Israelis: Portrait of a People (Golden), 248–49, 257, 323 (n. 14)

Jackson, Henry "Scoop," 258
Jackson, Mahalia, 212
Javits, Jacob, 258, 319 (n. 44)
The Jeffersonian, 240
Jet, 85–86, 183
Jewish Daily Forward, 13, 86, 272 (n. 12)
Jewish Labor Committee, 186
Jewish organizations: American Jewish Committee (AJC), 20, 21, 83, 108, 110, 115, 222–23, 242, 315 (n. 14); American Jewish Congress, 21, 83, 105, 110, 186, 211, 222; Anti-Defamation League (ADL), 21, 105, 110, 129, 222, 234–35; B'nai B'rith, 110, 263; and civil rights movement, 21, 105, 115, 222, 263; friction between Golden and, 222–23; Hebrew Sheltering and Immigrant Aid Society (HIAS), 20
Jewish Roots in the Carolinas (Golden), 74–75, 320 (n. 62)
Jews: in Atlanta, 106–7, 242; and blacks, 104, 109–11, 251, 252, 292 (n. 89); and Catholic Church, 223–24, 227; in Charlotte, 59–60, 67–68, 99–100, 107–8, 257; Christians' view of, 79–80, 99; in civil rights movement, 21, 105, 115, 211, 222, 257, 263, 315 (n. 11); and Communism, 104, 222; German and German-American, 20–21, 110, 191–93, 291 (n. 86); Golden's Jewish identity and, 17–18, 42–43, 100, 258; Judaism as one of "Big Three," 81, 99; King on, 252; and Leo Frank case, 21, 104, 242–43, 321 (n. 74); as merchants and peddlers, 102–3, 224, 251, 252, 290 (n. 65); migration to U.S. of, 10–11; name changes by, 277–78 (n. 109); Nixon on, 176–77; passion for education among, 16; postwar shifts among, 80–81, 256; religious-secular relationship among, 13–14; in South, 102–4; and southern segregation, 105–7, 134–35; stereotyping

Presley, Elvis, 86

Prince, Cecil, 119

Prinz, Joachim, 211

Progress and Poverty (George), 26

Prohibition and Politics (Hohner), 34

The Promised Land (Lemann), 117

Prostitutes, 24–25, 50, 274 (n. 44)

Protestant-Catholic-Jew (Herberg), 81

The Provincials (Evans), 102

G. P. Putnam's Sons, 137, 248, 257

Puzo, Mario, 137

The Race Beat (Roberts and Klibanoff), 54, 86

Race riots, 231

Racial discrimination: blacks seen as inferior, 54, 114, 115; in education, 115–16; in employment, 53, 54; Golden campaign against, 2–3, 5, 58–59, 86–87, 95, 116–17, 120, 121–22; Myrdal on, 51, 54, 85. *See also* African Americans; Segregation

Raleigh News and Observer, 179

Randolph, A. Philip, 84, 233

Raper, Arthur, 91

Ray, G. G., 65

Rayburn, Sam, 183

Ready, Milton, 52, 55–56

Reagan, Ronald, 259

The Rebellious Life of Mrs. Rosa Parks (Theoharis), 127

Redding, J. Saunders, 188, 306–7 (n. 101)

Reed, Adolph L., Jr., 291 (n. 87)

Remembrance Rock (Sandburg), 77

Reston, James, 62, 175

Ribicoff, Abraham, 319 (n. 44)

Richmond, Va., 118

The Right Time (Golden), 202, 248, 249, 257

Riis, Jacob, 25

"The Rise of the Goldbergs" show, 170

Roberts, Gene, 54

Robertson, Carole, 212

Robertson, Ken, 68, 139, 208, 250, 285 (n. 7)

Robinson, Jackie, 85, 89, 287 (n. 27)

Rodgers, Richard, 143

Rogers, Will, 144

Rogoff, Leonard, 81, 99–100, 103, 107, 266, 285 (n. 5)

Roosevelt, Eleanor, 91, 92; Golden and, 87, 130, 186; at Highlander Folk School, 129–30, 295 (n. 55); at University Settlement House, 20, 273 (n. 29)

Roosevelt, Franklin D., 34, 87, 211, 220; and civil rights, 84, 91

Roosevelt, Sara Delano, 91

Roosevelt, Theodore, 197

Rose, Peter I., 20

Rosenwald, Julius, 21

Rosten, Leo, 170

The Rotarian, 257

Roth, Philip, 170, 306 (n. 89); Golden criticized by, 185, 186–87; Golden reply to, 187, 306 (n. 97)

Rothschild, Jacob M. "Jack," 106–7, 290 (n. 76)

Round Table Literary Club, 26, 27–28, 148

Russell, Bertrand, 31

Rustin, Bayard, 84–85, 209, 251

Ryan, William Fitts, 311 (n. 57)

Rywell, Martin, 74, 270 (n. 6), 283–84 (n. 70)

Salisbury, Harrison, 204–5

Sandburg, Carl: *Abraham Lincoln*, 75; death of, 250; on Golden, 138, 140, 160; Golden biography of, 199–201, 310 (n. 32); Golden friendship with, 75–78, 153, 200; "Home Fires," 76; *Honey and Salt*, 200; portrayal of African Americans by, 77–78; Pulitzer Prizes of, 75, 77, 284 (n. 71); *Remembrance Rock*, 77; and Stevenson, 77, 92; support for Kennedy by, 6, 77, 199

Sandburg, Lilian "Paula" Steichen, 75, 76, 77, 246, 284 (n. 75)

Sanford, Terry, 177

Sanger, Margaret, 31, 76

Sanger, Paul, 321–22 (n. 1)

Sarna, Jonathan D., 13, 81, 110, 256

Saturday Evening Post, 86, 159, 183, 234